SHAMANS/NEO-SHAMANS

Shamans and shamanisms are in vogue at present. In popular culture, such diverse characters as occultist Aleister Crowley, Doors musician Jim Morrison and performance artist Joseph Beuys have been termed shamans. The anthropological construct 'shamanism', on the other hand, has associations with sorcery, witchcraft and healing, and archaeologists have suggested the meaning of prehistoric cave art lies with shamans and altered consciousness.

Robert J. Wallis explores the interface between 'new' (modern Western), indigenous and prehistoric shamans, and assesses the implications for archaeologists, anthropologists, indigenous communities, heritage managers, and neo-Shamanic practitioners. Identifying key figures in neo-Shamanisms, including Mircea Eliade, Carlos Castaneda and Michael Harner, Wallis assesses the way in which 'traditional' practices have been transformed into 'Western' ones, such as Castaneda's Don Juan teachings and Harner's core shamanism.

The book draws on interviews and self-reflective insider ethnography with a variety of practitioners, particularly contemporary Pagans in Britain and North America from Druid and Heathen traditions, to elucidate what neo-Shamans do. Wallis looks at historical and archaeological sources to elucidate whether 'Celtic' and 'Northern' shamanisms may have existed, he explores contemporary Pagan engagements with prehistoric sacred sites such as Stonehenge and Avebury, and discusses the controversial use by neo-Shamans of indigenous (particularly Native American) shamanisms.

Rather than discuss neo-Shamans as, simply, inauthentic, invalid culture-stealers, Wallis offers a more detailed and complex appraisal. He makes it clear that scholars must be prepared to give up some of their hold over knowledge, and not only be aware of these neo-Shamanic approaches but also engage in a serious dialogue with such 'alternative' histories.

Robert J. Wallis is Associate Director of the MA in Art History at Richmond, the American International University in London, and a Research Fellow in Archaeology at the University of Southampton. He has published extensively on the archaeology and anthropology of art, shamanisms and neo-Shamans.

SHAMANS/ NEO-SHAMANS

Ecstasy, alternative archaeologies and contemporary Pagans

Robert J. Wallis

Routledge
Taylor & Francis Group

LONDON AND NEW YORK

First published 2003
by Routledge
11 New Fetter Lane, London EC4P 4EE

Simultaneously published in the USA and Canada
by Routledge
29 West 35th Street, New York, NY 10001

Routledge is an imprint of the Taylor & Francis Group

Typeset in Garamond by Taylor & Francis Books Ltd
Printed and bound in Great Britain by MPG Books Ltd, Bodmin

British Library Cataloguing in Publication Data
A catalogue record for this book is available from the British Library

Library of Congress Cataloging in Publication Data
Wallis, Robert J.
Shamans/neo-Shamans: ecstasy, alternative archaeologies
and contemporary Pagans/Robert J. Wallis.
Includes bibliographical references and index.
1. Shamanism. 2. New Age movement. I. Title.

BF1611 .W33   2003
291.1'44–dc21   2002068282

ISBN 0–415–30202–1 (hbk)
ISBN 0–415–30203–X (pbk)

FOR MY GRANDMOTHER
GLADYS ROSA PRESS
1912–2002
WAES THU HAEL

[T]he Pagan renaissance is obvious. Bookstores are full of books on the ancient native religions. In Great Britain, you cannot avoid the Pagan network. They even have university professors who are openly Pagan. In Iceland, Paganism became an official religion in 1973. Everywhere in Europe ... [w]itness the return of the Druids, the shamans and the priests of the Gods.

> (Christopher Gerard, Belgian neo-Shaman,
> cited by Henry 1999: 3)

[W]e moderns have nothing whatsoever of our own; only by replenishing and cramming ourselves with the ages, customs, arts, philosophies, religions, discoveries of others do we become anything worthy of notice.

> (Nietzsche 1983 [1893]: 89)

[W]hy shamanism, why magic? We need them both.

> (Drury 1982: 100)

CONTENTS

CONTENTS

ILLUSTRATIONS

PREFACE

Autoarchaeology: what have neo-Shamanisms got to do with me?

> Shamanism is now a hard working word. A pedant might insist that the word can only mean whatever it meant to its original users, Siberian Tungus and their neighbours. Anthropologists might argue about its applicability to similar constellations of techniques, beliefs, traditional knowledge and authority in other cultures. They might also question its applicability to the activities of New Agers, Pagans or Therapists in America, Britain and elsewhere. Meanwhile, however, there are people who consider themselves to be Shamans or to be doing 'shamanic' things.
>
> (Harvey 1997b: 107)

Under cover of darkness on the morning of 19 June 1996, a number of stones of Avebury's Neolithic West Kennet Avenue were painted with white and black 'pseudo-magical symbols' (Carpenter 1998: 24), perhaps executed by 'New Age crazies' (Figure i) (*Antiquity* 1996). At the Summer Solstice a few days later, hundreds of neo-Shamans visited the Avebury monuments. Some of the less responsible practitioners left candle wax and scorch marks on West Kennet long barrow's sarsens, while others ascended Silbury Hill which is currently closed to the public. In the years since, more and more 'Pagans' have chosen Avebury as their place of pilgrimage. In June 1999, two more stones were vandalised, one daubed with the word 'cuckoo', and the other covered in red and green paint, and then, at the summer solstice 2001, scratch marks – apparently unreadable – were made in West Kennet. Other so-called 'sacred sites' have also been damaged by 'alternative' interest groups, from the 'restored' stone circle at Doll Tor, Derbyshire, to the 'napalm' damaged Men-an-Tol, Cornwall.

Despite these acts of 'vandalism', access to Stonehenge at the summer solstice reached a turning point in 1998, as one hundred people – a mixture of Druids, Pagans, neo-Shamans, archaeologists, locals and press – were allowed to walk freely among the stones and, if they wanted to, conduct 'rituals'. The non-confrontational nature of these proceedings resulted in access being made even easier the following year. The five-mile exclusion

Figure i Two Wiccans complete a ritual at Avebury's 1996 graffiti to elucidate who was responsible. The result is a psychic or trance drawing of the individual concerned, at the bottom of the photograph
Source: Courtesy of Calyx Multimedia

zone was officially removed for the first time in fourteen years, and anyone could reach the fence surrounding the stones. This event was not as peaceful as the year before since a number of people (variously named 'new age travellers', 'smellies', or 'hippies' by the press), 'invaded' (also a press term) the stones, some dancing triumphantly on the trilithons. More thought went into plans for the 2000 and 2001 solstices when 'open access' to the stones and landscape was provided for all. Scenes in 2001 were not only reminiscent of the original 'festival', but suggest that up to 14,500 people can gather at the monument with only five arrests and without major impact: the one misdemeanour I saw was just after dawn when an individual climbed a trilithon (not reaching the lintel) with a firework that created a scorch mark. These events at monuments on Salisbury Plain suggest a study of the diversity of 'alternative' engagements and their situation *vis-à-vis* British archaeology is timely indeed.

Such occurrences, however, are not restricted to the UK. On the contrary, they are reflected globally. In Peru, for instance, indigenous shamans have been commercialised by neo-Shamans who conduct 'spiritual tours' to ancient sites such as Machu Picchu. In South Africa 'white' sangomas might be accused of cultural appropriation when they learn shamanistic techniques from previously suppressed black Africans. This neo-colonialism is far more pronounced in the USA, where many Native Americans are extremely angry at what they see as the 'stealing' of their traditions by 'New Agers', be it mythologies, sweat lodges or ancient monuments. The ancient monuments of the Southwest, such as Chaco Canyon, have been implicated in complex debates between Native Americans, archaeologists and various alternative interest groups. This tension has been building for some years, at least since Carlos Castaneda's books prompted a deluge of hippie, Yaqui Indian-seeking pilgrims to descend on the Sonoran Desert in Mexico in the 1960s. But perhaps such appropriation originated much earlier, when the first ethnographers began 'playing Indian' in the USA (e.g. P.J. Deloria 1998), and antiquarians revived Druidry in the UK (e.g. Piggott 1968).

In this book I explore the socio-politics of ecstasy to show that despite the obvious sensationalism of these examples, the impact of such 'neo-Shamanisms' has been largely ignored. I attempt to redress this imbalance of study by exploring neo-Shamans with reference to their origins, practices, representations of the past in the present, engagements with archaeological monuments, and interactions with indigenous peoples. Despite the negative examples of neo-Shamanisms mentioned above, I in no way denounce practitioners outright but intentionally draw attention to the importance of the issues. Neo-Shamanisms are largely misunderstood, and in producing a well-rounded assessment, I make a point of discussing their positive contribution. Such issues demonstrate some of the implications neo-Shamanisms have for you, whether your angle is archaeological, anthropological, indigenous, and/or neo-Shamanic. But in answering a question, which I suspect many people may ask on opening this book – 'what have neo-Shamanisms got to do with me?' – I must also explain what neo-Shamanisms have got to do with me, Robert Wallis.

I came to this work as a trained archaeologist, but also with a personal involvement in neo-Shamanisms. This has created many tensions for me, tensions I am forced to resolve on a day-to-day basis. Most of all, my 'coming out' as a so-called 'neo-Shaman' is controversial. But where conventional anthropologists might promptly reject my findings based on my being 'native', recent movements in ethnography confront the fallacy of the insider–outsider dichotomy. This 'experiential anthropology' challenges those anthropologists concerned with going native to alter their view. Their fear is a colonialist hangover, a fear of descent into 'savagery' (perhaps most vividly revealed by Joseph Conrad (1989 [1902]). Experiential anthropology deconstructs the paralogism of absolute 'objectivity' and 'detachment', and replaces them with the nuanced understandings the 'insider's' view can bring. In challenging the impasse of going native, my theoretical and methodological considerations may be broadly characterised as 'post-modern', traversing concepts of alternative archaeologies, post-colonial discourse, queer theory and multi-sited ethnography. These ideas coalesce into what I call an 'autoarchaeology' in which self-reflexively considering and taking into account our own socio-political locations and motivations is crucial to understanding the past and representations of it in the present. Rather than beginning with shamanisms in the past, as in an archaeology of shamanisms, an autoarchaeology of shamanisms – which is of course intrinsically related – necessarily begins with neo-Shamanisms, in the present.

One of my aims in this volume is to encourage people who may currently think neo-Shamanisms have nothing to do with them to think again. In so doing, I explore diverse territory in which neo-Shamanisms are implicated. Indeed, each of the chapters has the potential to be a single book in its own right, and I have decided to take a broad view of neo-Shamanisms so as not to homogenise the issues. A new dialogue of this kind is at risk of superficiality, and I think many critics unwittingly fall prey to this; but, by examining neo-Shamanisms writ large and in specific instances a greater understanding is possible and an appropriate balance between generality and specificity is accomplished. Following this strategy, certain key issues arise which demand attention.

In Chapter 1, I present the sources which have inaugurated and inspired neo-Shamanisms, particularly the resources of anthropology and archaeology. I single out key individuals and sources of inspiration, but it is beyond the scope of this volume to examine all neo-Shamanisms; indeed, such a comprehensive claim would be rather suspect and certainly facile. Rather than attempt a 'complete' (whatever that would look like) representation or ethnography of neo-Shamanisms, emphasis is placed on archaeological and anthropological aspects. Hence, certain figures and issues are discussed in detail, while others are mentioned where such analysis requires it. The most popular neo-Shamanic practice in the West, for example, former anthropologist Michael Harner's core-shamanism (e.g. Harner 1990 [1980]), is scrutinised in depth. Core-shamanism, alongside other neo-Shamanisms, is criticised by scholars and indigenous spokespersons for decontextualising, universalising, psychologising and individualising shamanisms (e.g. Johnson 1995; Smith 1994). Neo-Shamans are also accused of the 'romanticisation of shamanism' (Atkinson 1992: 323), and ignoring the 'dark side of the shaman' (Brown 1989). I discuss these criticisms in detail, but my perspective is not the denouncing of neo-Shamans outright; indeed, there are misunderstandings of their aims because critics ignore their diversity.

Certain benefits of neo-Shamanisms, or ways they have contributed in various spheres, are realised in this exploration. In consequence, this is a more wide-ranging and 'balanced' examination of neo-Shamanisms compared to previous critiques. The key to recognising the positive and negative aspects of neo-Shamanisms is the diversity of practices and practitioners, rather than catch-all stereotypes.

Neo-Shamans' diverse uses of the past, discussed in Chapter 2, deeply involve historians and archaeologists. Neo-Shamans tend to hold romantic images of the past and utilise primitivist stereotypes of ancient peoples such as 'the Celts'. Notions of Celtic and Nordic (or more generally 'Northern') shamans in antiquity tend not to be entertained by specialist academics, but meanwhile neo-Shamans reinvent, revive or reconstruct these 'shamanic' traditions according to literary sources and archaeological evidence. I produce ethnographic examples of Celtic and Heathen neo-Shamanisms, but rather than simply deconstruct them due to their holding of 'spurious' beliefs about the past, I argue many of these neo-Shamans actually express awareness of the complexities and sensitivities of their practices. I also assess the evidence they cite to establish whether ancient Celtic and Nordic shamanisms are plausible. Though rarely acknowledged by academics, there is a valuable contribution some of these non-academic practitioner researchers make in reaching wider audiences and approaching 'old evidence' in new ways.

Appropriation of the past is found most directly at archaeological sites. Chapter 3 reports the increasing engagement between neo-Shamans and ancient monuments, with the primary case examples of Stonehenge and Avebury. The Stonehenge situation has been well publicised, but the less well-known detrimental activity at Avebury has now prompted negotiations between site custodians and other interest groups. I present the opinions of neo-Shamans, Druids, travellers and other 'alternative' groups. The expropriation of these monuments, ownership of and management of the past, and rights of access, involve many, from archaeologists (including academic archaeologists, field archaeologists, museum workers, and site managers) and anthropologists to religious and historical studies, politicians and the police. Yet until very recently, neo-Shamans and their peers have not been addressed seriously in site management strategies, and furthermore, the political nature of site presentation has not been adequately examined. Potential areas of dispute, such as a British reburial issue, are discussed as case examples. I examine the physical and intellectual 'exclusion zone' imposed on neo-Shamanic site visitors to demonstrate that where there has been tension between alternative groups and the authorities, unofficial strategies which attempt to harmonise the groups have been implemented.

Examination of neo-Shamanisms in Britain is contrasted with the situation in USA, my second case study, in Chapter 5. Neo-Shamanisms are particularly prominent in California and the Southwest, and the situation is all the more different for the involvement of native groups. Indigenous peoples worldwide, but particularly many Native American communities, are critical of neo-Shamans because to them they perpetuate racist stereotypes and embody a continuation of cultural imperialism. The plurality of Native American voices complicates the issues: some 'genuine' medicine people actively encourage neo-Shamans, claims of Indian ancestry for other teachers are questionable, and others have waged 'war' on neo-Shamanic appropriation. I compare the character of neo-Shamanic neo-colonialism with previous anthropological and archaeological approaches to indigenous peoples to illustrate a common core of disrespect. Chaco Canyon in New Mexico and the perspectives of neo-Shamans and Native Americans comprise a case example. The implication of site 'spirituality' in political contests of their marginalisation and the conflict between state authorities, native and neo-Shamans at these monuments is highly sensitive. This research highlights the diverse and often impassioned socio-political views concerning the contemporary roles of ancient sites.

These research considerations are timely and controversial in current archaeology and anthropology. I do not make inflated attempts to resolve sensitive political tensions, but venture some guidelines to inform these considerations which might reciprocally benefit all interest groups via informed research and much-needed communication. I hope this volume makes plain to the various interest groups that neo-Shamanisms have very much to do with us. If avoidance of the politics and ethics of neo-Shamanisms continues, hitherto neglected contemporary neo-Shamanic agendas for the archaeological past and ethnographic present will compromise all voices into increasingly difficult positions.

ACKNOWLEDGEMENTS

I am indebted to many people who have supported me and critically scrutinised my work over the past five years. Foremost, Thomas Dowson, for supervision and support beyond the requirements of an MA and PhD supervisor, and for constant encouragement ever since. For inspiration and advice I am also hugely thankful to Jenny Blain, Graham Harvey and Ronald Hutton. Unfortunately, Ronald Hutton's book 'Shamans' (Hambledon 2002) was not available before going to press – no doubt, it would have been essential reading while researching this volume.

I am grateful to the Department of Archaeology, University of Southampton (including some of its former members), especially Tim Champion, J.D. Hill, David Hinton, Andy Jones, Stephanie Moser, David Peacock, Brian Sparkes and Julian Thomas. Thanks also to Mary Baker, Chris Fowler, Jayne Gidlow, Sophia Jundi, Matt Leivers, Doug Murphy, and the Rock Art MA instructional postgraduates 1996–2001. I owe considerable thanks to Simon Crook and Ken Lymer for their kindred 'permeability' and thank my undergraduate and postgraduate students whose engaging discussions on some of these issues have contributed to the arguments set out in this volume.

I am also grateful to Brian Bates and Jan Fries who both directed me in the uncertainty of the beginning. Insightful comments on various drafts were welcomed from Jenny Blain, Simon Buxton, Simon Crook, Thomas Dowson, Ed Evans, Claire Gaudion, Darren Glazier, Martin Griffiths, Graham Harvey, Ronald Hutton, Merete Demant Jakobsen, Ken Lymer, Simon Macartney, Joan Townsend and Alex Woodcock. Funding from the University of Southampton School of Research and Graduate Studies, the Richard Newitt Fund and the Postgraduate Conference Attendance Fund, made various aspects of this research possible. I am grateful to Richard Stoneman, Julene Barnes and the helpful staff at Routledge for their support, and the three anonymous reviewers who offered highly constructive comments.

My British case study owes itself to the many 'neo-Shamans' (for want of a better word) who communicated with me, conceded to do interviews, allowed me to participate in their rituals, and discussed their very personal practices with me. In particular, thanks to Philip 'Greywolf' Shallcrass (BDO), Tim Sebastion (SOD), Gordon 'the toad' MacLellan, Shivam O'Brian of Spirit Horse Nomadic Circle, Leo Rutherford and Howard Charing of Eagle's Wing for Contemporary Shamanism, 'Runic' John, Barry of Coventry Earth Spirit, Malcolm, Gyrus, 'Carl' and 'James'. The work at Avebury and Stonehenge could not have been done without the assistance of Christopher Gingell and Paul Devereux; and Clews Everard, Tim Sebastion and Philip 'Greywolf' Shallcrass, respectively. On issues of site management and neo-Shamanism I benefited from discussions with David Miles, Melanie Pomerey, King Arthur Pendragon, Clare Prout/Slaney and Andy Norfolk.

The American case study was made possible by the Pueblo who offered their perspectives on a difficult and sensitive topic. Grateful thanks to Celestino Gachupin of Zia Pueblo, Petuuche Gilbert and Daniel Sanchez of Acoma, and Clay Hamilton of Hopi. I hope dissemination and publication benefit their tribes by further opening up awareness of the issues, and promoting dialogue where previously lacking. Christine Finn and Armin Geertz largely inspired this part of my discussion so I am grateful for their comments on various drafts, Wendy Bustard's encouragement and direction while in New Mexico were invaluable, and I thank Armand Labbé, who has been supportive without perhaps knowing it. On the West Coast, I thank Michael Harner of the Foundation for Shamanic Studies, and Diana Paxson and Rauðhildr of the Hrafnar community. Thanks also to Jeff McDonald, Mira Zussman, Tina Fields and Lisa Mertz of the Society for the Anthropology of Consciousness, and Jeff Hood in Santa Fe.

For permission to use quoted material and/or illustrations, I thank Carl McCoy (*Fields of The Nefilim*), Ward Churchill, *Cultural Survival Quarterly*, Caitlín Matthews, Calyx Multimedia, Eastern Counties Newspapers Ltd, Fulgur Ltd, Kenneth Grant, Mandrake of Oxford, Bernie Prior, The Sacred Trust and, for her line drawings, Sophia Jundi.

The companionship of Simon, Nathan, Mike, Martin, Dave, Dryw and Tim is ever a 'comfort and joy'. A final special thank you to my parents and Claire, for everything; to A.C. and A.O.S. for the beginning; and to L.L. and F.R. for now and, I hope, the future.

INTRODUCTION

A native at home – producing ethnographic fragments of neo-Shamanisms

> Before the mid-1960s, Shamanism interested only a few anthropologists and historians. Now travel agents are booking 'shamanic tours' [and] alternative healers advertise 'shamanic counseling'. Meanwhile a walk through any large bookstore will produce scores of titles with shaman, shamanic, and shamanism in them. In fact, 'how I became a shaman' is becoming a distinct literary category.
>
> (Clifton 1994: frontispiece)

> [G]iven the current place of shamans and shamanisms in spiritual movements and cultural commentary, it is incumbent on ethnographers to attend to the wider conversations both popular and academic, not only to devise new ways of being heard but also to engage reflexively these contemporary inventions.
>
> (Atkinson 1992: 321)

'Shamanism'[1] is in vogue at present. Anthropological interests have endured since the 1960s' explosion of studies on shamans, especially those who utilise(d) entheogens.[2] Archaeologists have constructed sophisticated shamanistic interpretations of the past, but their use of 'shamanism' is highly contested and accusations of 'shamania' (coined by Bahn 1996) and 'shamanophobia' (coined by Dowson 1996) abound (for critical discussion of issues surrounding these terms, see Wallis 2002b). In popular culture, various figures from Socrates and Shakespeare to Aleister Crowley, from Jim Morrison and Michael Jackson to the Pope, have been labelled 'shamans'.[3] Moreover, recent years have witnessed a growth in 'New Age', 'neo-', 'new' or 'modern' (or 'post-modern') shamanisms, a wide variety of 'spiritual' practices for personal and communal empowerment among Western[4] peoples. Despite numerous studies on shamanisms, the political and ethical sensitivities of neo-Shamanisms have gone largely unrecognised. Academia consistently marginalises neo-Shamans,[5] yet, ironically, there is more literature on shamanisms written by, or aimed at neo-Shamans than there are academic publications. Archaeology and anthropology, by virtue of their subjects of study, are deeply implicated in the rise of neo-Shamanisms; indeed their books are found juxtaposed with neo-Shamanic publications in all high-street bookshops. A particularly contentious area surrounds neo-Shamanic interactions with anthropology, archaeology and indigenous peoples; neo-Shamanisms are often regarded as 'fringe' and neo-colonialist, even 'the final step of colonisation' (Jacobs 1994: 307). Indigenous groups themselves express divergent views of neo-Shamanisms, from active encouragement to accusations of 'cultural genocide'. My study of neo-Shamanisms explores the complex and controversial issues neo-Shamanisms raise for archaeologists, anthropologists, indigenous communities, neo-Shamans themselves and related interest groups. In traversing and forging what is arguably a new field, the neo-Shamanic researcher must develop, refine and apply a careful and well-considered interpretative framework, what I term an 'autoarchaeology'.

Towards an 'autoarchaeology'

The impetus behind developing an autoarchaeology stems from a wide and far-reaching 'post-modern' shift in academic thought. The term 'post-modern' is fast becoming a cliché and overused to the extent that in the spirit of its deconstruction there is no single accepted meaning. Indeed, this plurality itself demonstrates that 'post-modern' is not a static term, that it must not replicate the catch-all mechanism of the metanarratives it deconstructs. Post-modern research, or research in the 'late modern age' (Giddens 1991), embodies a critique of the conventional logical positivist discourse derived from rationalist Enlightenment philosophy, which privileges the European, male, individual subject and the indisputable authority of scientific explanatory frameworks (see, for example, Lyotard 1986: xxiv). Detached scientific impartiality is no longer tenable, especially in social 'science', since the socio-political background of researchers inevitably influences and determines how data is interpreted and facts presented. In consequence, the worlds of archaeological and anthropological enquiry are no longer considered by many protagonists to be neutral and objective. Post-modernism has prompted researchers to be politically self-conscious and self-reflexive in their approaches (e.g. Crapanzano 1980; Cohen 1994; Denzin 1997; C.A. Davies 1999). One benefit has been an increased permeability of boundaries between disciplines and a trans-disciplinary methodology which C. Geertz (1983) terms 'blurred genres' and Strathern (1987a) refers to as 'pastiche'. The blurring of boundaries between archaeology, anthropology and religious studies, and even history and sociology in this book, promotes such an attitude.

The risk of post-modernism, on the other hand, is the extremity of judgmental relativism in which 'anything goes', where 'reality and fact are no longer certain' (Doty 1990: 269). A troubling result of post-modernism is an 'epistemological hypochondria' (Geertz 1988: 71), and in anthropology for instance,

> postmodernism has led, in the worst cases, to self-indulgent personal accounts [and] a kind of journalistic anthropology in which both theory and data are eschewed in favour of self-congratulatory literary flourishes. But the best practitioners have paid heeded attention to previously ignored alternative narratives and have developed a healthy critical stance towards the validity of anthropological research. These are constructive contributions worth emulating.
>
> (Lindholm 1997: 753)

To overcome fundamentalist relativism, it has become imperative that researchers move from a self-critical and perhaps self-destructive position, into an era of self-confidence (Ahmed and Shore 1995), and adopt a 'political standpoint which at the same time will articulate and challenge the assumptions framing not only the standpoints they challenge but also those they occupy ... standpoint specificity should be regarded as a resource, not a liability' (Wylie 1995: 268–270). This self-reflexive theme has been prominent in the theoretical and methodological stances of the auto-researcher, a position utilised and refined here for the purposes of approaching neo-Shamanisms. Indeed, examining the alterity of neo-Shamanisms requires a markedly alternative methodology.

Producing ethnographic insights into neo-Shamanisms necessitates a certain degree of qualitative autoethnography (see papers in Reed-Danahay 1997, particularly Motzafi-Haller; also Ellis and Bochner 2000; Blain 2002) and auto-anthropology, methodologies described as 'anthropology carried out in the social context which produced it' (Strathern 1987b: 17), or 'anthropology at home' (Jackson 1987). This self-reflexive position unites post-modern anthropologists who challenge the insider–outsider dichotomy in ethnography, and post-modern autobiographers who question the boundedness of individuality (Reed-Danahay 1997: 2). 'New ethnography' recognises the self-conscious, 'writerly quality of ethnographic treatises' (e.g. Clifford and Marcus 1986; Marcus and Fischer 1986; Rabinow 1988; Hammersley 1992), and the fertile opportunity for experimental writing (e.g. Ellis and Bochner 1996), with a 'self-consciously critical purpose'. The essence of such 'autoreferential poetry' (Fischer 1986: 195) is not that researchers are fabricating their ethnography. Rather, these approaches equip anthropologists with methodologies for approaching one's own culture ethnographically, an enterprise attesting to the fact that there is now a strong move for 'insider research'. In questioning the 'science envy' in branches of anthropology and archaeology which demand scholarly 'detachment', auto-anthropology opposes the dualism of the insider–outsider paradigm, and experiential anthropology radically alters the field technique of participant-observation by bringing into question not only the notion of 'going native', but also the seriousness with which we take the beliefs and practices of our 'informants' (with whom we engage in a two-way learning relationship; the label is perhaps better termed 'collaborators' or 'research assistants').

Challenging the insider–outsider divide

Ahmed and Shore encourage ethnographic research, ' "at home", not only among the marginal groups and minorities that exist within Western societies ... but also into the mainstream cultures of Western societies themselves' (1995: 27). Neo-Shamanisms are good subjects for this sort of ethnography, being simultaneously marginalised by the West, but also an increasingly acceptable aspect of middle England and America. Similarly, Marcus and Fischer (1986) urge self-reflexive anthropologists to use the 'self-as-subject' as an ethnographic category. Research of this kind blurs the insider–outsider divide. Furthermore, I agree with Favret-Saada, that it is vital for anthropologists to experience what they aim to understand. In her exploration of witchcraft in western France's Brocage, Favret-Saada realises the absurdity of neutral positioning in a situation where experience is everything: 'one must make up one's mind to engage in another kind of ethnography' (Favret-Saada 1980: 12). Such 'experiential anthropology' argues that anthropologists treat their own experiences as valid data (Turner 1994: 72; 1989). The perceived risk is of 'going native' with its 'fear of ostracism' (Young and Goulet 1994b: 8) from one's intellectual peers.

But, despite the stigma, the issue of going native is far less problematic in current ethnographic research. Up to a point, it is impossible to go native in the first place, since at a relativist extreme, we can only fully understand a culture if we have been raised in that social environment. And, when studying new religious components in our own culture we already are, in a sense, native (Salomonsen 1999: 7). The origins of concern at going native lie in an era when 'turning Indian' was seen as politically suspect, if not heretical, because turning your back on the West (the best), in favour of the 'savage' (the worst), was treasonous. In intellectual terms, the fear was of going against rationalist science in favour of primitive myth, and in religious terms, turning away from 'God', towards superstition. Going native has plagued anthropology at least since Lewis Henry Morgan and Frank Hamilton Cushing played at being 'Indian', and certainly since the likes of Michael Harner – anthropology professor turned major progenitor of neo-Shamanisms – consumed entheogens with his Amazonian Shuar shaman-informants in the psychedelic 1960s (see Chapter 1). Anthropologists have clearly been 'going native' for as long as they have pretended not to:

INTRODUCTION

Morgan's later anthropological work ... moved away from playing
Indian ... and focused instead on scientific paradigms that viewed
both Indian people and Indian pasts as objects – figures and histories of significant difference that were thus suitable for a detached
analysis. The anthropological discipline that eventually grew to
maturity around figures like Morgan gradually institutionalised this
subject-object dichotomy ... [E]thnography became an increasingly
powerful and influential method [but in] practice, anthropology
proved to be a problematic science at best, and its adherents
bolstered their intellectual authority by insisting on its objective
character. The insistence on ethnographic objectivity helped reinforce the perception that its primary research object – Indian people
– existed far beyond the pale of American society ... [P]articipant
observation – an insider approach that relied on empathy, subjectivity, and close contact with one's subjects – existed in continual
tension with the analytical system building of objective, outsider
comparative anthropology.

(P.J. Deloria 1998: 93)

In a hangover from our colonial and missionising past, anthropologists
today aim to get as close as possible to the culture they are studying, but
not too close. The criterion for closeness cannot be measured of course, just
as participant-observation does not 'specify accurately the kind of participation required' (Salomonsen 1999: 8). A case in point is Luhrmann (1989),
who researched Wicca (contemporary witchcraft) in Britain and has been
praised for:

preserving her anthropological integrity. 'The anthropologist', she
writes, 'is meant to become involved but not native' (p. 320).
Immersing herself in magical practices, she has nonetheless
succeeded in preserving her identity as an anthropologist ... anthropology at its very best.

(Flaherty 1991: 154–155)

Flaherty misses the point: since Luhrmann was initiated into witchcraft and
conducted rituals, she did go native, but in ceasing to be a coven member or
even a solo practitioner after fieldwork, apparently 'came back' again. But I
contend that Luhrmann may well have reached similar critical judgements
on Wicca had she remained 'native'. Pearson, a more recent autoethnographer of Wicca asserts, 'I do not ... consider myself to have broken the
anthropological taboo against "going native", for I already was native. The
situation has in fact been quite the reverse, "insider going outsider, going
native in reverse"' (Pearson 2001: 8). Indeed, the checks and balances in this
area are provided by peer review, a method considered – quite appropriately

5

– the mainstay of academic credibility. In effect, it does not matter how close anthropologists get, so long as their findings express the level of insight and constructive, critical evaluation which one's academic peers require for acceptable scholarship.

Participant-observation is an ethnographic field technique which requires revision in light of these comments (e.g. Tedlock 1991). Indeed 'direct observation' is an impossible ideal, indicative of 'pretension' (Salomonsen 1999), in that only a self-aggrandising 'detached' anthropologist would claim to be 'outside' and objectively unaffected, during an intense shamanic ritual for instance. This is even more the case in a Western setting where, as I have experienced at neo-Shamanic rituals, involvement is all or nothing. One cannot sit on the edge and take notes because being present necessitates taking part. As Salomonsen states:

> In the practice of modern mystery religions, you are either in, or you are not there at all. In my doctoral studies [I] had to put myself in the position of an apprentice, taking my own experiences seriously, observing the development of my own 'insight'.
>
> (Salomonsen 1999: 9)

Doing so entailed altering the current strategy of going native behaviourally ('participant-observation'), even emotionally ('empathy'), but not 'cognitively' (Salomonsen 1999: 7). Salomonsen calls this a 'method of compassion' which demands 'embodiment rather than disengagement', insisting that such an approach promises a healthy component of reflexivity in which constructive critical comment can be made (Salomonsen 1999: 9–10; see also 2002: 17–21). Rather than negatively influencing one's research, 'first hand experience may open the possibility to deep insight and the best description possible' (Salomonsen 1999: 8). Evidence of this is apparent in one other scholar's approach to Wicca, that of the historian Ronald Hutton who, in an interview for *The Independent on Sunday*, recounts his own experience at a ritual: 'he saw people's eyes change colour after they had become "possessed" by the goddess' (Stuart 2000: 22). This vivid experience of participation does not mean his *The Triumph of the Moon: A History of Modern Pagan Witchcraft* (1999) was marred by 'native' insights; indeed, the volume is a 'triumph' itself, not only for deconstructing the myth that Wicca is an unbroken tradition stretching back to the 'burning times' but also for vindicating Wicca as a religion relevant and valid for postmodernity.

If first-hand experience is fundamental to researching Wicca, then such also holds true when studying neo-Shamanisms, experiential 'spiritualities' wherein modes of verification depend on personal insight: unlike a Wiccan ritual with its detailed, 'revealed' ceremony, neo-Shamanic 'journeys' cannot easily be 'observed' or 'revealed'. Only by adopting an experiential ethnographer's role did I achieve what aims to be well-rounded perspectives on the various interest groups considered here. It also facilitated an ongoing addressing and redressing of my own partiality, my own perspective, in a politically explicit way which does not claim dubious credentials of objectivity and impartiality. Indeed, rather than threatening my academic credentials, I think they would be seriously open to question if I ignored my experiential approach or left it unsaid, for fear of ostracism. My intention is that such political explicitness actually promises a far more open-minded thesis. In making explicit my own positionality, however, I in no way wish to imply that I am on a moral high ground above other researchers of the subject, or above neo-Shamans, who of course are quite capable of speaking for themselves. In an era of transparency and accountability, my work is simply one way of telling peculiar to an archaeologist who, as I shall further extrapolate, is also a neo-Shamanic practitioner (or vice versa).

The fear of going native is related to a major failure in anthropology, perceived by Salomonsen (1999; see also Young and Goulet 1994a), to take the 'spiritual' realities of its 'subjects' seriously:

> A scholar who takes belief seriously and acknowledges that the people studied may know something about the human condition that might be personally valid also for the anthropologist, runs the risk of going native, and thereby the risk of abandonment by the scientific community.
>
> (Salomonsen 1999: 7)

One of the few anthropologists to 'go serious' is Edith Turner, who recounts fieldwork with her husband among the Ndembu of Zambia who believe in 'spirits',[6] a belief the anthropologists assumed they need not entertain because they were simply there to study these beliefs. In this positivist stance, as the Turners came to realise, 'we denied the people's equality with ours, their "coevalness"' (Turner 1992: 28). In one ritual, Turner 'sighted a spirit form' during a healing ceremony:

> I saw with my own eyes a large grey blob of something like plasma emerge from the sick woman's back. Then I knew the Africans were right. There is spirit stuff. There is spirit affliction: it isn't a matter of metaphor and symbol, or even psychology. And I began to see how anthropologists have perpetuated an endless series of putdowns about the many spirit events in which they have participated – 'participate' in a kindly pretence. They might have obtained valuable material, but they have been operating with the wrong paradigm, that of the positivist's denial ... Thus for me, 'going native' achieved a breakthrough to an altogether different

7

world-view, foreign to academia, by means of which certain material was chronicled that could have been gathered in no other way.

(Turner 1992: 28)

The 'positivist's denial' Turner speaks of is in fact a vestige of imperialism. It
tells the shaman or neo-Shaman that the 'spirits' or 'other than human
persons' they engage with are more symbolic and metaphorical than real,
and Turner compares such a standpoint with that of the colonialist
missionary 'sworn to eliminate their hosts' religion' (1992: 30). Just as
indigenous researchers have now, in response, developed 'decolonizing
methodologies' (Smith 1999), so insiders in contemporary and new
'Western' religions, particularly Paganisms, are effectively challenging the
stereotypical representations of their practices by non-practitioners, by
developing and refining reflective and reflexive insider-based methodologies.
The requirement then is, as Jackson points out:

> To break the habit of using a linear communicational model for
> understanding bodily praxis, it is necessary to adopt a methodolog-
> ical strategy of joining in without ulterior motive and literally
> putting oneself in the place of other persons; inhabiting their world.
> Participation thus becomes an end in itself rather than a means of
> gathering closely observed data which will be subject to interpreta-
> tion elsewhere after the event.

(Jackson 1989: 58)

Turner and Jackson, among an increasing number of researchers challenging
the insider–outsider divide, are advocating what I would term a 'queer'
methodology which disrupts normative anthropological methods of inquiry.
Indeed, there is a growing movement in anthropology for explicit confession
of the unusual experiences which occur when studying the 'religious'
domains of other cultures. Such experiences highlight how the 'irrationality'
of the Other – be it shamans or neo-Shamans – by virtue of its Otherness,
cannot be explored in scientific, rational terms which limit the interpretive
possibilities open to us. Rather than making judgements based on singular,
scientific reality, a more suitable hermeneutic framework for addressing
shamanic/neo-Shamanic experiences is according to 'multiple realities'
(Young and Goulet 1994a). Certainly, the unusual experiences I have had
during rituals and workshops are beyond scientific analysis, cannot be
subjected to 'truth value', and lead to a richer and nuanced understanding of
neo-Shamanisms (Young and Goulet 1994b: 11–12).[7] Experiential anthropology challenges the suggestion that self-reflexive and scientific
methodologies are commensurable, and this is a position I have found vital
to understanding neo-Shamanisms; an understanding facilitated by a number
of related theoretical discourses. But rather than reflecting eclecticism, the

various theoretical discourses I adapt to autoarchaeology address specific, albeit wide-ranging issues, central to an inquiry into neo-Shamanisms.

'Alternative' archaeologies and anthropologies

For the purposes of this study, Alison Wylie's assertion that 'evidence is never autonomous of theory' and that archaeology 'is always, in different ways and to varying degrees, a political undertaking' (Wylie 1995: 256–257) is apt. My autoarchaeological approach *vis-à-vis* neo-Shamanisms is not neutral and impartial, but rather a politically located representation informed by my situated standpoint (following Harding 1991). This 'politically self-conscious' exclamation, as Wylie (1995: 271) calls it, is increasingly being adopted by social scientists who recognise that only by being politically explicit can they do 'honest' research. The perspective of socio-political location used here not only necessitates reflexive examination of my own position but also provides an avenue into contextualisation of neo-Shamanisms as socio-political phenomena. As such, neo-Shamanisms mark just one example of the many alternative voices which are marginalised by academia. Suggesting that academia is a conservative institution which privileges its own views over others is not new. A challenge facing anthropologists and archaeologists in the contemporary arena is to accommodate alternative voices in their narratives. As Bender suggests (reflecting on Stonehenge):

> [J]ust as the past cannot be unhooked from the present, so academia cannot be unhooked from the larger body politic. Passively or actively we are involved. We might as well be active; might as well get involved over issues which are not really about access to a particular place but about access to knowledge, access to the past and to the land, and, ultimately, about tolerance. We might as well play a part in creating, to adopt Foucault's terminology, 'a counter-archaeology of social knowledge' ... part of the ethnographer's role is to document the complex engagement of this counter-archaeology with the symbolism and meanings of official discourse.
>
> (Bender 1998: 171)

From this standpoint, ethnographies of neo-Shamanisms involve writing what Schmidt and Patterson call 'alternative histories' (Schmidt and Patterson 1995). Wylie states that 'much crucially written history is not written at all' (Wylie 1995: 257), and here I write one of those histories using four inter-connected modes of acquiring knowledge. First, that of neo-Shamanisms; second, narratives of the past which neo-Shamans create; third, indigenous perspectives on neo-Shamanisms, and vice versa; and fourth, my own personal history which inevitably permeates this research.

Archaeologists have only recently come to consider 'world religions' such as Buddhism and Islam (e.g. Insoll 2001), let alone contemporary 'religious' practices such as neo-Shamanisms. The academic marginalisation of neo-Shamanisms reflects a hegemony implicit in archaeological/anthropological discourses, a hegemony which is evident in such works as *Cult Archaeology and Creationism: Understanding Pseudoscientific Beliefs about the Past* (Harrold and Eve 1995; see also Feder 1996), in which it is assumed that 'science' is the base-line, has the real answers, while alternative archaeologies are misguided 'pseudo-science'.[8] An unnamed *American Antiquity* reviewer cited on the back cover said of it: 'Now needed more than ever ... A very useful book', but rather than reinforcing outmoded stereotypes, what is really needed more than ever is a less sardonic approach to alternative archaeologies. The flaw in foundationalist epistemology is that it assumes 'orthodox' (correct) and 'fringe' (wrong) approaches are commensurable (Denning 1999a). This assumption is challenged by hermeneutics, in which multiple rather than single interpretations are encouraged. Instead of hegemonic terms like 'deviant', 'fringe', 'cult' or 'pseudo' archaeology, the less pejorative term 'alternative' should be used (Denning 1999a; see also interesting comments by Hiscock 1996). As well as writing alternative archaeologies into our discourse, this process reflexively promotes recognition of the socio-political motivations affecting the interest groups (in addition to Denning's research and my own, Stout [e.g. 2001] is one other archaeologist whose work follows this line of thought).

Denning suggests, for example, that 'popular archaeology books have at least partly replaced traditional religious wisdom', and neo-Shamanic representations of Celtic, Heathen and Neolithic shamanisms mark archaeological instances of this (Chapters 3–6), just as their representations and uses of indigenous shamanisms mark anthropological examples (Chapter 7). Denning continues,

> [M]ost archaeologists respond to such books with derision, or respond not at all. The books are seen as either bad archaeology, or nothing to do with archaeology ... underestimating the complexity of these narratives and ... their position in society, not to mention taking a rather narrow view of archaeology.
>
> (Denning 1999b: 95–96)

In contrast, my 'alternative' research is a representation and exploration of neo-Shamanic narratives which most directly affect archaeologists and anthropologists. It aims to show the extent to which neo-Shamanic approaches to archaeology, anthropology and wider society are important. Beyond simply challenging the stability of established academic discourse, some neo-Shamanic narratives disrupt conventionality in new ways which enhance the richness of anthropological and archaeological inquiry.

Academics can best view their role from the angle of historiography in which the historian cannot be separated from the history and histories always meet certain needs; thereby a more nuanced understanding of history is produced. An important feature arising from this hermeneutic approach is that the diversity of neo-Shamanic practitioners and perspectives is allowed to 'speak out'. In direct contrast to the foundationalist approach which 'exposes' frauds and makes monolithic judgements, exploring diversity recognises and represents multiple voices.

My exploration of neo-Shamanisms according to the diversity of practitioners is consistent with recent interpretative trends in 'shamanism' (e.g. Humphrey 1996; Thomas 1994; Harvey forthcoming) and rock art (e.g. Dowson 1998c) studies, which move away from generalities towards localised socio-political contexts of shamans, and which require examination of specificity and diversity. We require a theorising[9] of 'shamanism' in archaeology – an archaeology of shamanisms – and in his 1999a paper, Dowson argues definitions belie such requirements and that a conceptual shift is required in which we approach 'elements of shamanism' (or even less restrictively, shaman*isms*) and explore the diversity of them in specific communities, rather than 'define' or otherwise attempt to pin 'shamans' down to a check-list of features or specific 'religious' phenomenon (contra Price 2001b following Guenther 1999). These elements of shamanisms are: (1) agents consistently alter consciousness;[10] (2) these altered states are accepted as ritual practices by the agent's community; and (3) knowledge concerning altered consciousness is controlled in effecting certain socially sanctioned practices (after Dowson 1999a, in press); these themes underpin my theoretical and methodological considerations of the subject and, I hope, promise a more nuanced understanding of neo-Shamanisms than has hitherto been advanced.

In espousing this hermeneutic approach, I am not promoting judgmental relativism; representing multiple voices need not mean 'anything goes'. As Bender suggests, 'rather than float on a sea of relativity, one can position oneself so as to ask questions and propose interpretations that seem relevant to contemporary concerns' (Bender 1998: 5). Beyond deconstruction and multiplicity, constructive criticism is required and I have attempted to apply Wylie's suggestion that standpoint theory should be melded with empirical enquiry (1995: 272; also Wylie 1992), an empirical reflexivity in which not all realities are seen as fictions and *a priori* incommensurable. I evaluate critiques of neo-Shamanisms and present my own criticisms, particularly those surrounding representations of the past such as Celtic and Heathen neo-Shamanisms. But while established archaeology does not tend to entertain notions of Iron Age or Germanic shamanisms, my assessment of neo-Shamanic interpretations suggests they do make a contribution to archaeology. The key is to embrace a diversity of interpretative narratives which contribute to an ongoing debate, rather than promote a monolithic and judgmental view in which academic standpoints are privileged over other, alternative positions. This facilitates a range of conclusions and suggestions in an alternative archaeology and anthropology which challenges academic and social normativity, an activist approach most notably advanced by queer theorists.

Queering theory

Despite the contemporary meaning of 'queer', queer theory (e.g. De Lauretis 1991; Butler 1994) is not solely about gender relations or constructions of sexuality. Indeed, queer is not restricted to explorations of homosexuality, gender or sex. It begins by disrupting all forms of normativity, thereby not only 'reordering the relations among sexual behaviours, erotic identities, constructions of gender' but at the same time, 'forms of knowledge, regimes of enunciation, logics of representation, modes of self-constitution, and practices of community' (Halperin 1995: 62). In this way, it 'acquires its meaning from its oppositional relation to the norm. Queer is by definition whatever is at odds with the normal, the legitimate, the dominant' (Halperin 1995: 62). It is therefore open to 'anyone who feels their position (sexual, intellectual or cultural) to be marginalised' (Dowson 1998b: 84). Furthermore, it is not a 'unified', 'fashionable theory' doomed to be simply a passing fad, 'rather it is defined by one's practice in relation to an accepted norm' (Dowson 1998a).

Queer theory informs my research in two ways. First, this research is a dissonant act with regard to orthodox archaeological and anthropological discourse so that my own location is queer. In this, I am mindful of Halperin's warning:

> What makes 'queer' potentially so treacherous as a label is that its lack of definitional content renders it all too readily available for appropriation by those who do not experience the unique political disabilities and forms of social disqualification from which lesbians and gay men routinely suffer in virtue of our sexuality.
>
> (Halperin 1995: 65)

Meskell's use of queer in relation to Ancient Egyptian necrophilia (1998a), according to Dowson (1998b), marks one such example of misappropriation. In contrast, my involvement in neo-Shamanisms at an experiential level places me in a location with credentials reflecting the marginalisation Halperin refers to, and which are prerequisite to utilising queer theory. For instance, with my involvement in neo-Shamanisms and as a trained archaeologist, I have often felt torn between two irreconcilable opposites. I began my research feeling incredibly uneasy, trying to write an 'objective' account of a 'fringe' religion. But of course, this subject area resists 'objective' analysis and is sufficiently beyond mainstream research to foil my writing about it in a conventional academic way. On approaching my 'informants' I felt further uneasiness, being too academically (objectively) minded to engage with them in as intimate a dialogue as I would have liked. I have been able to resolve conflicts such as these by unloading the needless baggage of perceived scientific objectivity and by being up front about my own positionality to both academics and neo-Shamans. This has thwarted my conversations with some academics, but perhaps more importantly has considerably opened up my relationship with neo-Shamans and more liberal academics. Through a somewhat painful transformation into an autoarchaeologist, I have found that my perspective does not fall in either archaeological or neo-Shamanic camps, nor midway between the two, but marks a different – marginalised – position altogether. As an autoarchaeologist, I am claiming my own voice. Just as I cannot speak only as a 'neo-Shaman', to speak only as an archaeologist would downplay neo-Shamanic influences in my narrative. And to claim an objective standpoint from either position would ignore the influence of my work on neo-Shamans themselves. Scholars researching contemporary Paganisms, particularly 'insiders', are finding their research is agentic in Pagan, neo-Shamanic and other understandings and constructions of themselves; this is a fascinating state of affairs and it is incumbent upon these researchers to be self-reflectively responsive to their role in the construction and development of Pagan identities.

Combined with my academic training and the various benefits that embodies, my neo-Shamanic and autoarchaeological location places me in a unique situation from which to study neo-Shamanisms: as occupational atheists, archaeologists have only recently begun to study world religions (e.g. Insoll 2001), let alone new or unconventional religions and archaeology, or their own religious experiences and the effects of them on their work. In addition to this decidedly queer location, the second way in which queer theory informs my research is that neo-Shamanisms are also queer due to their marginalisation by the majority of Western society. As Dowson suggests, 'masculist scientific practice of archaeology downplays or denies a number of ways of knowing about the past' (1998a; see also 1999b), and neo-Shamanisms represents such marginalised ways of knowing. Essentially, queer theory facilitates appreciation of the peculiar nature of my own standpoint and those of neo-Shamans, *vis-à-vis* the normativity of Western society and academia. Indeed, a growing number of researchers are adopting a queer location, looking towards greater awareness and deconstruction of our backgrounds in metanarrative and dualism. A queer perspective recognises the diversity of neo-Shamanisms and how they cannot be generalised. Exploring this diversity reveals that while some practitioners have a very queer approach, radically reorienting conventional world-views, concepts of 'spirit' and gender distinctions, others are more conservative, even racist, homo-phobic, neo-colonialist or otherwise supportive of normative Western cultural values. These latter viewpoints are challenged in various ways by discursive neo-Shamans, offended indigenous communities and critical academics. So it is that neo-Shamans, as much as academia and Western discourse, are challenged by queer theory to redress themselves away from masculist representations of 'truth' and 'knowledge'.

Autoarchaeology and post-processualism

Dowson (1998a) argues that 'queer theory disrupts the normativity of archaeological practice, truly enabling a radical rethinking of the past in ways that post-processualism has failed to accomplish'. His claim that post-processual archaeology has failed to 'de-normatise its discourse' is important in my approach to the 'extraordinary[11] experiences' (Young and Goulet 1994a) of neo-Shamans. I think Dowson refers particularly to post-processualism's masculist bias, but it remains normative in other ways, especially when drawing on hegemonic discourses, Western philosophy and scientific paradigms (see also Hassan 1997; VanPool and VanPool 1999). I argue these difficulties inherent in post-processualism make it inadequate for approaching neo-Shamanisms, and that autoarchaeology is better equipped for such explorations.

Many post-processualists have moved substantially beyond hegemonic impositions by advocating plurality (e.g. Bender 1998). They have also been unfairly characterised as judgmental relativists because of this equality of interpretations.[12] It still remains, however, that many post-processualists implicitly privilege certain interpretations over others. Hassan (1997) incisively critiques Hodder's (1997) reflexive excavation methodology at Çatalhüyük for instance, arguing that where Hodder claims multivocality (e.g. Hodder 2000), it is still the white, male academic whose more 'legitimate' interpretations prevail over and above goddess spirituality. Nonetheless, Hodder's work, along with that of community and other archaeologists who are reflexively opening up and brokering their knowledge beyond academe, marks a significant develop-ment in archaeological practice (see also Lucas 2001 and various articles by UCL's Leskernick project, available online: http://www.ucl.ac.uk/lesker-nick/articles.html). Indeed, the contradiction Hassan identifies is not self-defeating since we all have particular and individual views to express – we need only be self-reflectively aware of them; but still, neo-Shamanisms and the perspectives of other interest groups are consistently marginalised by archaeologists. As well as failing to present multiple voices as it claims, post-processualism's sidelining of neo-Shamanisms also downplays the relationship between archaeology and wider culture (following Grimshaw and Hart 1995: 61), a political role it aims to accommodate.

Post-processualists consistently utilise Western philosophy to re-evaluate orthodox archaeology and inform their interpretations (e.g. papers in Holtorf and Karlsson 2000). Since Western philosophy is by and large atheistic, and in part founded in Christian dualism, I argue that it does not supply the means for approaching and appreciating the complexity of (neo-) shamanic world-views. Moreover, according to this 'atheist hegemonic discourse' (Ewing 1994; see also Berger 1980), 'religious' arenas are reduced to an entirely social phenomenon (e.g. Salomonsen 1999). I do not eschew sociological approaches to shamanisms; indeed, the emphasis in this volume is that a socio-political approach to shamanisms and neo-Shamanisms (and other contemporary 'religious' practices) is essential. But, such an approach is also limited if the 'spiritual' (for want of a better term) component is ignored, as post-processualists implicitly do (as, unfortunately do Dowson's 'elements of shamanism'). Where ethnographic or archaeological examples of shamans and 'spirits' are encountered by conventional archaeology, they are explained away in terms of functionalist, structuralist, symbolic or metaphorical models (but see the emergence of a greater sensitivity towards this latter issue in Dowson 1998c). Since Western philosophy cannot accommodate 'religion', so post-processualism, in line with its conventional forebears, retreats to the safety of 'symbol' (Hodder 1992) and 'metaphor' (Tilley 1999). These literary terms derive in part from semiotic anthropology with its emphasis on 'narrative', and the literary bent in post-modern social science which follows Derrida in 'reading' cultures as 'texts'.

This literary metaphoric approach is reminiscent of Turner's use of 'performance' and 'drama' (Layton 1997) to approach ritual, and in studies on shamanisms this continues to be manifest in the search for a definition of 'shamanism' in which the role of performance is held by some researchers to be a characteristic feature. Descriptions and analyses of shamanisms then involve the terms 'role-taking', 'performance', 'play' and 'theatre' (e.g. Siikala 1978; Hamayon 1993, 1994, 1998; but see Hultkrantz 1998c), and one researcher of neo-Shamanisms also utilises this approach (Lindquist 1997). To their credit, I think it important not to downplay or disregard the power of 'performance' in the theatre, the emancipatory value of children's 'play', or the empowering faculty of imagination as hailed by the neo-Shamanic 'imaginal realm' of some post-Jungian psychology (e.g. Noel 1997). Use of 'performance' to explore forms of embodiment, agency and mimesis (see especially Bakhtin 1993, and for a review Boddy 1994: 422–426), and to approach life in terms of a performance rather than regard some things as performed (e.g. ritual) but not others (e.g. work), is particularly informative (e.g. Bell 1998) – now also in archaeological praxis (Pearson and Shanks 2001); these authors problematise and theorise the issues and do not deny the seriousness of such 'performances'. But off-the-cuff use of 'performance', 'play' and 'imagination' is inappropriate when applied to shamanisms and neo-Shamanisms because of the deep-rooted connotations they imply of theatrics, fantasy and make-believe (see also Blain and Wallis in prep.) – a point also made by neo-Shamanic practitioners themselves (e.g. Horwitz 1998). Shamanic/neo-Shamanic experiences are not make-believe – shamans/neo-Shamans believe the 'spirit world' they interact with is real, very real indeed – and shamanism studies has in some more theorised quarters moved beyond conceptions of shamans as theatrical char-latans. Using 'performance' and other metaphors[13] for understanding and interpreting shamanisms/neo-Shamanisms therefore runs the risk of ignoring their seriousness and discredits practitioners. It may in part derive from a peculiarly atheistic, scientific perspective and reflects a deep-seated need on the part of Westerners to retreat into the comfort of metaphor rather than address the 'reality' of 'spirits' to shamans/neo-Shamans. Similarly, 'narrative' and other literary terms have been useful in relativising our discourses, but the use of literary metaphors as an interpretive strategy by post-processual archaeologists signals an ambiguous and safe location (rather than a politi-cally explicit one) which implicitly avoids the need to profess belief, even in one's own archaeological interpretation. Most importantly, one's own reli-gious or atheistic faith is ignored; it is assumed that the Western researcher and reader is atheist. In this way, while post-processualists often explicitly acknowledge their Western and socio-political biases, I think their approaches are more rooted in masculist, positivist, scientific discourse than some would claim. In questioning post-processualism, my queer autoarchae-ological approach to shamanisms and neo-Shamanisms challenges normative archaeological and anthropological discourse. As a self-reflexive position it owes much to the dissonant stances of feminist and queer theorists (e.g. Gatens 1991; Haraway 1991; Butler 1993; Dowson 2001a), though such theorists equally tend to be atheistic or at least rational materialist.

Post-colonial/neo-colonial concerns

Post-colonial theory and the issue of neo-colonialism mark a final line of inquiry which informs my approach to neo-Shamanisms. Neo-Shamanisms are, for example, expressions of the 'disembeddedness of radical modernity' (Johnson 1995: 174). This can be seen as resulting at least in part from the breakdown of colonialism and the advent of the post-modern epoch with its widespread disillusionment in Western, industrial, capitalist culture (e.g. Heelas 1996). My two geographical foci, North America and Britain, are two loci of the post-colonial empire where neo-Shamanisms are most promi-nent and polemical, and which compare and contrast in very different ways. Williams and Chrisman provide clarification of the related terms 'colo-nialism' and 'imperialism':

> [C]olonialism, the conquest and direct control of other people's
> land, is a particular phase in the history of imperialism, which is

16

now best understood as the globalisation of the capitalist mode of production, its penetration of previously non-capitalist regions of the world, and destruction of pre- or non-capitalist forms of social organisation.

(Williams and Chrisman 1993: 2)

In recognising the processes of colonialism and imperialism, post-colonial analysis 'increasingly makes clear the nature and impact of inherited power relations, and their continuing effects on modern global culture and politics' (Ashcroft *et al.* 1998: 1). Neo-colonialism, or 'new colonialism', is one manifestation of these 'continuing effects' and gives a better impression of their immediacy where 'post-colonial' gives a misleading sense of finality and closure. As is typical of neo-colonialist processes, some neo-Shamanic appropriations, or misappropriations, of indigenous culture are 'more insidious and more difficult to detect and resist than older overt colonialism' (Ashcroft *et al.* 1998: 163). Not only does the post-colonial culture of the West regard neo-Shamanisms as eccentric and harmless, so also do many neo-Shamans themselves. Indeed they often believe their utilisations of indigenous culture are sympathetic to the aims of indigenous people (although sometimes this may not be so in practice). Some neo-Shamans go even further, to erase native cultures from history by fantasising about a 'noble savage', or by suggesting they are incapable custodians of their shamanic inheritance which should be surrendered into more capable Western hands (as discussed by Root 1996: 93–94). This blinkered vision on the part of the West and its neo-Shamans makes it all the more difficult for affected indigenous cultures to resist neo-colonialism since their cries are written off as being political, paranoid, and/or sensationalist. Academics may also ignore neo-Shamanism's neo-colonialism according to these premises. Neo-Shamanic engagements are reminiscent of anthropological and archaeological approaches to indigenous communities which were an integral and operative part of the West's imperialist and colonialist past. Today, archaeologists and anthropologists may prefer to distance themselves from this colonial era, but:

> [The] romantic engagement of shamans in popular culture forces anthropologists to rethink their own roles and discursive stances vis-à-vis shamanic practice [... an example of] the predicament facing contemporary ethnography.

(Atkinson 1992: 323)

For those researchers who express a 'post-colonial hesitancy' (Vitebsky 1995a) to examine neo-Shamanisms and other neo-colonial manifestations, a dangerous predicament results. Neglecting analysis of neo-Shamanisms avoids our contemporary political and social roles, and rather than challenging the dissidents, may inadvertently sanction their neo-colonialist activities. Exploring aspects of neo-Shamanisms in light of post-colonial discourse and acts of neo-colonialism enables the formulation of certain perspectives and interpretations based on the problem of cultural appropriation. It also facilitates the formulation of guidelines for pragmatically addressing the issues.

Autoarchaeological 'ethnographic fragments'

The various theoretical and methodological considerations discussed above coalesce into an autoarchaeology. I have accordingly been politically explicit and self-reflexive with regard to my own socio-political location and motivations for undertaking this study of neo-Shamanisms. Autoarchaeology in other circumstances would certainly require very different theoretical and methodological considerations specific to the needs of the project. The sort of autoarchaeology I have detailed here has had major implications when gathering data during fieldwork. Not least because the subject matter is so diverse and fragmented – quintessentially post-modern – that attempting a singular and complete ethnography of neo-Shamanisms would be naïve, if not flawed. I must therefore be clear that what I present here is a 'partial' ethnography, or consists of 'ethnographic fragments' as I prefer to call them, but very detailed fragments nonetheless which I believe provide a suitable overview of these fascinating phenomena. My techniques for gathering the ethnographic fragments involved participant-observation, interviews, dialogues and assessments of written literature (e.g. Werner and Schoepfle 1987; Bernard 1988). However, the unconventionality of exploring an alternative subject necessitated a refining of these qualitative techniques when attending neo-Shamanic workshops/rituals and conducting interviews. Experiential anthropology was utilised at numerous neo-Shamanic workshops, aimed mainly at the beginner and where participants learn the techniques of 'shamanism'; and at rituals, where experienced neo-Shamans interact with their 'spirit world' in more complex ways.[14]

Conventional interview techniques proved limiting during the fieldwork. Rather than following a standard procedure which could be repeated, their format varied in each instance depending on the interest group involved – neo-Shamans, Native Americans and heritage managers. Some interviews, with Michael Harner (Director of the FSS) and Leo Rutherford (Eagle's Wing), for instance, were conducted using a tape-recorder and specific pre-prepared questions. These questions did not remain fixed, however, as new points and directions emerged during the interview and were followed. Rather than disrupting the interview process, this dialogic technique gathered information which would not have otherwise been possible. The value of this semi-structured and open-ended technique has been commented on by feminist researchers in particular (e.g. Reinharz

1992: 18; Moser 1995). It is useful, for example, in its space for openness, clarification and discussion.[15]

Using an audio tape-recorder, as in orthodox ethnographic interviews, was not possible with Native Americans interviewees. The familiar story of 'anthros' invading the 'res' and probing microphones where they caused offence and irreparable damage is an old (and recurring) one. I recognised at an early stage that Native Americans I met simply would not talk to me – certainly not in the way I wanted – if I produced a tape-recorder. A case in point, which also illustrates my need to develop an autoarchaeology, was with my first Native American 'informant' Clay Hamilton (Hopi Reservation, Arizona). A mistake I made here in the early stages of research was to (mis)represent myself (both to my own better judgement and to my 'informant') as the tape-recorder and pen-carrying anthropologist. He, unsurprisingly, mistook me for either another invading anthropologist or a culture-hungry neo-Shaman, or both, and, not to put too fine a point on it, suggested I leave the reservation! It was here that Robert Wallis the auto-archaeologist first emerged since I proceeded to be up front about my intentions: rather than seeking 'secret' information as both neo-Shamans and anthropologists might do, and have certainly been known to do, I was there to gather Native American perspectives on the appropriation of this secret information by the neo-Shamans and anthropologists themselves. This said, and with tape-recorder and pen left behind, Clay was pleased to discuss these issues.

In some instances it was also inappropriate to take field notes. At Hopi, for example, signs indicate that taking photographs, field notes, and making video and audio recordings are regarded as an intrusion and not permitted. Clearly, the third party of a literary or audio device would have negated the free flow of discussion in a head-to-head. I took audio and note recordings where permission was granted, but if these were prohibited then I relied on my oral memory, a faculty more appropriate and acceptable to formerly non-literate peoples, and immediately recorded my recollections of the interview on tape afterwards, off reservation. Appreciating the importance of orality in my interviews with Native Americans, and accounting for a distance of thousands of miles, it was difficult to follow up the interviews with email or snail mail, and any responses were dependent on 'Indian time'. Nonetheless, I think the chapter in question (Chapter 7) has not suffered from these diffi-culties but rather benefited from the insights derived from my self-reflectivity and transparency with 'informants'.

Taking field notes was not only at issue with Native Americans. At neo-Shamanic workshops it quickly became evident that note taking disrupted the event I was supposed to be unintrusively involved in. My scribbling endeavoured to be discreet at all times, but it was clearly inappropriate at workshops where silence was required, where I had my eyes closed or I was otherwise physically engaged for long periods, and/or where the other people present resented the 'left brain rationale' which requires notes and privileges intellect over experience. These were first and foremost, experiential workshops, not lectures, so my strategy was to respect the wishes of course leaders and participants and follow the post-interview note taking and tape-recording mentioned above. A final interview technique employed was via email. This proved successful since the respondents, such as Greywolf, were keen to be involved and replied promptly. The disadvantage here was, as Bender experienced, 'I found that email noticeably flattens their voices' (Bender 1998: 11). Fostering an engaging relationship over email was diffi-cult, but on the plus side, there was no problem in such instances with verifying points, having thoughtful breaks in the discussion, and continuing the dialogue over long periods.

These alternative interview techniques present a challenge to traditional ethnographic fieldwork, but are part of a movement towards new and different engagements with 'informants'. I question the singular authority of rigid question–answer interviews using a tape-recorder and have attempted to overcome the hegemonic relationship between interviewer and inter-viewee. This perhaps exemplifies 'ethnography as listening and speaking (rather than observing) and an ideal of anthropology as interpretive discourse' (Fabian 1983: 27). Researching neo-Shamanisms also shows that conventional participant-observation and interview technique are not always appropriate and it is not up to the ethnographer to impose a 'right' to 'intrude' and 'record'. Rather than compromising diligent fieldwork, these revisions can enhance ethnography and facilitate the production of otherwise irretrievable data. The techniques I employed suggest that in place of the terms 'informant' or 'subject', a collaborative relationship is most product-ive, thereby enabling a free-flowing, reflexive and, to all intents and purposes, friendly dialogue. Importantly, this dialogue should not end when the tape-recorder is turned off, the pen put away and hands shaken, but should continue well after the event. Email was vital here, especially with the American case study, in which a return to the field was logistically impossible.

Not only can autoarchaeology not be conducted according to conven-tional ethnographic techniques, but also, my personal involvement in neo-Shamanisms inevitably affects my methodological acquiring and inter-preting of field data. I emphasise again that this brings an idiosyncratic and nuanced understanding of neo-Shamanisms which would not otherwise have been possible. Of course it is *my own understanding*, but this is no less valid or diligent than a claimed 'objective' and 'detached' approach. Indeed, in light of my theoretical and methodological considerations, the avowed 'objective' researcher is more prone to criticism and deconstruction. Rather than leaving myself open to criticism in terms of 'bias' and 'going native', being politically explicit is a step towards bringing about an open-minded book. All ethnographic work is subjective to varying degrees; it is the critical assessment of peer review that determines the quality and value of the work, whatever its subjectivity.

In fostering this 'honest' approach, it quickly became clear that certain ethical issues were vital to the integrity of my research. The opportunity for anonymity was given and respected in all interviews without the loss of important contextualising information or hindering results. The use of inverted commas around pseudonym names indicates those persons who requested anonymity. Attempting the removal of hegemony required taking my 'informants' seriously as collaborators: '... as partners, not merely as subjects, as sources of insight, and as progenitors of new lines of evidence. The challenge is to find ways of creating such partnerships effectively where historical and archaeological research is concerned' (Wylie 1995: 267–268).

Writing 'informants' into interpretive ethnography as active human agents is in line with Strathern's argument for 'multiple authorship' (1987c: 288), and Doty's sentiment that 'the model for the new ethnography becomes dialogue-with, rather than objectifying-of, the other' (Doty 1990: 270). Such considerations incorporate an ethical dimension into my research which is often neglected by conventional anthropology and archaeology. Beyond a simply dialogic methodology, then, I consider my approach to be a useful move beyond claims of objective and impartial positivist discourse, and the solipsism of post-modernism, by ethically engaging with the interest groups in dialectic research (as advocated by Grimshaw and Hart 1995). This volume is not a 'literary flourish', a 'self-narrative' or a wholly subjective 'story' based on my own assessment of neo-Shamanisms; other voices speak, dialogues evolve and dialectic emerges. As well as roundly critiquing the interest groups, I also offer pragmatic guidelines which attempt to harmonise, negotiate and reconcile the conflicting, if complex, views. This aligns with Wylie's suggestion that,

> [T]he sociopolitics and culture of the institutions within which histories are constructed must be reshaped to ensure that they are inclusive of, and responsive to, the needs and histories of those whose history is at issue ... history should be undertaken 'for the people' ... [We] need to construct and present histories in an idiom that 'resonates' with – that is accessible to and engaging of – its popular audience.
>
> (Wylie 1995: 267)

As Giddens suggests, 'in a reflexive world, we are all knowledge producers' (1995: 276), and a key feature of new and alternative archaeologies and anthropologies is that they are relevant beyond or outside academic discourse. The future of our scholarship lies in its relevance to the contemporary world, requiring engagement with 'contentious issues and problems of wider public concern, and communicating with a wider audience than the

21

restricted community of academics that has hitherto been its arena' (Ahmed and Shore 1995: 16). My exploration of neo-Shamanisms attempts a significant contribution to the development of both academic discourse and public debate. This double impact is a challenge to the reflexive ethnographer who becomes a 'broker', negotiating ways of presenting the 'insider' view in ways that the 'outsider's' discourse can understand (Blain 1997), and inhabiting both worlds, indeed multiple worlds, simultaneously.

Multi-sited ethnography and neo-Shamanist pluralities

Negotiating these 'worlds', autoarchaeologically, is a politically active process. The laziest way to explore neo-Shamanisms would be simply to document the issues in an armchair approach. Unfortunately, many writers on neo-Shamanisms do just this; simply reading neo-Shamanic books, flyers and workshop outlines, perhaps in an attempt to keep the perceived 'fringe' at a suitable distance lest they become contaminated by alterity. In these instances, though many pertinent criticisms are raised, each researcher's monosyllabic voice intones the same stereotypes (e.g. Johnson 1995; Root 1996; P.J. Deloria 1998; Kehoe 2000) in which neo-Shamanisms are vilified. Few researchers engage with their subjects, but while those that do tend to have a more 'balanced' perspective, they unfortunately explore only one group of neo-Shamans, consistently producing 'single-sited' ethnographies (e.g. Lindquist 1997 on Seidr, see Chapter 3, in Sweden; and Jakobsen 1999 on core-shamans vis-à-vis the Greenlandic Angakkoq) or slim overviews (e.g. Harvey 1997b). The risk here is of short-sighted interpretations which extend laudable localised interpretations to a larger scale, thereby stereotyping neo-Shamanisms writ large. To improve on previous approaches my methodology involves a 'multi-sited ethnography' in which:

> [E]thnography moves from its conventional single-site location ...
> to multiple sites of observation and participation that cross-cut
> dichotomies such as the 'local' and the 'global', the 'lifeworld' and
> the 'system' ... testing the limits of ethnography, attenuating the
> power of fieldwork, and losing the perspective of the subaltern.
>
> (Marcus 1995: 95)

This approach is particularly apt with neo-Shamans who often, simultaneously, universalise shamanisms and appropriate local traditions. Operating within the 'global village' warrants a 'multiple-positioning' on the part of the researcher (see papers in Fardon 1995).

A comprehensive study of neo-Shamanisms requires this multi-sited approach because a single case study would confine itself to one group's/individual's peculiarities and idiosyncrasies. Hence, I have explored British and American cases in which 'micro-instances' such as Druidic and

Heathen neo-Shamanisms and the misappropriation of Native American culture have been singled out. Such a multi-sited approach requires an element of cross-cultural comparison. However, examining globalisation challenges the idea that cultures are bounded wholes which can be studied independently from one another. The ethnographic notion of going 'out', or 'into' the field to study a distant Other culture, is thereby disrupted (Ahmed and Shore 1995: 21), and the idea of 'cross-cultural' altered. Marcus suggests this moving between sites, or worlds, implicates the ethnographer as a 'circumstantial activist'. I take this to mean a political explicitness on the part of the researcher, a consistent renegotiating of political and ethical identity wherein each new site reflects and alters the ethnographer's relationship with the others (and Others). More than being a single 'boundary crosser' with 'dual identity' (Reed-Danahay 1997: 3) as an autoethnographer, the multi-sited autoarchaeologist of neo-Shamanisms has multiple lines to cross and consciousnesses to inhabit. In this sense, Lewis' (1986) comparison of anthropological and shamanic careers is notable. Rather than run the ethical risk of demeaning shamanic world-views by weighing them up against the Western crises and rites of passage experienced by anthropologists, however, the auto- and experiential ethnographer attempts access (with permission) to the shaman's/neo-Shaman's worlds. Researchers in this position tell their 'subjects' they are collaborating and prepared to take their experiences seriously. In applying this methodology to neo-Shamanisms I intend to follow what Marcus terms the 'peripatetic, translative mapping of brave new worlds' (Marcus 1995: 114). Before exploring the new worlds of neo-Shamanisms *vis-à-vis* archaeology and anthropology, it is necessary to appraise critically neo-Shamanisms. In the following two chapters I attempt such a review, in terms of the theoretical and methodological considerations discussed thus far.

1

'WHITE SHAMANS'

Sources for neo-Shamanisms

> fastest growing business in america
> is shame men shame women
> you could have a sweat same as you took manhattan
> you could initiate people same as into the elks
> with a bit of light around your head
> and some 'Indian' jewelry from hong kong
> why you're all set
>> (Extract from the poem *Shame On* [say it aloud] by
>> Chrystos, published in the activist anthropological
>> journal *Cultural Survival Quarterly*, Fall 1992: 71)

> [T]hese new practitioners are not 'playing indian' but going
> to the same revelatory sources that tribal shamans have trav-
> eled to from time immemorial. They are not pretending to be
> shamans; if they get shamanic results for themselves and
> others in this work, they are indeed the real thing.
>> (Harner 1990 [1980]: xiv)

Western fascinations with shamanisms have endured from at least the seventeenth century to the present day (Flaherty 1988, 1989, 1992;
Eilberg-Schwartz 1989). And while shamans were once deemed to be aber-
rant – 'the shaman: a villain of a magician who calls demons' (Petrovich 2001
[1672]: 18), 'shamans deserve perpetual labor for their hocus-pocus' (Gmelin
2001 [1751]: 27), 'shamans are impostors who claim they consult with the
devil – and who are sometimes close to the mark' (Diderot *et al.* 2001
[1765]: 32) – they are now perceived by neo-Shamans as inherently 'spiritual'
and in some way more 'in touch' with themselves and the world around them
than modern Westerners, providing 'a way back to greater balance with
nature' (Rutherford 1996: 2). The West's reception of shamanisms is intertwined with the emergence of neo-Shamanisms: various people over the last
four centuries, fascinated by the apparently bizarre antics of shamans, enthusiastically romanticised this so-called 'savage' into a pristine religious
specialist. Some people also directly associated themselves with these prac-

tices – sometimes naming themselves 'a shaman' – so radically different from and exotic to Western attitudes and aesthetics, and became neo-Shamans. Such figures, who received literature, resources and imaginative accounts of shamans and/or other 'savages', might include the antiquarians John Dee (1527–1608) and his assistant Edward Kelley, Enochian Magicians (e.g. French 1972), and William Stukeley (1687–1765) a.k.a. 'Archdruid Chyndonax' (Sebastion 1990: 97–98; see also Piggott 1989; Trigger 1989; Green 1997; L. Jones 1998). Also, some time later, the early ethnographer Lewis Henry Morgan, who in the mid-nineteenth century began a search for 'authentic America' in which 'playing Indian' was an integral part, consisting of men's secret societies in which participants wore Indian clothes, took Indian names and claimed guidance from Indian 'spirit guides' and 'visions' (P.J. Deloria 1998: 79). In true colonial fashion, inventing American identity required distancing real Indians, perceiving them to be already extinct or at least vanishing, to uphold an imperialist and romanticised idea of Indians past. The very real Native American struggle with social injustice and genocide was ignored. 'New ethnographers' thereafter continued to play Indian, such as Frank Hamilton Cushing, the famous ethnographer of the Zunis who enthusiastically embraced a 'white Indian' identity. He wore Zuni clothes and decorated his New York home in replica of a Pueblo Kiva (Deloria 1998: 119). Indeed, to 'study' the Zunis, Cushing had to 'be adopted, he had to be made into a Zuni, and this required that he undergo the same social and ritual procedures which all Zunis underwent' (Roscoe 1991: 127). Perhaps only following this process was Cushing, as a 'white' or 'neo-' shaman, fully able to write his 'Remarks on Shamanism' (1897).

Neo-Shamans of the twentieth century include, I contend, a variety of artists and occultists. Greenwood (2000), similarly, draws attention to the influence of 'shamanism' on the practices of modern magicians, and Tingay (2000: 38) notes the influence of 'shamanism' on Madame Blavatsky, the mother of theosophy. Other individuals worthy of mention include the occultist Austin Osman Spare (1887–1956), whose idiosyncratic system of 'atavistic resurgence' (Spare 1993) incorporated sexual excitation and orgasm combined with 'will' and 'image' in a technique of 'ecstasy'. 'Spirit familiars' (well known to shamans) were encountered, 'automatic' or trance drawings of them made (Figure 1.1), and the Native American spirit 'Black Eagle' was a major source of Spare's ecstatic inspiration (e.g. Grant 1973, 1975, 1980, 1991 [1972]; Grant and Grant 1998). Similar shamanic other than human helpers are evident in the artwork of Australian witch Rosaleen Norton (1917–1979) (Figure 1.2) (Drury 1993). The poet Jerome Rothenberg, more recently, claimed that various romantic and visionary poets, including Rainer Maria Rilke, Arthur Rimbaud and the Dadaists, all represented 'neoshamanisms' (Flaherty 1992: 4; see also Rothenberg 1985). Modern artists such as Marc Chagall (1887–1985) and Vasily Kandinsky (1866–1944) were also neo-Shamans, with occultism, mysticism and folklore influencing their

Figure 1.1 The Self in Ecstasy (1913) by occultist and trance artist
  Austin Osman Spare

Source: Courtesy of Kenneth Grant.

work. Kandinsky regarded the artist as a shaman (Rosenthal 1997: 20–21), as, more recently and famously, did Joseph Beuys (1921–1986). Tate Modern's tribute to Beuys (part of the 'Bits and Pieces' collection display in the *Landscape/Matter/Environment* gallery) states he 'was no ordinary sculptor. He was also a shaman', and Beuys himself claimed 'everybody is an artist'. Reflecting on these two comments, I have wondered whether Beuys also thought 'everybody is a shaman'. Caroline Tisdall, Beuys's biographer (Tisdall 1979), agreed the link is appropriate (pers. com.).

Beuys has been termed a 'shaman' for a number of reasons. He was rescued by Tartars after the Stucka plane in which he was radio operator crashed in the inhospitable conditions of the Crimea during the Second World War. The Tartars revived him, badly burnt and freezing, with fat and felt insulation, and these substances became a primary inspiration for his work; he wrapped himself in felt for hours at a time, for instance, and wore a felt trilby hat he termed 'shamanic' during the performance of *Coyote*. He viewed felt and fat as alchemical substances, felt being both an insulator and a filter, and fat being an insulator with a unique state which fluctuates

Figure 1.2 Nightmare by Rosaleen Norton, 'a clear indication of the artist's
trance technique' (Drury 1993: 27)

Source: Courtesy of Mandrake of Oxford.

between solid and liquid. Beuys regarded the plane crash as an initiatory-
like experience, likened it to a death and rebirth, and also endured a
long-lasting breakdown which he viewed as a rite of passage essential to
being an artist. Beuys's words 'show your wound' espoused the view that
vulnerability is the secret to being an artist, the term wound here perhaps
alluding to the indigenous shaman as a 'wounded healer'. Many of Beuys's
paintings are entitled *Shaman*, and the techniques he employed to produce
the drawings entitled *Coyote*, as well as the performance of *Coyote* (New York
1974) itself (see Tisdall 1976, 1998), were certainly mimetic of shamanistic
consciousness-altering practices: wrapped in an enormous piece of felt,
wearing the trilby and 'sulphur [another alchemical substance] boots', and
wielding a cane walking stick which he perceived as a 'conductor', Beuys
spent three days in a room caged with a live coyote, accompanied by a tape-
recording of chaotic turbine sounds. The question was 'who was caged?',
and in performance dialogue with the animal, the coyote took over,
urinating and defecating on the *Wall Street Journal* – which Beuys deployed

as a statement against capitalism (Beuys was a candidate for the Green Party but became disillusioned by it).

Of interest to a study of alternative approaches to archaeology and shamanisms, one of Beuys's 'Bits and Pieces' exhibits is entitled *Tramstop Archaeology* (1976), various entheogens including magic mushrooms and *Datura* are integral fabrics in some of these pieces, and finds of bog bodies are known to have inspired Beuys's sculptural works. Further, Beuys defined the spiral (organic or implosive), split-cell and diamond (crystalline or explosive) shapes from the Neolithic passage tomb art of Newgrange (Boyne Valley, Ireland) as 'The Three Energies of Newgrange', inferring that the 'ancient Celts [*sic*] had a sophisticated knowledge of physical and spiritual energies' (Tisdall 1998: 72). According to one artist ('Ricky') speaking at Tisdall's celebration of Beuys's 'Bits and Pieces' works (an open event at Tate Modern entitled 'Shamanism and Healing'), his obsession with the red stag (also the elk, both of which Beuys perceived as 'spiritual' and figure strongly in his art) 'brings us back to Alta Mira'; further, 'he was a Celt, he was a shaman', and Tisdall suggests the megalithic *The End of the 20th Century* (1983–1985) makes reference to Stonehenge. Art, archaeology and shamanism are, I think, united in Beuys's works which explicitly challenge the elitist dealer-critic system: in Beuys's world-view, archaeology, the everyday (in a similar vein to Duchamp's readymades) and shamanism – particularly healing (of nature, individual, society and planet) – are embraced by the term 'art'. So, as had happened in previous centuries, the shaman/neo-Shaman in the twentieth century was relegated to the realm of the bohemian artist (e.g. Tucker 1992). In all, shamanisms and neo-Shamanisms have, without doubt, deeply permeated new religious movements and other aspects of society, such as art, in the modern era.

Neo-Shamans re-emerged in the academy when anthropologists, following an interlude of Boasian 'scientific' methodology, again went 'native' and trained as shamans during the 1960s, and psychologists experimented on the entheogenic substances some shamans consumed, such as the chemical derivative LSD (e.g. Grof 1996 [1975]). Many such anthropologist researchers, in South America particularly, participated in entheogen-orientated rituals which enabled first-hand encounters with shamanic realities. Examples of these neo-Shaman 'anthros' include Michael Harner (1990 [1980]), Carlos Castaneda (arguably not an anthropologist, see below) and Douglas Sharon (1978), who, following initiation into the traditional shamanic practices they were studying, brought shamanisms to the West – and/or took neo-Shamans to the host culture – for spiritual consumption. These events neatly coincided with the widespread use of LSD and other entheogens, and emergence of a counter-culture in search of alternative lifeways and spiritual fulfilment. Aldous Huxley's (1959) experiments with mescaline (chemically linked with LSD), in particular, inspired them to explore shamanic realms, and Timothy Leary, the controversial 'godfather of acid', encouraged them to adopt an alternative lifestyle with the mantra 'tune in, turn on, drop out'. These neo-Shamans of the 1960s and 1970s enthusiastically consumed popular anthropology books on shamanisms (such as Castaneda 1968; Furst 1972; Harner 1972, 1973a). Following this historical trajectory, the closing decade of the twentieth century and early years of the twenty-first witness growing reproduction and reification of neo-Shamanisms with increasing numbers of people employing aspects of shamanisms in their occupations and turning to 'shamanism' as a path for personal and communal empowerment.

Characterising neo-Shamanisms is a complex endeavour (e.g. Hess 1993) and a variety of potentially useful terms fail to embrace its diversity sufficiently. Terms such as 'crisis cults' are inappropriate since while neo-Shamanisms may express a crisis in Western religious thinking, related to the 'crisis of modernity' (Lyon 1993), they have no leader or organisation that warrants the term 'cult'. 'Revitalisation movements', or 'marginal religious movements' (Wilson 1974: 596–627) better reflect the situation, although neo-Shamanisms are too fragmented to be simply a movement, and only some neo-Shamanic groups such as road protestors (e.g. Letcher 2001) readily lend themselves to Maffesoli's (1996) post-modernising of the term 'tribe'. Lindquist (1997) argues 'neo-shamanism' is a 'subculture', but I think practitioners are rarely socially 'deviant' in the sense that this term may imply: neo-Shamanisms are increasingly becoming less marginalised and more integrated into society, and thus cannot be characterised as counter-cultural (as described by Roszack 1970). But just as neo-Shamanisms are not simply counter-cultural, so they are not simply 'New Age' (Lewis and Melton 1992). Where New Agers 'honour spirit above matter' (Harvey 1997b: 122), the Pagan element in neo-Shamanisms suggests a spirituality which is often earth-orientated. Indeed, neo-Shamans and Pagans often use New Age as a derogatory term, denoting a shallow, woolly approach to spirituality (see also Pearson 1998; Shallcrass 1998: 168), with one Pagan suggesting 'newage' be pronounced 'rather unkindly, as in "sewage"' (Fleming n.d.b).

With often highly pluralised beliefs and practices, neo-Shamans are influenced 'arguably' by a syncretism of reactionary thought and post-modernism, although describing neo-Shamanisms in terms of 'modern', 'post-modern', etc. is rather academic and artificial: most neo-Shamans and others in society are unfamiliar with, or at least not interested in, these terms; they are simply living their lives. This does not negate their use however, since such terms allow academics to appreciate the socio-political locations of neo-Shamanisms within their own intellectual framework, and such labels also need not deny social agency and individual sensibilities. At their most modern, individualistic and conservative, neo-Shamans teach business executives how to contact 'spirit guides' which can help them make more money (though that might be too harsh a criticism of Heather Campbell's workshops, also author of *Sacred Business* [Firth and Campbell

1997], who conducts neo-Shamanic workshops for business managers).
Western capitalism has influenced them in their 'sacralization of the self'
and fostering of 'New Age capitalism' (Heelas 1992). But where some live
happily as business people in a capitalist marketplace, others destabilise the
fabric of modernism. At their most post-modern, neo-Shamans execute
dissonant acts which render conventional metanarratives of gender defunct
(see Conclusion). Neo-Shamanisms may thereby embody a number of socio-
political locations, including counter-cultural, being socially integrated,
modern and post-modern. In this diversity, neo-Shamanisms reject attempts
at simplistic classification (following comments by Heelas 1993 and Lyon
1993 on New Age). Terming neo-Shamanisms 'counter-cultures', 'subcul-
tures' (Lindquist 1997) and 'movements' seems to miss the point; we might
rather speak less pejoratively, plurally and simply, of 'neo-Shamanisms'.

'Indigenous' critics have used the terms 'whiteshamanism' (Rose 1992)
and 'plastic medicinemen' (Churchill 1992) to describe Westerners 'appropriating' their traditions. 'Neo-shamanism', coined by Rothenberg (e.g.
1985), has become a widely used academic term for this cultural interaction,
although 'modern shamanism', 'new shamanism', 'urban shamanism' and
'contemporary shamanism' are also widely used. 'Neo-Shamanisms' may be a
more appropriate, sensitive and critical orthography: (1) it distinguishes
'Western' forms from those in 'indigenous' communities, where 'modern',
'urban' and 'contemporary' may not; (2) pluralising, cumbersome though it
may be, embraces diversity and difference, rather than generalities and metanarrative;[1] (3) capitalisation locates, rather than downsizes neo-Shamanisms
alongside established 'religions' such as Christianity, and is sensitive to neo-
Shamans themselves, reflecting both freedom of expression and the diversity
of practitioners who may respond with exasperation to ethnographic labels
(e.g. Høst 2001); (4) the lower case 'neo-' prefix (also in 'shamanisms' when
referring to 'indigenous' practices) suggests the terms 'shamanisms' and
'neo-Shamanisms' are Western inventions, and avoids pinning down, in
metanarrative, a variety of practices (both neo-Shamanic and shamanic) to a
fixed and named type; and (5) while the -ism does not indicate 'an organised
system ... a reification constructed from disparate lifeways' (Harvey forthcoming), but rather a suffix which acknowledges similarities, so the prefix
neo- does not denote inauthenticity, like quasi- (I hope it is not too reminiscent of other neo-s such as Neo-Nazi, as has been suggested to me). Indeed,
while it may be useful to contrast shamanisms with neo-Shamanisms, the
diversity and sometimes permeability of both suggest a sharp distinction is
misleading. And here I must enter a debate on the issue of authenticity and
validity with the inevitable, if simplistic and I think naïve, question 'are
neo-Shamans shamans?'.

When responding to this question, the term 'shaman' can arguably be
seen as self-defining: essentially, people calling themselves shamans *are*
shamans since the term is invented and means different things to different

people. Such relativism would, however, ignore the reality of situations where neo-Shamanic approaches to shamans are blatantly neo-colonialist. It would also run the risk of suggesting neo-Shamans are the *same* as shamans; in most cases, particularly in instances of neo-colonialism, they most certainly are not. But not all neo-Shamans are neo-colonialist and, in recognising this diversity, I think it is possible to differentiate some neo-Shamans who are more like indigenous shamans or make constructive contributions to them from those who are not (see following chapters). But in some cases a distinction between shamans and neo-Shamans is misleading. Where shamanisms are being urbanised, such as in Peru (e.g. Press 1971; Joralemon and Sharon 1993) and Buryatia (Humphrey 1999), or being taught by Michael Harner and other core-shamanists such as among the Sami and Inuit (see, for example, Hoppál 1996; Khazanov 1996; Townsend 1999), dichotomous terms neglect the dissonant, unpredictable and nuanced reality (see especially Chapter 7).

Critics of neo-Shamanisms tend to fall into a methodological trap of comparing neo-Shamanisms with indigenous shamanisms, when, as I have stated, the plurality of both, and their engagements, indicate they may or may not be commensurable. In simplistic terms critics, then, logically, move on to pose the question 'is neo-shamanism authentic, or valid?', with responses most often in the negative. There is certainly a snobbish and derisive tone in much literature on neo-Shamanisms: real shamans are perceived to be culturally distant and Other, and therefore 'authentic'; neo-Shamans are invented, deluded and specious. In one sense this shamanism vs neo-Shamanism dichotomy might arguably reify a primitivist or noble savage stereotype of indigenous peoples. At the very least it is shamanophobic and reveals a hypocritical attitude taken by those anthropologists who suggest there is no such thing as 'static' tradition or culture, but who discriminate against neo-Shamans because they are not apparently part of a 'tradition' and appear, at least on the face of it, to be piecemeal spiritual consumers in the global village. In true logical fashion, the question 'is neo-shamanism authentic, or valid?' begs another question: 'when does a new religious path or set of paths become traditional and authentic?', or at least, at which point are they perceived to be so?

In essence, the authentication process itself is the core issue: simply put, neo-Shamanisms, in all their variety, become valid when countless people practise the techniques and get results 'for themselves and others', as Harner puts it (1990 [1980]: xiv, and see my comments in later chapters). Besides, debates over authenticity and the invention of tradition have arguably been resolved by various sections of the social sciences, from anthropology and history to religious studies. As Herzfeld states:

[S]uch terms as the 'invention of tradition' ... suggest the possibility of an ultimately knowable historic past. Although traditions are invented, the implicit argument suggests, there ought to be something else that represents the 'real' past. But if any history is invented, all history is invented. We should not view one kind of history as more invented than others, although its bearers may be more powerful and therefore more capable of enforcing its reproduction among disenfranchised classes.

(Herzfeld 1991: 12)

Indeed, the issue here, rather than being one of authenticity vs inauthenticity (following papers in Bromley and Carter 1996), validity vs invalidity (e.g. De Mille 1976), of divergent or competing perspectives, or even one of academic discourse versus public understanding, is of multivocality and forms of knowledge and power, and whether scholars of neo-Shamanisms should, in the pluralist and multivocal climate of post-modernity, not only examine the authentication process but also be prepared to embrace such pluralities and engage with them dialogically, rather than dismiss them as 'fringe' and 'eccentric'.

It is far too easy to set up 'neo-shamanism' as a 'straw man' and accuse it of being inauthentic, impure, fuzzy, etc. But in approaching neo-Shamanisms we are not always dealing with coherent, clear-cut belief systems, and nor should we expect to be. We are dealing with people's actual experiences and behaviours which are often syncretic and dissonant, even contradictory – involving cognitive dissonance, as psychologists like to term it – and perhaps on the face of it, muddled, messy, etc. It is not only inappropriate, but also beside the point to criticise neo-Shamans for not practising what academics think neo-Shamanisms or shamanisms should or do look like: the real issue is not one of authenticity or inauthenticity, but one of power; these critics assume they have the power to make such charges. But, as an autoarchaeologist producing 'ethnographic fragments' of neo-Shamanisms, I argue the positivist dichotomies (of authenticity/authenticity, validity/invalidity, etc.) constructed, and empiricist approaches taken, by some critics are incompatible with the 'nature of the beast(s)' – neo-Shamanisms – and with current social research methods. This does not require that we accept or embrace all neo-Shamanisms without criticism in a hyper-liberalist discourse which ignores neo-Shamanisms implicated in neo-colonialism, racism, homophobia, etc. It does require that we address the diversity of neo-Shamanisms and shamanisms, and the subtleties of their engagement and interaction.

Given my emphasis on diversity, and on the convergence of some neo-Shamanisms and shamanisms, it is impossible to examine 'neo-shamanism' as if it were a single entity, since the diversity of practices and practitioners resists such a metanarrative, and there are no fixed boundaries: as well as convergences between indigenous and neo-practices, there are also clear similarities between aspects of neo-Shamanisms and a number of traditions in contemporary Paganisms. 'Paganism' (neo-Paganism in the USA) is an umbrella term most commonly used to refer to a variety of contemporary Western 'nature-based' spiritualities or religions such as Wicca (modern witchcraft), Heathenry, Druidry and Goddess Spirituality (see Chapters 3 and 4, also Harvey 1997a, 1997b; Weller 1997). For the purposes of this discussion, however, the term 'neo-Shamanisms' is employed to describe and explore pervasive shamanic (or more correctly neo-Shamanic) elements in these traditions. Wiccans, for instance, frequently hail 'shamanism' as the origin of their religion (e.g. Adler 1986; Starhawk 1989), even, according to Clifton (1994: 7), stating 'witchcraft is European shamanism'.

The Pagan Federation is a British organisation founded in 1971 'to provide information on Paganism and to counter misconceptions about the religion. The Pagan Federation works for the rights of Pagans to worship freely and without censure' (as stated on their website: www.pf-pf.html). Their 'Information Pack' makes clear the relationship between Paganisms and neo-Shamanisms:

> [S]hamanic practices are an underlying aspect of all expressions of pagan religion and there are those who would describe themselves as Wiccan, Druidic or Women's Mystery shamans. Bearing this in mind, there are, however, a growing number of men and women who see themselves on a specifically Shamanic path.
>
> (Pagan Federation 1996: 10)

It is, therefore, perhaps a little perplexing that 'Paganism' has become the popular generic term for these traditions instead of 'shamanism' since, as Puttick (1998) convincingly argues, 'shamanism' is perceived to be global and timeless where 'paganism' is originally located, strictly speaking, in Classical antiquity, and, as I have said, Paganisms are permeated by neo-Shamanisms in various respects – more than neo-Shamanisms are influenced by Paganisms at least. In this regard, I consider my use of 'neo-Shamanisms' well suited for approaching neo-Shamanic aspects of contemporary 'pagan' spiritualities.

Three sources have had, and continue to have, a particularly prominent impact on neo-Shamanisms (see also Noel 1997; Bowie 2000), and, I would argue, academia. The first, Mircea Eliade's *Shamanism*, a cross-cultural study of 'Archaic Techniques of Ecstasy' (Eliade 1989 [1964]), the second, Carlos Castaneda's eleven Don Juan books discussing a form of shamanism in Mexico's Sonoran Desert (e.g. Castaneda 1968), the third, Michael Harner's *The Way of the Shaman* (1990 [1980]; for a mixed book review, see Murphy 1981), a how-to manual. If they have not had direct contact with these works, then there has certainly been indirect influence via the many neo-Shamanic authors who draw on them (e.g. Andrews 1982; Kharitidi 1997 [1996]; Wilcox 1999) and in the workshop circuit which spreads their messages. Neo-Shamanic authors are also clearly well networked, citing each other in their own publications (e.g. Harner citing Castaneda, Rutherford [1996] citing Castaneda and Harner, and most authors citing Eliade).

If academic researchers have considerable influence on practitioners, then the same is true vice versa; this contra the neo-Shamanophobic assertion that the revival of shamanistic interpretations in archaeology 'is *unrelated* to the growing popular interest in shamanism in the context of alternative spiritual philosophies' (Price 2001b: 10, my emphasis), as made clear, for example, by the citing of the independent (and for the purposes of this book, neo-Shamanic) researcher Paul Devereux by rock art academic Thomas Dowson, and vice versa (e.g. Devereux 1992a; Dowson 1999c). It is impossible to ignore, furthermore, the widespread impact the 'psychedelic' 1960s had on academic approaches to shamanisms, particularly given that many of those in psychedelia were young academics themselves, such as Castaneda and Harner. And currently, as well as reading books and articles about themselves (e.g. Harvey 1997b; Hutton 1998a, 1999), neo-Shamans increasingly network with the academics 'studying' them. Philip 'Greywolf' Shallcrass, for instance, an informant we meet in following chapters, tells me the work of Professor Ronald Hutton has greatly informed him, and many contemporary Pagans hold Hutton in high regard. The likes of Hutton and Harvey attend conferences where the atmosphere of scholar-meets-practitioner is encouraged. Such forums I have attended, where these encounters take place, include the annual Society for the Anthropology of Consciousness meeting in the USA, the Re-Enchantment conference on contemporary Paganisms at King Alfred's College, Winchester (1996), and Shamanism in Contemporary Society conference at the University of Newcastle (1998; reviewed by Woodman 1998). Such engagements between academics and neo-Shamans are hardly surprising given that there have always been distinctly permeable boundaries between the two. In the second half of the twentieth century, academic anthropologists and psychologists became deeply – experientially – involved with the indigenous shamans they studied and/or entheogenic substances they consumed, and so at the start of the twenty-first century scholars of Wicca, Druidry and other traditions engage experientially with Pagan communities. Rather than simply reading books as 'armchair shamans', then, many neo-Shamans are active seekers of shamanic knowledge: the individual, agentic quality of neo-Shamanic practices must not be forgotten. Indeed, while 'academic' research, in the form of Castaneda, Eliade and Harner, has provided some pinnacle texts and resources, there are significant indigenous players in the growth of neo-Shamanisms. Certain indigenous shamans have encouraged the participation of Westerners in their rituals: for instance, Peruvian shaman Eduardo Calderon (e.g. Joralemon 1990), Native American Lame Deer, and seminars for core-shamanists were given in California by a Siberian shaman, 'the last remaining male shaman of the Ulchi tribe' (Grimaldi 1996: 7).

Nonetheless, the primary significance of Eliade, Castaneda and Harner necessitates a close examination of their various impacts on academia, neo-Shamanisms and indigenous groups. Michael Harner's pervasive impact on shamanisms and neo-Shamanisms has prompted most discussion and criticism of neo-Shamans. Harner's work and a variety of other neo-Shamanisms are appraised here, but where other critiques are overly negative and sneering, my analysis posits certain useful contributions neo-Shamanisms make to shamanisms. Neo-Shamanisms have been acknowledged as 'revitalising new traditions' in Paganisms, for instance, and giving benefits to the shamans and indigenous cultures borrowed from Harvey (1997b, 1998). I attempt a fair (yet inevitably personal) assessment of neo-Shamanisms, but one that does not equivocate where judgements must be made.

Mircea Eliade: 'forefather' of neo-Shamanisms

One of the first signs of our fascination with all things 'shamanic' in the second half of the twentieth century, is *Shamanism: Archaic Techniques of Ecstasy* (Eliade 1989 [1964]). This monumental work is, without question, the definitive cross-cultural work on 'shamanism'. Some scholars and most neo-Shamanic practitioners uncritically accept Eliade's stance without question (e.g. Carrasco and Swanberg 1985a). A quote from Noel demonstrates the impact this book has had: 'This master scholar, the most significant precursor to the New Shamanism, really its forefather, was Mircea Eliade' (Noel 1997: 23). Few researchers have evaluated the man or critiqued the book, but of those who have, many agree 'Eliade is "the greatest living interpreter of the whole world of primitive and archaic religions"' (Carrasco and Swanberg 1985b: 4, quoting T.J. Altizer). In sharp contrast, growing numbers of critics are placing Eliade and his approach to the history of religions in context, specifically his 'armchair anthropology' and the impact of a literary imagination on his supposedly factual work (e.g. Smith 1987). Weighing both views, we can properly see both Eliade's exceptional, creative view of shamanisms and his biased peculiarity.

One of Eliade's driving forces – cultural evolution – was a major trend in shamanism studies and has since been reified by neo-Shamans. His aim was to locate 'shamanism' within the history of religion, a quest that went hand in hand with attempting an etymological derivation for the term. The misguided idea, in my view, of a primal Indo-European shamanism based on the 'original' Siberian model has resulted, alongside the hailing of a singular shamanism as the oldest of all religions, even the proto-form of many established religions. While such speculations are intriguing, their basis, along with etymological forays, largely derives from outmoded evolutionary frameworks (see also Lewis 1993: 361) and culture-historic approaches. These have of course been proven inappropriate because of their Eurocentric and racist use of 'primitivism' *vis-à-vis* 'civilisation', with an erroneous emphasis on innatist 'progress'. Just as prehistoric religions are unlikely to have been 'simple' or less evolved than monotheism, so 'shamanism' is not 'primitive' or an undeveloped residue of prehistory. The commanding impact of Eliade as a religious evolutionist has reified such misnomers.

Eliade and other researchers also distinguish between 'black' or 'primitive' and 'white' or 'pure' shamans, and 'authentic' and 'inauthentic' forms of possession (Hultkrantz 1998a). These classifications have ethnographic precedents, in Central Asia for example (see Wallis in prep.), but such examples are more subtle and nuanced than Western binary distinctions between 'good' and 'evil'. And while Harner suggests that in the Himalayas shamanism and possession fuse but in 'pure' shamanism this blending does not occur (Harner and Doore 1987: 15), such value-laden judgements reveal more about the biases of Western researchers than they do about ethnographic realities. As Lewis argues, 'Shamanism and spirit possession regularly occur together and this is true particularly in the Arctic *locus classicus* of shamanism' (Lewis 1989: 44; see also Blacker 1975: 26; Lewis 1984, 1989, 1991 [1988]; but see, for example, De Heusch 1982; Rouget 1987). Studies on shamanisms have clearly been plagued by numerous outmoded interpretations which have since been reproduced by neo-Shamans.

As well as inappropriately promoting evolutionary and binary oppositional interpretations of shamanisms, Eliade's approach was heavily influenced by his Christian beliefs (Smith 1987). During his work on *Shamanism* Eliade produced a novel, *The Forbidden Forest*, in which Noel (1997: 28–41) finds the consistent theme of, and focus on, notions of 'upward flights' and 'celestial vistas'. Noel suggests Eliade's devout Christianity, with its focus on ascension to heaven, deeply influenced this 'shamanovel'. Literary criticism aside, Noel proposes that Eliade's relationship with Christianity and obsession with celestial ascent also affected his factual writing on shamanisms. In *Shamanism*, Noel finds consistent favourable referral to shamanic ascent to upper worlds to the negative discussion and exclusion of descent to lower worlds. There are roughly double the references to ascent than descent, a count reflecting not the preponderance of shamanic ascent cross-culturally, but Eliade's personal bias (see also Balzer 1997: xvi). Elsewhere, he uses the words 'infernal' and 'demons' when describing lower shamanic worlds, but 'spirits' and 'supreme beings' to address upper worldly entities, concepts clearly dictated by a Christian world-view. It seems Eliade was either purposefully or subconsciously searching for what he perceived to be the most fitting in 'shamanism' to reflect aspects of Christianity.

Indeed, this Christian perspective influenced other aspects of Eliade's research on shamanisms. Within the history of religion, Eliade's aim was clearly to elucidate the earliest religious form. This quest for 'archaic ontology' is criticised by Geertz (1993), among others, for its primitivism according to which tribal peoples are perceived by the West to have inherited the simplest and therefore most archaic forms of religion. To Eliade, this religion was 'shamanism'. He also distinguished a 'true' or archaic shamanism as distinct from spirit possession, which was seen as being more corrupt, historically more recent, and subject to decline, degeneration and 'decadence' (Eliade 1961: 155; 1989 [1964]: 507, n. 34); hence, according to Reinhard (1976: 15), Eliade's motivation for the subtitle 'archaic techniques of ecstasy'. Rather than showing shamanisms to be backward, as previous researchers had erroneously done, Eliade perceived shamanism as the true, 'paradisal', Edenic religion in which a Supreme Being reigned: during ecstasy the shaman 'recovers the situation as it was at the beginning [and] re-establishe[s] the "paradisal" situation lost at the dawn of time' (Eliade 1989 [1964]: 99). Of course a pristine or 'true' shamanism *vis-à-vis* a later and debased possession, or an archaic vs a degenerate shamanism, never existed (see also Reinhard 1976: 14), except in the minds of Eliadean scholars.

Eliade's implicit agenda was to search for examples of celestial ascent, a Supreme Being and comparable themes in shamanisms and 'primitive' religion, to authenticate his belief that all shamanistic religions displayed a global Ur-Christianity. Seeing *Shamanism* in terms of this religious and political manifesto sheds new light on how and why Eliade represented shamanisms in the way he did. I agree with researchers who suggest *Shamanism* consistently reveals the spiritual bias of its author to the detriment of his cross-cultural representation of shamanisms (e.g. Noel 1997; Reinhard 1976). While the volume does explore shamanisms from a vast array of cultures and was in many ways a first step in the right direction for presenting shamanisms in a positive and popular way, its presentation and focus must not be accepted unquestioningly. One author portrays Eliade as 'an Aristotelian shaman' (Nolan 1985: 117), but also shows that Eliade's religion was decidedly un-Pagan: the essay 'The Terror of History' 'insisted that man had one last choice: Christ or nihilism' (Nolan 1985: 109). This theme of attempting to redirect spiritually impoverished Westerners also influenced Joseph Campbell's quest for perceived primitive Christianities, clearly indicating how Western notions and impositions of 'supreme deity' and Edenic religions have permeated studies on shamanisms (see also Reinhard 1976: 14).

While these criticisms are valid, other aspects of Eliade's work are overlooked. Noel's point, for instance, that Eliade's literary imagination dominated the writing of *Shamanism* stretches a little too far. Followers and critics all consider Eliade a remarkable scholar, so that being an accomplished novelist need not mean his academic work is somehow more fictitious than factual. In any case, his attempting 'an integrated humanistic endeavour in the academies' (Carrasco and Swanberg 1985d: 35) in some respects anticipates current trans-disciplinary efforts in academia. In the past, positivism may have provided reason for scholars to dismiss reflective and intuitive understandings in favour of cold 'science', but we now realise absolute objectivity is the real fiction. Among other 'subjective' approaches, and in Eliade's own words, 'literary creation can be considered an instrument of knowledge' (Eliade 1985b: 23). It is perhaps Eliade's unique 'conception of the alternating modes of the creative human spirit, the "diurnal," rational mode of scholarship and the "nocturnal," mythological mode of imagination and fantasy' (Carrasco and Swanberg 1985c: 17) which gave him an ideal perspective from which to write *Shamanism*. As he suggests:

> [S]ome of my literary creations contributed to a more profound understanding of certain religious structures, and ... sometimes, without my being conscious of the fact at the moment of writing fiction, the literary imagination utilized materials or meanings I had studied as a historian of religions.
>
> (Eliade 1985b: 18)

We must bear in mind that in *Shamanism* Eliade was attempting a 'scientific' work which he clearly acknowledged was distinct from, but not uninfluenced by, his literary career. Certainly, the novelist in Eliade affected his presentation of *Shamanism*, and his Christianity and evolutionism influenced the interpretations. In all its brilliance and failings, *Shamanism* was and is a highly influential work. Recognising this, alongside his academic credentials in the 'history of religions' (rather than anthropology or ethnography) and theological bias, allows us to examine both the problematic areas of his approach and the uniquely productive angle Eliade brought to the study of shamanisms.

Neo-Shamanisms are better understood, appreciated and critiqued when we balance Eliade as person, Christian, novelist and scholar. Eliade may have predicted the rise of neo-Shamanisms: 'interest in shamanism and the awareness of the psycho-mental risks involved in hallucinogens, may have another consequence in the near future: helping contemporary Western man undergo sickness ... as a series of initiatory ideals' (Eliade 1985a: 16). *Shamanism* stands as the major text which inspired and continues to inspire many scholars to explore shamanisms, and neo-Shamans to consider undertaking their own shamanic 'journeys'. Unwittingly, Eliade had 'great influence on Europe's Pagan revival' (Henry 1999: 1). But in emphasising the symbolic and cosmological aspects of 'shamanism' and downplaying socio-political diversity, Eliade paved the way for universalism. And, as the primary source on shamanisms for neo-Shamans, his metanarrative is reproduced over and over again. Noel sees Eliade as the 'forefather' of the 'New shamanism', but this is not entirely true; a thirst for shamanisms and things shamanic permeated Western society long before Eliade's study. Also, if 'the neoshamanism movement was founded on fiction', as Noel has it, the ethnographic data itself might also be discredited, something indigenous shamans would

surely contest (that is not to say such data should not be approached critically). While Eliade did provide ethnographic examples and a definition
which neo-Shamans now apply, he did not provide the impetus for actually
attempting to practise shamanisms in the West. To elucidate that penulti-
mate event in the history of neo-Shamanisms, I next explore a second major
inspirational figure, Carlos Castaneda.

Carlos Castaneda: literal or literary shaman?

The work of Castaneda undoubtedly represents the single most prominent
effect of neo-Shamanisms on anthropology, and indeed, anthropology on
neo-Shamanisms. Nevill Drury suggests, 'One can argue that, the academic
efforts of scholar Mircea Eliade notwithstanding, Castaneda was the first
person to make the shamanic perspective accessible to westerners' (Drury
1989: 81). I would add that where Eliade and other academics only
presented shamanisms to the West, Castaneda's work, in a radical shift,
encouraged Westerners to become shamans themselves. But, in the three
decades since his first publication, and now with eleven books as best-sellers,
with the very likely possibility of posthumous works, along with a video
trilogy to boot, the debate continues to rage over the question 'is Castaneda's
work a fake?'. By the early 1990s, Carlos's books had sold over eight million
(Fikes 1993: 14), were translated into several languages, and had prompted
'a small industry of Castaneda-explaining, Castaneda-debunking, and
Castaneda-plagiarizing' (Clifton 1994: 4–5). More works struggling with
the applicability of Carlos's work have been produced than Castaneda's books
themselves (e.g. Olson 1978)! And, the enigmatic Yaqui brujo or shaman
'don Juan du Matus', Castaneda's shaman informant, has been hailed as
presenting the most important paradigm since Jesus (Pearce 1976). In the
USA, Britain and elsewhere, Castaneda's neo-Shamanic followers aspire to be
'Toltec Warriors'. These practitioners of the 'new Toltequity' might also
name themselves 'double-beings', 'dreaming' men or women, or more recog-
nisably anthropological classifications such as 'nagual' (e.g. Saler 1979
[1967]). Academics might rather term them neo-Shamans than use this
latter indigenous-specific term, but there are many more people who have
been influenced by Castaneda's books than just these practitioners. Almost
any Druid, Witch and Chaos Magickian, indeed any Pagan or alternative
spiritual seeker, will likely have read Castaneda – if not, then they will have
heard of him and will be familiar with the gist of his narratives. Whatever
their perspectives on the factuality of the books, most neo-Shamans will
agree the content affected them deeply. In recent years, the increasing
numbers of Castaneda-orientated workshops attest to the fact that
'nagualism' is now more popular than ever. Clearly any examination of neo-
Shamanisms, and shamanisms for that matter, requires entering the curious
world of Carlos Castaneda.

Castaneda claimed to have met Don Juan for the first time in 1961, while researching medicinal plants in Mexico. Over the four years 1961–1965, Castaneda said he was apprenticed to Don Juan as a shaman. The first publication of these experiences *The Teachings of Don Juan: A Yaqui Way of Knowledge* (1968) became an instant best-seller for the University of California Press, and the same work was submitted as a Master's dissertation. Its main themes surround use of entheogenic plants to gain supernatural power and knowledge, a subject wonderfully timed for consumption in the psychedelic 1960s. *A Separate Reality: Further Conversations with Don Juan* (1971) charted Carlos's continued shamanic training between 1968 and 1970, in which Don Genaro, a shaman colleague of Don Juan, appears. With *Journey to Ixtlan* (1972), the third book, Carlos received a PhD; it describes how shamanic 'alternate reality' can also be accessed without the use of entheogens, again nicely timed for a post-psychedelic audience. The relationship between Carlos and Don Juan continues in *Tales of Power* (1974), yet at this point I need say little more about the content of the books, for we are not even halfway through the full list of Castaneda's works, and the many shamanic experiences he describes now become repetitive. Perhaps, at first, Castaneda was not set on a money-spinner, but by the fourth book he must have been. At first, and with the backing of academic qualifications and the UCLA anthropological department, Castaneda's work was critically acclaimed. Notable old-school American anthropologists including Edward Spicer (1969) and Edmund Leach (1969) praised Castaneda, alongside more alternative and young anthropologists such as Peter Furst, Barbara Myerhoff and Michael Harner.

The authenticity of Don Juan was accepted for six years, until Richard de Mille and Daniel Noel both published their critical exposés of the Don Juan books in 1976 (De Mille produced a further edited volume in 1980). Most anthropologists had been convinced of Castaneda's authenticity until now – indeed, they had had little reason to question it – but De Mille's meticulous analysis, in particular, debunked Castaneda's work. Beneath the veneer of anthropological fact stood huge discrepancies in the data: the books 'contradict one another in details of time, location, sequence, and description of events' (Schultz in Clifton 1989: 45). There are possible published sources for almost everything Carlos wrote (see especially Beals 1978), and at least one encounter is ethnographic plagiarism: Ramon Medina, a Huichol shaman-informant to Myerhoff (1974), displayed superhuman acrobatic feats at a waterfall and, according to Myerhoff, in the presence of Castaneda (Fikes 1993). Then, in *A Separate Reality*, Don Juan's friend Don Genaro makes a similar leap over a waterfall with the aid of supernatural power. In addition to these inconsistencies, various authors suggest aspects of the Sonoran desert Carlos describes are environmentally implausible, and, the 'Yaqui shamanism' he divulges is not Yaqui at all but a synthesis of shamanisms from elsewhere (e.g. Beals 1978).

The controversy does not end here. Castaneda's estranged wife recently wrote in detail about how Carlos was hardly new to shamanisms when he 'met' Don Juan. Like other seekers of his generation he had been influenced and inspired by alternative spiritual thinkers and psychedelic explorers, particularly Aldous Huxley and Timothy Leary (M.R. Castaneda 1997). It is also interesting to note the academic politics of the time. Awarding Castaneda a PhD was encouraged by the phenomenologist Professor Garfinkel, whose belief in reality as social construction convinced the critics that Castaneda's 'alternate reality' vis-à-vis 'ethnographic actuality' should be academically acceptable (e.g. M.R. Castaneda 1997). Furthermore, both Myerhoff and Furst largely supported the ethnography as true, but they are stunningly critiqued on their own merits by Fikes (1993), who perceives methodological corruption in the contemporary UCLA anthropological team. Granted, Fikes is a staunch Boasian, yet it is interesting that Myerhoff and Furst portray Medina as traditional Huichol when his shamanic practices are largely urbanised and distinct from more 'traditional' reports. This does not stop Medina being a 'real' shaman of course, but Myerhoff and Furst seem to have neglected to mention Medina's social background and, in an attempt to promote him (Medina and other Huichol shamans have been commercialised for neo-Shamanic consumption by Brant Secunda), presented Medina's practices as an unchanged and pristine form of shamanism; hardly scrupulous ethnography. Further intrigue surrounds Castaneda when he was not forthcoming in addressing the accusations of fakery as they emerged, and indeed may have vetoed their dissemination: Noel's first book on Castaneda did not reach fruition due, he thinks, to the clout of Castaneda's publishers (Noel pers. com.).

Politics and personal grudges aside, there is little to merit belief in Castaneda's work as anthropological 'fact'. He neglected to produce field notes on request, eventually claiming they were destroyed in a basement flood. When he did respond to the critics, Carlos was mysterious and elusive, particularly with arch-enemies De Mille and Noel, all adding to his enigmatic persona. Most problematic of all, Castaneda's apprenticeship to Don Juan to become a 'man of knowledge' required him to 'erase personal history', resulting in several inconsistent versions of his own biography. Part of the problem in accepting Castaneda's work, then, is that it is hard to accept Castaneda himself. Indeed, which Carlos? There are multiple versions of where Castaneda was born, who his father was and the rudiments of his life story up to entrance into UCLA, most of them peddled at one time or another by Carlos himself. He even disputed his marriage to Margaret Runyan Castaneda and the fathering of her child (M.R. Castaneda 1997). Carlos revelled in enigma and enjoyed confusing people as he attempted to 'stop the world' shamanically. Even more strangely, the public image of an eccentric Carlos was hardly consistent with the reclusive, moderate and sober man who rarely presented himself in public. Awaiting his appearance at a rare lecture, Clifton relates:

[M]y friends had joked about expecting a beaded and feathered
shaman who would walk without leaving footprints; for now, I will
assume that the short-haired man in the conservative suit, who
looked a lot like one of my junior-high Spanish teachers, was indeed
Castaneda.

(Clifton 1994: 5)

Carlos almost invited people to expose him, and that, rather than destroying
him, gave his work ever greater publicity and mystery.

To date, the 'Toltec Warrior' followers of 'Don Carlos' steadfastly testify
they have met, even practised nagualism, under Don Juan or his fellow
shamans in Mexico (e.g. Douglas 1980; Matson 1980; Wilk 1980). Few
scholars believe Don Juan is a real person and in the final analysis with no
other supportive data, rigidly supportive anthropologists demand instead
that we 'believe' in Castaneda (see papers in De Mille 1980), 'believe' in the
'truth' of the books: Michael Harner told Richard de Mille that Carlos's
work is '110 per cent valid since it conveys a deep truth' (Noel 1997:
91–92). Noel remarks on how neo-Shamans 'avert their eyes from any
controversies over factual reliability … if they are aware of this issue, they
often declare "it doesn't matter" whether the writings are fact or fiction …
they seem to find its "principles" factually persuasive' (Noel 1997: 38–39).
The danger of universalising shamanisms and devaluing the individual experiences of indigenous shamans, alongside the under-cutting of their truth by
a fake shaman, here, is clear. But, De Mille adds that it is Castaneda's
methodology, and the alternate shamanistic reality he presents, that we are
asked to believe, rather than the ethnographic 'facts' themselves, which are
certainly fictitious:

> Castaneda wasn't a common con man, he lied to bring us the truth.
> His stories are packed with truth, though they are not true stories,
> which he says they are. This is not your familiar literary allegorist
> painlessly instructing his readers in philosophy. Nor is it your fear-
> less trustworthy ethnographer returned full of anecdotes from the
> forests of Ecuador. This is a sham-man bearing gifts, an ambiguous
> spellbinder dealing simultaneously in contrary commodities –
> wisdom and deception. That's unusual. It may be important. And it
> needs straightening out.
>
> (De Mille 1976)

It certainly is 'important', to anthropologists, neo-Shamans and indigenous
people, and De Mille does a thorough and exhaustive job of 'straightening' it
out. He and others undoubtedly revealed Carlos 'the multifaceted "literary
shaman"', 'Carlos the Trickster' (Schultz in Clifton 1989: 45). But perhaps
the greatest concern for academia is that Castaneda's work exemplifies a

stunning and embarrassing parody of normative anthropological practice. The research is presented as fact, but the field notes are lost, the results are qualitative and therefore not repeatable, and the methodology is unconventional, even dangerous (involving entheogen ingestion). Additionally, the publications are more populist than academic and read more like an autobiography than a positivist ethnographic record. Many anthropological supporters of Carlos were steadfast in their 'belief' in Don Juan and the 'truth' of the writings, not because they were naïve but because they required the material to be presented as 'scientific anthropological facts'. Presentation as normative anthropology legitimated both their belief in the universal shamanic 'truth' of the work and their own approaches to shamanisms. This is representative of the time: although educated in Boasian methodology a new generation of anthropologists were embedded in the psychedelic era of 1960s' liberation. They were, understandably, inspired by Castaneda's ability to portray the bizarre and fantastical (to Western minds) world of the shaman in a new, exciting way; a way unlike most positivist ethnography that many people – laypersons and anthropologists – could identify with. In his 'magical autobiography' (Clifton 1989) Castaneda made shamanisms more personal and approachable. The books were timed perfectly, when people were ready and willing to take on 'shamanism' as an ethnographic concept, and an experiential approach which was forward-looking for its time (even though in Castaneda's case it was fictional). Unfortunately for experiential anthropology, Castaneda's tale is bogus in every other way, so giving the methodology a poor entrance into anthropology. And had Castaneda actually been reflexive and candid – and quite simply honest – about his 'novelistic' accounts, the literary turn in anthropological method of the 1990s might have had an earlier introduction into the discipline.

Castaneda certainly inspired me, as he has countless other spiritual seekers and budding archaeologists/anthropologists. But the only 'belief' in Castaneda I might profess is in his unconventional but promising experiential approach, or claims for one at least. That doesn't stop his works being 'anthrofolly' and purely fictional, for which Carlos deserves due discredit. Nor does it mean we should forget how indigenous people were exploited in the process:

> The behaviour encouraged by reading Castaneda's books and the influence the books have had on his readers (including their disruption of certain Native American societies Castaneda's books sensationalised), are issues which have been almost completely overlooked ... Thousands of readers seeking an alternative to chemical psychedelics headed for the hills of southern Mexico ... The local Indians were overwhelmed by the sheer number of hippies and appalled by their manners.
>
> (Fikes 1993: 36–38)

Castanedaesque neo-Shamans may have brought some financial benefits to the Huichol, but the effect was also to 'disrupt community life and subtly change traditional religious behaviour' (Brown 1997: 163), and deplete their Peyote resources which are so essential to ritual life. But this does not stop Castaneda's books being 'spiritually' valid to neo-Shamans. Furthermore, while they are ethnographically inauthentic, the narrative they present – in terms of experiential methodology – is certainly anthropologically valuable. The work is meaningful anthropology then, but only as the shamanovel Noel suggests, a remarkable historical phase in the history of anthropology looking towards experiential anthropology. That Don Juan never existed and that Castaneda's apprenticeship was only with himself and the shamans he read about make it problematic for mainstream anthropologists. It does, however, present a marvellous critique of anthropological practice and a new, previously unaccepted approach to shamanisms, a methodology alone – were it actually implemented – which is worthy of a PhD: an experiential, participatory, insider, phenomenological approach.

The absolute bizarreness of this whole Castaneda controversy must bewilder those largely unfamiliar with it. This in turn fuels the power of the Castaneda story, and Carlos must have relished that awe of mystery. I write this, rather aptly, soon after Castaneda's death was announced, and that, unsurprisingly, is yet another riddle. Strangely, the public was not informed until three months after Carlos died, and various stories surround the events of his death. The version favoured by acolytes of Carlos is that physical death was superseded by a spiritual death in which Castaneda's spirit transcended material existence:

> Carlos Castaneda left the world the same way that his teacher, Don Juan Matus did: with full awareness. The cognition of our world of everyday life does not provide for a description such as this. So in keeping with the terms of legalities and record keeping that the world of everyday life requires, Carlos Castaneda was declared to have died.
>
> (As stated on the website www.castaneda.com;
> see also M. Brown 1998; Wood 1998: 8)

The shamanic death of their founder marks a culmination point for the Toltec Warriors. From their perspective, 'Saint' Castaneda – whom most of them will never have met – has crossed over to the otherworld near to a celebrated date in Western history, surely a fortuitous omen. Henceforth, Nagualism looks set to flourish in the new millennium. Castaneda's teachings remain fabricated lies to most of us, yet they have taken on biblical proportions to his aspirants. Whatever we choose to believe, Carlos Castaneda was certainly the greatest anthropological trickster, who, significantly, presented shamanisms in a way which made people want to be shamans.

Michael Harner: disseminating 'core-shamanism'

The current tide of neo-Shamanic authors, Castaneda spin-offs, testify to the enduring appeal of 'how I became a shaman'. Uniquely, Castaneda's work simultaneously prompted what could be called an 'academic-shamanophobia' and popular 'neo-Shamania'. But with 'shamanism' at the time Castaneda presented it, becoming a shaman, doing 'shamanism' oneself, required being apprenticed with a mystical and distant anthropological Other, involving arduous physical and mental trials including the ingestion of potentially lethal entheogens. Until that is, Michael Harner, once professor of anthropology, provided safe and simple techniques for making neo-Shamanisms a pragmatic possibility, via an easily accessible set of procedures which did not involve the danger of entheogens: 'Harner Method' 'Core-Shamanism'. Harner chronicles his relationship with shamanisms in *The Way of the Shaman* (Harner 1990 [1980]: Chapter 1), a book described as the 'definitive handbook on practical shamanism' by 'the world's leading authority on shamanism' (Harner 1990 [1980]: back cover). Castaneda himself praises Harner: 'wonderful, fascinating ... Harner really knows what he's talking about' (Harner 1990 [1980]: back cover).

Harner's encounters with shamanisms began with fieldwork among the Untusuri Shuar (Jivaro) peoples of Ecuador during the years 1956–1957 (Harner 1972). Then, with the Conibo of the Peruvian Amazon, he underwent his first shamanic experience by ingesting the entheogenic Ayahuasca vine. Following this, and with the aim of acquiring tsentsak (other than human helpers), Harner returned to the Shuar in 1964 and learned use of the entheogen maikua (*Datura brugmansia*). He visited them again in 1969 and 1973, and also, apparently, learnt ways of practising shamanisms without entheogens from various North American shamans: the Wintun and Pomo in California, the Coast Salish in Washington and the Lakota in South Dakota. Following his profound shamanic experiences, Harner believed he should bring similar shamanic awareness to his fellow Westerners: 'Now it seems time to help transmit some practical aspects of this ancient human legacy to those who have been cut off from it for centuries' (Harner 1990 [1980]: 19). As a result, Harner founded the 'Center for Shamanic Studies: a non-profit incorporated educational organisation' in New York in 1983, currently the Foundation for Shamanic Studies, Mill Valley, California. To many anthropologists, 'going native' may have lost Harner his academic credibility, but this has not deterred neo-Shamanic adherents who say they reap immeasurable benefits from his teaching of core-shamanism.

Harner and colleagues teach courses in experiential shamanisms ranging from beginner to advanced throughout the Western world – including North America, Australia, the UK and Europe – the most widespread of which is *The Way of the Shaman: The Shamanic Journey, Power and Healing; The Basic Workshop*. With the shamanic journeying technique Harner teaches in this workshop, participants are taught that anyone can induce altered consciousness, or trance, which Harner names the 'shamanic state of consciousness' (SSC). Harner is in 'essential agreement with Eliade' that 'shamanism' is a type of ecstasy, but argues its 'distinctive feature is the journey to other worlds in an altered state of consciousness' (pers. com. See also, for example, Harner 1988a and Vitebsky 2000: 56).[2] This is the characteristic feature of his core-shamanism according to which shamans access 'an altered state of consciousness – at will – to contact and utilize an ordinary hidden reality in order to acquire knowledge, power, and to help other persons' (Harner 1990 [1980]: 20). Entering this state, usually induced by monotonous drumming, though other instruments may be employed, facilitates the core-shamanic 'journey', referring to the out-of-body travel or magical flight described by Eliade, and experienced during the LSD 'trip'. During the core-shamanic experience people lie down and relax with their eyes closed or covered. The journey begins by entering the earth at a place well known in the physical world such as a cave, and experients then fall, slide, fly or travel by some other means down a tunnel and into a 'spirit world'. Here aspirants meet and interact with 'spirit helpers' and 'power animals' and, as they become more adept, learn to heal sickness and to divine. It is stressed by advocates that the spirit world encountered is 'real', not imaginary (or imaginal, as post-Jungians prefer), and that the experiences are not guided visualisations but non-structured visits to the spirit world. The basic framework of relaxed posture, tunnel experience and entrance to the spirit world is the only guideline.

These core-shamanism techniques are probably the most widely known and practised in the West, and Harner's techniques have been highly influential on neo-Shamanisms and indeed the New Age, as L. Jones notes:

> The rhetorical strategy of combining anthropological data, myth, personal experience narrative, and visualisation exercises, the emphasis on drumming ... and a listing of workshops and mail-order sources for further information, has become the paradigm for most current mystical handbooks.
>
> (L. Jones 1998: 197)

I attended Harner's 'basic workshop', conducted by Leslie Kenton (representative of the 'Faculty' in England until Simon Buxton of the Sacred Trust, http://www.sacredtrust.org, was appointed), in London over a weekend in April 1997 (Figure 1.3). This seminar provided a suitable experience of how beginner-level Harner Method neo-Shamanism is taught and practised, and I also interviewed Harner in San Francisco in April 1998. I am mindful, however, of being accused by core-shamanists, as Noel (1997) has been (Grimaldi 1997), for critiquing core-shamanism based on limited experience gained by attending a single, basic workshop: techniques taught at this

Figure 1.3 Leaflet advertising neo-Shamanic workshops in 1998 with Leslie
Kenton and Sandra Ingerman. I attended a 'core-shamanism' basic
workshop with Kenton. Ingerman teaches more advanced courses
on the neo-Shamanic healing methods of Soul Retrieval and
Shamanic Extraction

Source: Courtesy of Simon Buxton/The Sacred Trust.

workshop have come under the closest scrutiny and criticism (see, for
example, Zinser 1987; Willis 1994; Johnson 1995; Harvey 1997b; Jones
1998; Jakobsen 1998; 1999). On the one hand, there are more advanced
courses core-shamanists can attend, including 'soul retrieval' and 'shamanic
counselling training', but on the other hand, many neo-Shamans may only
ever attend the basic workshop, so criticism of it alone is not without merit.
And meanwhile, many other neo-Shamans practise very differently.
Although I have not attended advanced Harner workshops, my discussion of
his work derives from my surveying literature on the subject (e.g. Harner
1988b; Ingerman 1991), from my experiences in the workshop and follow-
up 'journeying sessions' alone and in groups over a two-year period, from
Harner's responses to my interview questions, and from the perspectives
people have expressed during my five years of research, comprising

published or verbal critiques and appraisals. I feel these core-shamanism studies and experiences alongside my familiarity with other neo-Shamanic practices, provide sufficient data with which to appraise core-shamanism and other neo-Shamanisms in the following and subsequent chapters.

2

PLASTIC MEDICINE MEN?

Appraising the 'Great Pretenders'

Selling shamanic journeys is a multimillion-dollar business today. Some sellers, such as Michael Harner, believe they are assisting clients to 'cross the shamanic bridge' into contact with spirits, to heal ills and extend cosmic knowledge. Some sellers appear merely earning a living. A few can be dangerous ...

(Kehoe 2000: 81)

A shaman belongs to his people, be they human or non-human ... And there the shaman's obligation lies: to serve those who come to him ... [but] he is not necessarily there to be nice to anyone ... A shaman is fierce or tricky or gentle because he sees a way in that for his people to find their own paths through life, not because he is bitter or vindictive.

(MacLellan 1999: 117–118)

Having introduced how neo-Shamanisms are constituted and examined the background of historical influences, I turn in this chapter to the ways in which neo-Shamans have been and can be appraised critically. Four main charges are made against Harner and neo-Shamanisms more widely:

1 Decontextualising and universalising
2 Psychologising and individualising
3 Reproduction and reification of cultural primitivism
4 Romanticising of indigenous shamanisms.

Paradoxically, these misappropriations of shamanisms largely reproduce pervasive themes in the study of shamanisms such as evolutionism, which, as I have argued, equally misunderstand shamanisms (see also Boyer 1969; Noll 1983, 1989). In exploring these criticisms, it is important to note that critics tend to treat core-shamanism and other neo-Shamanisms as a single entity, thereby privileging Harnerism and both stereotyping and neglecting

49

other neo-Shamanisms. Jakobsen (1999), for instance, is one of the few scholars to study neo-Shamanisms in detail, but I feel she has made the error of concentrating mainly on core-shamanism (see also Townsend 1997, 1999) and its manifestations (such as the Scandinavian Centre for Shamanic Studies directed by Jonathan Horwitz 1989) and contrasting this with her own indigenous example, the Greenlandic angakkoq.

Jakobsen suggests, for example, 'the power of the specialist is what neo-shamanism is attempting to eliminate ... the knowledge of the shaman is no longer of an esoteric character but instead available to all' (Jakobsen 1999: 217). While some neo-Shamanisms (or at least core-shamanism) can be criticised for proposing anyone can be a shaman, not all neo-Shamanisms can be characterised in this way. Indeed, many clients might compare the visit to a neo-Shaman with that to a doctor: the visit is made because the healer is perceived to be a 'specialist'. Furthermore, when shamanisms are explored worldwide, notions of the shaman as a 'specialist' with 'esoteric' knowledge are not universal, particularly the specialist 'master of spirits'. Among Southern African Bushmen (San) shamans, for instance, the shaman's vocation is open to all, and as Lewis argues (1989 [1971]), possession (not requiring mastery over spirits) is an integral part of some shamanisms. Jakobsen's conclusion only holds true for core-shamanism (even this is an oversimplification) and the singular case study of the angakkoq. But it is by no means the case that the angakkoq should be regarded as any more representative of shamanisms, or more 'pristine' (as the cover of her book argues), than other instances worldwide. Notions of 'pristine', 'real' or 'authentic' shamans are a Western imposition based in no small part on the misguided search for a singular 'proto-' shamanism, and ignore the agentic urbanisation of shamanisms in many places which cannot be regarded as less authentic or valid. Further, a more nuanced understanding of neo-Shamanisms is achieved by undertaking a multi-sited ethnographic approach. I next address the four criticisms listed above which scholars tend to levy at neo-Shamanisms (particularly core-shamanism). While I am in agreement with these criticisms in some respects, my discussion, in contrast to that of many other publications, is not restricted to criticisms of neo-Shamans. I also remark on various positive contributions made by neo-Shamans to the term 'shaman', to shamanism studies, and to indigenous shamans themselves, which are consistently overlooked.

Decontextualising and universalising

Following Eliade, Harner's definition of 'shamanism' has had considerable influence on perceptions of shamanisms among neo-Shamans (and some academics), particularly his selection of features he deems fundamental to all shamanisms: entering a 'shamanic state of consciousness', 'journeying' to other worlds' and 'healing' comprise the crux of his core-shamanism and are consistent with Eliade's understanding of 'shamanism'; features apparently universal to shamanisms the world over. The emphasis is clearly on what is perceived to be shamanic universally across space and time. Between earlier publications (Shuar ethnography [1972] and the edited volume *Hallucinogens and Shamanism* [1973a]) and the neo-Shamanic bible *Way of the Shaman* (1990 [1980]), Johnson believes Harner shifts 'from the particular to the universal, from the locative to the utopian' (Johnson 1995: 171). Given that the 1973 volume is markedly more eclectic than that of the previous year, this shift seems only to have taken one year, but nonetheless Harner has indeed decontextualised aspects of shamanisms from original 'owners' in the 1980 book. As Harvey comments for neo-Shamanisms more widely, 'Shamanism has been appropriated from these societies (rarely if ever given or exported by them), distilled into a set of techniques and re-contextualised for modern urban societies' (Harvey 1997b: 108). Among core-shamanists particularly, there is no need for 'cultural baggage' or the trappings of traditional shamans, only the techniques of shamanisms are required. As Harner told me:

> I teach core-shamanism in which we are attempting to have everything the same ... and that's a hard job ... because we are trying to find the basic principles that are common to most shamanic practitioners in most societies, and teach those basic principles without all these elaborations and specialisations that make them a product of each cultural context.
>
> (Harner pers. com.)

But by downplaying the role of cultural specificity, Harnerism and other neo-Shamanisms can be accused of homogenising shamanisms and, worse, ignoring the peoples whose 'techniques' have been 'used' (others may be correct in preferring the terms 'borrowed', 'appropriated' or 'stolen'). While reference to the Shuar, Conibo or other native shamans may be made, it is reasonable to suggest that from the way Harner presents core-shamanism in his book, a neo-Shaman need never know about traditional shamans in order to learn the techniques. Indeed, in a troubling equation, native shamans are merely used to legitimate neo-Shamanic techniques. Whether this is intended or not (for core-shamanism does have benefits for practitioners and native groups, as I state below), core-shamanism removes indigenous people from the equation, and their 'religion' is reduced to a set of 'techniques'. In this way, traditional shamans and the often harsh realities of modern indigenous life need not be encountered, and certainly would not match up to the romantic image.

Criticisms in terms of decontextualising and universalising have been made of other neo-Shamans: Felicitas Goodman and her work on shamanic trance postures, for instance. Goodman claims that various prehistoric remains and the imagery of certain indigenous artistic traditions point towards specific stances which can automatically induce trance (e.g. Goodman 1986, 1988, 1989, 1990) – it is claimed that all people have the potential to promote trance via these postures. As well as to such ethnographic instances as the shaman and bear 'spirit' carving from America's Northwest coast, Goodman applies this approach to the so-called 'wounded man' depicted in the shaft-scene of the famous cave of Lascaux in the Dordogne.[1] Goodman suggests that if we take the bird-headed stick and Bison as upright, the wounded man is positioned at a 'thirty-seven degree angle' (Goodman 1990: 22). By achieving this angle (with some form of support), Goodman argues trance can be induced easily. From the perspective of rock art research, this marks a good example of how such imagery is inappropriately interpreted with the modern, eighteenth-century definition of 'art', particularly when encountered in expensive coffee-table books, since there is actually no reason to compare cave paintings with two-dimensional canvases. Indeed, there is nothing to suggest where 'upright' is in the paintings – they are viewed inappropriately as 'framed' or subject to modern Western aesthetic rules. I think Goodman's aim is admirable, for there are connections between the postures some shamans assume and altered consciousness (e.g. San shamans in Southern Africa). But shamans combine specific combinations of trance-inducing practices, so the assumption that simply sitting as an 'African Diviner' or reclining at thirty-seven degrees automatically induces trance is highly tenuous. I attended a workshop in which these postures were taught (not by Goodman) and found them to be utterly ineffective. Indeed, the participants were quite impressionable and the workshop leader fished for the responses he wanted and put his words into their mouths, to authenticate the claims made about the postures. Geertz's stinging assessment of Goodman's methodology and results posits her essentially misleading aim to 'strip away cultural specificity and you will find the universal human' (Geertz 1993: 369). Like Harner and other neo-Shamans, Goodman's practices decontextualise and universalise shamanisms.

In contrast to traditional shamanisms, shamanic experiences are portrayed by many neo-Shamans as being safe and, by virtue of their universality, available to be practised by anyone. Harner Method neo-Shamanism is in sharp contrast to the Shuar and Conibo traditions Harner learnt and on which he based the techniques. In one harrowing shamanic experience Harner ingests maikua for the first time:

> [W]as my shamanic quest worth the danger? ... thought vanished as an inexpressible terror rapidly permeated my body. My companions were going to kill me! I must get away! I attempted to jump up, but instantly they were upon me. Three, four, an infinity of savages wrestled with me ... their faces were above me, contorted

into sly grins. Then blackness. I was awakened by a flash of lightning followed by a thunderous explosion. The ground beneath me
was shaking. I jumped up, utterly in panic. A hurricane-like wind
threw me back down on the ground ... Lightning and thunder
exploded all around ... My companions were nowhere to be seen.

(Harner 1990 [1980]: 15–16)

Harner's testimony makes plain how learning to be a shaman can be a
dangerous and potentially life-threatening endeavour. His 'core-shamanism',
though, is:

tame by comparison ... : a series of safe, simple, short 'experiential
exercises'. The experimenters remain in control and face only
aspects of themselves – worrying and perhaps frightening, but
nonetheless safe and controllable. Harner ... tries to divorce healing
Shamanism from its more aggressive manifestations ... many neo-
shamans ignore the aggressive elements of Shamanism or treat them
as something allegedly different – 'sorcery' – as if the techniques,
beliefs and experiences were of a completely different type.

(Harvey 1997b: 112)

Many neo-Shamans clearly avoid what Brown (1989) calls the 'dark side of
the shaman', such as battling with evil spirits and death threats, which are a
common part of the shamanic vocation (see also Jakobsen 1998, 1999).
Core-shamanism basic workshops for instance, suggest you do not accept
insects, reptiles or carnivores as other than human helpers or power animals
(see also Jakobsen 1999: 191). This is due partly to the negative connotations associated with these creatures in the West, when in indigenous
shamanisms such creatures may be the most powerful of helpers because
they are the most difficult to deal with. Understandably, but unlike indigenous shamanisms, core-shamanism recommends less dangerous creatures to
ensure beginners feel 'safe'. Some neo-Shamans are clearly very aware of this
misappropriation. As neo-Shaman Gordon 'the toad' MacLellan told me:

I sympathise strongly with the Native American feelings that the
teachings have been stolen, but also recognise that Western people
are gaining from the experiences. I suppose my balance is where
does respect lie?: are people being true to the source of such rituals?,
are these evolving as they encounter new forces?, are the people
using them claiming a Native American shamanic heritage? On
balance I am wary and feel that a lot of teachings are taken piecemeal, choosing the gentle bits and missing the fullness of tradition
by avoiding some of the less palatable (to Western tastes) stuff. We
hear a lot about the sweat lodge, pipe ceremonies and some dances,

but more rarely of full vision-quest, yuwipi ceremony, piercing sundance, or skin and flesh going into rattles.

(MacLellan pers. com.)

MacLellan draws attention to the neo-Shamanic aim to embrace that which
is appealing and downplay the negative aspects of shamanisms, a neat
example of scientific/Western compartmentalising and of separating that
which to its originators is inseparable: where there is healing for many
shamans, there is danger, and this cannot be viewed in terms of a Christian
dualistic cosmology of good and evil.

Also in contrast to indigenous shamanisms, core-shamanism emphasises
that the shamanic state is controllable. While this might, at first glance,
compare with the shaman's 'mastery' of spirits in some cultures, this need
for control actually contrasts with the same. Jakobsen asserts that neo-
Shamans prefers to avoid the concept of mastery since it has negative
connotations for Westerners (Jakobsen 1999: 206), in effect another
example of how neo-Shamanisms decontextualise shamanisms. The
emphasis on 'control', on the other hand, is important in core-shamanism
because the shaman's path can be conveyed as safe and suitable for teaching
in a workshop scenario. It may also represent an attempt to de-stigmatise
shamanisms following decades of oppression in indigenous communities by
colonising cultures and religions (e.g. Soviet communism). The logic is that
if we can show shamans to be competent and normal rather than raving
mad, then the persecution of shamanisms can be discouraged. The aim is of
course praiseworthy, but using the notion of shamans' control over trance to
demonstrate this is spurious. Such endeavours to present shamanisms positively should challenge Western stereotypes and prejudices rather than
impose more of the same. Emphasising 'control' over trance, or contrasting
shamanisms (controlled) with spirit possession and mediumship (uncon-
trolled) is one such example. Similarly, Lewis suggests that such
delineations are rather arbitrary when we consider the diversity of shamanic
practices. Where other researchers regard shamanisms and spirit possession
as 'antithetical phenomena', I have marked that Lewis regards shamanisms,
possession and mediumship as comparable (Lewis 1989 [1971], 1993).
Approaching spirit possession and shamanisms as disparate in fact derives
from impositions of binary oppositions and cultural evolution (as discussed
earlier under Eliade). Pervasive themes in studies on shamanisms such as
these illustrate how many stereotypes and misunderstandings of shamanisms have come about (see also Holm 1980) and been reified by
neo-Shamans. While the emphasis on control in Harnerism promises the
technique is safe to practitioners, it also reveals the Western need for
'control' (over consciousness, emotions, finances, etc). Contrasted with
'world religions' with an omnipotent, all-seeing, untouchable Supreme
(consistently male) Being and their hierarchies of priesthood, shamanisms

may be perceived as less dogmatic and more egalitarian, with the tools for unlocking one's own spirit allies and direct contact with the divine – shamanism as a democratic, and in some instances activist, 'spiritual' path. But no such precedent of security, safety and democracy may be found in all indigenous shamanisms.

Taussig (1987, 1989) demonstrates indirectly this point in his study of colonialism in the Colombian Putomayo, which, to Stoll (1987), suggests reads like a Yage hallucination itself. He draws attention to the shaman as negotiator and negotiated in a deeply political process which destroys any belief in shamanisms as fundamentally safe or benevolent, and disrupts the stereotypical notion of colonialism as a one-way process of domination and acculturation. According to Taussig, coloniser and colonised engage on multiple levels of negotiation and contest; the colonised are not passive and reactive, but proactive. Shamanic careers and their rituals are open-ended; there is always a tension in the air, an aura of unpredictability, and the potential for 'dismantling all fixed notions of identity' (Taussig 1989: 57). Rather than there being a strictly followed narrative pattern and a cathartic shamanic 'healing', the nature of shamanisms is consistently undetermined with no certain or known outcome (though Western observers might expect one). The ritual may be unsuccessful, disputes may not be resolved, the shaman's other than human helpers may depart and the career end abruptly. This ongoing nature of unpredictability waxes and wanes alongside the desired catharsis and constancy, just as shamans themselves often struggle with malevolent and benevolent other than human helpers, sorcery and healing. Shamanic vocations are culturally constituted so the shamanic world itself is also political and in perpetual change. Recognising the uncertainty of the shamanic office allows Taussig to deconstruct the 'classic' Western model of shamanisms in which shamans are perceived to be largely male, dominating figures who control social relations and charismatically master their communities. The uncertainty of shamanisms in Taussig's experience shows how this image is a fabrication by Western observers imposing their masculist ideals inappropriately. It is also reified by those neo-Shamans who, on a more idealistic level, portray shamanisms as being safe, controllable and desirable.

Because shamanisms are often perceived in the West to be inherently 'safe', 'controllable' and 'universal' to all human cultures, its 'techniques' are presented as freely accessible to all. They are, as Hutton notes:

> represented as available to anybody prepared to devote the necessary time and trouble to them. In Siberia, shamanism was a gift bestowed upon rare individuals, often burdensome and unwelcome. To that extent the new employment of the term concealed more than it revealed about its origins.
>
> (Hutton 1993: 11)

Such accessibility also does not hold true for shamanic societies other than those in Siberia. In Bushman society, for instance, everyone has the potential ability to heal – to experience n|om ('boiling energy': e.g. Katz *et al.* 1997) – yet not everyone becomes a shaman. The shamanic experience is viewed with a healthy fear because it is painful and involves 'death' as well as healing. In Bushman and other societies, the shaman is called to the vocation: perhaps a sickness threatens a person's life and other than human persons come to that person and heal them so that they can go on to heal others – the well-known 'wounded healer' metaphor (Halifax 1982). Certainly, though, very few shamans would say they choose to be shamans; in many pre-industrial societies shamanic experience is known to be painful and hazardous. Worse, among some Siberian reindeer herders, having a shaman in the family is recognised as being a death curse (Vitebsky 1998). There is, then, a decontextualising of shamanisms by neo-Shamans where what seems useful and safe is enthusiastically adopted, while the potentially dangerous is atrophied. Also, the spirit-helpers do not choose the neo-Shaman, the literature encourages people to become shamans of their own accord.

In a final example of decontextualising, beyond their downplaying of diverse traditional shamanisms in favour of a 'core-shamanism', Harnerists can also be accused of promoting core-shamanism to the exclusion of other neo-Shamanists. Harner intends his 'shamanic state of consciousness' (SSC), for example, as a distinction from ordinary states of consciousness (OSC) so that the unusual world of the shaman can be made easily understandable to Westerners. It is also meant to encourage its equal if not superior status and thereby de-stigmatise native religions. Furthermore, it makes the SSC more acceptable to us than ASC (altered state of consciousness) which might hint at entheogen misuse. Credible as this endeavour sounds, the SSC, I think, implies that only certain religious practitioners are able to enter it – shamans/core-shamans, privileging them and their 'SSC' over and above other ecstatics and altered states. Moreover, SSC suggests an exclusive division between ordinary and shamanic awareness, where non-Western peoples may make far less a rigid distinction (as with good and evil). Perhaps 'altered consciousness' serves as a better term to suggest that awareness is simply (yet profoundly) altered: shamans frequently describe altered consciousness as being more real than the ordinary state, but there is not a rigid distinction between them.

Political bias of a comparable sort is evident in Harner's de-culturing of shamanisms. Responding to my suggestions in our interview that shamanisms are inherently political, Harner suggested that the healing aspect – requiring the journey into spirit – is paramount in defining and understanding shamanisms. Politics, on the other hand, is an aspect of cultural baggage that is either added onto the essence or does not typify shamanisms: 'Shamanism, as I said, is not a religion. The spiritual experience usually becomes a religion after politics has entered into it' (Harner and Doore:

1987: 15). Such a view is not uncommon: Houston, for example, follows Harner in suggesting 'shamanism' is 'prepolitical' (Houston 1987: vii). In direct contrast, I think shamanisms, like all aspects of society, are inherently political from the outset: shamanisms do not begin in an apolitical vacuum and then become socially embedded – they are social and therefore political from the outset. Shamans are social beings whose experiences, the images they 'see' and the 'spirits' they interact with, are religiously and socially guided, as well as politically embedded (the extent to which these three can be disengaged is of course disputed). As Atkinson's study of Wana shamanism illustrates: 'Wana seek shamanic powers for a variety of reasons ... [but] if they persist, sooner or later they will find themselves operating in an arena that is at once ritual and political' (1989: xii). Harner and Houston might object to my 'culturist' angle, but their neglect of the politics of shamanisms is itself a political position. Core-shamanism aims to remove culture, which removes politics, to leave a perceived bare bones of 'shamanism'. Practitioners are thereby free from responsibility to traditional shamans and from the bonds of cultural politics to practise a perceived acultural and apolitical spirituality. This is less to do with shamanisms and more an integral part of New Age ideology in which the post-modernist (and arguably capitalist) belief is held that individuals are responsible for social ills so that social change is effected by individual action and personal development (Vitebsky 1995b: 195). Arguing that core-shamanism (which to Harner *is* traditional shamanism) is politically neutral is therefore a politically motivated act embedded within Western discourse.

A similar example of core-shamanism exclusivity is apparent in the work of Townsend (e.g. 1988, 1997, 1998, 1999). Townsend, like Jakobsen, is one of the rare academics to have taken the time and effort required to explore neo-Shamanisms in some detail. I do take issue, though, with her distinction between 'Neo-shamanism' and 'Core shamanism': the value of this distinction within her 'Western shamanic spirituality' banner, or for that matter between 'traditionalist' (core-shamanism), and 'modernist' and 'eclectic' (both aspects of neo-shamanisms), is obfuscated by the fact that her research clearly privileges core-shamanism over the rest of what she terms 'Western shamanic spirituality'. While she is not a core-shamanism practitioner herself, she has conducted experiential fieldwork in that area (pers. com.), which may indicate a reason for her bias. Having explored various neo-Shamanisms experientially myself, I suggest core-shamanism cannot be singled out in this way. Indeed, I find Townsend's rationale for distinguishing core-shamanism rather troubling when she uses the terms 'pure', 'universal', and 'core' to describe it, where neo-Shamanisms are 'pseudo-', 'invented', 'idealized', 'eclectic' (Townsend 1997, 1998, 1999). In direct contrast, I think core-shamanism is as much an 'invention' or 'idealized' as the other aspects of neo-Shamanisms Townsend derides. I do agree that many neo-Shamanisms suffer from romantic, primitivist and universalist assumptions, but I extend such analysis to core-shamanism. Further, I would not go so far as to characterise all neo-Shamanisms in this way since that would ignore diversity and neglect those practitioners who make positive contributions.

Individualising and psychologising

The transportation of shamanisms from indigenous to Western contexts since the 1960s is part of a larger process of globalisation: in the 'global village' almost any cultural facet, wherever it originated, is readily available via electronic means. In cyber-space, I can enter Hungopavi village on the Hopi web page, surf the hyper-reality of techno-shamanism, or hear an Australian 'shamanic' didgeridu. In the spiritual marketplace thus created, Johnson rightly suggests that an inevitable individualising is inherent in neo-Shamanisms:

> a plurality of religions ... leads to ... a focus on individual agency, choice, 'needs' and preference in the religious 'marketplace' ... an obsession with the 'self', subjectivity and reflexivity ... [and] the discourse of mobility – individuals are free and capable of converting to any religious system in any place and at any time.
>
> (Johnson 1995: 174)

Besides the underlying liberal capitalism in contemporary religions thus influenced, Vitebsky (1995b: 194) cites Kleinman's identification of a 'psychologising process' in the West since the Second World War, wherein psychology has filled the vacuum left by the dissolving of religion. Unsurprisingly, studies of shamanism have undergone their own phase of psychologising, transforming the early perception of shamans as psychotics (Czaplicka 1914; Kroeber 1940; Devereux 1956, 1961; Murphy 1964; Neu 1975; Silverman 1967; but see Handelman 1967, 1968) into adept psychiatrists (e.g. Opler 1936; 1961; Lévi-Strauss 1963; Jilek 1971; Torrey 1974; Peters and Price-Williams 1980; Downton 1989; Groesbeck 1989; Senn 1989). Again drawing on such literature and influenced by the many psychologists who advocate experiential engagements with shamanic experiences (e.g. Villoldo and Krippner 1986; Walsh 1990; Bates 1996; Wilcox 1999), neo-Shamanisms have often psychologised shamanisms. By practising the Harner Method or Goodman trance postures, for instance, the shamanic experience becomes simply a set of techniques removed from their original cultural and community contexts. Shamanisms are sanitised for the West and brought 'up to date', often compared with psychotherapeutic and psychiatric techniques. In this way, Vitebsky suggests neo-Shamans water down the traditional shamanisms in his area of specialism – Siberia – and 'internalise' the cosmology with myths simply representing psychological metaphors

(Vitebsky 1995b: 193, 200–201). The Siberian tripartite cosmological world is removed from the environmental and social context in which it is embedded, and imbued instead with Jungian archetypes; the 'teacher within', the process of 'individuation', an 'inner landscape'. Rather than travelling into a 'real' spirit world, neo-Shamanic journeys are often perceived as being trips into oneself, and 'Soul Loss' involves healing emotional wounds rather than the actual retrieval of someone's lost soul. Healing also becomes a psychological process because it is difficult for Westerners imbued with Cartesian and scientific world-views to accept a 'spiritual' cause for illness, either derived from malevolent shamans or from the 'spirits'. In all, this process of psychologising suggests many neo-Shamans find it difficult to embrace shamanisms and their ideologies in their entirety.

Despite the widely held maxim 'all things are connected', neo-Shamans tend to separate themselves from the cosmos and from traditional shamanisms as cultural packages. Either the spirits are 'within', as in a psychology of shamanisms, or the spirits of 'nature' are idealised and set apart from a cruel and destructive humanity in environmentally oriented neo-Shamanisms. Radical environmentalist neo-Shamans might also understand shamans to be traditional resource managers, but rather than being 'caretakers of the earth' in which animal rights philosophy and an earth-orientated imperative are implicit, the indigenous shaman resource manager is quite different (see also Vitebsky 1995b: 200). The game animals are persuaded that they must be killed (in return for some form of offering/sacrifice) and shamans use their abilities to direct game into traps or to cross the path of the hunter's aim. Vegetarianism or veganism is not an option in most native shamanisms and the web of interactions between people and other species in indigenous communities is often not repeated in neo-Shamanisms. Instead, there is a one-way reaping of benefits. Neo-Shamans ritualising in field or forest invoke and gain healings from the other than human persons present there, but often no benefit is returned to the land. The ideas of 'spirits' and 'nature' are embraced, but direct engagement with habitus-based shamanic cosmology is often sidestepped. Shaw, in particular, from the perspective of deep ecology – a radical environmental philosophy – has monitored this process among neo-Shamans in Australia. Here, as elsewhere, shamanic techniques are based on a consumer ethic in which it is acceptable virtually to vampirise nature without reciprocal return of even the most basic kind, such as recycling waste (Shaw in prep.a, in prep.b). To the indigenous shaman, in contrast, reciprocation within the community and with the other than human persons of nature (in positive and negative ways) is implicit in what shamanisms are.

Some neo-Shamanisms, because of their individualised, psychologised and consumer-based slant, may be accused of selling 'rapid results', in terms of 'spiritual' development and healing (e.g. Atkinson 1992: 322). Gordon 'the toad' MacLellan notes there is an increasing trend for 'get-in-quick-and-do-it weekend courses that may be valuable in self-development but do not make shamans, which is a much longer, slower process and calls for an ongoing commitment that many people are not prepared to make' (pers. com.). Core-shamanism techniques, in particular, have been subject to this sort of criticism, and Harner does little to refute them when stating that what a shaman can do in a few minutes takes a yogi many years (Harner 1990 [1980]: xiii); the comparison is hardly credible. The arduous traditional shamanic vocation is not a psychological tool for self-discovery or empowerment which can be used for five minutes with dramatic results, but if we look at the plethora of books and workshops available, shamanisms are certainly 'packaged' by neo-Shamanisms and undergo a 'commoditization' (Vitebsky 1995b: 199).

Many critics object to this 'spiritual commerce' (Brown 1997: 144–145), although the form of exchange is normally the essence of dispute. People find money tainted and non-spiritual, yet many shamans have always received a form of payment for their services. The standard price for training with the indigenous shaman Harner leant from, for instance, was a shotgun. Brown (1997: 144–145) cites Marx and Simmel, who disliked the idea of 'money' as an abstract measure of value, imbued with a moral emptiness, and this idea seems to be behind the thrust of those who criticise neo-Shamanisms. In wider perspective, Brown also remarks that Mauss (1990 [1950]) showed how in non-Western cultures, materiality is consistently permeated by spirituality/religion. It is important to be aware of where the accusations of overt materiality in neo-Shamanisms arise. The motivations for such criticisms are (understandably) politically derived when Native Americans, in particular, have their traditions appropriated and sold on by neo-Shamans (see Chapter 7). But though we can accuse neo-Shamanisms of commodifying shamanisms and peddling quick-fix spirituality, and though we can criticise a number of well-publicised individuals of charging extortionate prices (particularly in Los Angeles e.g. Lynn Andrews), to accuse neo-Shamanisms of 'selling' shamanisms is misleading since it ignores the devices of exchange almost all indigenous shamans employ.

Neo-Shamanisms may also be accused of at once decontextualising, individualising and psychologising shamanisms when they remove the social contexts and community focus of traditional shamanisms. I have argued that essential to understanding shamanisms is a social or community context: the shaman's office is embedded within a community and cannot operate without that sanctioning. Neo-Shamanists, in contrast, often conduct their practices alone and in private, as Hutton observes:

> The new shamanism consisted essentially of a set of gentle meditations and visualisations, instead of the frenetic and dramatic performances of the Siberians. They were private to the practitioner or carried on by groups, rather than being displays before audiences.
>
> (Hutton 1993: 11)

More specifically, core-shamanic journeying is most often done for oneself and the neo-Shamanic vision quest is a solitary ritual. The journey in traditional shamanisms, on the other hand, is rarely done for the shaman's own benefit; and the 'vision quest' of certain Native American cultures is a very personal experience, but the teaching is brought back to the community and shared (that is, to the wider community rather than the paying community at a workshop). Indigenous shamanisms would not function were it not for the social. In contrast to indigenous shamanisms, there is little community or even an after-shamanic-experience forum for core-shamanism practitioners. Indeed, many I have met complain that there is no 'after-workshop' opportunity for communal interaction. Harnerists essentially teach the practice, then you are on your own. Only the more seasoned and dedicated practitioners go on to form drumming groups where practitioners come together to journey (for oneself or each other) and share experiences. For the most part, neo-Shamanisms are not community-practices (but see next chapter). Where shamans are reciprocally situated within their communities, neo-Shamanists emphasise healing oneself, the personal shamanic journey to empowerment and the 're-enchantment of everyday life' (Moore 1996).

Cultural primitivism and archaism

Further appropriation and misappropriation of traditional shamanisms surround the perpetuation of racist stereotypes of indigenous peoples by neo-Shamanisms. Early ethnographic notions of Indians as *Naturvölker* (natural peoples) and medicine 'men' who work a 'spirit world' in harmony with nature, reified the Western primitive premise. Kehoe (1990) describes how inauthentic 'plastic medicine men', such as Hungry Wolf and Grey Owl, reinforced these stereotypes in their 'teachings' of native spirituality (e.g. Hungry Wolf 1973). Rather than actually promoting respect and sensitivity towards native peoples, as perhaps intended, these authors, paradoxically, promoted mistaken and outmoded ideas of primordial peoples (e.g. Bowman 1995a), what Geertz (1996: 405) calls the 'tradition/modernity paradigm that essentializes uncritical stereotypes glorifying tradition and vilifying modernity'. Believing they are getting closer to the native shaman's viewpoint, some neo-Shamans see Native Americans and Australian Aborigines in particular to be in harmony with nature. This has a troubling subtext which reifies cultural primitivism since, if they are in harmony with nature, then they must also be controlled by it. This approach illustrates the need of many socially dislocated post-modern Westerners to reconnect with their own indigenous pasts, the search for the 'autochthonic shaman' (Mulcock 1998) or ancient 'primitive' (e.g. Torgovnick 1990). With Indians past and present being invented, reinvented and romanticised by neo-Shamans, their representations should evoke reflective responses rather than disdain from

anthropologists and archaeologists whose own disciplinary culture reproduced cultural primitivism in the first place.

Rather surprisingly for a former professor of anthropology, Harner's
manual plays on the terms 'primitives' and 'savages', not with the typically
racist connotations of evolutionism or inferiority, but turning cultural primitivism on its head. Indeed, this reversal of the Western stereotype of native
shamans as ignorant and superstitious savages, to become the all-wise healer
in contact with higher (than Western) realms, is consistently evident in neo-
Shamanisms. Rather than sensitively regarding native peoples, this reverse
discourse has the unfortunate effect (which may or may not be intentional) of
defining shamanic cultures in terms of their (naturally) harmonious and
(simplistically) superior religion. Harner also suggests differences between
shamanisms and forms of sorcery, in that shamans heal while sorcerers harm
(pers. com.). He states that sorcery exists where people 'stray from good
purposes with shamanism' (Harner and Doore 1987: 7). This idea is rather
too simplistic, I think, based on a Western view and Christian dualism, the
black and white of good and evil. In actuality, shamanisms are far greyer. The
distinction may hold for the groups where Harner did his fieldwork in South
America, but the misleading implication is that such beliefs apply worldwide
and this is what practitioners and teachers of core-shamanism suggest (similar
primitivist tendencies were repeated at a Harner workshop I attended).
Harner's distinction is politically motivated, however, since most beginners
in core-shamanism prefer to conceive of shamanisms as positive and healing
phenomena, a world apart from the evil Satan and demons of occidental
cosmology. Unfortunately, neo-Shamans may then assume only healing
shamans are real shamans, to the exclusion of other indigenous shamanisms
and the problems facing such communities today. Furthermore, Harvey
points out that 'some Pagans appropriate shamanic techniques without
returning any benefit to the "donors", they appear to be "playing Indians"
and some even insult the "Indians" by continuing to use the derogatory term
"Red Man"' (Harvey 1997b: 120). The misconception of 'Red Indian' rein-
forces romantic notions of Indians past, who were never red, pristine or
Edenic, in a perpetuation of Indianness which ignores real Native Americans
in the present. If they refer to native peoples, then neo-Shamans ought to be
aware of the contemporary marginalised situations facing indigenous peoples
today. Few would wish to be a part of the racist mindset presenting Native
Americans as 'Red Indians', 'primitive' and 'closer to the animals'. And
certainly any neo-Shamanic author, especially if he/she is a trained anthropologist, should be acutely aware of the subtleties of language and terminology.

Hand-in-hand with neo-Shamanisms and shamanophobia, cultural primitivism is not simply a modern manifestation:

> With no change in the basic thinking, 'Indian' has replaced the
> Classical 'Scythian' as the label for the fabled Naturvölker. Cultural

primitivism, constructed as the opposition to civilisation with its discontents, has been part of Western culture for close to three thousand years.

(Kehoe 1990: 207)

Kehoe's historical context illustrates the in-built Western need to hanker after a Golden Age, Eden and harmonious primal cultures. But far from being perfect or 'better' than the West, as Krech (1999) has it, indigenous cultures past and present are not necessarily exemplary of 'sustainable living' or 'walking in balance with nature'. For example, early Native Americans may have contributed to extinction of the three-toed giant ground sloth (Steele 1996), the last tree on Easter Island was cut down by indigenous populations (Bahn 1993), and the indigenous population of New Zealand (Aotearoa) was destroyed by colonising Maoris (now themselves oppressed by white colonisers) (e.g. Mead 1997: 222–231). Of course I do not intend these instances to demonise native peoples, but it is important to remember that when considered in their own social and natural environment, that is not contrasted with the industrialised West with its problematic effects on this planet, indigenous peoples do not necessarily 'retain a primordial wisdom that could heal our troubled world' (Kehoe 1990: 194). Indeed, there is no reason why they should be more environmentally friendly or socially cohesive than us; this is an opinion we have very clearly imposed on them. Not unexpectedly, intellectuals are no exception to the notion of cultural primitivism. Åke Hultkrantz is a well-known writer among academics and neo-Shamans of books on Native American religions, as well as shamanisms (e.g. Hultkrantz 1973, 1978, 1998a, 1998b, 1998c). However, Hultkrantz's 'primal wisdom peoples' view of indigenes parallels that of both Hungry Wolf and Harner, and assumes an authority over the people they study: 'convinced of [Western culture's] "inauthenticity," they define for themselves the mission of bringing their "knowledge" of American Indian spirituality to the peoples of modern Europe and America' (Kehoe 1990: 195). With these three authors in particular the familiar relationship between academic and neo-Shamanic 'appropriation' and neo-colonial imposition of cultural primitivism is plain.

Further misunderstandings of shamanisms are perpetuated when the notion of archaism is used to describe, locate and typify them. Harner presents 'shamanism' as an 'ancient human legacy' (Harner 1990 [1980]: 19), Rutherford (1996: 1) states it is 'the oldest way in which humanity has sought connection with Creation'; at least MacLellan (1999: 1) points out it is only *possibly* the oldest kind of organised spiritual expression' (my emphasis). This impression of shamanisms as ancient, undoubtedly heavily influenced by Eliade's catchy subtitle 'archaic techniques of ecstasy', has not been scrutinised sufficiently. This is perhaps because a preoccupation with dating, antiquity and the primordialness of material culture and humanity affects archaeology (e.g. Holtorf and Schadla-Hall 1999; also Holtorf 1998) as much as it does neo-Shamanisms – it is one reason many of us are drawn to archaeology in the first place. Nevertheless, such a widespread understanding of shamanisms surely requires unpacking, particularly in light of increased archaeological attention to shamanisms past (e.g. Lewis-Williams and Dowson 1999 [1989]; Clottes and Lewis-Williams 1998; Price 2001a).

Shamanisms are consistently used to exemplify the enduring nature of 'primitive' ecstatic religions, oft described – misleadingly – as 'the key to religion' (Riches 1994), 'the world's oldest form of religion' (Vitebsky 2000: 55), 'the real "Old Time Religion"' (www.shamanism.org/, Foundation for Shamanic Studies web site), 'the oldest spiritual discipline known to human kind' (Kokopelli neo-Shamanic workshop flyer), and a way of getting 'back to the Palaeolithic with acid-house rave' (cited by Vitebsky 1995a: 153). It is also claimed to be the oldest artistic tradition or beginnings of art (Lommel 1967), the origins of acting and performance, even the cause behind the spark of human consciousness and language (e.g. De Rios 1984), and 'the shaman: the gay and lesbian ancestor of humankind' (Jeter 1990: 317). These notions are typically Western and monolithic, locating shamans and shamanisms in a distant, homogeneous, and perhaps Edenic, past which again neglects the injustices facing contemporary shamans and their marginalised communities. As with 'Indianness', a 'shaman-ness' is sought after, but not the contemporary shamanisms which are often, to some extent, acculturated or 'tainted' with modernism. Cave painters, however, did not consider their images to be the beginnings of Western or any other artistic tradition, nor did those individuals who 'first' (another Western assumption) communicated with other than human persons consider themselves the earliest religious practitioners. The search for these linear and highly improbable origins rests only with chronocentric Westerners, both neo-Shamans and scholars: neo-Shamans are not the only ones problematically to describe 'shamanism' as the oldest religion or to use this presumed antiquity to add legitimacy to their practices, because this idea, as with many others I have discussed, stems from academia (e.g. Eliade 1989 [1964]) and popular science (e.g. Rudgley 1993; Allen 2000).

Romanticism

In the same vein as, and akin to, the reinforcement of archaic primitivism, is the romanticising of shamanisms by neo-Shamans (Figure 2.1). As Harvey suggests, Shamanic cultures are 'perceived to be closer to nature, simpler, more wholesome, more spiritual (but not dogmatic or god-controlled), more ecological and more human than "modern", "civilised" life' (Harvey 1997b: 110; see also Jakobsen 1999: 177–180). Of course these are impositions on shamanic cultures: I have mentioned Harner's misleading characterisation of the 'savage' and shaman as wiser and more environmentally aware than Westerners (1990 [1980]: xiii). Atkinson (1992) encounters further evidence

Figure 2.1 Flyer advertising neo-Shamanic workshops, illustrating
how some neo-Shamanisms romanticise shamans
Source: Courtesy of Bernie Pryor

of romanticising when Drury opens his book with mention of an Iban shaman Manang Bungai who used monkey blood to fake a shamanic battle with an incubus. He thinks this is not 'true shamanism', which 'is characterised by access to other realms of consciousness' (Drury 1982: 1). Atkinson correctly ascertains '[t]hat would certainly be news to many shamans practising world-wide' (Atkinson 1992: 323). An idea of a 'true' shamanism is a Western construction: Manang is a fake in Drury's terms, not on his own terms or in the eyes of the culture he practises in. If he were a fake, though, he probably wouldn't deserve financial support from Harner's institution; that would be reserved for a real shaman.[2] Atkinson's reflective statement: '[t]he romanticising of shamanism by its current Euroamerican promoters is also unsettling for anthropologists (despite – or perhaps because of – their own familiarity with romantic tropes)' (Atkinson 1992: 323) is pertinent: anthropologists have fallen where their neo-Shaman contemporaries now do – in terms of 'romantic tropes' – as I have suggested in the lives of, for example, Lewis Henry Morgan and Frank Hamilton Cushing. Neo-Shamans

65

frequently draw on academic literature which portrays shamans in terms of cultural primitivism and romanticism, so it is unsurprising that they should reproduce the same stereotypes. Due to enduring orientalising desires of Western culture, the motivations for neo-Shamanisms appear to have changed little since first encounters with shamanisms, and we still struggle with the antagonistically exciting contradiction of both fearing and eradicating the 'savage' Other, whilst desiring simultaneously the 'freedom' and 'primitivism' of the very same 'wild man'. Such contradictory cultural primitivism and romantic notions of a Golden Age are persistent in Western history (see also Albanese 1990).

There is a final valid criticism of neo-Shamanisms which is both romanticising and decontextualising: the genders of shamans. Where the Evenk term *šaman* is not gender-specific, neo-Shamans have applied the term *shamanka*, for female practitioners. *Shamanka* is not indigenous Siberian but

Figure 2.2 Leaflet advertising neo-Shamanic workshops for women
Source: Courtesy of Simon Buxton/The Sacred Trust.

derives from Russian, -ka being a feminine suffix (e.g. Chadwick 1936a, 1936b; Basilov 1992). *Shamanka* first appears in neo-Shamanic use, according to Hutton (1993), with the 'Celtic' neo-Shaman and writer Caitlín Matthews (e.g. 1995), and the idea might represent the worthy aim of empowering women practising neo-Shamanisms (Figure 2.2). On the other hand, I think it might equally reify Western gender stereotypes (something scholars of shamanisms are not immune to, e.g. Oosten 1989: 334), increasing the distance between men and women, ignoring any differences within genders, and neglecting the third or multiple genders apparent in many traditional shamanisms. The same seems true of Gabrielle Roth's (1990) extremely popular 'five sacred rhythms' shamanic dance which rigidly separates male and female dance forms, 'flowing' being female and 'staccato' male. This female *vis-à-vis* male notion is embedded in the classic Western world-view and is therefore commonplace in neo-Shamanisms and (until recently) academia. In academic studies on shamanisms, on the other hand, Laufer infers from Siberian communities where the terms *udagan*, *utygan* and *ubakxan* for female shamans occur that there is a female origin for all Siberian shamans (Laufer 1917: 367). Notwithstanding the evolutionary bias here, Western binary oppositions of gender are imposed by scholars and neo-Shamans onto cultures which may not hold such rigid distinctions. Where the counter-cultural tendencies of neo-Shamanisms could produce a queer and dissonant challenging of Western gender relations and stereotypes, then, many neo-Shamans, like their academics counterparts, instead reify fabricated and normative concepts of male, female, heterosexual, etc.

A 'Humpty Dumpty word': seeing to 'extra pay'

I have outlined certain problems and contradictions with neo-Shamanisms and their approaches to traditional shamanisms. Neo-Shamans frequently fall foul of mistaken nostalgia for 'primal shaman wisdom' and reduce 'shamanism' to its lowest common denominators with token or no thanks to indigenous shamans. It is important to stress very clearly, though, that where shamanisms are extremely diverse, so neo-Shamanisms are heterogeneous. Vitebsky argues '[t]hese movements are inchoate and barely studied, so that any generalisations can be no more than tentative' (Vitebsky 1995b: 192). With my views against universalising, I err further on the side of caution: it is impossible to make generalisations about neo-Shamanisms. The harshest of the criticisms I have mentioned applies to the less scrupulous aspects of neo-Shamanisms where they embody an archetypal expression of Western consumerism and commodification. Continuity of cultural imperialism is not too harsh a charge in these instances, especially where the theft of religious traditions occurs (see Chapter 7). But to characterise all neo-Shamans under this tainted banner would be a misrepresentation and too many critics, while criticising the way in which neo-Shamanisms universalise and decontextualise, do exactly the same to their victims (particularly Kehoe 2000). In many respects neo-Shamanisms can be seen to make worthwhile contributions to the term 'shamanism', to studies on shamanisms and, perhaps most importantly, to the shamanic cultures from which they 'borrow'. 'Shamanism', according to Harvey,

> is a Humpty Dumpty word. During her journeys 'through the Looking Glass' Alice endured a bizarre conversation in which Humpty Dumpty claimed to be able to use a word to mean just what he wanted it to mean, 'neither more or less'. If a word like 'glory' or 'impenetrability' is made to work hard, carrying unusual or idiosyncratic meanings, Humpty Dumpty says he 'pays it extra'. 'Shamanism' is now a hard working word.
>
> (Harvey 1997b: 106)

Harvey goes on to explain why 'shamanism' is a 'hard working word', and suggests we see towards giving it 'extra pay':

> If Shamanism has become an exercise in self-discovery and self-empowerment, such goals are not to be belittled in our age. But to consider this as the essence of Shamanism is to devalue the word and those from whom the original techniques were acquired. How then is Shamanism to be paid extra? What can be added or combined with lessons learnt from traditional Shamans that will not be merely Western self-therapeutic techniques by another name?
>
> (Harvey 1997b: 112)

Despite the connotations of capitalism and a patronising 'pat on the back' of indigenous shamans which may be perceived in the term 'extra pay' when used without Humpty Dumpty's explanation (which, clearly, Harvey does not intend), I can think of no better way of describing the process in operation, except perhaps as a 'contribution'. There are numerous ways neo-Shamans can be seen to be returning benefits to shamanisms, such as using the term sensitively, raising awareness of the injustices faced by indigenous communities, and undergoing experiences which are directly comparable with indigenous shamanisms.

A first example of extra pay involves Western approaches (be they academic or neo-Shamanic) to shamanisms which do, of course, immediately alter shamanism, but it would be naïve to think this engagement cannot be beneficial or useful. The term 'shamanism' is itself a case example, transforming a set of practices from a culture-specific (Evenk) reality to a cross-cultural Western invention; but approaching indigenous practices in terms of shamanisms can be rewarding, furthering academic understanding (e.g. Humphrey 1996), and raising awareness of the modern predicament shamanistic cultures face (e.g. Vitebsky 1995b); and exploring prehistoric ritual and religion in terms of shamanisms also brings new insights (e.g. Bradley 1989, 1997; Creighton 1995, 2000). The term may also be used sensitively by neo-Shamans, for example those not calling themselves shamans at all; to do so would be egotistical, inflated or at least a little suspect, and to an extent disrespectful to traditional shamans (Harner, MacLellan and Rutherford, pers. com.). In this way, the term 'shaman' becomes honorific among neo-Shamans: 'you don't call yourself a shaman, other people do' (Barry, pers. com, environmental educator and 'shamanic practitioner'). Many neo-Shamans are modest and unpretentious: Jonathon Horwitz (Scandinavian Centre for Shamanic Studies) says, 'It is not me who is working but the spirits' (quotation from Jakobsen 1999: 183). Treating the term and practices with care and respect perhaps honours and respects traditional shamans. It also reveals something of the authentication processes in neo-Shamanisms which, interestingly, cohere with the majority of authentication criteria suggested for shamanism by Jensen (1996), especially where it is the shaman's/neo-Shaman's community which negotiates authenticity (thereby aligning with Dowson's third 'element of shamanisms'). Except, that is, in instances where neo-Shamans choose to become 'shamans', when, in contrast, the vocation is consistently thrust unwantedly upon individuals in indigenous contexts. This in turn reveals the socio-political location of some neo-Shamanisms contra shamanisms, in the self-authenticating and individual-orientated capitalism of the contemporary West – as mentioned above, neo-Shamanisms often individualise shamanisms.

Furthermore, Hoppál (1992b: 204) suggests a fundamental alteration of indigenous shamanisms in Harner's Method when the person to be healed either makes the 'journey' on their own or accompanies the shaman. In traditional contexts the patient may be instrumental in the rituals but it is the shaman who makes the journey – often perilous – to the spirit world. How can this radical shift contribute to shamanisms? Perhaps the relocation of indigenous shamanisms into Western contexts itself, and the empowerment it brings to practitioners can be seen as a contribution, bringing new benefits (to the West at least) and new meanings to the term shamanisms rather than devaluing it. Nevertheless, neo-Shamanic focus on the 'heal thyself' metaphor reflects an obsession with the individual in contemporary capitalist society and emphasis on the individual inner journey, personal psychology and explanations according to Jungian archetypes suggests neo-Shamanisms psychologise shamanisms, leaving them open to 'the risk of solipsism' (Johnson 1995: 175). But to stereotype all neo-Shamans in this way would homogenise the subtlety of the situation: many other neo-Shamans avoid the problems of Western terminology and its failure to apprehend the non-Western correctly, and in similarity to their traditional counterparts express specific beliefs in spirit worlds (rather than archetypes) and spirits outside themselves (rather than 'within'). In occupying a demonstrably shamanic way of being, with spirit-helpers, 'supernatural' forms of healing and sometimes entheogenic assistance to enter trance, some neo-Shamans are radically critiquing the received wisdom of objective science all around them.

In addition, in the instance of romanticism, critics may overemphasise the division between neo-Shamanisms, social location, and traditional shamanisms. Many neo-Shamans are realistic in acknowledging they cannot return to an idyllic primal lifestyle or religion and that their needs are an expression of radical modernity. Further, they express active interest and concern with the society in which they live, the indigenous societies they draw on, and the 'natural' environment which accommodates them. Brown (1997: 79) contrasts the intrinsic political element of shamanisms with the apolitical stance of neo-Shamans, yet many neo-Shamans are embedded in highly political trajectories and counter-cultural locations. Where neo-Shamans are critiquing society and its conventional religious and social values, for instance, they are different to indigenous shamans because their stance is not integrated into a wider community. But their social values and their recognition of them make neo-Shamans active political agents rather than blind automata. The lack of community (e.g. Clifton 1994: 6) in neo-Shamanisms is particularly true of core-shamanism,[3] but over-representation of Harnerism to the exclusion of other facets of neo-Shamanisms by both critics and core-shamanists is a misrepresentation of the whole. Other neo-Shamans 'cannot journey on behalf of their society, which is largely indifferent. They can, however, journey in the hope of an improvement in the conditions of that society' (Jakobsen 1999: 190). Where a sense of community has been lost in urbanised, consumerised and capitalist Western culture, neo-Shamanisms have, for some practitioners, revived community-focused activities, and a sense of belonging and identity is formed where previously lacking.

Other neo-Shamans speak of the 'community' of other than human persons with which they engage and negotiate, the close-knit relations they have with their neo-Shamanic group members, even the shamanic support they provide for the dying, dead 'ancestors', and recently bereaved in wider society (e.g. Heathen neo-Shaman Bil in Conclusion; Matthews 1997). Here, the shamanic vocations of 'master of the animals', psychopomp and community healer are enacted in a Western setting. In addition to the loss of community in neo-Shamanisms, Vitebsky (1995b) suggests that many locative aspects of shamanisms, such as 'ancestor worship', tend to be 'lost in transit'. In the global village, neo-Shamans are free to choose those aspects they wish to take on board, but locative elements are not always atrophied. In the example of ancestor worship (a difficult term at the best of times, denoting primitivism and blind superstitious belief), many neo-Shamans stress the importance of ancestors (especially Heathens, see Chapter 3): some groups and individuals not only celebrate ancestor days, such as Halloween, but also communicate with their ancestors and divine future events via ancestral intermediaries. Again, the diversity of neo-Shamanisms is downplayed if sweeping generalisations are applied. Instances of community healing and ancestor worship are comparable with traditional shamanic communities, going some way towards paying shamanisms extra.

This does not mean of course, that neo-Shamanisms are the same as traditional shamanisms. Brown may be near to the mark when suggesting neo-Shamanisms are most like traditional counterparts where shamanisms have been urbanised (1997: 81). In such circumstances (e.g. Balzer 1993) indigenous shamans may adopt practices previously not encountered (such as Christian icons), blend cultural facets and interact with new types of helper-spirits (including Christian saints) (e.g. Press 1971; Joralemon and Sharon 1993). Similarly, some techno-shamans using the Internet believe their surfing of cyber-space compares with shamanic journeys through the spirit world, and they use the worldwide web as an electronic divination device or Ouija board (Brown 1997: 125) just as, they suggest, shamans use animal entrails and bones as oracles. At the same time as comparing shamans and neo-Shamans, these examples apparently differentiate between the two – as the world becomes increasingly Westernised, though, we ought not to be surprised if traditional shamans 'journey' on the net too. Another massive disjuncture between the political localities of indigenous shamanic revivals and neo-Shamans is nationalism. Among the Sakha of Siberia, for instance, and in Tuva, reviving shamanism in the aftermath of communism has been a potent force in revitalising ethnicity, allowing reconnections with past identities and the re-creation of new ones (e.g. Hoppál 1996; Khazanov 1996). In contrast, while there are a number of nationalist Celtic (e.g. *Touta Dumnonioi* at http//www.homestead.com/dafydd/declaration2.html) and Heathen (e.g. Asatru Folk Assembly) groups, other neo-Shamans find nationalism tainted with right-wing politics and racism and, in their cosmopolitan ideology, resist cultural boundaries. Other practitioners, while not being nationalist, are attempting to re-establish their cultural roots by exploring 'Celtic' and 'Nordic' shamanisms (see chapter 3).

Comparing shamanisms and neo-Shamanisms favourably seems laudable in some instances, but criticisms of Harner's techniques for being safe, in contrast with traditional shamanisms, seem to stand well. On the other hand, this criticism ignores the possibility that the shamanic experiences he encourages are profound and might be dangerous – as I have suggested, many critics base their analyses on limited, basic workshop experiences. For no reason other than his prominence in neo-Shamanisms, Harner has been singled out as a figure for attack from critics. Certainly, he has altered shamanisms into techniques for a Western audience, providing experiences of sufficient alterity to warrant gentle beginnings. But there are more advanced techniques which are less public and reserved for the more dedicated, dealing with darker aspects of 'spirits' and more treacherous parts of the spirit world, such as in the Scandinavian Center for Shamanic Studies (a core-shamanism-based institution) 'Shamanism, Death, and Dying' course. The criticisms regarding safety concern only aspects of Harner's method aimed at beginners, who, if they want to learn shamanic techniques, must for obvious reasons of health and safety be introduced carefully. Advanced techniques are only taught once the aspirant has gained sufficient experience and knowledge. Harner's neo-Shamanism, then, is not only for the safety of your living room. At a workshop I attended for instance, a healing was performed which involved the extraction of a malignant 'spirit'. Formerly, core-shamanic methods made the extraction by sucking out the spirit with the mouth and then spitting it out to be neutralised by the earth, a technique Harner learnt in the Amazon (which is practised elsewhere, e.g. in Tibet [Peters 1997] and Nepal [Spilman 1999]). This practice has been replaced by working the spirit out with the hands because it was felt sucking the spirit out was too dangerous; less experienced practitioners might allow the spirit to enter themselves, hands, in contrast, can 'throw' the spirit away. Another expression of the risks involved with neo-Shamanic healing occurred when I attended a different neo-Shamanic healing group. The spirit removed was not the romantic unicorn or grandiose eagle power animals of naïve neo-Shamans, but a malevolent snake which had been causing severe illness in the client and, if not correctly extracted, could have harmed the neo-Shaman. Clearly, utilising these techniques, interacting with these spirits and dealing with terrible diseases is not a matter to be taken lightly. Like traditional shamanisms, there are definite dangers in neo-Shamanic practices.

Critics of neo-Shamanisms tend to direct their accusations at the Harner Method because it is the most popular and widely known. However, my communications with neo-Shamans and exploration of neo-Shamanic literature indicate there are many people who do not associate themselves with Harner. Again, I stress that neo-Shamanisms are extremely diverse: their approaches to shamanisms vary and they express experiences and opinions which are different from those of Harner. Some suggest their introduction to neo-Shamanic practices was not one of choice, but they were 'called' and suffered severely at times, in similar ways to traditional shamans. Howard Charing, co-founder of Eagle's Wing for Contemporary Shamanism, UK, described to me how a near fatal and almost disabling lift crash led to communication with spirits and a subsequent healing. Only later did he come to call these practices 'shamanism'. In another interview, Howard's colleague Leo Rutherford suggested his 'classic mid-life crisis' resulted in an awareness of the shamanic spirit world which reoriented his understanding of the world. As a result of these experiences, both shamanic practitioners relinquished their affluent white-collar lifestyles to be involved with the (mostly financially unproductive – according to them) teaching of 'practical shamanism'. Another informant, 'Carl', explained that while conventional scientific methods were unable to help a psychopathological condition and drug abuse, communication with spirits allowed a self-healing. In retrospect, and having read Castaneda, he understands his experiences as 'shamanic'. Furthermore, Wiger's (Bend and Wiger 1987) biography reports how sex and drug abuse, prostitution and multiple personality disorder were overcome with the shamanic techniques she now teaches (see also Stafford 1990).

These incidents mark aspects of neo-Shamanisms which are comparable with shamanisms by virtue of their harrowing initiatory ordeals and ongoing undesirable practices. Harvey rightly claims: 'Shamanism is not a technique available to anyone, but a calling which is not always welcome. Shamans are distinguished from their neighbours not by their beliefs but by the intensity of their experiences. Anyone can take the same drugs' (Harvey 1997b: 109). In the examples cited above, the individuals did not 'choose' shamanism. Rather than a 'safe' spirituality, they faced experiences which compare with traditional shamans and, they suggest, shamanisms provide the best framework for them to comprehend and contextualise their encounters. Clearly neo-Shamanisms are not just for the living room; they are reported to be potentially life-threatening and dangerous (see also Drury 1982; Fries 1993). Such descriptions parallel the initiatory sickness and self-healing of shamans worldwide; they are 'wounded healers'. Descriptions of neo-Shamans dealing with the 'soul-loss' of hospitalised patients close to death is also not for the faint-hearted (e.g. Matthews 1997; see also Bil in Conclusion). These testimonies exemplify Harvey's idea that some neo-Shamans substantially change their views beyond safe and acceptable Jungian (and other) psychological models. Critics should seriously consider examples such as these before universalising neo-Shamanisms in stereotypical ways, under the self-help therapy and New Age banners of 'Safety', 'Jungian' or 'Romantic'.

I have argued that in some respects shamanisms are substantially devalued by neo-Shamanisms when the techniques are simply for self-discovery and empowerment, and more akin to Western psychotherapies. But while Harner might be accused of teaching psychological techniques rather than ecstasies, and merely dressing up New Age visualisation techniques in shamanic clothing with an overemphasis on 'visions', the experiences of core-shamanists suggest a more complex picture. They point out that the shamanic journey is an unstructured one, and their experiences of synaesthesia (wherein the experience is not visualisation but a blending of the senses) compare with native shamanisms. There are also neo-Shamans who confront conventional gender stereotypes because their experiences question conceptions of what it is to be 'male/female' and 'heterosexual'. Like the shaman 'Berdache',[4] who embodies multiple genders, Brown notes that shaman-like 'Channels' (Channelers) make crossings of gender in their channelling of spirits (Brown 1997: 93). These experiences prompt the channels to reconsider binary oppositions and adopt more subtle understandings of gender. Furthermore, some male neo-Shamans say their experiences with altered states allow significant transformations of gender understandings. Seidr workers in particular (see Chapter 3) work with and may become possessed by goddesses and female spirits, in incidents which disrupt normative understandings of gender and sexuality (e.g. Blain and Wallis 2000). These encounters with the 'spirit world' present a significant challenge to Western philosophical scepticism, theories of perception and biological reductionism, and give credit to indigenous cosmologies.

Other instances of paying shamanisms extra are witnessed in neo-Shamanic interactions with native groups which draw considerable attention to cultures formerly and currently marginalised and missionised. Following neo-Shamanic interest, Siberia (among other non-Western areas), for instance, 'became a place of interest, however faintly, to many who would not otherwise have been concerned with it at all' (Hutton 1993: 11). Indeed, beyond the slight naïveté of the Living Treasure award (see Chapter 7), Harner does emphasise the complexity of shamanic cultures (they are not evolutionarily simple) and the value of their modes of awareness (altered consciousness is not simply an aberration). In these sorts of example, neo-Shamanisms are giving back to the cultures from which they 'borrow' by raising Western awareness of them and Western concern for their future in the modern world. The question of whether this is appropriate, desired or required by native peoples, is altogether different (see Chapter 7).

In his examination, Harvey remarks on how extra pay is given to shaman-isms when Paganisms use aspects of them to revitalise their traditions. Foremost in this regard is the raising of 'power' in Wicca (modern Witchcraft), which has drawn largely on indigenous shamanistic practices. Raising power or energy is essential to spell working and most other ritual exercises of Wicca, and indeed most Pagan practices, and as Harvey states, '[s]hamanism has, however, provided a wider context in which to understand and celebrate it' (Harvey 1997b: 117). Harvey refers specifically to the prac-tices of altering consciousness and using 'shamanic' tools such as drums and rattles. There is also the assertion among Wiccans that 'Witchcraft is a shamanistic religion' (Harvey 1997b: 116, citing Starhawk 1989: 40) and they often draw on the idea of witchcraft as European shamanism, from the Palaeolithic to Middle Ages, to better understand and give meaning to their own religious path. Interestingly, Harner's discussion of medieval witchcraft and entheogens may be one source for this idea (Harner 1973b). While there are problems with decontextualising and universalising shamanisms in Wicca (rattles and drums denote shamanism, prehistoric witchcraft=shamanism=a homogenous entity), it is apparent that shamanisms provide a historical context for some contemporary witches to work with, and that it gives greater meaning to their practices. If this draws attention to shamanisms, complica-tions with academic studies of shamanisms and the contemporary plight of indigenous shamans, then Wicca's use of shamanisms, despite the polemics of that usage, is making a demonstrable contribution to shamanisms.

If the word 'shaman' brings new meanings to witchcraft, then ideas such as the 'wounded healer', the shamanic 'rattle' or 'drum', 'shamanic road protesting' (e.g. Butler 1996) and 'shamanic singing' utilise 'shamanism' as a buzz-word with all sorts of connotations quite different from the original. The motive behind use of the term in these examples is to give greater meaning to the 'drum' or 'song', and therefore it does not wholly devalue or decontextualise the term. To cite Harvey again, 'when anthropologists described shamanism people recognised similarities and resonances with familiar experiences and ideas. Anthropology gave people a name that could be attached to things they were already doing and added different techniques' (Harvey 1997b: 110). Rather than representing aspects of the 'shaman', the word 'shaman' is removed from its original context, but it would be short-sighted to accuse neo-Shamanisms of simple 'appropriation' here: the word is used to add and convey meaning and authenticity, however problematic the process of giving meaning and authentication may be.

Neo-shamanisms provide a contemporary stage for change in the work of people such as the aforementioned Gordon 'The Toad' MacLellan, an Environmental Educator (MacLellan 1994, 1995, 1997, 1998, 1999). For him, the 'environment' is not romanticised or objectified (Harvey 1998), a fact in sharp contrast with the criticisms Shaw levies at neo-Shamans (Shaw in prep.a). MacLellan suggests neo-Shamanisms worthy of favourable comment can be neatly characterised in terms of three types of healing: 'the first helps to heal people's relationship to themselves, the second helps to heal people's relationships to one another and the third helps the community to communicate with its relatives in the other-than-human world' (cited in Harvey 1997b: 118). As he told me, in his everyday occupation, 'The Toad' aims to 'revitalise the links between people in cities and countryside, their land, and spiritual connection with the land. This may encourage greater respect for the planet we live on, place we live in, and people we live with' (pers. com.). In contrast to Shaw's assertion that neo-Shamanisms give little benefit back to the nature spirits invoked, Greywolf (joint head of the British Druid Order) told me that for him and many other druids, there is 'a sense that making ritual at [ancient sites] energises and benefits both the sites themselves and the land around' (pers. com.). Many neo-Shamans express similar awareness of environmental issues, and a few are involved in environmental campaigning, such as road protesting. The Dragon Environmental Network, for instance, has in the past worked magic in attempts to stop trees being cut down and disrupt construction machinery. If they do not echo the political embeddedness and engagement with 'nature' that traditional shamans embody, these direct and political interactions with 'the environment' may at least mark a positive contribution to the term 'shamanisms'.

Vitebsky (1995b: 185), however, sees this as part of the delocalising inherent in processes of neo-Shamanic appropriation: the eristic principle in shamanisms – a people's precarious position in a world permeated with both natural and socio-political dangers – is either lost in New Age ideals of 'love' as the universal principle, or reworked into psychological or environmentalist agendas. But again, not all neo-Shamans adhere to this delocalisation formula, and I think some devalue neither the meaning of shamanisms nor the cultures borrowed from. MacLellan's environmental education, for instance, employs neo-Shamanisms alongside environmentalism in an active way. He is engaging directly with the communities he works with, rather than just working alone, sporting a Greenpeace sticker or speculating on environmental apocalypse. In this sense I agree with Harvey that neo-Shamanisms move 'towards being properly shamanic ... the word is paid extra: it is honoured as a force for change, an imperative in the growth and evolution of Paganism ... an important part of the postmodern critique of society' (Harvey 1997b: 117–122). The positive socio-political context of some neo-Shamanisms and their benefits is becoming evident: where some practices and approaches to shamanisms conform to the criticisms I have discussed, there are others which cannot be written off as simply a symptom of modernity and neo-liberalism. Furthermore, neo-Shamanisms are, in these respects, similar to traditional shamanisms, being socially embedded and active agents of community.

Discussion of neo-Shamanic contributions would be incomplete without mention of 'alternative' archaeologies. Most archaeologists are familiar with, if not sceptical of and amused by, Dowsers and 'ley lines', in particular. Neo-Shamanisms have contributed to new understandings of the latter in the work of Paul Devereux, who considers leys as 'spirit tracks' used by prehistoric shamans for out-of-body travel (e.g. Devereux 1992a). A convincing presentation of this idea was given in a BBC documentary (October 1997; Millson 1997) which focused on the Nazca lines of Peru and advocated their shamanic purpose above other theories such as landing sites for alien craft (see also Devereux 2001). Devereux's neo-Shamanic scholarship is also evident in the popular *The Long Trip: A Prehistory of Psychedelia* (1997). As Harvey points out, 'This, at least, is evidence that the term "shamanism" is now working hard to incorporate and give new explanations for existing beliefs' (Harvey 1997b: 117). Ethnographic records of shamanisms provide new insights into a previously 'fringe' theory, and rather than making it even more alternative, this shamanistic approach better explains material found enigmatic by academic researchers, and has come to be acceptable to some of them (e.g. Dowson 1999c). The rise of shamanisms in this sort of interpretative work, apparent in the recent *3rd Stone* and *At the Edge* journals (now a joint publication, *3rd Stone*) alongside long-established circulars such as *The Ley Hunter* (recently dissolved), shows how shamanisms are being paid extra. Many archaeologists may not agree with these interpretations of material culture, of course, but where they are reluctant to examine 'religion', and often devalue the term 'ritual' as a dumping bag for non-utilitarian evidence, alternative archaeologists tackle this data with enthusiasm. Indeed, neo-Shamanic interpretations question traditional compartmentalising and stereotypical attitudes in which politics, economics and religion are interpreted separately, and point towards an intrinsic link between these social aspects in non-Western societies. When neo-Shamans interpret neglected 'ritual' evidence, academics are likely to express disquiet, but 'fringe' research since the 1960s, perhaps because of its usefulness, seems to have prompted academic interest. The shamanic approach to rock art, for instance, owes a considerable debt to neuropsychological experiments into altered consciousness. Clearly academia, areas of post-processual archaeology included, must shed some elitism and prejudices in order to appreciate the value certain neo-Shamanic approaches bring to some difficult material.

As shamanisms must be explored in all their diversity, so in this chapter I have demonstrated the variety of neo-Shamanisms. I have identified aspects that can be critiqued and duly deconstructed, but have also made a point of representing some of their contributions to studies on shamanisms, shamanic cultures and the term 'shamanism'. As such, it should now be quite obvious how and why neo-Shamanisms have grown popular as spiritual/religious practices in the contemporary West: some neo-Shamans perceive shamanic cultures to be freer, closer to nature and more in tune with spirituality, but some of them also acknowledge the context of shamanisms in specific socio-political relations, embedding their own practices in community. To understand neo-Shamanisms fully, it is important not to let the term become a monolithic construction in which the problematic aspects of practices and world-views dominate discussion. Where other writers overemphasise the negative aspects of neo-Shamanisms, singling out Harner and core-shamanism specifically, I have attempted a well-rounded analysis: Harnerism is not the whole story, but rather part of a wider socio-historic picture, and it is not without its own contributions. Where some neo-Shamans may universalise, romanticise or psychologise shamanisms, others use shamanic experiences actively to transform their Western world-views towards shamanic modes of perception, understanding and ways of interacting with their world(s). Reflecting on these considerations it becomes more difficult, I think, simply to separate shamanisms and neo-Shamanisms in terms of 'authenticity' alone. Vitebsky, among others, considers 'neo-shamanism' to be inauthentic:

> it can never authentically recapture the holistic vision which is the rationale for its own striving. It is unable to transmute mere contradiction into the powerful totalising function of paradox ... [I]ndigenous knowledge, when transplanted and commoditized, comes to take on the fragmentary nature by which it is appropriated. This is surely why indigenous or local knowledge must always

remain epistemologically marginal to global knowledge. The one thing global culture cannot recapture is the holistic nature of indigenous knowledge.

(Vitebsky 1995b: 201)

Many writers echo Vitebksy's sentiments, and while I think they are applicable to many aspects of neo-Shamanisms, I do not think they are true universally. Where some neo-Shamans sufficiently alter their world-view (towards the shamanic) to be ideologically distinct from Western culture, this need not automatically isolate them in the fragmented epistemological vacuum of post-modernity. Their life-transforming experiences empower their world-views to the extent that, while they are often discordant with the West, it is nevertheless socially integrated – into neo-Shamanic communities. A new sort of shamanic local knowledge is thus produced, validated (if not authenticated) by anthropological resources, direct contact with indigenous communities, personal and communal experiences. Certain neo-Shamanic individuals and communities seem to have accomplished this: MacLellan's work is a good example, I think, along with the 'Seidr' and 'Hrafnar' communities examined in the next chapter. I consider these neo-Shamans not only to be giving 'extra pay' to shamanisms, but in their radical challenging of the conventional West and forming of new shamanic communities, to be empowering the term 'neo-Shamanisms' beyond the New Age stereotype and beyond a dislocated individuality symptomatic of capitalist economies. While it is essential to recognise that neo-Shamanists are different from their traditional counterparts, it is also plausible in these instances to argue that their close similarity to shamanisms is beyond dispute. This is particularly evident when neo- and indigenous shamans engage and the former even teach the latter: some shamanisms and neo-Shamanisms thus blur into a neither–neither category, exemplifying the character of neo-/indigenous shamanisms as affected by processes of globalisation (see Chapter 7). My considerations in the current chapter and that preceding it are based on historical analysis and a generic (though self-consciously not generalised) approach to neo-Shamanisms. The remaining chapters examine neo-Shamanism in greater and specific detail with case examples in which the impact of neo-Shamanisms on archaeology and anthropology are assessed: specifically, Celtic and Heathen neo-Shamanisms, British 'sacred sites' and indigenous communities.

3

TALIESIN'S TRIP,
WYRD WODEN

Druid and Heathen neo-Shamans

Celtic Shamanism derives from the native traditions of North-West Europe. The shamanic contribution of the Celts and their predecessors has been overlooked until now, and is one of the last shamanic traditions to be explored.

(Matthews 1991a: rear cover)

The central world-image of the Germanic religion is the World Tree ... Odin, the god of shamans, hangs himself from the tree Yggdrasil and by doing so, obtains the secret knowledge of the runes.

(Metzner 1994: 49)

While anthropologists at least make occasional discussion of neo-Shamanisms – albeit most often with derogatory remarks – archaeology has yet to recognise many of the implications neo-Shamanisms have with regard to its ideas and objects of study. There has been comment on 'New Age archaeology', as Meskell negatively calls it, particularly in terms of Goddess worshippers whose beliefs are influenced by the work of Marija Gimbutas (e.g. Gimbutas 1974) and her Goddess-orientated interpretations of the famous site of Çatalhüyük in Turkey (e.g. Jencson 1989; Meskell 1995, 1998b). A number of authors also consider the contemporary Druids (e.g. Piggott 1968), especially in light of incidents surrounding Stonehenge in the 1980s (e.g. Chippindale et al. 1990; Bender 1998). But following the same line of thought as many anthropologists, archaeologists tend to regard the New Age, Paganism and neo-Shamanisms – as with all alternative archaeology – negatively (but see Finn 1997; Denning 1999a, 1999b), if, that is, they recognise it at all. To be fair, archaeologists are less likely to be sympathetic to the eccentricities of neo-Shamans than anthropologists who often meet entheogen-taking and spirit-travelling indigenous shamans on a regular basis. Even so, there is as yet no serious examination of neo-Shamanisms or related Pagan practices and their impact on archaeology, despite some of the distant ancestors of both archaeologists and neo-Shamans being the antiquarians, with Dee, Aubrey and Stukeley among them. This neglect of research is unprecedented and does not reflect an insignificant research area. On the contrary, neo-Shamanic engagement with the past is considerable and accelerating. In this chapter, I explore the manner in which neo-Shamans use the past to inspire, legitimate and validate their practices and beliefs, and the extent to which this implicates and requires the attentions of archaeologists and other specialists.

Archaeologists and historians ought to be concerned, for instance, by neo-Shamanic interpretations of 'Celtic' and 'Northern' religions in terms of shamanism. Both these ancient European paganisms are much-debated subjects in academia, indeed archaeological researchers in particular generally prefer to avoid the subject of religion and focus on what they perceive to be safer aspects of past communities such as economy and social structure. That such rigid distinctions between social and religious spheres of life are unlikely to have been operating in the past makes an emphasis on the former to the exclusion of the latter arbitrary and short-sighted.[1] A compartmentalising, positivist and empirical interpretative framework does not seem to be the ideal tool for gaining entry to 'spiritual' aspects of the past, aspects which conceivably permeated all levels of society. This is particularly true when we appreciate that interpretations of Celtic and Anglo-Saxon social structure or politics are no less likely to be subjective and motivated by contemporary politics, nationalism and romance than are notions of Iron Age and 'Dark Age' religions (e.g. Stanley 1964; Dietler 1994; James 1999). 'Religion' and 'ritual' – itself arguably an unhelpful term, 'a product of post-Enlightenment rationalism' (Brück 1999: 313, but see Grimes 2000) – are used as catch-all terms in the meanwhile when evidence just doesn't fit anywhere else: what 'ritual' means is a question *someone else* ought to deal with, of course. Unsurprisingly, many archaeologists distance themselves from such issues by avoiding religion all together.

This avoidance of religion has left free rein for non-academics to approach and interpret the material. Where shamanism was once used briefly and tentatively by Anne Ross (1967) to understand Celtic Paganism (but now see also Creighton 1995, 2000), neo-Shamans have enthusiastically embraced and revived the idea. Over the past decade or so, it is increasingly evident that notions of Druidic and Runic shamans are gathering momentum (e.g. Bowman 1993, 1994, 1995b, 2000; L. Jones 1994, 1998). And surely specialist academics should be aware of how 'their' data is being used by other 'non-specialist' researchers, including researchers from other disciplines. Psychologists in particular are producing popular books (e.g. Metzner 1994; Bates 1996) which interpret various archaeological data in terms of shamanism. And, quite simply, a volume on Celtic shamanism will receive a wider audience than an expensive academic text on Iron Age religion. Ancient religions are discovered, reconstructed, revived, created or invented (depending on viewpoint) by neo-Shamans, based on sources of archaeology, history, literature and ethnographic analogy. Orthodox researchers might term this an inauthentic 'invention' of tradition, but this is not only rather too simplistic, but also, and more accurately, erroneous (as detailed in Chapter 1).

In the example of neo-Shamanisms it would be remiss to shrug off neo-Shamanic interpretations as 'made up' and give them no further attention, when, as this chapter demonstrates, there are clearly significant ramifications for archaeologists and other academics – in terms of publications, for example. Neo-Shamanic interpretations might go largely unnoticed by academics due to publication in the popular sphere, but 'authoritative' academic explanations in expensive and obscure books and journals are eclipsed by these alternative approaches to the data found on 'mind–body–spirit' bookshelves. Perhaps more troubling for 'conservative' archaeologists, it has become common practice to shelve certain archaeology volumes (particularly those discussing megaliths) alongside those of the 'mind–body–spirit' variety. It seems timely that archaeologists should not only be aware of these neo-Shamanic representations of the past, but also, as a matter of course, that they should be responding to them. In addition, and as I hope this chapter demonstrates, out-of-hand dismissals of neo-Shamanic publications might, just might, be neglecting valuable interpretations. The current chapter presents case studies of Celtic and Heathen[2] neo-Shamanisms, consisting of two partial ethnographies – ethnographic fragments[3] – of Druid (Celtic) neo-Shamanisms and Heathen/seidr neo-Shamanisms. A commentary follows to elucidate how these contemporary practices relate to traditional shamanisms, if at all, leading into Chapter 4, which assesses the integrity of the evidence to enquire into the possibility that Celtic and Nordic shamanisms existed.

Celtic shamanism and Druidic shamans

Neo-Shamans approaching European shamanisms are most often contemporary Pagans,[4] falling into three categories, in order of popularity: Wicca, Druidry and Heathenry. Practitioners in all three are diverse, making definition of them difficult, but it may be agreeable to most to describe Wicca (derived from the Anglo-Saxon *wicca*, probably meaning witch: e.g. Pollington 2000: 52) as an initiatory religion in which practitioners revere divinity in nature as manifest in the polarity of a goddess and god (with female often privileged over male); affectionately termed 'the only religion England has ever given the world' (Stuart 2000: 20, citing Hutton 1999: vii). Wicca has been considerably influenced by shamanisms in a number of respects, for mention of it appears in many core texts (e.g. Farrar and Farrar 1984; Starhawk 1989). Some Wiccans even term their religion 'Shamanic Wicca', 'Shamanic Craft' and 'Wiccan-shamanism' (e.g. Adler 1986: 430–434; Luhrmann 1989: 134, 329); and to emphasise the point, Scott Cunningham's best-seller (sold 400,000 copies by the twenty-ninth edition, 2001) claims Wicca 'is a shamanic religion' (Cunningham 2001 [1988]: 4) and 'we are the shamans' (ibid.: 13). Practices such as inducing trance, working magic, divination, interacting with spirits and animal familiars, and healing via supernatural means are certainly reminiscent of many shamanistic practices. Of interest to archaeology is the way in which some Wiccans claim descent from prehistoric European shamanisms. This idea was popularised in the first part of the last century by Margaret Murray, whose first book *The Witch Cult in Western Europe* (1921) argued that those persecuted during the late medieval witch trials were members of an extant ancient pagan religion. Her second contribution, *The God of the Witches* (1933), 'asserted the doctrine that the horned god of the greenwood had been the oldest deity known to humans, and traced his worship across Europe and the Near East, from the Old Stone Age to the seventeenth century' (Hutton 1999: 196). Hutton's thorough historical research has most persuasively deconstructed Murray's arguments, and his presentations at major Pagan conferences have done much to disseminate these findings among those Wiccans who had previously held Murray's interpretations as fact. With Wiccan academics now conducting research, rigorous scholarship blended with insider knowledge is providing greater insight into the historical data, thereby changing the ways in which both medieval Witchcraft and contemporary Wicca are represented and understood.[5] The work of Vivienne Crowley (e.g. 1994, 1998), Wiccan High Priestess and established academic, is notable here. As illustrated in the previous chapter, academics such as Eliade, Castaneda and Harner have had, and continue to have, a major influence on the growth of neo-Shamanism, and since Wicca is one of the most studied traditions of contemporary Paganism, so major academic authors such as Vivienne Crowley, and more recently Ronald Hutton, have considerable influence on contemporary Witchcraft's evolving view of itself (e.g. Hutton's 2000 argument against Wicca as an unbroken Pagan tradition).[6]

The more feminist and goddess-oriented branches of Wicca, by virtue of a common ancestry, in many ways resonate with the so-called Goddess movement. As I have said, Goddess Spirituality has been heavily influenced by the work of Marija Gimbutas (e.g. Gimbutas 1974), for whom the famous Turkish site of Çatalhüyük is a Goddess site *par excellence* (e.g. Jencson 1989; Meskell 1995). Current engagements between adherents to Goddess Spirituality and archaeologists at the site (and off-site over the Internet) are somewhat strained due to conflicting approaches and interpretations. Despite Hodder's claims for a self-reflexive archaeological process at the site, which accommodates both archaeological strategies and alternative goddess views (e.g. Hodder's web site: http://catal.arch.cam.ac.uk/), other archaeologists see the practice being far removed from the ideal (e.g. Hassan 1997). Meskell (1999) argues the differences between Pagans and academics are so fundamental that there is little room for fruitful negotiation. Of course, this should not promote avoidance of the issues, and, as I shall demonstrate, there are various instances where productive dialogues have flourished. It is interesting to note at this juncture that Gimbutas was not the first to suggest Goddess interpretations of archaeological data (e.g. Hutton 1997a, 1998a). Hutton suggests the precedent was set not only by Margaret Murray, who 'whole-heartedly endorsed the idea that the prehistoric European and Mediterranean world had worshipped a single supreme female deity' (Hutton 1999: 273), but also by the archaeologist Jacquetta Hawkes, who portrayed Neolithic European communities as living in harmony with the earth and worshipping a single mother-goddess that personified nature (Hutton 1999: 278–279). Hutton (1999: 280) goes on to point out that such figure-heading archaeologists as O.G.S. Crawford, Vere Gordon Childe and Glyn Daniel declared 'their belief in the veneration of a single female deity by New Stone Age cultures' (e.g. Crawford 1957; Childe 1958; Daniel 1958). While some archaeologists today might rather forget the fact, their predecessors are strange but intimate bedfellows with neo-Shamanic approaches to the past, a past that cannot be ignored due to its repercussions in the present.

Druidry is a case in point. It is perhaps, after Wicca, the second most popular branch of contemporary paganism in Britain today. As is well known, Druids are inspired by the Iron Age druids and all things 'Celtic' which are perceived to relate to them, from medieval and romantic Welsh and Irish literature to archaeology and the legacy of early antiquarians such as William Stukeley, aka 'Archdruid Chyndonax' (Sebastion 1990: 97–98). A number of authors consider the relations between druids past and Druids present (e.g. Piggott 1968; Green 1997; L. Jones 1998), but while Modern Druids endure as an object of ridicule among many archaeologists and historians, the negative stereotypes are being transformed (e.g. Hutton 1997b). The idea that Druids claim descent from ancient Iron Age orders, for instance, is increasingly being replaced – among both Druids and academics – by recognition that Druidry is very much a tradition situated in the modern era (e.g. Harvey 1997b). Emma Restall-Orr, joint-chief of the British Druid Order (BDO), for instance, has a sensitive approach to the problems of D/druidic terminology and genealogy:

> Druidry is sometimes easier to define through what it is not, and so is the BDO. It is not a source of teaching for an ancient faith or culture reconstructed. It is not aiming to proclaim a definitive Druidry, be it 3000 years old, 200 or 10.
>
> (Restall-Orr 2000)

Even so, Druidry's antiquity is at least as old as archaeology (Hutton 1996), stretching back to the early antiquarians mentioned in Chapter 1, and the two are arguably 'blood brothers', as Tim Sebastion of the Secular Order of Druids proclaims (Sebastion 2001).

The plethora of Druid Orders illustrates how diverse contemporary Druidry is; sixteen alone are listed for Britain in the *Druid's Voice* magazine

'Druid Directory', and there are more orders in Europe, the USA and Australia. With such a plurality of Druidic voices in the world today, it is not possible – as with all the traditions I discuss in this volume – to present a single picture of what Druidry is, although there are consistent themes which have been amply documented elsewhere (e.g. papers in Jones and Matthews 1990; Carr-Gomm 1996; Harvey and Hardman 1995; Harvey 1997b, 2000b). To illustrate the relationship between Druidry and neo-Shamanism, a topic as yet unexplored, it is worth discussing the work and practices of Kaledon Naddair, for instance, who suggests 'Pictish and Keltic shamanism is the native initiatory system practised by the ancient Druids'. Naddair founded the shamanic-based 'College of Druidism' in 1982. He describes the use of native shamanistic Celtic incenses formulated from native plants which revives the 'power smoke of the [Druid] shamans' without the use of entheogens. He also recounts how, on one occasion, 'just like a traditional Shaman I acted as a channel ... and whilst I allowed a mighty Keltic God to speak through my body, my own higher consciousness was instantaneously teleported to a far-off steep hillside' (all quotations Naddair 1990: 94). We meet Naddair again in Chapter 5, when I discuss his interactions with British rock art, but to document Druidic neo-Shamanisms more thoroughly beyond his very idiosyncratic exploits, I next detail an e-mail interview I conducted with Philip Shallcrass, joint-chief of the British Druid Order, one of the most prominent figures in British Druidry.

I first met 'Greywolf', as Philip is known by his Druidic name, at the Contemporary Paganism conference held at King Alfred's College, Winchester, in September 1997. The 'shamanic' tale behind how Greywolf received this Druidic name, among other topics, cropped up in our discussions. Our dialogue illustrates how various examples of historic and archaeological evidence, and indigenous (mostly Native American) traditions, are used by one Druid to inspire his shamanic practices and world-view. Our dialogue also illustrates that Druids are not blind to the sensitivities and problems of their practices when borrowing from indigenous cultures, archaeology and history, and how their interpretations of the evidence are not entirely romantic. It would certainly be simplistic to generalise, but given that the British Druid Order is one of the largest in Britain, much of what Greywolf says does reflect Druidry more generally. In this regard, he is clearly an influential figure, with pragmatic involvement at Gorsedds and a profuse publications record (e.g. Shallcrass 1995, 1996, 1997a, 1997b, 1997c, 1998; and, *The Druid's Voice: The Magazine of Contemporary Druidry*, *Tooth and Claw: The Journal of the British Druid Order* and *Gorseddau: Newsletter of the Gorsedd of Bards of the Isles of Britain*, of which he is editor and major contributor). My questions have been tailored slightly from the original interview to facilitate a more consistent flow of dialogue, but Greywolf's responses are reproduced as he stated them, and I am very grateful for his permission to use this material here.

Ethnographic fragments: Philip 'Greywolf' Shallcrass, a Druid shaman

RJW: Greywolf, tell me please, how your Druidry might be regarded as 'shamanic'?

GREYWOLF: I avoid using the term shamanism wherever possible since it is, or at least should be, a culturally specific term for spirit workers in Siberia who have particular understandings of the universe and particular ways of working within that understanding. The kind of Druidry I practice works with the spirits of the land, is of the creatures who inhabit the land, of the gods and of our ancestors. The work we do is about communication, seership, healing, rites of celebration, rites of passage and teaching. Some of this could come under the far too broad definition of 'shamanism' now being bandied about as a catch-all term for working with spirits.

RJW: What other practices of yours might compare with shamanism?

GREYWOLF: I sometimes use a drum as an adjunct to moving myself and/or others into altered states of awareness. I use a rattle for calling spirits, for cleansing ritual space or individual's psychic space or for tracking spirit paths. I use incense for cleansing and purification, referred to by the old British term *saining*, a practice similar to the Native American concept of smudging. I journey into the spirit world to find healing for people. I look to the spirit world for guidance and information.

RJW: Do you think your practices could be described as deriving from 'Celtic' and/or 'British' shamanic tradition(s)?

GREYWOLF: Druidry is, essentially, a native European (more specifically British) way of communicating with and responding to the spirits of place, of the gods and ancestors and of the natural world. Given that definition, it is British or European because it relates directly, spirit to spirit, with the spirits of Britain or Europe. What we do is Druidic because we define Druidry as the native spirituality of these lands. If we were Siberian, we'd describe what we do as shamanism. All 'shamanic' practices are responses to local spirits and the natural world, local variations occurring because the practices are painted in the distinctive colours of their native lands.

Celtic is a term I try to avoid since its meaning and value are dubious. Celtic identity was invented in three stages, first by linguists in the eighteenth century looking at linguistic similarities and trying to define them, secondly by archaeologists in the nineteenth century seeking to define groups of similar artefacts found in Europe, thirdly by writers of the so-called 'Celtic twilight'. Until fifty years ago, hardly anyone living in the so-called Celtic countries would have identified themselves as Celtic. They were Scottish, Welsh, Irish, Manx, Cornish,

Breton. Likewise, the inhabitants of Iron Age Britain and Europe would not have recognised the term. They were a diverse collection of tribal peoples with a multiplicity of tribal gods, having little in common beyond membership of a linguistic group and the use of iron. OK, I exaggerate, but not a lot. 'Celtic' may describe a language group adequately, but beyond that it is fairly meaningless. It does not describe a single ethnic group, a political or social entity, a group of beliefs or anything else much.

My group is called the British Druid Order, understanding the term British as referring to the *Pretani*, the Painted People, the pre-Roman inhabitants of the islands of Britain (and Ireland), our earliest named ancestors. The name Britain covers at least two and a half thousand years of our history, the same length of time that Druidry has been in the historical domain.

RJW: What sort of historic, literary and archaeological evidence would you use for interpreting Druidic shamanism?

GREYWOLF: There is plenty of evidence for 'shamanic' type practices among druids. E.g. the references in Irish manuscripts and Hebridean folklore to druids wearing feather cloaks in which they fly. The insular manuscript sources are full of tales of Otherworld journeys that have clear parallels with spirit journeys undertaken by 'shamans' in other cultures. Many of these are undertaken at or into prehistoric burial mounds, others in caves, under the surface of lakes or across the sea.

A practice called 'the cell of song' carried out in the bardic colleges of Ireland, Wales and Scotland up until the seventeenth century is clearly a survival of a type of incubation oracle widely known throughout pagan Europe and beyond. Bards were shut in windowless cells for a day and a night, their heads wrapped in plaids, to incubate a poem on a given subject. This is a type of sensory deprivation with parallels in insular literature and folklore where people were wrapped in bull hides in order to have oracular dreams. In Ireland, the druid under-going the Bull-sleep had incantations chanted over him by other druids to ensure the veracity of his dream visions.

The poetry of *Amergin* and *Taliesin*, in which poets refer to having been many different animals, people and things through many periods of history, seems sometimes to relate to shape-shifting, at other times to represent either a series of incarnations or a spiritual identification with the creatures that border on universal consciousness. There are, however, numerous clear references to shape-shifting in insular literature and folklore. Irish tradition refers to a type of enchantment called *fith-fath* by which people are transformed into animals. *Fintan mac Bochra*, regarded as a fount of wisdom by the Irish *filidh*, transforms into an eagle, a salmon and a stag. The Welsh *Mabinogion* also contains stories of animal transformations. *Lleu Llaw Gyffes* transforms into an eagle, other characters become deer or wolves. The Story of Taliesin has the bard and the goddess Ceridwen both going through a series of animal transformations. Various methods of divination are outlined in insular sources, some of which involve sacrificing and eating the flesh of a 'taboo' animal, while others involve a kind of psychometry, others the casting of lots or the study of the behaviour of certain birds or animals. There are also references to druids communicating with the dead, i.e. with the spirits of the ancestors.

The archaeological evidence is perhaps less clear, but points in similar directions. From the Neolithic period through to post-Roman times there was an interest in thresholds and a desire to place spirit guardians near them. These were represented by human or animal burials sited near entrances to sacred enclosures or shrines. The burial of a thirty-year-old woman in the ditch near the southern entrance to the Avebury henge is a case in point. Before she was buried a fire was lit on which a collection of herbs, animal bones and small objects such as chalk balls were burnt. These may well have been the working tools of this Bronze Age 'medicine woman'. Megalithic tomb-shrines such as the West Kennett Long Barrow were provided with narrow entrances through which it was possible to crawl in order to deposit new bones or bring out bones for use in rituals at the entrances. The tomb-shrines give the strong impression that they were constructed to represent the body of an earth mother goddess. Entering within them seems likely to have represented a spirit journey as well as a physical one into the realm of the ancestors.

RJW: Greywolf, tell me about your namesake and how the wolf spirit is important to you.

GREYWOLF: I've been working with wolf spirit energy most of my life, but more consciously since a vision that came to me in a sweat lodge some years ago. The sweat lodge was run by a Lakota-trained medicine woman and was in Lakota style, only held in a field in England at a Druid camp. In introducing us to the four quarters the medicine woman mentioned coyote as one of the animal guardians. This jarred in my mind a little since I knew that coyotes had never walked the part of the earth I was sitting on. I asked myself what the local equivalent would have been and the word 'wolf' jumped into my mind. At the same moment a full-grown grey wolf appeared in the lodge, curled up in the central fire-pit. The red-hot stones in the pit were held within his body. He got up and looked at me, inviting me to follow him. I got up (in spirit) and left the lodge. Outside, instead of the English field, there was the side of a snow-covered mountain. The wolf led me up the slope to the tree line where he bid me go back to the lodge, promising that we would meet again. I went back to my body.

The next day, I thought about the vision and that I should try to find something that would link me with the spirit of the wolf.

However, in almost forty years of life, I had never set eyes on hide nor hair, tooth nor claw of a wolf, so I thought it unlikely I would find anything. Returning home, I got a message from a friend inviting me to a garage sale at his parent's house. The first thing I saw when I arrived was a pelt lying across an old water tank. I looked at it, hardly believing my eyes. 'What's the skin?' I asked. 'Wolf' said my friend. I told him the story of the lodge and my vision and he gave me the hide. It turned out to be six small hides from juvenile wolves stitched together. I added beaded strings as ties and made it into a cloak.

The next ritual event I was invited to was a gathering of witches who were to feast on venison. I was vegetarian, but, for the wolves, decided to go along. The feast was preceded by the tale of how the stag had been hunted and killed and how the meat had been prepared. The haunch of venison was brought to the table with reverence and honoured by all those present. As I ate the first mouthful I felt the hides on my back begin to ripple with life and heat that radiated through my body. After forty years in a bag in an attic, my wolves were eating again. I discovered that I could trade forms with the wolf who had come to me in the sweat lodge. I could slide my consciousness into his body and travel in spirit as a wolf. In this shape I was able to find my way through the spirit world with ease. After the wolf-skin cloak came to me I found that I had a pack of six young wolves I could call on for assistance. I became their alpha male, the pack leader. I began to howl under the moon, calling the pack to me.

In a rite at Avebury I was given a Seneca wolf chant. I found it hard to recall the exact form of the chant although two people gave it to me again on four subsequent occasions. Instead, it took on its own form. I think this is because the wolf spirit of this land is a little different from that of North America, even though my wolf skins came from Canada. I later incorporated my version of the chant into a song called *Lord of the Wildwood*.[7] The song and chant in combination have sometimes shifted me into the spirit world while singing. The wolf who came to me in the sweat lodge is my teacher, friend and guide and also my helper when needed. He has a clearly defined personality and a name. The six young wolves who make up my spirit pack also have their own personalities (some quite mischievous!). Wolf in general, or the archetype of wolf, is my power animal, i.e. the creature whose energy I call upon most frequently when I need additional strength to teach, guide, heal, etc. Since working with wolf energy I have found that I tend to attract other wolf people and wolf-related gifts such as pictures, a claw, wolf lichen, articles about wolves, etc.

RJW: You mention the Lakota sweat and Seneca wolf chant, and I know that you have had some involvement with indigenous groups. Can you tell me about your relationships with Native Americans and comment on any problems you might perceive surrounding neo-Shamanic appropriations of their traditions?

GREYWOLF: I have a very good relationship with Native Americans. There are many Native Americans who dislike white folks ripping off their traditional spirituality or being wannabe Indians. When I explain that what I do is teach and practise Native European spirituality we get on fine. As I said, I work with spirits of the land, of the natural world, of the ancestors. This gives me a common understanding with people who work with these things in other traditions. There is a common understanding that we are working in the same areas, just expressing what we do through localised language.

RJW: Your comments reflect your sensitivity to the issues concerning the 'stealing' of native traditions. But still, you mention use of the Lakota-style sweat and Seneca wolf chant, so how do you feel about that? Is that not appropriation? Would you say instead, that using a sweat over here can be 'Native British' and therefore does not involve a stealing of Native American tradition: there is some evidence for sweat lodges in prehistoric Britain, I believe?

GREYWOLF: The sweat lodge that I went into that first time was carried out in Lakota style. It was conducted by a Dutch medicine woman, trained in Lakota tradition by Chief Archie Fire Lame Deer. She has great integrity (and is also a Druid). I have spoken with one Native American elder who has utterly disowned Lame Deer because of his willingness to teach non-Native Americans about his people's traditions. I went into that sweat lodge not because it was Lakota but because it was there and because I trusted the people involved. Since that first time I have (as have several other people I know) been working on reconstructing a native British, Druidic sweat lodge. The physical construction of the lodges I use is the same bender-type construction that the Lakota use.

There is ample evidence that similar lodges were built throughout Britain from about 3500 BCE through to about 850 BCE in England, much later in Ireland. The difference is in the ritual. I have used various paradigms from insular literature and from my own understanding of the spirits of the land and of the ancestors to construct sweat lodge rites. The essential process is the same: the communal construction of the lodge, offerings made to the spirits of place, the gods and ancestors, positioning the fire and the lodge itself with reference to the cardinal points, drumming and chanting around the fire while the rocks are heating, honouring the four directions within the lodge, making prayers. The purpose is the same: purification, sometimes as an adjunct to prayer or healing, sometimes as part of a vision quest. What *is* *different* is the spiritual language and the detail. When we make offerings into the fire or into the earth when we are constructing the lodge we will use native herbs such as vervain, mistletoe or mugwort rather than tobacco or sage. When we honour the four directions, we do so through our understanding of native Druid tradition. The gods we call upon to guide us are 'our' gods, the ancestors we call to are those of 'our' blood and spirit. The Seneca wolf chant started off as a Seneca wolf chant but worked its way through my psyche and came out as something that bears only a passing resemblance to the chant as I was originally given it. I didn't realise this until others who knew the original chant pointed out to me how different my version is. Sparked by the inspiration of the Seneca chant, I seem to have produced a native British wolf chant!

Heathenry and seidr

Having briefly discussed shamanistic aspects of Wicca and presented my dialogue with the Druid Greywolf, I next explore the third popular branch of paganism known to its practitioners variously as Heathenry,[8] Heathenism, or more loosely the 'Northern' tradition, with such terms as Ásatrú ('allegiance to the gods', specifically the Æsir), Odinism or Odinist (orientated to the god Odin) and Vanatrú ('allegiance to the Vanir'), denoting preferences for specific deities. Contemporary Heathens utilise Norse and Icelandic literature and mythology, and Viking and Anglo-Saxon migration period history and archaeological sources[9] to revive and reconstruct a Heathen religion for the present. In the same vein as other Pagan traditions, Heathenry takes many forms and there are a variety of functioning groups worldwide. In the UK there is Odinshof, the Odinic Rite (e.g. 1998) and Hammarens Ordens Sällskap (see their web site: http://www.geocities.com/hammarens/); in the UK and USA the Ring of Troth, in Europe the Ring of Troth European Branch (e.g. Ring of Troth 1997); in the USA the Ásatrú Alliance, the Odinist Fellowship, Rune Gild and Ásatrú Folk Assembly; and in Iceland Ásatrú has been an official religion since 1973 (e.g. Berg 2001), with its own burial ground in Reykjavík. Smaller localised groups known as 'Hearths' meet regularly and are comparable, in size and function, with a Wiccan 'Coven' or Druidic 'Grove'. Harvey's (1995, 1997b) discussions of Heathenry alongside other Pagan traditions mark the most comprehensive and erudite academic survey to date (from a popular practitioner angle, see Pagan Federation 1997). He suggests practitioners are steadily growing in numbers and the practices are advancing in 'coherence' (Harvey 1997b: 53). There is no need for me to replicate what Harvey ably details, but there is a great deal of room to explore the shamanistic elements in Heathenry which, in similarity with Wicca and Druidry, are mostly only touched on by other ethnographers of the traditions.

The concept of shamanism may permeate Heathenry more than any other contemporary Pagan tradition because more associations between the two have been drawn (whether correctly or not, and whether by academics or Pagans) in the historic and archaeological records (e.g. Davidson 1964; Simek 1993). Numerous aspects of the god Odin and goddess Freyja for instance, may display aspects of shamanism, and Heathen neo-Shamans may have one or both of these deities as their patrons because of their associations with *seiðr*, a ritual practice perhaps shamanistic in nature. *Seiðr*[10] is an obscure practice of 'magic' in the Northern sources which is often disreputable and related to 'sorcery'. While a number academics argue that *seiðr* was a shamanic technique (e.g. Davidson 1993: 77, 137; Simek 1993), and Heathens consistently do likewise, there are certainly both academics (Price pers. com.) and neo-Shamans (e.g. the detailed considerations of Gundarsson 2001) who challenge this view. I have met numerous Heathen shamanistic and/or seidr practitioners in the UK and USA; for instance 'Runic John', from Lancashire, whose patron deity is Woden[11] and who gives 'rune readings' and 'shamanic healings'. When conducting runic divinations for clients, John says he enters a trance in which Woden sits behind him and covers his right eye with his hand (in Norse mythology, Odin sacrifices one eye to gain wisdom). At this point, John knows he has the 'sight' to be able to read the runes. In Figure 3.1 John is seen sending a malignant 'spirit' into

Figure 3.1 'Runic' John, Heathen neo-Shaman, completing a shamanic healing. John has extracted a malignant 'spirit' from the patient and is slamming it into the ground where it will be absorbed into Helheim, a Heathen term for the Lower World of Nordic Cosmology. On the ground in front of him is his shamanic rattle, and he wears Thunor's hammer around his neck

91

the earth where it will be absorbed and recycled, having just extracted it from a patient. And in Figure 3.2 John is seen possessed by Woden during a public ritual, stood rigid and transfixed by the ecstatic inspiration of the god. Moments later, John was then possessed by the fertility god Freyr and shape-shifted into a wild boar (Freyr's tutelary animal) while in the 'spirit world' (an experience he later recounted), and to the surprise of onlookers, fell to hands and knees and charged around grunting and snorting, nose to the ground, churning up dust.

Heathenry is as diverse as any other branch of Paganism and John's practices are no less idiosyncratic. Examining Heathen shamanisms in examples beyond the individual practitioner, I next discuss two specific sets of practices – forms of seidr and a form of heathen possession – pioneered by a more widely publicised group, the Hrafnar community in San Francisco led by Diana Paxson. I interviewed Paxson and 'Rauðhildr' of Hrafnar and took the role of participant-observer in a Hrafnar shamanic possession ritual in March 1998 (thereafter we communicated by email). Later, in August 2000, I took

Figure 3.2 'Runic' John is possessed by the shaman-god Woden in a public ritual, 1998

on the experiential role of seer in a seidr, and a year later I acted as a guide for the seer, in both instances with a community of Pagans and Heathens in Hampshire, England. In August 2001 I had the opportunity to meet Paxson a second time during her visit to England, and we discussed various issues further. Having just participated in a seidr with a core-shamanic group (led by Karen Kelly – see citations below) in Cambridge, she took time out of her busy schedule to meet with me at the Rollright Stones in Oxfordshire, before conducting an oracle work seminar with Caitlín Matthews (whose work with John Matthews is discussed below) in Devon. The location and circumstances of our meeting, along with the effects on the development of a 'new religious movement' of American and British neo-Shamans networking and collaborating in workshops might, in it own right, make ideal ethnographic subject matter for this book! In addition to my interviews and discussions with Paxson and Rauðhildr, the ethnographic fragments of neo-Shamanic seidr and possession presented here have benefited from my communications over the last five years with the seidr-worker and anthropologist Jenny Blain (e.g. 1997, 1998a, 1998b, 1999a, 1999b, 2001, http://home.freeuk.net/wyrdswell/), whose volume dealing exclusively with seidr/seiðr has recently been published by Routledge (Blain 2002).

Ethnographic fragments: Hrafnar community (San Francisco) seidr and possession

When I met Paxson in 1998, we talked and I took notes as she shopped and prepared her home for that evening's ritual. The subjects of being 'possessed by Odin' and 'communicating with ancestor spirits' seemed out of place for me in a conventional American supermarket and around a kitchen table, but then I reminded myself that indigenous shamans similarly treat their experiences matter-of-factly. The mundane locations reinforced for me the fact that to neo-Shamans and indigenous practitioners shamanism is not bizarre or eccentric, as an ethnographer might perceive it, but is deeply implicated in everyday actions. Paxson described her spiritual background to be in eclectic areas including Women's Mysteries, Ceremonial Magic and Qabbalah. She became interested in shamanisms after reading Michael Harner's *Way of the Shaman*, and at the same time took an interest in Heathenry. At a Harner workshop, Shamanisms and Heathenry coalesced when, unlike the 'safe' experiences of other workshop attendees, Paxson had a traumatic encounter with a 'clichéd' (as she put it) Raven spirit (Odin has two Raven helpers, Huginn and Muninn), and the God Odin who asked 'Just how serious about shamanism are you?'. The implication was that to become a shaman great sacrifices had to be made and a new world-view adopted which is unconventional, challenging and discordant with Western society; being a shaman was not going to be easy. After this initiatory experience, Paxson began working with the runes as a divination device, and her contacts with a

Scandinavian graduate student pointed her in the direction of historic and archaeological sources. A year of research and experience later, Paxson says she had sufficient knowledge and experience to 'retrieve European shamanic techniques of *Seidr*', and she has since written widely on the subject (e.g. Paxson 1992, 1993, 1997, 1998, 1999).

Along with other seidr practitioners (e.g. Campbell 1999; Fries 1993; Høst 1999; Kelly 1999; Linzie 1999; Pedersen 1999) – whose practices are diverse, often differing significantly from those of Paxson – Paxson uses sources such as the *Eiríks Saga rauða* and the Eddic *Voluspá*, a myth describing the 'seeresses prophecy', to inspire reconstructions of seidr séance's today. Eirik's saga is especially noteworthy, as it vividly reports around one thousand years ago, how a seeress or *völva* (also known as the *Seiðkona, Spákona*, or *Spákóna*) engages with the 'spirit world' for a Greenlandic community. And in the *Voluspá*, a myth from about the same time but with themes of some antiquity, Odin travels the treacherous road to the gates of Hel (the realm of the dead)[12] to summon and question a seeress (see especially Ellis 1943). Commenting on her reconstructions of seidr from past evidence and having practised seidr for over eight years at the time of our most recent conversations, Paxson states, 'I don't know exactly how they did it, but this works!' At the time I was in San Francisco, Paxson said around six people from the Hrafnar community (numbering around twenty to thirty) attend seidr sessions in the Bay area. They meet once a month and practise seidr for the wider Heathen community at (Pagan and Heathen) festivals and workshops in the USA, such as Trothmoot. The format for a seidr session is very specific and participants dress for the part, wearing Viking clothing and jewellery based on historic and archaeological sources. The location is similarly prepared with a ritual 'high seat' reconstructed from Eirik's saga which is carved in Scandinavian style. During the rite, the *völva* sits in this elevated position (though in seidr sessions I have attended, the elevation is not mandatory) and the other community members form a circle around her. While the *völva* or *seiðkona* is female in the ancient sources, there is mention of the *seiðmaðr* or male Sorcerer (plural *seiðmenn*) (e.g. Simek 1993: 280), and both men and women assume the position of seidr-worker today.

The seidr session or séance is orchestrated as follows: two main figures are prominent in the proceedings, the *völva* and a 'guide' who sings and chants the *völva* and other seidr-workers into trance (though often all present may sing). The text of the songs is based on Nordic mythology and the music is based on medieval sources. The guide keeps a watchful eye on the proceedings, a necessary precaution because trance is a potentially unpredictable condition and up to a point all members gathered enter an altered state. The guide's singing, often narrating a journey into the otherworld, takes everyone to Helheim where the *völva* communicates with ancestors and other than human persons. But only the *völva* enters a deeper state of trance in

94

which she goes through the gates of Helheim and into the realm of the dead: the format of the songs as sung by the guide means that at a specific point in the chant the *völva*, and only the *völva*, enters Helheim. Paxson describes the experience of entering Helheim as one of 'dropping' or 'falling', which is reminiscent of indigenous shamanic descriptions of entering the spirit world. Once the *völva* is accustomed to being in Helheim, a dialogue begins between guide and *völva* in which extracts from Odin's speeches in the Norse myths may be recited, particularly from the *Hávamál* (sayings of the high one) *Vafþrúðnismál* (Vafthrudnir's sayings) and *Grímnismál* (Grimnir's Sayings). The *völva* is thereby encouraged to communicate with the community and vocalise descriptions of the territory of Helheim so the ritual can then move on to the oracular prognostications of the *völva*. The other members of the community gathered besides the *völva* and guide, currently gathered at the gates of Helheim, then put questions to the *völva*, who experiences visionary imagery and other extrasensory perceptions influenced by her presence among the dead and/or other than human persons.

Often, at first, the *völva*'s information is enigmatic. In one incident, for example, the questioner asked 'should I change jobs?' and the *völva* 'saw' a mouse busy digging for seeds in a large field, which seemed to be a mammoth task. The *völva* reported this imagery and the questioner made sense of it: she was a biologist specialising in rodents in grassland habitats and currently working as a waitress to make ends meet. The mouse imagery told her that progress was not being made in her current situation and that career changes did have to be made. In other instances, the *völva* may need to interpret the imagery and give advice to the questioner, but it is not uncommon for the questioner to understand immediately what is meant and therefore not require the *völva*'s counselling. During the séance a deity, spirit of the dead or other spirit-helper may, exceptionally, possess the *völva*, but Paxson stated that generally it is easiest for the *völva* to act as a medium for the information given by the 'spirit' to the questioner. Similarly, Blain (see previous citations) describes an experience of 'partial possession' during seidr: 'At times it simply becomes easier to let the deity speak through you than to pass on somebody's questions and the deity's answers, but only if you know who/what you're dealing with' (pers. com.). The intensity of many 'beginner' experiences requires vigilance on the part of experienced seidr-workers. 'Watchers' are present at all times to ensure the ritual proceeds carefully. At times, the strong emotional responses of some questioners to the information given them might require the support of seasoned practitioners. Alternatively, inexperienced seidr-practitioners may leave a part of their 'soul' behind in the spirit world so trained *völva*s must make shamanic soul retrieval journeys to Helheim, similar to but not the same as those practised by core-shamanists and indigenous shamans.

Paxson says the seidr séance has proven very popular among the Heathen and Pagan communities she has worked with, and all participants find it extremely empowering. Seidr has not gone uncontested, however, and there is some division over its reconstruction and practice, a theme I revisit in some depth, in the concluding chapter. In the meantime it is interesting to note that since Paxson has been practising seidr, a second ritual has been developed which utilises a possession technique. The impetus for this practice came when a deity first possessed a Hrafnar practitioner – the Scandinavian scholar mentioned above – an unexpected happening which required explanation and contextualisation. Paxson went on to research the historic sources and ethnographic texts, and believes she has found examples of possession in the Norse texts, particularly the earlier material. A possible example is in the *Saga of King Óláfr Tryggvason* (*Flateyjarbók* 1) in which an idol of Freyr is described as being carried around the country in a wagon, accompanied by his 'wife', a priestess (*gyðja*). The hero of the tale, Gunnar, fights with the idol and takes its place, whereupon the Swedes are well pleased the god can now feast and drink, and are even more pleased when his 'wife' becomes pregnant! The tale is written from the perspective of the Norwegians and if read at face value is a jive at the gullibility of the Heathen Swedes who believe Gunnar's impersonation of Freyr to be real. If interpreted as a possible example of possession, however, as Paxson would suggest, then it may have been common practice among the Swedes for a person to take on the part of a deity and let the deity speak through them when needed. In this case Gunnar is the 'shaman', or whoever else was accompanying the *gyðja* before being usurped by him: Gunnar's struggle with Freyr would actually be a fight with the previous shaman.[13] Paxson also noticed how traditional shamanic societies often incorporated possession into their rites (e.g. Lewis 1989 [1971]), and to build on the fragmentary Nordic evidence with contemporary possession techniques, she studied and took part in the rituals of an Umbanda community in San Francisco. Umbanda combines elements of Christianity with indigenous Brazilian and African religions, is related to Candomblé, Voodoo and the Ifé (e.g. Deren 1975; Fatunmbi 1991), and is growing in popularity throughout South and North America. Essentially, Paxson combined an ethnographic analogy with Old Norse sources to reconstruct a Heathen possession technique for the present.

During a Hrafnar possession ceremony certain individuals who are already accomplished seidr-workers, become possessed by Odin; they are 'ridden' by Odin whose principal means of travel is his eight-legged horse Sleipnir.[14] In effect, the possessed become the horse vehicle for the god. As with seidr, in which anyone can seek to become a *völva*, the position of Odin's horse is also available to everyone, but also as with seidr, the process is long, hard, demands commitment and therefore is not chosen by everyone. In similarity with seidr, the possession ceremony, which lasts about one and a half hours or more, follows a strict procedure. It begins with an explanation of what is going to happen, so all persons present are fully aware of the format, any dangers and the responsibility involved. Everyone is then purified with smouldering herbs, candles are lit, and each person is blessed with appropriate runes in preparation for their journey. A horn of mead is passed around and each participant makes a toast to Odin, giving either informed consent in the wish to become a horse of Odin or passing the opportunity on this time. Singing based on Nordic sources then follows to invoke the god into the ritual and into those participants who are willing. As they become possessed the participants adorn themselves in garments which have been made available to them and which are characteristic of Odin, including a wide brimmed hat, a long cloak and an eye patch to represent his missing eye. They may also hold a tall staff and carry a tobacco pipe and drinking horn. When Odin possesses he is said to 'want a party'[15] and often eats, drinks heavily and smokes tobacco. There is a process of negotiation here, though, as each 'horse' requests Odin to take the effects of these substances with him, post-possession: 'if the deity isn't prepared to play by the rules then he's not invited – you can always say no' (Paxson, pers. com.).

Having satiated his material desires Odin moves among the non-possessed to give oracular advice. Dialogues occur between Odin and devotee, with questions asked and answers given. This is perhaps the most important part of the rite, when people may be challenged by Odin to make changes in their lives or to take on advice which is unexpected, a happening described by participants as a profound and empowering experience. Being a trickster God, though, Odin can also be devious; the advice is not always 'good'. At the end of the rite Odin returns to *Asgard* (the realm of the *Aesir* gods in Norse mythology) and the possessed waken from trance. The effects of the alcohol and tobacco on the participants is said to recede once possession ends; indeed, many of them only smoke and drink heavily when possessed by Odin. After the ritual, the evening ends with a socialising feast during which experiences can be discussed and the friendship bond of the group strengthened. Having noted the inspiration for this technique derives from both Norse sources and Paxson's long-term experiences with Umbanda, it is worth pointing out that Odin equates with *Baron Samedi* (both are lords of the dead), whose devotees wear top hat and cloak when possessed by him, during which time he likes to party by drinking, eating and smoking (e.g. Deren 1975). Those he possesses are known as 'horses' because he is said to 'ride' them (e.g. Lewis 1989: 51). Hrafnar's reconstruction of Heathen possession from the Nordic sources obviously borrows heavily from Umbanda, but even so the parallels between Heathen and Umbanda mythology and terminology are striking.

Comments on the ethnographic fragments

Various issues arise from the ethnographic fragments which are important to a study of neo-Shamanisms. This commentary provides, at first glance, confirmation that like other neo-Shamans these practitioners romanticise and misrepresent shamanisms past (if they existed at all) and present. But more importantly this analysis facilitates a deeper understanding of these Celtic and Heathen tradition neo-Shamans who, like Gordon MacLellan (whom we met in Chapter 2), challenge widespread stereotypes of themselves by being aware of and effectively responding to the criticisms aimed at them, as we shall see. Where other evaluators of neo-Shamanisms present monolithic surveys which ignore its heterogeneity, my presentation of specific case examples and the opinions of practitioners aims to present a picture which better reflects aspects of neo-Shamanisms' complexity and subtlety.

It is worth noting, first, that in similarity to other Pagans but in contrast to 'wannabe' shamans, and 'cardiac celts' (Bowman 1995b), Greywolf suggests he did not choose to become a shaman. He did not *convert* to Paganism because he feels it has been with him all his life. Like many native shamans who cannot refuse the call of the spirits or inherit their skills from ancestors, Greywolf was, he believes, destined to be a shaman Druid. In a similar vein, not all members of Hrafnar's community choose to become seidr-workers or seek to be possessed by Odin. These positions are of great responsibility, are potentially hazardous and are not to be taken lightly; not everyone succeeds in becoming a *völva* or horse of Odin.

Furthermore, Rauðhildr of Hrafnar related a shamanic initiatory experience to me, which, in involving experiences of death and dismemberment, is quite comparable with traditional shamanic accounts. Rauðhildr says she went on a journey to visit the Maurnir, who in Nordic cosmology are female giants. They dwell in a cave and she went there, 'naïvely' she says, because she thought it would be 'interesting'. She was, at this time, attempting to journey to all of the denizens of the nine worlds of Nordic 'shamanic' cosmology. The Maurnir were there and saw her, and asked why she was there. The Maurnir have much wisdom, and she asked (naïvely again, she says) if they would teach her, if she could learn from them, and share in their wisdom. They said no, they couldn't teach her. But, if she wished she could become part of their wisdom. She agreed this would be a good thing. So they ate her. They threw aside the bones, as they ate her. Her bones were lying on the cavern floor, when Loki (the trickster deity) appeared and started singing and dancing, calling to the gods and goddesses to put her back together again, which they eventually did. This very personal, disturbing (and in part comical) account testifies I think to the fact that neo-Shamanisms – or at least aspects of Heathen neo-Shamanisms – are not entirely safe, and can involve frightening experiences. Similarly, Greywolf told me about his involvement with the 'darker' side of shamanisms:

> [T]he traditional shaman often fights against the calling, kicking and screaming all the way, and usually undergoes extremely painful experiences to learn. The neo-shaman signs up for a course of work-

shops and listens to New Age music. This obviously oversimplifes, but, from experience I know that there is a good deal of truth in it. My own path into spirit work has more parallels with the traditional than the neo approach. As a child, I used to fight demons who flew in through my bedroom window. I was the archetypal misfit/outsider. I spent some years driving myself to the edge of psycho-spiritual endurance and beyond. I suffered a major breakdown at the age of eighteen, complete with 'initiatory' visions. The only things I lacked were a culture that understood in any meaningful way the nature of the experiences I was going through and a living teacher who could offer guidance. The pain of the path is something very little stressed. That's why I want to write my book: *Sex, Fear and Death: A Guide to Modern Druidry*. I sometimes feel guilty about teaching Druidry as I know that if people are to fully connect with it, they will suffer deeply. It then becomes a question of weighing the benefits against the harm. The benefits are expanded awareness to an extent that can be positively ecstatic and the ability to help others. The harm is the potential for ego-mania, madness or death.

(Greywolf, pers. com.)

The 'misfit/outsider' experiences are surely different in indigenous contexts, where shamans are often vital community members, than in the fragmented, post-modern society of the West, yet other aspects of Greywolf's initiatory experiences are certainly very reminiscent of indigenous shamanisms. In the instances of these Celtic and Heathen neo-Shamans, then, shamanisms are not simply a matter of choice, and safety is not necessarily part and parcel of the deal. In accordance with other neo-Shamans I have mentioned, and with indigenous shamans, these practitioners are chosen by the spirits and may even be plagued by them.

Practices aside for a moment, use of the term 'shaman' by Greywolf and Paxson is also of interest since, in contrast to other neo-Shamans, they seem to use it carefully. Their comments on shamanisms are not universalist or acultural, and the term is used sensitively: as illustrated by his comments above, Greywolf is cautious not to refer to his own practices as 'shamanism', and, as Paxson told me, she does not think Hrafnar seidr is the same as shamanisms in indigenous communities, since it is not only a reconstructed rite but is also reconstructed for contemporary Westerners whose needs and experiences may be markedly different from those of indigenous shamans and their communities. In these ways, particularly by perceiving Druidic and Hrafnar neo-Shamanisms to be explicitly different from traditional shamanisms, respect is given to the integrity of the term 'shaman' and to indigenous shamans themselves. By virtue of their interest in native cultures, both these practitioners have had significant interaction with indigenous communities. They are not armchair neo-Shamans and rather than simply taking what they want from indigenous shamanisms as some anthropologists and neo-Shamans are known to do, Greywolf's and Paxson's approaches to indigenous culture are markedly intelligent, sensitive and respectful. Indigenous people are not romanticised and the aim is certainly not to be like an 'Indian'. The aim is to practise one's own – British or Northwest European – shamanism, rather than to steal someone else's. Paxson stated she was fascinated by Native American traditions, but her main concern is with a 'European tribal heritage' and connecting with that to be on a level footing with Native Americans. In a meeting with Native Americans not long before our interview in 1998, Paxson was introduced by them as 'practising what we do but in European terms', and, she said, this is exactly the kind of response she aimed for. The Hrafnar seidr and possession techniques, as well as Greywolf's methods, are quite different from Harner's core-shamanism, then, which avoids cultural specificity. By locating their practices in specific 'Druidic' and 'seidr' circumstances, these neo-Shamans do not immediately homogenise shamanisms. There is an intrinsic cultural component which is vitally important, providing context and content for the imagery and experiences. Hrafnar neo-Shamanism has the 'fibre' – as Paxson put it – which people are looking for.

Despite their concerted efforts to avoid appropriating and offending indigenous shamanisms, certain problems with Greywolf's and Paxson's approaches endure. Fully aware of the problems of appropriation, Greywolf did attend a 'Lakota-style' sweat lodge, and even if there is evidence for 'indigenous British' sweat lodges, the inspiration for understanding them to be so derives from Native American sources. Nonetheless, experimental archaeology points towards the use of Bronze Age sweat lodges as precedent: British Druid Order member Mark Graham (1998/9; see also Richardson 1998; Weir 2000) reports on his collaboration with archaeologists Barfield and Hodder in an experiment to reconstruct such a sweat lodge from the evidence of 'burnt mounds'. Around 3,000 piles of such enigmatic heat-shattered stones are found beside British waterways, perhaps heated to boil water and cook meat (see, for example, Ó'Drisceoil 1988), or, as Barfield and Hodder (1987) suggest and the experiment hoped to show, used to heat a Bronze Age sauna. The construction and ritual of a Native American sweat lodge, the ethnographic example on which they drew, are easily transferable. To Native Americans this borrowing may rather be an appropriation, but for Graham and other users of the lodge in Britain such as Greywolf, people who do not follow a Native American tradition, 'it was a way of recon-necting with our ancestors[16] and reclaiming our own indigenous sweat lodge tradition' (1998/9: 24).

Graham's lodge was constructed from hazel poles with a canvas covering, and the stones were heated on an open fire. These were placed in the lodge and participants then entered and poured cold water over the stones to create steam, a reaction which causes the stones to shatter. The more water was added, the more steam was produced, and the hotter the lodge became, inducing altered consciousness in the participants. The ritual accompanying the sweat was based on 'rounds' during which a break is taken from the intense heat by opening the door of the lodge. Graham's lodge had four rounds, 'one for each of the elements' (1998/9: 25), but the sweat can last much longer, sometimes through the night. The sweat lodge experiment, conducted as part of Birmingham City Council's Archaeology Week, was successful: the ceremony produced the desired spiritual result for the neo-Shamans, and the archaeologists confirmed that the stones 'had exactly the same shatter pattern as the ones on the burnt mound' (Graham 1998/9: 25). Despite 'borrowing' inspiration for their sweats from Native America, Greywolf, Graham and other neo-Shamans doing 'British' sweats – for which there appears to be archaeological precedent – are at least endeavouring to disassociate what they do from Native American examples.[17] To quote Greywolf again,

> [M]ost of the people I know who work with sweat lodges in Europe have drawn inspiration from and usually had direct experience of Native American sweat lodge rites. All are also aware of the tensions existing around this issue. However, they are using that inspiration to establish a native European sweat lodge that once existed but had been lost. Native American teachers have been generous enough to help us recover this important part of our spiritual heritage. For this, we are sincerely grateful ... Now that many folk are beginning to work sweat lodges in Britain with the spirits of our own land and ancestry, we can acknowledge our debt to our Native American friends whilst abandoning any idea that we ourselves have to pretend to BE Native Americans.
>
> (Greywolf, pers. com.)

Whether Native Americans are prepared to accept the British sweat as legitimate and not an appropriation of native traditions remains to be seen, but of course, Native American opinions are unlikely to be singular (see Chapter 7).

Different issues surround Paxson's 'borrowings' from Umbanda. The problem of appropriation exists in this situation, I think, although it is less of a problem than in the Native American example. This is simply because Umbanda is itself a syncretic religion which is derived from (or has borrowed from) a variety of sources, and its practice is not restricted to a particular culture or community, as is apparent with much Native American religion. So Paxson's borrowing from Umbanda is hardly a unilineal appropriation from 'them' to 'us'. The contention might instead, from an archaeological/historic perspective, surround the analogy made between ancient Norse sources and contemporary Umbanda. While the striking similarities between the deities and mythologies involved beg the circular question 'Where does appropriation begin and reconstruction or interpretations end?', it is worth bearing in mind that there is little similarity between the two cultures, even if possession techniques may have been practised in both.

In all, the sensitive approach to indigenous peoples and – for the most part – careful use of specific ethnographic examples seems to let these neo-Shamans off the appropriation hook. Indeed, they may give 'extra pay' to shamanisms because of that sensitivity and care. It is really up to native people themselves to judge this matter, of course, and from the responses Greywolf and Paxson have received thus far, it appears there is general approval. Apart from the general avoidance of borrowing from indigenous religions, one further reason for this approval might be the emphasis on community focus which is consistent for many Native American ceremonies and these neo-Shamanic rites. Hrafnar neo-Shamanism is fundamentally interactive, for the community provides the reason for the *völva* to journey to Helheim, and the *völva*s, in response, feel their practice is legitimated and supported by the community. Rauðhildr stated that for her the maxim 'to honour is to serve' reflected this. Commenting on possession, she expresses a strong degree of responsibility: '[We] ask Woden to come and ask him to walk in us. This is not to be taken lightly ... it is not for beginners.' Paxson expressed a similar commitment to community: during trance she thinks it important to 'watch over' and take care of the people involved because the experiences are consistently unusual for Westerners and may be overwhelming. Indeed, she said, Hrafnar uses more 'checks and balances' than traditional shamanisms do because Western culture is not well prepared for such bizarre experiences. And, Jenny Blain (see previous citations) states:

> What's very hard to convey is the feeling of the room where the ritual [takes] place, and the intensity of it ... It isn't like anything else, to experience seidr in that environment where there's about forty of fifty people in the room, all ages, and they almost all have a pretty good clue as to what's going on, and real questions to ask and the answers are intensely meaningful to them. The extent of community involvement, and hence the intensity of the ritual, is something that doesn't (in my albeit limited experience) happen elsewhere.
>
> (Blain, pers. com.)

Like indigenous shamanisms, there is clearly a strong community element in the seidr rituals.

Similarly, Greywolf's neo-Shamanism involves the wider Druidic community when, for instance, the movement of the seasons is celebrated at the eight Pagan festivals. At the two Beltane (Mayday) ceremonies conducted by the British Druid Order at Avebury which I attended there were hundreds of people present, celebrating the beginning of summer with ritual and song (Figures 3.3 and 3.4). Greywolf and Bobcat (e.g. Restall-Orr 1997) – joint-chiefs of the British Druid Order – lead these rituals, invoking gods and goddesses, conducting many a hand-fasting (Pagan marriages), and child naming/blessing. In a similar vein, it is interesting to note how wider Pagan connections are starting to provide inspiration for new community practices. After meeting Paxson and Blain at the 2001 Midlands Pagan Federation conference and discussing oracular seidr, Greywolf commented,

> [I]t struck me as strange that the seidr tradition should be under-going such a dramatic and widespread revival, yet no one in the Druid community seems to be taking a similar approach to the practice of awenyddion. I think this situation should change and wonder if maybe we can help that process along?
>
> (Greywolf, email to Paxson and Blain 29.08.01)

Awenyddion is, according to Greywolf, a practice similar to oracular seidr described by Giraldus Cambrensis in his twelfth-century *Description of Wales*:

> [A]mong the Welsh there are certain individuals called Awenyddion who behave as if they are possessed ... When you consult them about some problem, they immediately go into a trance and lose control of their senses ... Words stream from their mouths, incoherently and apparently meaningless and lacking any sense at all ... and if you listen carefully to what they say you will receive the solution to your problem. When it is all over they will recover from their trance, as if they were ordinary people waking from a heavy sleep ... They seem to receive this gift of divination through visions which they see in their dreams.
>
> (Greywolf n.d.)

The extent to which Giraldus' statement is a reflection of reality in twelfth-century Wales is not of concern to me here – interesting from an ethnographic point of view is how these Heathen and Druid members of the Pagan community are engaging with one another, and, inspired by each other's trance practices, developing new ones; in this instance looking towards development of a new Druidic neo-Shamanic practice which is communally empowering, just as seidr is for Heathens. I can only speculate that similar exchanges are happening elsewhere in the Pagan community.

When compared with traditional shamanisms, the community element in Hrafnar and Druidic neo-shamanisms is of course implicated quite differently, as we would expect. Indeed, as I have emphasised, shamanisms and

Figure 3.3 A ritual procession of Druids around Avebury henge at Beltane in 1998. They are led by Greywolf

Figure 3.4 Druid ceremony at Beltane, the Devil's Chair, Avebury

neo-Shamanisms are very different. But in contrast to other neo-Shamanisms, this community emphasis in some Heathenry and Druidry means it resonates more favourably with the traditional shamanisms it in part emulates. Acknowledging these similarities and differences between shamanisms and neo-Shamanisms allows us to avoid metanarratives, and explore the complexities and idiosyncrasies of both.

The way in which these Celtic and Heathen neo-Shamans approach the historic and archaeological sources is significant: their reconstructions of Celtic and Norse religion from various sources may be somewhat unorthodox to the specialists. No small proportion of academics will contend the sources cannot be interpreted this way, that too many liberties – the influence of Umbanda, for instance – have been taken, and that Hrafnar's reconstruction of a Norse possession technique is therefore misguided. They might suggest further, there is simply too little evidence to reconstruct these religions to the extent that they can be practised reliably today, and that these neo-Shamans cannot claim their practices are the same as those among the Celts and Norse. Most unsettling for historians and archaeologists must be that while these neo-Shamans may be avoiding the issue of indigenous appropriation, their claims to the past are equally problematic. This final issue is the most difficult to resolve, since academic argument itself is built on diversity of interpretation, let alone having to contend with 'fringe' neo-Shamanic input. That is, unless a more liberal, post-processual and queer standpoint is taken, in which archaeologists' interpretations of the past are not seen as commensurable with those of neo-shamans. It is interesting also that these neo-Shamans are aware of academic criticisms, and respond by agreeing with them, in part. Greywolf has no qualms about the fact that his Druidic practices are not the same as what the original druids did: Druidry has a firm foot in the present and seems, as Greywolf's comments testify, to be less romantic about Iron Age prehistory than critics suggest. For the most part, the critics' perceptions of contemporary Pagan Druidry are clouded by the image of Victorian Druidry (e.g. Piggott 1968), but the two strands barely resemble each other.

Commenting on the differences between what Hrafnar does and what her 'ancestors' may have done, Rauðhildr says, 'We are not them, so what we do is not exactly what they did. But it works ... We are lucky that the gods and ancestors have allowed us to cobble all this together and make it work.' She adds, 'If the seiðkona walked into our seidr she would recognise it and the spirits, but she'd probably look funny at us and I wouldn't blame her!'[18] Rauðhildr recognises the issues facing contemporary Heathens are different to those the Norse faced, and, that her background in 'women's mysteries' affects her perception of the Norse past; she cannot be entirely objective and must address personal biases. By and large, then, Hrafnar members appreciate that their practices are not the same as those of their 'ancestors'. More important for them than interpreting what Nordic shamanisms *were* like is that these reconstructions are valid and valuable for the *present*. Similar careful thought is afforded the term *seiðr*. Paxson thinks the sources should not be seen as entirely representing shaman*isms*, but that aspects of them – when shape-shifting and oracular divination occurs, for instance – may be shaman*istic*. She also argues that Hrafnar possession cannot strictly be called 'shamanism' because of its difference from indigenous shamanisms. Again, the practice is referred to as shaman*istic*. Hrafnar seidr and possession are not for intellectual amusement and are not a re-enactment, but they are a serious spiritual and/or religious practice, and, to all intents and purposes, one that is consistent, systematic and, for its practitioners, effective. The interpretations and reconstructions may be said to 'fit' the evidence (whether acceptable to academics or not) to the extent that they are not entirely speculative; if they were, such inauthenticity might well undermine the contemporary practice. Important differences are clearly recognised between what Hrafnar is doing, what the ancient Northern peoples did, and what native shamans do.

In the final analysis and with some disquiet about appropriation of the past and indigenous sources, I think Greywolf's Druidry and Hrafnar's seidr are not a world apart from traditional shamanisms. Apart from similarities in cosmology and 'techniques', both an honest and open-minded perception of their own practices, and, for the most part, a distinct respect for indigenous shamanisms which avoids appropriation, exemplifies how these neo-Shamans give 'extra pay' to shamanisms. Can we also say, however, that neo-Shamanic engagement with the past gives 'extra pay' to, that is furthers our understanding of, prehistory (and history)? Despite any positive spiritual, social and personal results from their practices, the problem still remains for academics that neo-Shamanic interpretations of the past are problematic, in places a distortion, even an appropriation. Addressing this argument, the next chapter discusses in detail the sources used to reconstruct Celtic and Northern shamanisms, and evaluates the possibility that Celtic and Northern shamanisms existed.

4

'CELTIC' AND 'NORTHERN' SHAMANISMS?

Contesting the past

The use of the runes for divination was the province of a special class of shamans.

(Howard 1985: rear cover)

Caitlín Matthews and her colleagues are not really concerned with the past, so much as with the present and the future ... One aspect of this is her imposition upon Celtic lore of a lot of Native American religion, such as the totem, the spirit-quest and the shamanic vision. There are actually no precise parallels for any of these in ancient Celtic culture.

(Hutton 1991: 144)

Having presented ethnographic fragments of Druid and Heathen neo-Shamanisms and noted academic avoidance of such literature, practices and interpretations – even from the perspective of 'appropriation' – I examine, in this chapter, the historic and archaeological sources neo-Shamans cite as evidence for these shamanisms past. After discussing the Celtic and Northern sources in turn, I conclude by evaluating the usefulness of approaching both in terms of shamanisms.

Celtic shamanisms

Though it is not a widely accepted idea, a number of academics have, over the past hundred years or so, suggested Celtic religion may display shamanistic aspects (e.g. MacCulloch 1911; Powell 1958; Rees and Rees 1961; Eliade 1989 [1964]; Chadwick 1934, 1942, 1966; Ross 1967; Piggott 1968; Nagy 1981; Taylor 1994, 1996; L. Jones 1998; MacKillop 1998; Aldhouse Green 2001a, 2001b). Of these, note that most are non-archaeologists (focusing their attentions on literary sources), and that the suggestions of the trained archaeologists (strictly speaking, Piggott, Powell, Ross, Taylor) are by no means conventional in Iron Age archaeology. Drawing on literary sources and exploring other sources are academics from disciplines other than archaeology and history (e.g. Melia 1983; Lonigan

107

1985), and neo-Shamanic practitioners (e.g. Naddair 1990; Matthews 1991a, 1991b, 1991c, 1999; Cowan 1993; Conway 1995; Matthews 1995, 1996, 1997; Laurie and White 1997). Difficulties immediately encountered by these interest groups (whether they acknowledge it or not) concern the nature and definition of the concepts 'shamanism' (e.g. Wallis 1999) and 'Celt' (e.g. James 1999), and the nature and representation of the evidence used to argue for Celtic shamanistic practices. I begin by answering briefly the questions 'Who were the Celts?' and '*If there were* Celtic shamanisms (for this is by no means certain), what evidence remains of them?'

Before recent revisions of the term 'culture' and simplistic conflations of material remains with culture-boundaries, archaeologists suggested the Celts were a 'civilisation' of 'Indo-Europeans' who were the first to use iron and colonised Europe west of the Danube from *c.*1000 BCE (e.g. Powell 1958; and for a major critique of the idea, see James 1999). But strictly speaking the term 'Celt' is a linguistic convention, the Celtic language being divided into Brythonic (P) and Goidelic (Q), both of which survive in modern form in parts of Britain, Ireland and Brittany (e.g. Thurneysen 1993 [1946]). While they do not therefore denote a racial or ethnic category, 'Celt' and 'Celtic' as they are used today (among academics and in popular culture) implicitly refer to a distinct people and culture. However, in terms of material culture, in terms of the primary data available to archaeologists, it is difficult to distinguish the Celts from their neighbours. Indeed, according to both material culture and linguistic data, and by virtue of geographic distance, the Celts themselves were regionally variant: simply put, Gaulish Celts were similar to but not the same as Irish Celts (Moore 1994: 937). Although the 'linguistic' definition of the Celts is broad, it remains the accepted terminology – 'Celt' has an undeniable 'currency' – and archaeologists and Celticists have little choice but to battle with its generalising, nationalist (James 1999), but useful nature. In the popular realm, though, 'Celtic' is a buzz-word (see Chapman 1992; Bowman 1995b, 2000), frequently used unreservedly to mean many things, from the Neolithic passage tomb at Newgrange (e.g. Graves 1961 [1948]: 101–105) to silver jewellery and rock music

Combination of the term 'Celtic' with 'shamanism' therefore doubles the contention and at first appears contradictory. According to classical authors, the Celts[1] were 'noble savages'; they had a strict and complex social hierarchy with all the attributes of 'civilised' agricultural peoples. According to culture historians, they had 'evolved' considerably from the 'simple' and 'savage' society associated with shamanisms. Though current archaeological theory avoids such loaded terms as 'civilisation' and deconstructs notions of social evolution and similar racist, elitist approaches to the past, academia struggles to loosen the tie with these ingrained concepts. Many neo-Shamanic publications reinforce them all the more strongly because they rely on outmoded classic texts (e.g. MacCulloch 1911) which reproduce them, and because neo-Shamanisms are predominantly unfamiliar with contemporary archaeological/culture theory –

though not exclusively; I have pointed out exceptions such as the Druid Greywolf whose comments on 'Celtic' and 'shamanism' are sensitive to the difficulties. For academics I suggest the 'elements of shamanisms' here advocated (see previous citations and p.11) would be the best line of approach to the evidence, to elucidate how Celtic religion was shamanistic, if at all, and provide political and geographic specificity. Certainly, the complexity of Celtic society is no judge as to whether it was shamanistic; aspects of some religions are best understood when approached with the term 'shamanisms' even if their character is not what is conventionally[2] considered shamanistic, that is occurring in hunter-gatherer[3] societies (Eliade 1989 [1964]: 375–379; De Rios 1974, 1984; Emboden 1978, 1989). From this standpoint I explore some of – for this is by no means a definitive or exhaustive account – the possible evidence for Celtic shamanisms in two parts: first, sources used by academics and neo-Shamans, and second, data used exclusively by neo-Shamans.

Academic approaches to Celtic shamanisms

Descriptions of the Celts by classical authors, however subjective and politically motivated, may suggest shamanistic practices. Strabo refers to the Celtic intellectual-religious caste which had three divisions (Ross 1967: 80). The *vates* were practitioners of divination, sacrifice and poetry, the *bards* were poets and storytellers, and the *druids* were associated with philosophy and theology. Caesar records that druids were also teachers, healers and judges (Hutton 1991: 170). Clearly the distinction between all three is unclear (Chadwick 1966: 23) and their activities are closely linked. Indeed, with Roman suppression the druid's political function was fulfilled by the poet. Relying only on descriptions by classical authors, the vates, bards and druids assumed offices which might be described as shamanistic. The word 'vate', for instance, is argued to be cognate with the Irish *fathi*, meaning a prophet or seer, from the root meaning 'inspired' or 'ecstatic' (Powell 1958: 183). Eliade mentions: 'the *fili* (Irish poet) ate raw bull's flesh, drank the blood, then slept wrapped in the hide; during his sleep "invisible friends" gave him the answer to the question that was troubling him' (Eliade 1989 [1964]: 382). Eliade may be referring to the 'bull dream', a rite of divination described in *Togail Bruidne Da Derga* (Hutton 1991: 193), according to which druids in Ireland chose each king of Tara. The druid gorged on the flesh of a sacrificed bull, then 'fell into a trance while incantations were recited over him, and on recovery he was able to prognosticate' (Powell 1958: 183). MacCulloch, similarly, discusses bardic 'trance utterances' or 'illumination by rhymes', which caused ecstatic states (MacCulloch 1911: 249). He also mentions the Scottish Highlands *taghairm* ceremony, in which people bound in cow skins were left in a desolate place where spirits inspired their dreams (MacCulloch 1911: 249–250, see also Spence 1995 [1945]). A comparable rite in the ninth-century Irish *Sanas Cormaic* (Cormac's Glossary) induces the poetic inspiration and prophecy of *imbas forosnai* (great light/knowledge which enlightens/illuminates). Having chewed the flesh of a pig, cat or dog and then placed it on a flagstone near a door, the *fili* (also *filé*, plural *filid*) or 'poet' chants over it, and both his palms, asking that his sleep will not disturbed. He then puts his palms on his cheeks and sleeps for three days and three nights, after which time he may achieve *imbas forosnai* (MacCulloch 1911: 248; MacKillop 1998: 239). Perhaps the meat was sacred and contained an entheogenic substance which induced altered consciousness, or perhaps, as suggested by Karl and Minard (2002), the consumption of excessive quantities of carnivore liver induced *Hypervitaminosis A*, with the altered consciousness-associated symptoms of migraine, drowsiness, diplopia, nausea and vomiting, increased intracranial pressure, limitation of motion, cranial nerve palsies and desquamation of the palms and soles – the latter being intriguing since there is an emphasis on the palms in the extract from *Sanas Cormaic*.

These descriptions, though not entirely reliable – particularly because they are regionally and chronologically diverse – may display shamanistic aspects, although these interpretations are tentative at best. Altered consciousness was, perhaps, induced by such circumstances as ingesting bull's flesh and blood (and perhaps the entheogen it contained), by chanting, and/or by isolation. In this way, the subject achieved poetic inspiration while sleeping and thereby divined knowledge. Analogously, ethnography records how traditional shamans often use 'sleep' and 'dreaming' as descriptions of trance experiences (Eliade 1989 [1964]; Lewis-Williams 1992: 59; Sales 1992: 26; Whitley 1992: 97). Added to this ethnographic analogy is the data from neuro-psychological experiments on trance subjects which has been much debated in rock art research (see Wallis 2002b for a review), and, perhaps surprisingly, applied to Iron Age coinage. Creighton (1995, 2000) argues, quite persuasively, that geometric and distorted anthropomorphic imagery on some of these coins is derived from trance experiences, possibly influenced by entheogens (see also Green 1998: 200). Evidence for entheogens in Britain (though not explicitly their use) is not uncommon (e.g. Tomlinson and Hall 1996: table 2, 6.2): large quantities of henbane (*Hyoscyamus niger*) and the seeds of the opium poppy (*Papaver somniferum*) were found in the Late Iron Age and Roman levels at Farmoor (Thames), and the early first millennium BCE site of Wallingford (Oxon.), respectively (Creighton 2000: 52); and on the Continent, traces of cannabis were found in the Hochdorf Hallstatt D wagon-burial (Sherratt 1991: 52). In whatever ways trances were induced, altered consciousness and coin production were, Creighton contends, agentic in the negotiation and contestation of power, with the coin as a whole – its colour and composition dictated by precious metals, its indication of status and wealth, its depiction of mythological imagery – beguiling those who came into contact with it; this idea resonating I think with Gell's theory of art as a 'technology of enchantment' (Gell 1998). The least convincing evidence for shamanisms here may be the coins themselves, since unlike rock art, where often huge and complex panels may be approached productively in terms of shamanisms and the universality of human neuro-psychological processes (e.g. Lewis-Williams and Dowson 1999 [1989]), coins display only limited imagery in a compact medium and so arguably do not provide a sufficient dataset. Perhaps more convincing is the way in which Creighton connects the 'fortification' imagery often seen during migraine experiences – a series of chevrons appearing on the inner curve of a crescent – to the basketry compass-work on the Latchmere Heath mirror (Figure 4.1), suggesting:

> [T]he engraving of such complex patterns on what we can presume to be polished metal would add a shimmering appearance to this image [cf. Gell's 'technology of enchantment' once more]. The association with mirrors is particularly telling, as these are often associated with passages into other realms.
>
> (Creighton 2000: 49, my parenthesis)

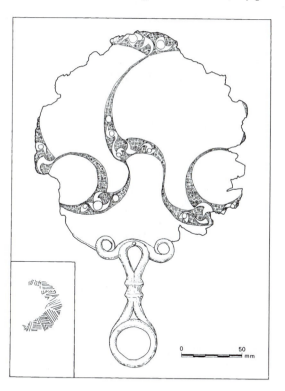

Figure 4.1 Basketry compass-work on the Latchmere Heath mirror compared with inset of the 'fortification' imagery often seen during migraine experiences (a series of chevrons appearing on the inner curve of a crescent)

Source: Line drawing by Sophia Jundi.

Whatever its shortcomings, Creighton's analysis is the most detailed archaeo-logical argument for a form of Celtic shamanism to date, and unlike the literary sources, numismatic data might be coupled profitably with other local (in space and time) archaeological finds to provide a more complete picture.

Religious knowledge among the Celts, then, according to various academic interpretations of both historic and archaeological material, was plausibly 'achieved through trances, frenzies or stimulated inspiration of some kind' (Powell 1958: 183). But there are other references to the druids in the literary sources: arguing for Celtic shamanisms, Ross recounts how '[t]he chief Druid of the King of Ireland is described as wearing a bull's hide and a white speckled bird's head-dress with fluttering wings, a typical shamanistic appearance' (Ross 1967: 83). Donning this equipment, *Mog Ruith* 'rose up, in company with the fire, into the air and the heavens' (Ross 1967: 333).[4] The costume may be attributed to his shamanic animal helpers, and the scene of levitation is perhaps a description of a shamanic experience. On this note, Piggott suggests:

> [H]ere and in other ritual and ecstatic contexts of the use of bull-hides, we may indeed have a fragment from a very archaic substrate of belief. Here too we might place such evidence as the sacrificial deposits of horse-hides or ox-hides, represented by the surviving skulls and leg bones, recently identified in the votive find in La Tene itself: this 'head-and-hoofs' practice, known from the late third millennium BCE onwards in South Russia, was a feature of recent shamanism in the Altai and elsewhere.
>
> (Piggott 1968: 164)

Furthermore, Tacitus describes the druids in Britain; their 'blood stained groves, the howling priests, their arms uplifted to heaven' (Ross 1967: 83). Tacitus's statement exemplifies the ambiguous nature of the classical sources: he may simply be misrepresenting the 'savage' Celts for political ends. But, howling and screaming may refer to shamanistic chanting or singing, a common technique of trance induction. The posture of the priests is also interesting in this example, being characteristic of many inspirational reli-gions, and it is often assumed by shamans (e.g. Lewis-Williams and Dowson 1999 [1989]: 77; see also discussion of the 'Cernnunos' figure on the Gundestrup cauldron, below).

Ross, Powell, MacCulloch, Eliade and even Piggott all suggest that examination of the sources suggests a Celtic priesthood who were not unlike the shamans of the North Eurasiatic zone. Indeed the evidence cited so far indicates Celtic priests utilised 'techniques of ecstasy' such as dancing, chanting, ingesting entheogens and undertaking shape-shifting soul flights to obtain 'special' knowledge. While I think it safe to suggest these activi-ties are shaman*istic* and that seeing them in this light might be advantageous for approaching Celtic religions, it would be stretching the interpretation too far to argue the Celtic priesthood consisted of 'Celtic shamans'. Such a suggestion would require that Celtic religious practices are *socio-politically contextualised* in space and time. Shamanisms become vague and misunderstood when the importance of shamans' socio-political specificity is ignored. Exploring the evidence for Celtic shamanisms as I have done is useful up to a point; then social, historical, spatial and temporal idiosyncrasies must be elaborated upon to elucidate whether the evidence is suitable for positing 'Celtic' or any other 'shamanisms'. That, however, is not a task for this volume.

Neo-Shamanic interpretations of Celtic shamanisms

Popular 'neo-Shamanic' literature on Celtic shamanisms often cites the same evidence described above, but also goes one step further to use Celtic vernacular sources, materials too problematic for consideration by academics because of their wide chronological distribution and the hazards of translation. Most often utilised are the Welsh manuscripts *Canu Taliesin*, the Book or Song of Taliesin and *Hanes Taliesin*, the Story of Taliesin, both referring to the poet Taliesin, who may have existed, and which contain poems dealing with prophecy, fantastic imagery and supernatural themes. Because of the questionable historical origins of these themes, the reliability of such fragmentary evidence, and because of the difficulty of translating medieval Welsh into English, interpretation of the Taliesin manuscripts has, largely, been avoided. Except that is, by 'Celtic shaman' and researcher of the 'Western mystery traditions' for well over three decades, John Matthews, who, with contributions from his wife Caitlín (Figure 4.2), devotes a book to shamanic interpretations of the translated Taliesin manuscripts (Matthews 1991a; similar, though less extensive, work has since been undertaken by Shallcrass 1997b). Matthews confesses, 'much has been taken for granted ... hidden meanings have indeed been sought out ... we have often had to take a leap in the dark' (Matthews 1991a: 5), but this caveat aside, the main problem with interpreting these sources, in terms of shamanisms or otherwise, is the reliability of the manuscripts themselves.

Due to ambiguities in translation, eighteenth-century 'pseudo-Celticists' tailored manuscripts (fabricating some passages) to fit neatly their ideas of 'primitive' religion (Hutton 1991: 320). These mistranslations later appeared in Lady Charlotte Guest's *Mabinogion*, probably the most widely read of Welsh mythological tales. Indeed, the *Mabinogion* greatly influenced Robert Graves's (1961 [1948]) *The White Goddess*, a book of immense popularity among contemporary Pagans, though predominantly regarded as speculative by academics[5] (indeed Graves is said to have regretted writing the work: Hutton 1991: 145). Around the same time, Williams (published in English in 1968, somewhat later than his 1940s' research) scrutinised the

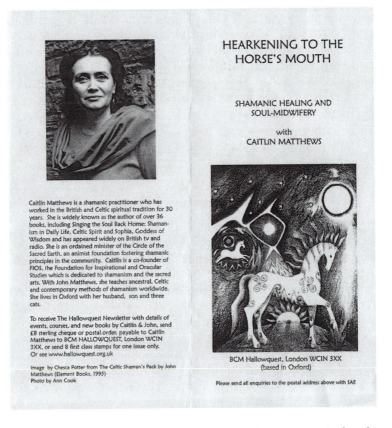

HEARKENING TO THE HORSE'S MOUTH

SHAMANIC HEALING AND SOUL-MIDWIFERY

with
CAITLÍN MATTHEWS

Caitlín Matthews is a shamanic practitioner who has worked in the British and Celtic spiritual tradition for 30 years. She is widely known as the author of over 36 books, including Singing the Soul Back Home: Shamanism in Daily Life, Celtic Spirit and Sophia, Goddess of Wisdom and has appeared widely on British tv and radio. She is an ordained minister of the Circle of the Sacred Earth, an animist foundation fostering shamanic principles in the community. Caitlín is a co-founder of FIOS, the Foundation for Inspirational and Oracular Studies which is dedicated to shamanism and the sacred arts. With John Matthews, she teaches ancestral, Celtic and contemporary methods of shamanism worldwide. She lives in Oxford with her husband, son and three cats.

To receive The Hallowquest Newsletter with details of events, courses, and new books by Caitlín & John, send £8 sterling cheque or postal order, payable to Caitlín Matthews to BCM HALLOWQUEST, London WC1N 3XX, or send 8 first class stamps for one issue only. Or see www.hallowquest.org.uk

Image by Chesca Potter from The Celtic Shaman's Pack by John Matthews (Element Books, 1995)
Photo by Ann Cook

BCM Hallowquest, London WC1N 3XX
(based in Oxford)

Please send all enquiries to the postal address above with SAE

Figure 4.2 Leaflet advertising Caitlín Matthews's neo-Shamanic practice based in Oxford, which offers shamanic healing and soul-midwifery, based on 'Celtic shamanism'

Source: *Hearkening to the Horse's Mouth* leaflet, copyright Caitlín Matthews 2002. Title image by Chesca Potter. Photo by Ann Cook.

Canu Taliesin and showed they are a mixed bag of dates and orthography and only a small number are actually attributable to Taliesin, a quasi-mythical figure (Hutton 1991: 320). The earliest *Canu Taliesin* manuscript is thirteenth century (1275) and Hutton argues that the orthography of the 'mystical' poems it contains – with which Matthews is primarily concerned – is in the style of the twelfth or thirteenth century, well after the Christian conversion and therefore unlikely to contain shamanistic references. He attributes the manuscript to the Welsh *Gogynfeirdd*, a group of 'fairly early poets' (1080–1350) who revived earlier poetic themes in a nationalist reaction to the Norman incursions. Socio-political change was so rapid at this time it is thought these bards were linguistically and culturally very different from those who preceded them by only two centuries, and that they were, moreover, devoutly Christian; it seems there is little connection between the *Gogynfeirdd* and the pagan past, and that even if there were, their Christian prerogative would have censored any vestiges of paganism. The *Hanes Taliesin* is probably even less reliable than the *Canu*, the earliest manuscript being sixteenth century, although, like the 'battle' poems of the *Canu Taliesin*, its content and style suggest ninth-century (or earlier) origins (Hutton 1991: 322).

While supernatural themes (discussed below) in these manuscripts at first glance provide some persuasive data for a form of Celtic shamanism, then, such interpretations are immediately thwarted by issues of the manuscripts' historic reliability, subject as they are to the lens of translation, confusing genealogy, questionable antiquity and the hands of Christian writers. Indeed, characters in the *Hanes Taliesin* are apparently deified from their human or semi-human origins: Ceridwen, for instance, appears in no other early Welsh literature; Hutton argues she was created for this tale alone and that the *Gogynfeirdd* turned her into a semi-deified muse. She has, more recently and paradoxically, been fully deified by neo-Shamans as an archetypal Welsh pagan goddess. Considering how the *Gogynfeirdd* emphasised and played on their powers of inspiration and prophecy (Hutton 1991: 322), it is no surprise that the *Hanes* is infused with such themes as *Ceridwen* and her cauldron of inspiration, and that these themes, in turn, resonate with neo-Shamans.

All things considered, Hutton concludes:

> [the] supernatural beings of the *Gogynfeirdd* are of no interest to the student of pre-Christian beliefs ... But, as has always been recognised, paganism did bequeath an enormous legacy of superstitions, literary and artistic images and folk rituals to the culture of later ages.
>
> (Hutton 1991: 324)

As is recorded, for example, in the research of Lewis Spence (1995 [1945]). Hutton rightly proposes the obscure, supernatural themes of the mystical poems cannot be subjected to literal historic translation. And, as a historian concerned with finding documented proof, he finds there is none to demonstrate the *Gogynfeirdd* or their Christian predecessors knew of earlier texts or traditions. Rather than end the story here, though, there remains arguably the possibility of (1) a role for folk/oral transmission, and (2) interpretations which avoid literal translations of myth, both of which might still be worthwhile considering. Though we know little of sixth- to thirteenth-century oral traditions in Wales, and though I am by no means a scholar of Celtic languages, I will speculate more than Hutton does on the possibility (though not the probability) that the *Gogynfeirdd* might have inherited shamanic themes in their work via oral transmission, and, although there is no known evidence of it, other manuscripts. Entertaining the idea that Taliesin was potentially a shaman may give a stronger impression of the extent to which Matthews has speculated in his interesting and extensively researched work. Alongside this shamanistic approach to Taliesin, I consider the Irish hero Fionn MacCumhail, for whom there are more reliable manuscripts.

A starting point is that, in the case of the Taliesin manuscripts, and as supported by similar themes in other myths, the shamanistic approach mentioned above (see also p.11) might tease out shamanistic specifics without generalising shamanisms, the Celts or decontextualising the sources. While the fantastic style of the poetry demands that meaning is open to a variety of interpretations, a shamanistic approach perhaps provides a useful interpretative entrance point. When assessing the fantastic imagery of the 'mystical' poems, for example, it is worth noting that shamans consistently have unusual ways of describing trance experience. We might call them 'metaphors', but to shamans these metaphors, such as 'death', are real, lived experiences: Bushman shamans, for instance, believe they *'die'* in trance (Katz 1982: 116), and this belief must be taken *seriously* (to take it literally would miss the point). 'Metaphor' is a problematic term extracted from Western literary discourse which does not do justice to non-Western, non-literary shamanic experiences. In recognising this limitation, 'metaphor' may remain a useful term for explaining alien shamanic experiences in terms understandable to Westerners. In this regard, aspects of the Celtic mythologies may contain 'metaphoric' meanings which allude to shamanisms, allusions the Christian writers were unaware of. The Taliesin poems describe superhuman feats and supernatural themes which may represent metaphoric pagan-shamanistic meanings. Of course these cannot be equated with Bushman or other shamanisms, but they can be compared and contrasted with them. The sixteenth-century *Hanes Taliesin* text (in ninth-century or earlier style) recalls the origin of Taliesin, which, as Matthews proposes, may be a metaphoric description of Taliesin's shamanic initiation in his pre-shamanic form as Gwion Bach. The aged sorceress Ceridwen brews a cauldron intended to confer inspiration on her ugly son Afagddu ('utter darkness'). Gwion Bach watches over the cauldron, but a boiling drop of the brew lands on his finger. He sticks the painful finger in his mouth and immediately obtains wisdom. Ceridwen is enraged and Gwion flees from her, transforming himself into a hare, a fish, a bird and a grain of wheat. Ceridwen, for her part, changes into a greyhound, an otter, a hawk and a hen, respectively. As the hen, she swallows the grain of wheat that is Gwion who is then reborn from Ceridwen as Taliesin ('shining brow'), the inspired poet (Williams 1968: xvi–xvii).

The *Hanes Taliesin* is argued, conventionally and at face value, to be a telling of fantastic deeds, nothing more. Another possibility is that shaman-istic aspects may be described in the story: the ingestion of a magic brew, the attainment of great knowledge/inspiration-ecstasy, shape-shifting into animal helpers, battling with an enemy in the supernatural realm, and the shamanic initiation of rebirth. Despite Matthews's detailed interpretation of Taliesin as a shaman, and identification of other possibly shamanistic themes, it is impossible to avoid the enigmatic nature of the Taliesin poems, some of which are written in the style of the *Gogynfeirdd*, all of which have questionable antiquity, chronology and originality, making them poor examples with which to argue for Celtic shamanisms. The Irish myths of Fionn MacCumhail in the Fenian Cycle (one of the four major cycles of early Irish myth), on the other hand, parallel that of Taliesin, have firmer dating (though still well within the Christian period with earliest written sources from the eighth century), and though the mythology is equally fantastical to the modern mind, it may display similar shamanistic themes. In one medieval tale the hero Fionn is taught druidry by Finegas (Fionn the Seer), who catches the 'salmon of knowledge' and entrusts Fionn to cook it. While cooking, a blister grows on the salmon's skin. It bursts and splashes Fionn, who thrusts the burning thumb in his mouth. Immediately, Fionn achieves great knowledge. This incident marks the beginning of Fionn's 'seer-poetry' (O'hOgain 1988: 17). There are variations on the theme of Fionn's achieving supernatural knowledge in the *Feis Tighe Chonáin* of the fourteenth or fifteenth century, though its themes link it back to the eighth. In one account, Fionn is hunting near a well and *sí*-dwelling (burial mound) guarded by three otherworld maidens. The *sí*-dwelling opens and, on entering, the maidens pour well water into Fionn's mouth, which confers on him inspirational wisdom (O'hOgain 1988: 133–134). The motifs of a 'wise-drink' and a journey to the otherworld are recurrent in tales about Fionn, and a consistent element of shamanic practice is, of course, the profound journey to a spirit world which may be facilitated by the ingestion of entheogens.

Shamans worldwide describe and recollect past trance experiences in stories using fantastic metaphors (e.g. Halifax 1979), and the Celtic 'otherworld' describes a comparable realm of other than human persons (see also Karjala 1992). Fionn's eating or drinking of a substance which confers knowledge may be a metaphor for the ingestion of an entheogen. His initial experience may represent a shamanic initiation, and entering the otherworld via the *sí*-dwelling may represent a metaphor for entering trance (see also O'hOgain 1988: 67). Likened to some indigenous shamans, Fionn is described as a diviner and prophet (O'hOgain 1988: 133): whenever he sucked his thumb (burnt by the cooking salmon) 'that which was unknown to him would be revealed' (O'hOgain 1988: 56), a practice perhaps similar to the divination procedures of *teinm laída* and *díchetal do chennaib* at which Fionn is said to be adept and which focus on the hands (MacKillop 1998). A link between Fionn and shamanic ritual has been suggested – 'Fionn had the function of visiting the realm of the dead in order to gain knowledge. This is a shamanic practice ... and Irish tradition ... furnishes much evidence of it' (O'hOgain 1988: 17, 21; see also Nagy 1981) – though O'hOgain does not embellish upon this general contention to provide spatio-temporal or socio-religious specificities of these practices among the diverse communities in 'Celtic' Ireland.

In the light of these comments, I speculate that the legends of Taliesin (unreliable) and Fionn (more reliable) originally described shamanic experiences in the form of fantastic 'metaphors'. Comparable figures are the Irish Cú Chulainn and Oisin, and the Welsh Pwyll and Gwydion. Recurrent shamanistic-type motifs in all these myths might suggest the Taliesin manuscripts speak of earlier and forgotten shamanic traditions, pre-dating the manuscripts themselves. Moreover, this multiple-myth evidence, despite its difficulties, at least provides further support in terms of quantity and reliability for Matthews's thesis. Hutton thinks the deified Taliesin characters were fabricated by the *Gogynfeirdd*, but this does not rule out the possibility that these figures were perhaps once mortal persons who undertook heroic deeds, or perhaps Celtic shamans who journeyed to the otherworld and then related their trance experiences to their communities through storytelling (see also L. Jones 1998: 67–68). The descriptions, by virtue of their otherworld origins, were inevitably fantastic, and the tales became invested with greater imagination and inventiveness in subsequent accounts. When eventually written down, the underlying shamanic structure to the poems perhaps went unrecognised by the devoutly Christian scribes. If they were aware of the pagan meanings of such obscure imagery, it is perhaps more likely they would have suppressed or destroyed the poems.

As is apparent from these myths, a recurring motif in Celtic myth and religion is the ability to shape-shift, and neo-Shamanic authors such as Matthews rely heavily on shape-shifting as evidence for shamanisms, since the metamorphosis of shamans into animals and other beings is common worldwide. Like Taliesin, Fintan, the druidic teacher of Fionn, is described as changing his form into 'a salmon, an eagle and a hawk' (O'hOgain 1988: 17). Also, the Irish Amairgen sings a 'ritual chant' boasting profound knowledge and shape-shifting experiences (MacCulloch 1911: 356). It is thought Fionn was King Mongan of Ireland (O'hOgain 1988: 21) and Mongan shape-shifted into the forms 'of every beast ... a deer ... a salmon ... a roving wolf ... a man' (MacCulloch 1911: 358). Various descriptions suggest the druids were also capable of shape-shifting. Assuming the form of a woman allowed the druid Fer Fidail to carry off a maiden. Another druid took the form of 'fair' Niamh to deceive Cú Chulainn, and the priestess of Sena could transform into animals (MacCulloch 1911: 322–323). His pejorative terminology and outmoded assumptions aside, MacCulloch suggests the druids were shamans who 'hypnotised' people into believing in druidic shape-shifting, and 'hallucinated' others into thinking they had transformed, 'as Red Indian shamans have been known to do' (MacCulloch 1911: 323).

Celtic literature is not the only place where plausible evidence for shape-shifting is found. Iron Age iconography and metalwork are full of the inter-connecting forms of humans and animals which, Green (1986) suggests, represent shape-shifting gods and heroes. The Gaulish deity Cernnunos is particularly associated with shape-shifting and is frequently depicted with antlers, associated with snakes, and in one example at Cirencester god and snake fuse (Green 1986: 197). Perhaps the depictions represent a shaman's trance experience of being transformed into spirit-helpers, since shamans worldwide show themselves as therianthropes in their art. Rock art of South African San shamans, for instance, depicts transformed shamans as buck-headed snakes, and, interestingly, the similar ram-horned snake is an image frequently associated with Cernnunos. Again, these two are not directly comparable but a neuro-psychological, somatic, link is not implausible. The connection between Celtic shape-shifting and shamanisms has been suggested by a number of academics (e.g. Powell 1958: 183; Green 1986), so perhaps interpreting Celtic iconography and the vernacular texts as evidence for the shape-shifting shaman is not beyond the remit of acceptability. Certainly, the Celts had an intimate relationship with their natural surroundings: an integral part of Celtic religions, according to Green, was respecting the 'spiritual' (or what 'the West' would call 'super'-natural) elements residing in nature. They honoured qualities of strength, speed, courage, virility, ferocity and cunning visible in the wild animals around them (Green 1986: 167). These qualities are also honoured by shamans who are empowered by them when they transform into animal helpers.

Alongside the Taliesin 'evidence', the Gundestrup Cauldron marks the neo-Shamanic evidence for Celtic shamanisms *par excellence*. The god 'Cernnunos' and his attendant animals are thought to be depicted on this silver vessel found in northern Jutland, Denmark in 1891 (Collis 1997 [1984]: 11), which was ritually dismantled and deposited in a bog. Possible 'Celtic' influences in the Gundestrup Cauldron's imagery may lend support to the notion of Celtic shamanisms. Matthews thinks the imagery depicts the 'World of the Shaman'; in particular, a shaman figure accompanied by animal spirit-helpers and other mythical creatures, and dead warriors being brought back to life in a cauldron of rebirth (Matthews 1991a: 12–13, 35, 38). Indeed, the posture of 'Cernnunos' seems significant, and suggestive if not of ecstatic trance, then of deep meditation – seated with legs crossed, arms raised, with a torc and ram-headed serpent in either hand. Taylor notes the figure is 'sexually ambiguous', perhaps related to ritualised transvestism, and mentions this alongside 'steppe shamanism' and 'tantric yoga', 'as interlinked systems of ritual specialization in the Eurasian later Iron Age' (Taylor 1996: 269, see also Taylor 1994: 381, 397–398, 400–402). This statement somewhat homogenises the issues, and the unqualified use of 'transvestite' is deeply problematic (discussed further in Conclusion). But I think Taylor's discussion of multiple genders and shamanisms[6] to be worthy of further study, and his suggestion that the silversmiths 'were ritual experts' themselves, who may have 'presided in the rites' in which the cauldron was involved also to be interesting, especially since the powers and social standing of smiths, among other metal-workers, are often closely affiliated or contrasted with shamans in some Siberian and Mongolian communities (e.g. Eliade 1989 [1964]; Vitebsky 1995a).[7]

In addition to these shamanic interpretations, to the upper right of 'Cernnunos' is an image usually identified as a boy riding a dolphin (e.g. Megaw and Megaw 1990), though the clear scales and grooved fins on the creature suggest it is actually a fish. Perhaps, adding to the shamanistic interpretation of the cauldron's imagery, this depiction can be read as an 'underwater' metaphor for trance experience: among South African and North American shamans, the experience of entering trance was described as submergence, drowning or the feeling of going underwater (Lewis-Williams and Dowson 1999 [1989]: 54–55; Whitley 1992: 97). Of the apparently non-Celtic depictions – the majority of the imagery – the cauldron has elephants on one plate: the dots covering them may portray realistic adornments, as elephants are decorated in parts of the world today, and/or they might equally refer to the geometric 'entoptics' (Lewis-Williams and Dowson 1988) perceived in some trance experiences. In addition, the 'scene' depicted on the base of the cauldron (Figure 4.3) is interpreted by Collis (1997 [1984]: 12) as a small figure slaying a bull (bull-slaying deriving from Iranian mythology [Taylor 1994: 402]), but since the sword is aimed at a dog and the human is perhaps only 'looking' at the bull, it is also possible this is a shaman figure on an otherworld journey who is attended by animal helpers, including the typical bull and dog motifs of Celtic mythology, as well as what may plausibly be interpreted as a lizard – a prominent animal helper among a variety of shamans (e.g. Whitley 1992) due to its liminal nature (being reborn each time it sheds its skin, darting in and out of cracks in rocks, able to re-grow lost parts of its tail, and so on).

Plant motifs on the cauldron are not mentioned in the literature I have encountered, but since the shape of the 'leaves' may represent deadly nightshade (*Atropa belladonna*), a species of ivy, henbane (*Hyoscyamus niger*) or mandrake (*M. officionarum*), perhaps the plant is entheogenic (linking here with research on coinage by Creighton 2000, discussed above). These plants have been linked (convincingly or otherwise) to the ecstatic sabbats of medieval European witchcraft which may have involved out-of-body journeys to the supernatural realm (Harner 1973b; Heiser 1987). The Gundestrup plants are also reminiscent of the entheogenic seed pod of the opium poppy (*Papaver somniferum*) – particularly those depicted either side of the serpent, the 'nipple'-topped head of the 'magic' mushroom (*Psilocybe semilanceata*) – especially those present between Cernnunos's antlers, and the Celts might also have made use of the fly agaric (*Amanita muscaria*) fungus. While this may be stretching the interpretation of such a stylised motif far enough, Graves goes further, with problematic notions of culture contact and diffusion, when he suggests *Amanita*

Figure 4.3 Base of the Gundestrup Cauldron. Traditionally interpreted as imagery
of a bull sacrifice, the human figure (whose sword points at the dog and
who is looking only at the bull) may be a shaman on out-of-body travel
accompanied by animal spirit-helpers

Source: Line drawing by Sophia Jundi.

was the 'gift' wrapped in straw by the Britons and passed from 'tribe to tribe',
to eventually reach the ecstatic oracle of Apollo in Delphi (Graves 1969: 3–4).
Nonetheless, the use of entheogens by the Celts cannot be ruled out. Apart
from the wise-drink motif linked with Fionn, there is also mention of a druidic
'drink of oblivion', linked by MacCulloch to shamanism, ecstasy and hallucina-
tions (MacCulloch 1911: 324). According to Pliny, the Celts were
knowledgeable about the magical properties of plants (Pliny, *The Natural
Histories* XVI, XIV, cited in Kendrick 1927: 88–89); therefore, it would be
reasonable to suggest they were familiar with their medicinal *and* entheogenic
properties.

The Gundestrup Cauldron possibly displays shamanistic aspects, and although
there may be 'Celtic' influences which make this ideal evidence for neo-Shamanic
interpretations of Celtic shamanism, Celtic origins are uncertain: probably made
during the second or first century BCE and with apparently 'Gaulish' representa-

tions, it was first thought to have been made by Celtic smiths in France, while finds in the southern Balkans now point towards origins in the Black Sea/Central Europe but with 'Celtic' influences. Imagery on the silver cups from a burial at Agighiol, Romania, on the other hand, is stylistically resonant with that on the Gundestrup Cauldron, and although I have not encountered such interpretations in any published literature, I think shamanistic motifs may be prominent in this example also (Figure 4.4). The antlers of one deer appear exaggerated, perhaps reflecting a somatic trance experience of transformation and attenuation; and the multiple legs of another hint at polymelia, the experience of being multi-limbed; while the large eyes of the creatures depicted might indicate subjects' dilated pupils after entheogen ingestion. Such an interpretation might be supported if the original contents of the cup were known. Returning to Northern Europe and the Gundestrup Cauldron, the extent to which this source provides viable evidence for Celtic shamanisms is certainly unclear, although it is worth considering that the 'barbarian tribes' of Europe were not separated entities and likely traded products and ideas. As Taylor says:

> [The Gundestrup Cauldron] in many ways encapsulates the whole problem of our understanding of Thracian, Dacian, and Scythian society. Put simply, these societies were not tightly bounded. On the one hand, they existed within a developing world system with many shared elements and on a long time-scale, and, on the other hand, they were composed of a plethora of small, local, short-lived cultural groupings within which these elements were given meaning.
>
> (Taylor 1994: 401)

Figure 4.4 Silver 'cups' from a burial, Agighiol, Romania. Shamanistic themes might include dilated pupils (induced by entheogens) and a multi-limbed deer (the trance experience of polymelia) with elongated antlers (the trance experience of transformation and attenuation)

Source: Line drawing by Sophia Jundi, after Collis 1997 [1984]: 1b.

Neo-Shamanic authors tend to focus on the Gundestrup Cauldron as archaeological evidence for Celtic shamanisms, although Matthews briefly mentions other examples. There is the Temple of Nodens at Lydney, Gloucester, with possible evidence for shamanic 'sweat lodge' conditions (Matthews 1991a: 56–59; see also Reide-Wolfe 1997 and Weir 2000 on Celtic sweat lodges). There is also Iron Age rock art in Valcomonica, Italy, which could be interpreted in terms of shamanisms (e.g. Matthews 1991a: 43): I suggest there are human figures, their arms raised (possibly an ecstatic pose), which have antlers (perhaps transforming into deer helpers) and strange protrusions (which may be manifestations of supernatural power) from their elongated (a classic sensation of trance experience) bodies. Further, an intriguing and widespread Iron Age practice not mentioned elsewhere, to my knowledge, as plausibly shamanistic, is the depositing of different species of animal bones arranged to represent a composite creature; a cattle head, horse torso, legs of pig and sheep, and so on (Hill 1995; see also Green 1997: 87). J.D. Hill[8] (pers. com.) suggests that in examples such as this, a shamanistic exploration might be rewarding.

Clearly, there are many lines of 'Celtic' evidence that *can* be interpreted 'shamanically', but whether they *are* shamanic, rather than something else, is difficult to assess; all too often, the data 'fits' a number of interpretations. Leaving aside the possible use of entheogens and sweat lodges, it is shape-shifting which is most commonly used to argue for Celtic shamanisms, but it is impossible to argue convincingly that Celtic shape-shifting represents a form of Celtic shamanism absolutely. There are shape-shifting references in early Irish literature which might not suggest shamanistic associations, for instance. In *The Dream of Angus*, the otherworld being Cáer and her supernatural followers take on bird form (Gantz 1981: 111–112). In *The Wasting Sickness of Cú Chulainn*, the hero attacks two otherworld swans who later return in human form and beat him (Gantz 1981: 157). Shape-shifting in these cases is simply attributable to supernatural beings, not shamanisms. On the other hand, elements in the same stories may also be interpreted as shamanistic (see also Rees and Rees 1961: 236). Cáer is also a magician and wears a 'swan cloak' (Ross 1967: 306), and since MacKillop (1998: 380) points out that Ibormeith, 'yew berry', is the agnomen of Cáer, I might speculate that the toxic, if not entheogenic, properties of the yew seed are of significance here.[9] Could the wearing of the cloak and transformation into a bird be a metaphor for entering trance and shape-shifting into a spirit-helper? In *The Conception of Cú Chulainn*, there is sleep-inducing singing, and in one translation the birds he attacks submerge under water when one of them is hit (Ross 1967: 307). Would it be too far-fetched to suggest that a technique of ecstasy and underwater metaphor for entering trance are hinted at in this story?

Ultimately, I think it would be asking too much of the Welsh and Irish sources and the ethnographic material rigidly to argue for shamanistic associations. As L. Jones suggests, '[t]he belief that there is a pre-Christian religious system underlying the literatures of the medieval Celtic countries is one tool for reading those literatures, but not the only one' (L. Jones 1998: 229). And, as Hutton notes, the fantastic themes of the Taliesin manuscripts are not exclusively Welsh (nor, in my own example, are the feats of Fionn exclusively Irish): 'the marvellous child, the person who is swallowed and then reborn, the accidental tasting of a dish which confers great gifts' are all common in other Euro-Asian mythologies (Hutton 1991: 322). It would be ridiculous to propose all these manifestations are a result of the prevalence of shamanisms (though Indo-European scholars might instead propose a shamanistic *origin*). Since only very tentative interpretations can be made, to what extent can we really say there were Celtic shamans? Is it not a sweeping generalisation which ignores the diversity of the Celts, shamans and the evidence? The same questions apply to 'Northern shamanisms', so I respond to them after next examining the 'evidence' for Northern shamanisms and end by considering the two case examples together.

Northern shamanisms

As with Celtic shamanisms, few academics raise the subject of Northern shamanisms; that is, among the Germanic, Scandinavian, Anglo-Saxon and Icelandic settlers of north-west Europe (e.g. Davidson 1964, 1980, 1993; Crossley-Holland 1980; Simek 1993; Arnold 1997: 153, 165; North 1997: 84; Dubois 1999; Leto 2000; Price 2000, 2001b). But there is a proliferation of 'non-academic', neo-Shamanic literature (e.g. Pennick 1989; Fries 1993, 1996; Aswynn 1994; Linsell 1994; Jones and Pennick 1995: 111–164) which is also written by academic non-specialists (e.g. Glosecki 1986, 1988; Metzner 1994; Bates 1996) and non-academic specialists (e.g. Pollington 2000). This close link between academic and neo-Shamanic approaches renders a separation between them – as I have done with the Celtic evidence – unwieldy. Various archaeological and literary sources are utilised in these interpretations,[10] but particularly mythology surrounding the god Odin, skilled in magic and sorcery, and 'who ruled and practised the art which is the most powerful of all and is called *seiðr*' (*Ynglinga* saga 7). Eliade (1989 [1964]), for example, devotes most of his chapter 'Shamanic ideologies and techniques among the Indo-Europeans', to Odin and his shamanic aspects (with brief reference to the Irish Celtic *Fili* poet, mentioned above). Shetelig and Hjalmur Falk (1937) and Davidson (1964) provide greater details, particularly with regard to the etymology of Odin (or Odhinn). Odin is argued to be cognate with the Old Icelandic adjective and noun *óðr*, meaning 'mad, frantic ... furious, vehement', while the noun *óðrm* (m.) can be 'mind, feeling ... song, poetry' (Zoëga 1961 [1910]: 323). As Wotan the name relates to the modern German *Wut*, meaning 'fury', 'intoxication', 'possession', 'rage', 'wrath'; and as Woden, the derivation is the old English *wôd*, meaning 'angry', 'obsessed' (see Davidson 1964: 147; Fries 1993: 208; Bates 1996: 169–170). All these cited authors relate this etymological evidence to the 'ecstasy' of shamanisms.

Other shamanistic themes are identified easily in the mythology of Odin. In *Ynglinga* saga 7, Snorri tells how Odin can 'shift his appearance ... in the shape of a bird or animal' while his body would lie (in trance?) 'as if he were asleep or dead'. In the Norse myths Odin rides (the shamanic journey) his eight-legged horse Sleipnir (a spirit-helper[11]) to the worlds (shamanic other-worlds) comprising the Yggdrasil tree (shamanic world tree). According to the *Hávamál* he hangs himself in Yggdrasil, pierces himself with his own spear and after nine nights (shamanic initiation) he receives wisdom of the runes. Yggdrasil means 'Horse (or steed) of Yggr (i.e. Odin)' or 'terrible steed', perhaps a shamanic metaphoric link to Odin riding Sleipnir. Odin has the ability to shape-change at will (perhaps a shamanic ability while in trance), and he is 'lord of the dead', collecting the souls of warriors after battle during the 'wild hunt' of the Valkyries and supervising their journey to the afterlife (possibly the shamanic role of psychopomp). Furthermore, Odin has animal helpers (which might be shamanic other than human helpers): two ravens – Huginn ('thought', 'mind') and Muninn ('the thought', 'memory') – who perch on his shoulders and bring news of happenings in the world tree, and two wolves – Freki and Geri. In Snorri's telling of the myth about the mead of poetry (*Skáldskaparmál* 1, but see divergence of *Hávamál* 104–110)[12] he changes into both snake and eagle, and apart from the eagle being a symbol of Odin as 'All-father', there is an eagle which sits at the top of Yggdrasil and a snake (or wyrm/dragon) at the bottom (*Niðhoggr* 'one striking full of hatred'). Elsewhere in the myths and sagas, it is likely that Odin was one of the *Æsir* who learnt *seiðr* from Freyja (*Ynglinga* saga 4), wakens a seeress in a necromantic rite while travelling to Hel (*Baldrs draumar*), gives statements of Gnomic wisdom or 'kennings' which reflect techniques of magic and an ability to foretell the future (*Hávamál*; *VafÞruðnismál*), possibly undergoes 'shamanistic rituals' of 'torture, starvation and heat' (Larrington 1996: 50; *Grímnismál* 1–2) and consults the preserved, severed head of the giant Mímir for divination (*Ynglinga* saga 4; for an alternative view of Odin simply as god of the dead and not a shamanic deity, see Grundy 1995).

This etymological and literary evidence (see also Buchholz 1971) surrounding Odin is most commonly used to support the idea of Northern shamanisms. Many Heathen neo-Shamans, who are often very familiar with this literature and aware of Odin's attributes, have Odin as their patron deity, Freyja being a goddess equivalent. Indeed, Freyja also displays plausible shamanistic aspects, though few scholars have recognised this: whereas Dubois (1999) discusses Freyja's (and Odin's) *seiðr* practice and makes plausible links between *seiðr* and local Sami shamanism (a connection suggested earlier by Strömbäck 1935,[13] Johnston and Foote 1963: 79, and with some reservation Mack 1992), there is no mention of shamanisms and such links in the detailed discussions of Freyja and *seiðr* by Näsström (1995, 1996a, 1996b) or Grundy (1996) – despite Näsström's (1996a) paper being in a volume entitled *Shamanism and Northern Ecology*, she prefers the term 'sorcery' over 'shamanism', yet the former is not explicitly defined. As well as referring to the practice of *seiðr*, Freyja's character may refer to shamanistic themes when she makes use of a falcon guise (*Þrymskviða* 2–5; *Skaldskaparmal* 56), and, like Odin, raises the dead (in her form as Hildr) (*Flateyjarbók*), acts as a trickster deity (in the form of Gefjon) (*Ynglinga* saga 5; *Gylfaginning* 1), and endures a trial of fire (in the form of Gullveig): 'three times they burned her, three times she was reborn' (*Voluspá* 21).[14] Other data cited for Northern shamanisms includes the *Berserkir*, *Ulfheðnr* and *Svínfylking* warriors who fight in bear, wolf and boar form, respectively, and wear the skins of these beasts, perhaps denoting Odin-like shamanic frenzy and the ability to shape-change (such imagery may be depicted in the sixth-century CE helmet panels [e.g. Jones and Pennick 1995: plate 8.7] from Torslinda, Öland, Sweden; see also Arent 1969). Sherratt (1995b: 16) even suggests the *Berserkir* frenzies may have been entheogen induced. In terms of both shape-shifting and the shamanic motif of flight, it is worth citing Budd and Taylor's discussion of Wayland the Smith, who, while 'laughing', 'rose in the air' (*Völundarkvida*, Larrington 1996: 108):

> [M]etal-making and magic-making can easily go together as, for example, in the story of Wayland the Smith (also Volundr, Wieland) – lord of the elves and a cunning swordsmith – who is able to fly with wings he has made himself (although this motif is often referred back to the Daedelus myth, it is better connected to visual narratives in northern metal iconologies depicting shamanistic flight).
>
> (Budd and Taylor 1995: 139)

There are also a number of descriptions of '*seiðr*' in the sagas (e.g. *Egils* saga 59; *Laxdœla* saga 35; *Vatnsdœla* saga 10; and *Gísla* saga 18), although, interestingly, these are markedly different from the positive effects of *seiðr* in Eirik's saga and in neo-Shamanic ritual, more akin to Näsström's 'sorcery'. But these examples are less compelling evidence for shamanisms than are those surrounding Odin, and second to that, the practice of *seiðr* in Eirik's saga, which, as discussed above, is reconstructed by contemporary Heathens in a neo-Shamanic practice.

The most detailed recording of *seiðr* is in *Eiríks Saga rauða* (e.g. Magnusson and Pálsson 1965), according to which a seeress or *völva* performs a 'séance' for a Greenlandic community suffering a famine. Many features of this tale may, according to neo-Shamans and some academics, hint at shamanistic practices. The *völva* eats a strange porridge before the ritual, containing the hearts of various creatures. She wears unusual clothing such as a black lambskin hood lined with cat's fur and cat skin gloves. Furthermore, a pouch at her waist contains various (unstated) charms, perhaps similar to those found in a pouch from a female grave at the Fyrkat site, Denmark, which included the bones of birds and small mammals,[15] and entheogenic henbane seeds.[16] She also holds a long staff topped with a brass knob which is studded with stones, and she sits on a ritual platform with a cushion of hen-feathers beneath her. Viewed shamanistically, the items of dress may indicate the *völva*'s relationships to her other than human helpers, and her characteristic staff may act as a connection with the earth, or it may symbolise the world tree Yggdrasil. However, this view is at variance with some academic (non-practitioner) interpretations (e.g. Price, pers. com.). Thus attired, the seeress' *seiðr* proceeds: the verses which enable the spirits to be present are sung or chanted, and in communication with that realm, the *völva* prophesies a better future for the community and for each person who asks her questions. Contemporary seidr-workers use sources such as this to reconstruct and revive the seidr séance.

Archaeological evidence found in 'ritual' contexts and which might suggest shamanistic practices is enigmatic. I have mentioned the finds of henbane, for example, and given the archaeological testimony for entheogens in Britain (e.g. Tomlinson and Hall 1996; Sherratt 1991), there might be finds of other entheogens in future. A likely candidate is the nightshade family, perhaps deadly nightshade (*Atropa belladonna*) or black nightshade (*Solanum nigrum*), the former being rather more poisonous than the latter, but intriguingly known as *dwale* or *dwayberry* in Old English (Pollington 2000: 145). *Dvale* is interesting, for its use in the Old Norse dwarf name *Dvalinn*, 'slow' or 'sleeping' one (Simek 1993 [1984]: 67), 'sleeping' perhaps referring to effects occurring after ingestion, and, further, for its linguistic link to the Danish *dvale*, 'stupor', thus *dvaleboer*, 'stupor' or perhaps 'trance' berry (cf. modern 'daftberries'). Nightshade is also known in Germanic as *walkebeere*, 'berry of the valkyries' (Devereux, pers. com.), the valkyries of course linked to 'death' – a shamanic metaphor in this instance, perhaps – and to the plausibly shamanistic god Odin. Of course these links cannot replace hard archaeological data, and the henbane remains are all that is known to date. As Creighton argues, however,

> it is only a matter of time before a proper programme of residue analysis begins to place on a solid rather than anecdotal footing the use of [entheogenic] plants in British prehistory. The problem then becomes fitting them into a social context.
>
> (Creighton 2000: 52)

Until then there are two other interesting sources at our disposal: pagan art and funerary remains. Studies of Germanic art have been seriously bogged down with issues of formal analysis, style, and the origins and diffusion of style, from Salin's (1904) classic work to more recent examinations (e.g. Whitfield 1999). Interpretative work is sparse and limited in scope (e.g. Shepherd 1998). There is an all too cursory reference to 'shamanism' in Speake's analysis of raptors in Anglo-Saxon 'animal art' (e.g. imagery on Grave 1, Vendel, Uppland): 'the interpretation must be that the birds represent the mind of Odin as seer or shaman' (Speake 1980: 82), which provides yet another example of how scholars use the term 'shamanism' in a liberal, off-the-cuff way. Nonetheless, the earlier examples of Germanic art are replete with (possibly shamanistic) themes of transformation – images of humans interlinked with animals and foliage (e.g. Dickinson 1993a), and ambiguity – that certain images were 'deliberately designed to deceive the eye ... which have more than one meaning, depending on the angle at which they are viewed' (Leigh 1984: 41). Furthermore, the mixing of human and animal funerary remains in Anglo-Saxon pagan cremations has recently been approached in terms of shamanisms – an 'ideology of transformation' (Williams 2001). I think both Speake and Williams use the term 'shamanism' far too uncritically, but a shamanistic line of enquiry might prove profitable in both cases if conducted with greater methodological rigour (i.e. the 'elements of shamanisms' here advocated, see p.11).

Runes and runic inscriptions are more often cited by both academics and neo-Shamans as evidence for shamanisms. They are certainly more than simply an alphabet; scholars point to their use as a magical tool (e.g. Page 1995), and some even tentatively suggest they may have been used as a divination device (e.g. Elliott 1989 [1959]). Etymologically, the Old English *rūn* means 'mystery, secrecy, hidden knowledge', and archaeological contexts do suggest at least magical significance:

> [P]articular words or phrases with an apparently mystical significance – alu, for example – appear often in the runic record, as do seemingly nonsensical or repetitious strings of characters with no evident practical purpose. Likewise, the carving of individual runes on weapons or in places where they could not readily be seen, such as on the underside of grave-markers, seems to attest to some magical significance.
>
> (Orchard 1997: 134)

The source *par excellence* for the runes as an oracle among neo-Shamans and some scholars is Tacitus who describes Germanic divination in the first century CE:

> They retain the highest opinion for omens and the casting of lots. Their method of casting lots is always identical: they cut off a

branch of a nut-bearing tree and cut it into strips, which they inscribe with various marks and cast entirely at random onto a white cloth ... [The] priest ... gazing heavenwards, picks up three strips one at a time and interprets their meaning from the inscribed signs.

(*Germania* 10, translated by Mattingly 1948)

The 'marks' and 'signs' he describes may be runes, but opinions vary (e.g. Mattingly 1948: 108–109), and while most academics dispute the link,[17] neo-Shamans enthusiastically cite the source as evidence for runic divination. Michael Howard, for instance, is not atypical when suggesting 'The use of the Runes for divination and magico-religious purposes was the province of a special class of shamans' (Howard 1985: rear cover). While evidence for runic divination appears enigmatic, it is certain the runes were used for magical purposes, as described in various Icelandic sagas, such as *Grettis saga* 79 and *Egils saga*. A witch in the first example carves runes to destroy Grettir and reddens them with her blood, and in the second case, Egil similarly carves and bloodies the runes on a horn of ale, which, thanks to this act, shatters because it contains poison. Egil also visits a farm where a girl is sick, discovers the cause of the sickness to be runes inscribed to make her fall in love with the carver, so he carves further runes to cure her. In material culture, runes often form coded messages which may be equivalent to magical spells, inscribed onto weapons and items of jewellery, among other artefacts (e.g. the sword-pommel from Faversham with a 'Tiw' rune, the inscribed urns from Loveden Hill, and the Bramham Moor rune ring).

Interestingly, 'few of the runic inscriptions on early Anglo-Saxon objects have been interpreted' (Arnold 1997: 152; see also *Mitteilungen* 1935; Wilson 1959: 159). The alu runes mark a good example, found in over twenty inscriptions (such as the 'Tiw' runes stamped onto pottery from Spong Hill Anglo-Saxon cremation cemetery, Norfolk, e.g. Welch 1992: figure 60) from the third to eighth centuries (e.g. Pollington 1995: 72–80). The most widely accepted current interpretation is that it is connected to the 'Hethetic alwanzahh "to charm", Greek alúein "to be beside oneself", Old Norse ol "beer" ... [T]his suggests alu had a basic meaning of ecstasy, magic' (Simek 1993: 12–13), perhaps related, I suggest, to the poetic mead of inspiration Óðrœrir, 'the one that stimulates to ecstasy', drunk by Odin (see note 12). Furthermore,

[A] frequently recorded practice was the carving of runes into bits of wood, which was supposed to have a significance in harmful magic as well as in death magic. Runes were less used for their magical importance as letters composing individual words, but rather as concepts. Thus the repetition of certain concept runes (such as th = thurs 'giant', n = naud 'plight') were supposed to emphasise the message.

Simek 1993: 200–201)

So the evidence does point towards a magical as well as a utilitarian written use (if the two can be disengaged pragmatically) for the runes. But the neo-Shamanic use of the runes as an oracle really only has precedent in the enigmatic description by Tacitus. Perhaps the runes were used for this purpose in antiquity, but from an ethnoarchaeological perspective there is no certainty. Proponents of the runic oracle, on the other hand, assert the 'evidence' for and from the past for the present. Indeed, alongside the Tarot cards and I Ching, Runes are one of the most popular divination systems available with numerous books (e.g. Thorsson 1984, 1987; Howard 1985; Pennick 1992, 1999; Taylor 1992; Fries 1993; Aswynn 1994; Linsell 1994) and rune sets for sale. Neo-Shamanic interpretations of runes also include the practice of 'runic yoga', according to which, postures can be assumed to invoke the runic 'energies'. Such postures are derived from, for example, inscriptions on the Golden Gallehús Horns from South Jutland. Rune 'sounds' may be combined with the postures, and both are used to induce altered consciousness. Consequently, widespread public opinion differs significantly from the academic attitude, in that runes are believed to be (and to have been so in the past) for magic and divination, even yoga, rather than simply a form of script.

When isolated from the wider Germanic evidence there appears to be the least evidence for runes-as-oracle and for shamanisms *per se* in Anglo-Saxon England. Yet the psychologist Brian Bates presents a picture contrary to this in his *The Way of Wyrd: Tales of an Anglo-Saxon Sorcerer* (1983), a novel popular with neo-Shamans which describes the experiences of a Christian monk who is initiated and trained by an Anglo-Saxon 'shaman'. For Bates, the evidence for these practices is concrete: 'the book reveals the teachings of a remarkable Western path to psychological and spiritual liberation ... every event and detail of the teachings has been reconstructed from the Anglo-Saxon evidence' (Bates 1983: dust cover, front flap). This is also the view taken in his second book (1996), a manual for contemporary Anglo-Saxon shamans, *The Wisdom of the Wyrd: Teachings for Today from our Ancient Past*. In these volumes the 'evidence' is used to illustrate how 'Anglo-Saxon shamanism' existed, as well as its psychological and 'spiritual' value for people today. As with most neo-Shamanic literature, it has its problems: the *Time Out* review states '*The Way of Wyrd* ... reads like a fusion of Carlos Castaneda's *Teachings of Don Juan* and Tolkien's *Lord of the Rings*', which, from the academic standpoint I have taken in Chapter 2 with regard to Castaneda, could be as much criticism as praise. The novel is primarily an integration – and certainly an ingenious one – of shamanic metaphors and a specific vision of early Anglo-Saxon England, both of which are subject to a process of

130

psychologising; mythological beings and god forms are particularly affected, to make this 'indigenous spirituality' consumable for the Western mind.

Bates pays particular attention to a certain manuscript (MS Harley 585), the *Lacnunga*, which he calls the 'Anglo-Saxon spellbook' (discussed more recently in fuller detail by Pollington 2000):

> a collection of magical/medical remedies probably recorded by Christian monks in the tenth century, but reflecting a tradition several hundred years earlier ... [detailing] the medical practices of pagan practitioners operating within the indigenous Anglo-Saxon culture.
>
> (Bates 1983: 10)

Anglo-Saxon scholars may agree with Bates up to this point, but most would not agree with his suggestion that the manuscript's magical content is also shamanistic. Bates similarly uses shamanism as a reference point for other features central to his Anglo-Saxon shaman's world-view. *Wyrd* is an Old English term perhaps referring to 'fate' or 'destiny', but this meaning is not widely accepted (e.g. Stanley 1964). According to Bates, though, it was,

> a way of being which transcends our conventional notion of free-will and determinism. All aspects of the world were seen as being in constant flux and motion between the psychological and mystical polarities of Fire and Frost ... Following from the concept of *wyrd* was a vision of the universe, from the gods to the underworld, as being connected by an enormous all-reaching system of fibres rather like a three-dimensional spider's web.
>
> (Bates 1983: 11)

Furthermore, Bates believes, 'The Anglo-Saxon sorcerer dealt directly with *life-force*, a vital energy which permeated everything ... The manipulation of *life-force* was central to the sorcerer's healing work.' The shaman also 'dealt directly with spirits' (Bates 1983: 12–13).

I think in these themes it is clear that Bates's interpretations are, unfortunately – for Anglo-Saxon specialists at least – rather speculative, and have indeed been heavily influenced by Castaneda. Certain feats of Bates's Saxon sorcerer Wulf and his apprentice Brand directly compare with Don Juan's and Carlos's experiences; for instance, superhuman leaps, 'hunting' magical plants, losing one's soul to the spirits, bizarre visions and dreams, and being trained by an enigmatic sorcerer. Suggesting a form of Anglo-Saxon shamanism in light of Castaneda's unreliable work is problematic in itself, but it is also impossible to ignore that many of the aforementioned feats of Wulf and Castaneda are widespread in shamanic communities. Bates's notion of indigenous shamanisms though is not far removed from Harner's core-shamanism in that certain 'universal' features are found in one culture and perceived to be appropriate for fitting onto another, features which perhaps fit easily onto any other 'magician', 'sorcerer' or 'healer', particularly when the evidence (from Anglo-Saxon England) is so fragmentary and enigmatic. This is not to say Anglo-Saxon shamanisms were an impossibility, for as well as the archaeological evidence worthy of investigation in light of shamanisms (e.g. Storms 1948; Meaney 1981, 1989; Wilson 1992; Dickinson 1993b; Arnold 1997; Semple 1998; Williams 1998), there is much evidence for pagan beliefs, magic, elves, witches and other supernatural beings and occurrences in literary and other sources (e.g. Bonser 1925, 1926, 1962; Hübener 1935; Armstrong 1944; Davidson 1950; Branston 1957; Gelling 1962; Crawford 1963; Ryan 1963; Thun 1969; Page 1964, 1970; Barley 1972; Stuart 1976; Herbert 1994; North 1997). Paganism is not, in itself, evidence for shamanisms, of course, and while *The Way of Wryd* (Bates 1983: 103–108) gives a wonderfully evocative narrative of a healing in which a horse is cured of elf shot – a persuasive pagan recontextualisation of the 'charm for a horse' from the mid-tenth century (e.g. as translated by Griffiths 1996: 204) – healing *per se* also does not denote shamanisms.

Indeed, Bates has certainly universalised the evidence for a neo-Shamanic audience. His original aim was to reconstruct Anglo-Saxon 'shamanism', as exemplified by the novel, but much of his evidence in the later book is from a wide range of north European sources, not only Anglo-Saxon. And while the novel promises 'implications for ... the contemporary search for spiritual meaning' (Bates 1983: dust cover, front flap), the second book is clearly marketed as a manual through which 'we can once again rediscover and reclaim our sacred heritage' (Bates 1996: rear cover); that is, a neo-Shamanism rather than an Anglo-Saxon shamanism. Bates thinks the material from Celtic, Nordic, Anglo-Saxon and Bronze Age (to name but a few periods and cultures) sources can be collectively examined to support a 'North European shamanism of our ancestors'. For example, he follows Shetelig and Hjalmur Falk (1937: 415) in discussing the 'bags' found in Bronze Age Danish burials in terms of shamans' medicine bags, positing that they contain objects pertaining to *seiðr* (Bates 1996/7: 10). Such a suggestion is compelling, but might be more acceptable to specialists if the interpretation were specific to Bronze Age Sweden, rather than presented alongside an array of other evidence for the rather imprecise category of north European 'shamanism'.

Promoting Bates's view of Anglo-Saxon/Germanic 'shamanism' is Glosecki, who has written in great depth about Old English literary sources and some archaeological evidence (Glosecki 1986, 1988, 1989). He also is not an archaeologist, but a scholar of Old English; intimately familiar with literary sources but evidently (as his publications make plain) not a specialist with regard to contemporary shamanism studies and/or archaeological approaches. For instance, his use of anthropology involves accepting uncritically early theories of Lévi-Strauss and Mauss (which is not to deny their landmark works), so reproducing and reinforcing prejudices and problems of primitivism, culture evolution and structuralism. Furthermore, he does not provide chronological context or geographical specificity for some of the archaeological evidence, which, of course, would be a statutory requirement in archaeological papers.

Glosecki's archaeological work draws attention to the prevalence of animals in Germanic art, and the way in which animals and humans are integrated along with other interlacing ornament, and he suggests such motifs may be influenced by shamanistic experiences (see also Shepherd 1998: 66–67, 94). Typical examples include a variety of men-between-monsters and so-called 'horned-dancers' or 'horned-warriors' (e.g. Hawkes *et al.* 1965) depicted on, for example, sixth-century helmet panels from Torslinda, Öland, Sweden (discussed above, see also, Jones and Pennick 1995: plate 8.7), and the men-between-monsters portrayed on, for example, the Sutton Hoo purse lid. The latter Glosecki interprets as representing possibly an Ulfheðnr warrior with two wolves, or as a shaman depicted with wolf 'spirit'-helpers who are whispering esoteric knowledge to him. In addition to the archaeological evidence, Glosecki's analysis of Old English poetry is incredibly detailed, although the interpretations may be a little overstretched, such as the argument that references to the bear in *Beowulf* are vestiges of totemism and shamanism. Nonetheless, from the perspective of the study of Anglo-Saxon literature, Glosecki's approach is wonderfully refreshing, as summarised by Jolly: 'By using the "primitive" concept of the shaman, Glosecki shocks the reader out of the anachronism of reading Anglo-Saxon poetry through the lens of modern aesthetics and reverence for the classical texts canonized in the literature curriculum' (Jolly 1996: 15).

Glosecki's research into Anglo-Saxon literature has been followed by Pollington (2000), who draws attention to shamanistic aspects of Leechcraft ('healing') in Anglo-Saxon England. Pollington is, correctly in my view, more reluctant to infer shamanisms from the sources; but still, like those of Glosecki, aspects of his discussion of shamanism as a 'simpler stage in the development of human culture', and as a form of 'psychosis' (pp. 57–58), for example, are heavily influenced by outmoded culture-evolution and shamans-as-epileptics concepts, respectively. Nonetheless, aspects of Pollington's research are striking: he concludes the section 'the Læce as shaman' with a passage of Old English Gnomic Poetry from the *Fates of Men* which may allude to shamanistic themes of flight:

> In a wood someone must from a high tree
> fall wingless – he will be in flight nonetheless,
> dances in the air until he can no longer be
> the tree's fruit. Onto the roots he then

sinks in dark spirits, bereft of his soul
he falls to earth – his spirit is on its way.

(Pollington 2000: 67)

Where neo-Shamanic approaches to Northern shamanisms might prove difficult for academics to consider (such as with Paxson's use of Umbanda as an ethnographic analogy for elucidating Norse possession practices), use of the evidence by non-specialists such as Bates, Glosecki and Pollington, though exciting in some places, is clearly far too sweeping and generalist for archaeologists and historians. A myriad of hitherto unrelated data is employed to support the individual case for an Anglo-Saxon shamanism in Bates's account, and, in a circular argument, the case thereby for a universal 'shamanism' among all the Celts, the medieval Icelanders, Bronze Age Danish, etc. Jan Fries and most noticeably Nigel Pennick are among those who also suggest a rather vague Northern 'shamanism' using data which in Pennick's case at least is rarely referenced, and is widely variant in space and time; 'Northern' now meaning any place and time in Europe, and the interpretation assuming some sort of grand unified European or Indo-European heritage (e.g. Pennick 1989; Fries 1996) – archaeologists would no doubt prefer to see evidence for more localised shamanisms, and their sociopolitical specificity. Such homogenising may be all the more difficult for academic specialists to digest, given that the search for Anglo-Saxon and Germanic paganism has been rife with prejudice, nationalism and romantic assumptions, often with reference to so-called 'Indo-European' origins.

The archaeologist Gustav Kossina (*Die Herkunft der Germanen*, 'The Origin of the Germans', 1911) lies at the root of these issues (e.g. Arnold 1990). Kossina claimed archaeology to be 'the most national of sciences and the Germans as the most noble subject for archaeological research' (Trigger 1989: 163). In his culture-historic approach to archaeological remains Kossina argued that stylistically similar assemblages of artefacts directly reflect similarities in culture and ethnicity. By mapping the distribution of artefacts which characterised specific cultural groups, he argued to have discovered where specific cultures had lived. Kossina thereby argued that archaeology established the right to territory, so that wherever allegedly German artefacts were found, the land must by right be German. After his death, the Nazis eagerly adopted Kossina's research and one of the first things the SS did when Germany expanded its territory into foreign lands was to excavate in search of German artefacts to legitimate its territorial claims; all perceived 'anti-German' artefacts, particularly Roman remains, were systematically destroyed. The SS also revived interest in Norse religion and culture since it was believed to represent that of their Aryan forefathers. Well-known symbols appropriated by the SS include the two Sowilo runes which make up its abbreviation (though they are incorrectly shaped), and the swastika – originally a good luck symbol associated with Thor found on numerous artefacts

134

across northwest Europe (and, intriguingly, in diverse material culture from the late Neolithic/early Bronze Age so-called 'swastika stone' on Ilkley Moor, Yorkshire, to ancient and contemporary religious artefacts in India).

In light of this disturbing past, it is all the more troubling that Anthony (1995) points to similarities between the Nazi culture-historic approach and Gimbutas's eco-feminist interpretations of evidence for 'the goddess' in ancient Europe; both use/d the idea of an Indo-European 'culture' to fit archaeological data into a particular mould. In addition, there is a revival of 'Aryanism' in right-wing European political (e.g. Biehl 2000; Poewe 1999) – including some so-called 'Green' – and Heathen organisations (e.g. Gallagher 1997). This is a topic worthy of further academic investigation (and is something I intend to explore in future work), especially since concepts of the Indo-European 'culture' emerge repeatedly in neo-Shamanic literature. Such research is much needed, not only to address issues of the far right which undoubtedly exist in some sections of Heathenry, but also to respond to the misleading view that Heathenry itself can be characterised as far right in outlook. It is surprising, for instance, that having deconstructed the myth of satanic child abuse, La Fontaine (1999), oddly, incorporates discussion of 'Heathenism/Odinism' into a section entitled 'Satanism and Satanic Mythology': the paper presents a rather confused assessment of the subject which verges on the monolithic and evidences an unfamiliarity with the diversity of Heathenry. It is particularly welcome then, that Bates and neo-Shamanic colleagues, in writing for a post-modern spirituality-orien-tated audience, have not become entangled in issues of nationalism and racism, and in the case of Fries (1993) at least, this contemporary Heathenry is explicitly distanced from the National Socialist politics of the past.

Archaeologists may have avoided interpreting Germanic religions, but their distance from such controversies as totalitarian archaeology in Nazi Germany may have allowed for Bates and colleagues more easily to approach the material. Bates and company at the very least deserve applause for re-assessing the sources in light of shamanisms, and thereby making a contribution to the richness and variety of interpretations which, in a post-processual vein, is essential to debates regarding perspectives on the past. Furthermore, aspects of Bates's research *are* intriguing: the suggestion (Bates 1996: 180) that Freyja's (as Gullveig) trials by fire (*Völuspá* 21–22) are comparable with Odin's shamanistic tests (*Grímnismál* 1–2) is to the best of my knowledge entirely new. And while it is not clear whether the seeress' engagements with spirits in Eirik's saga constituted out-of-body travel – for the practice may equally have involved simply mediating spirits in other, mediumistic ways – it is interesting that Bates suggests her elevated position in the high seat and cushion of hen feathers may pertain to shamanic flight. Furthermore, before Bates no one had examined the *Lacnunga* in terms of shamanistic themes. Academic specialists need not take the entirety of these arguments on board, but certainly aspects of such research are valuable.

Some of these books, notably Bates's novel and Pennick's work, give the immediate impression of presenting a singular 'truth' about the past, but I think the more obvious aim of such writers is more concerned with the present than the past, and how the past can be used to empower neo-Shamanic spirituality (Figure 4.5). In this sense, it is not wholly correct to deconstruct their work in archaeological terms since academic and neo-Shamanic approaches are not commensurable. As Bates suggested when I spoke with him, the strategies for writing works aimed at neo-Shamans are very different from those for works written and read by academics. Despite my academic contentions with Bates's work, he may be applauded for attempting to make 'Dark Age'[18] religions a little less dark, and for presenting them to a wider audience. It is important for academics to get their ideas into the popular realm, and where many researchers do not, Bates has at the very least done just that. The works of Bates and Pennick, then, alongside the likes of other experiential writers including Fries, Paxson and Greywolf, mark examples of how neo-Shamans make bold, new approaches to 'old' evidence.

Did Celtic and Northern shamanisms exist?

In this chapter I have discussed many different lines of evidence presented by academics, academic practitioners and neo-Shamans, to illustrate how

Figure 4.5 Effigies of the Anglo-Saxon runes *Ing* and *Daeg* are burnt in a ceremony celebrating Beltane

elements of Celtic and Northern religions may be shamanistic. Some evidence is less convincing and more problematic than others, and the sources themselves are consistently enigmatic and very much open to interpretation. Classical and medieval authors were not authorities on these foreign religious traditions and often met their neighbours under antagonistic circumstances. Their concentration on the outlandish aspects of the religions, such as those discussed here, was inevitable and invented polemics probably had a major role to play. The vernacular Celtic texts are hard to date, often do not accord, their meanings are elusive, and Celtic and Norse literature was mostly written by Christian monks hostile to paganism. Archaeological evidence moreover is fragmentary and enigmatic, and authors tend to universalise its chronological and geographic contexts. And finally, terms such as 'Celt' and 'Shaman' are universalised openly and misleadingly with unsatisfactory implications.

On the other hand, my scepticism aside, it is possible the ancient texts do have hidden meanings which allude to shamanisms, that the classical and Christian writers may have recorded some vestiges of Celtic/Nordic shamanisms, and that some archaeological evidence is plausibly explained according to this phenomenon. In her detailed discussion of the Celtic sources, L. Jones (1998) suggests that if Celtic shamans existed, then at first glance, the most likely candidates for the role would be druids, with Taliesin hailed as the druid-shaman-bard *par excellence*. In this regard, I have provided a variety of examples according to which certain activities of the druids may be shamanistic. However, having gone on to cite the example of Fionn as well as that of Taliesin, I must draw attention to Jones's argument that in the Welsh and Irish texts there are more references to shaman-like warrior-hero-poets such as Fionn, Cú Chulainn and Owein than there are to druids-as-shamans. This is a remarkable revision of the druid-as-shaman stereotype promoted by academics, and a challenge to the same stereotype favoured by neo-Shamans, who tend to avoid such martial associations as the warrior-hero. Jones also argues that where antiquarians such as Stukeley once closely linked the druids to Christianity and various saints, this association has been dropped – even ignored – by neo-Shamans, who prefer the notion of druid-as-pagan-shaman. The history of ideas attests that, depending on our biases, the ancient druids are whoever we want them to be: we impose our ideas onto the past. However, I think the sources are not sufficiently malleable to support any interpretation: indeed they are sufficiently robust to suggest not only that aspects of Celtic Christianity may have involved altered consciousness (which is not to say saints were shamans), but also that pagan shamanistic themes were preserved, which could indicate that there were pagan Celtic shamans.

A central problem is that each strand of evidence – for either Celtic or Northern shamanisms – cannot stand alone, in its own right, and indicate shamanisms. And brought together, such themes as ecstatic rituals, shape-shifting, communication with ancestors, the ingestion of entheogens, the casting of lots, and so on lose their chronological and geographic contexts. Considered together or alone, these sources do not portray shamanisms, only shamanistic activities, and to rely on these as proof of shamanisms would reify the spurious check-listing of features to define a singular and monolithic 'shamanism'. Indeed, both neo-Shamanic and academic writers often do little to explain what Celtic and Northern shamanisms were actually like, only pointing out examples which represent them; that is, the methods and techniques of shamans, not 'shamanism' itself as it is socio-politically constituted. Recognising the spirit world activities of shamans, the 'religious' component in shamanisms, is arguably a vital factor. But it is not the complete picture. Shamans are social beings, so to be able strongly to argue for such shamanisms we must socially and politically situate Celtic and Northern shamans in specific, localised, chronological and geographic circumstances.

Recent studies have promoted a theorising of Celtic and Northern archaeologies, revaluating our understanding of 'barbarians' and socialising the sources (Samson 1991; Ausenda 1995; Frazer and Tyrell 2000). Unfortunately, to date, no academic or neo-Shamanic author suggests such socio-political specificity for Celtic or Northern shamanisms. For the Northern example, only those discussing the *völva* in *Eiríks Saga rauða* provide some degree of specificity, and it cannot be inferred from this alone that one Greenlandic colony was shamanistic in its world-view, let alone other Northern societies. And in the Celtic example, Creighton comes closest to a specific form of shamanism in his numismatic analysis, drawing attention to the druids, vates and bards as the most likely candidates for practitioners of trance in the Middle to Late Iron Age of Southern Britain, but he is hesitant rigidly to impose the term 'shamans' on them (Creighton 2000: 54); and as I have mentioned, Jones's argument for the warrior-hero as shaman as opposed to druid-as-shaman is also persuasive. Acknowledging the difficulty of imposing 'shamans' on the evidence, and the possibility of a close link between coin producers and practitioners of altered conscious states, Creighton argues there 'may have been no conceptual difference between a ritual specialist and a metalworker' (Creighton 2000: 54), and he thereby avoids having to give a specific name to these 'metalworkers/ritual specialists'. But it is worth noting that in communities where smiths and shamans exist, the roles are often markedly defined (e.g. Vitebsky 1995a: 84), so it is equally likely that there was some division between the two and therefore a specific role for 'Celtic shamans' rather than the general and vague 'ritual specialist'. It is also noteworthy that although Creighton does not avoid the term altogether, he is certainly reluctant to argue for a form of Celtic shamanism in his example, reflecting a wider shamanophobia (as discussed by Dowson 1999a) in archaeology, which has yet to recognise how the term 'shaman' has a currency which cannot be avoided, and that the 's' word need not be a monolithic one.

138

For 'Celtic' and 'Northern' shamanisms, which are more acceptable to scholars, to take shape, it is imperative that the term shaman is theorised (not avoided or used uncritically) and that any cited evidence for shamanisms be contextualised, not universalised. The academic cry 'there is not enough data' in this regard is exhausted, as Yates argues: 'archaeological data are not limited, only the minds that interpret them' (Yates 1993). To achieve the social, cultural, temporal and spatial specificity needed to elucidate agreeable interpretations of Celtic and Northern shamanisms, *to embrace diversity*, the sources are best explored in any future analysis by following a similar avenue to the 'elements of shamanisms' discussed previously (p.11). Until then, Matthews's assumption that 'beyond reasonable doubt Celtic shamanism did exist' (Matthews 1991a: 1) is too bold a claim, though the possibility of Celtic shamanisms certainly deserves more rigorous examination; and in terms of Northern shamanisms I cannot disagree with Davidson's (1964: 119) more conservative (than Matthews's) proposal that 'shamanistic practice was so widespread in the heathen north as to have left a considerable impact on the literature'.

Notions of Celtic and Northern shamanisms are aimed predominantly at a neo-Shamanic audience, so academics are unlikely to encounter them, and, even if they do, to consider them seriously; the interpretations are just too 'alternative'. This is as much a setback for academia as it is for neo-Shamanisms: the 'alternative' neo-Shamanic view reigns supreme in the public sphere, where the academic 'truth' is eclipsed; being unaware of and unresponsive to these neo-Shamanic interpretations can only worsen the situation. This state of affairs is also not advantageous for neo-Shamans because input from and dialogue with academics would surely look towards advances in and refinements of their experiential practices, a case of two minds working better than one. This meeting of minds is workable and I already see it in action, if rarely, such as at Newcastle University's Shamanism in Contemporary Society conference in 1998, the annual Anthropology of Consciousness meeting, and the 1999 Permeability of Boundaries? conference in Southampton (reviewed by Kaye 2000), of which I was an organiser (Wallis and Lymer 2001). The direction future research takes among both academics and neo-Shamans is of major significance.

Whatever the past was like, it would be a mistake to dismiss the reconstruction and practice of these contemporary Celtic and Heathen religions as invalid or inauthentic. Jones thinks Druidry *is* valid in the contemporary world – '[c]ontemporary neo-druidism deserves to be studied in its own right, rather than dismissed as fringe lunacy' (L. Jones 1998: 229) – nonetheless she cannot resist the occasional jive at Druids. She states, '[t]he Celtic shaman turns out to be an eco-nanny' (ibid.: 201):

These inner quests of the Celtic shaman are fizzy and warm, exciting but not particularly dangerous, like the pony ride at the amusement park ... The encounter with the Otherworld basically comes down to sightseeing and acquiring souvenirs ... Harner's Jívaro shamanism is more than a little scary – if you screw up you could lose your soul. In Matthews' Celtic shamanism, you have little to do besides lose your dignity ... no doubt he would advise including a hanky in your crane bag.

(Jones 1998: 200–201)

Comments framed in this way, however incisive and amusing, actually reify the 'fringe lunacy' stereotype she suggests we dispel. While archaeologists and other academics with interests in the past have their misgivings – perhaps thinking neo-Shamans make 'inappropriate' 'appropriations' of ethnographic analogy and 'misread' the literary sources – these reconstructions *are* deeply empowering for contemporary practitioners. Indeed, the growing number of practitioners – Paganism is said to be the fastest growing religion (as is Islam, Bahai, etc.!) – suggests 'it works'. In that it 'works', and in that Druidic and Heathen neo-Shamans have in various ways contributed to debates on shamanisms, from respecting native shamans to challenging normative Western stereotypes, I think in some cases they give 'extra pay' – a constructive contribution – to shamanisms, past and present. At the very least, if academics continue to prove reluctant to engage with neo-Shamans directly, the published work of these neo-Shamans should be of significance to archaeologists. As Hutton argues,

It is a classic case of a situation in which the experts are feeding the public with information while leaving it free to make such imaginative reconstructions as it wishes ... Druids are well placed to take advantage of it ... indeed, it is almost a duty on their part to do so, for the more people who are involved in the work, and the broader the range of plausible pictures imagined, the healthier the situation.

(Hutton 1996: 23)

Archaeologists and historians may in some respects be custodians of the past, but they are not the owners of the past, nor do they have exclusivity to the market of ideas concerning the past. Indeed, popular neo-Shamanic books about the past are a reckoning force for academics, and since the notions of 'Celtic' and 'Northern' shamanisms have widespread popular currency, archaeologists and other specialists cannot afford simply to dismiss these ideas as 'fringe'.[19] I find comments in the vein of the following rather perplexing, therefore:

[M]any archaeologists differ sharply from neo-shamanist opinion, finding it hard to credit any link (beyond basic inspiration) between ancient practices and modern neo-shamanic rituals often given the same name by their adherents. This is not in any way an expression of doubt as to the sincerity of modern Pagans, but merely to question the privileging of their understanding of ancient religion above those of anyone else.

(Price 2001b: 11)

Archaeological and neo-Shamanic interpretations are, first, not commensurable, and, second, logically is it not also true that archaeologists tend to privilege their understandings of ancient religions above non-professional interest groups, including neo-Shamans, when we know archaeological interpretations are, in their own way, subject to bias and subjectivity (for discussion of similar ethical issues, see papers in Pluciennik 2001)? The implications of neo-Shamanisms for archaeologists do not end with claims to the intellectual past, however. According to many 'native British neo-Shamans', particularly Druids, places where ritual practices 'work best' includes archaeological sites (Neolithic tombs, for instance), described as 'sacred sites', where rites of ancestral communication take place. I turn to neo-Shamanic interactions with archaeological monuments in the next chapter and illustrate how they present other challenges – hitherto largely unexplored – to the archaeological community.

5

'SACRED' SITES?

Neo-Shamans and prehistoric heritage

'Is Stonehenge worth it?' was a question we were all asked ...
At one level, the answer has to be 'No'; but, at another, and
more strongly, it has to be 'Yes', if only because the
Stonehenge issue was not only about Stonehenge. For decades
now, events at Stonehenge have continued to reflect in minia-
ture the changing spirit of the larger society in which it
stands. What we see in this mirror for our times is about
ourselves, all of us, including you – our past and our present
and, some would say, our future too.

(Chippindale *et al.* 1990: 8)

The condition of heritage, particularly damage to and the destruction of
ancient sites is a matter of concern to archaeologists, yet where the impact of
'tourists', unscrupulous land owners and farmers is often recognised (e.g.
English Heritage 1995; Jones 1998; Morris 1998), the actions of Pagans,
Druids, neo-Shamans and others with 'spiritual' interests in such places are
less often addressed. Indeed, neo-Shamanic engagements with the past affect
archaeologists most directly in relation to archaeological sites, as Derbyshire
archaeologist John Barnatt came to realise:

In the spring of 1993, shortly before the Spring Equinox, the stone
circle at Doll Tor [Derbyshire] was seriously damaged when persons
unknown 'restored' it prior to holding rituals there. In 1994 archaeological excavations and restoration were undertaken after the
removal of several newly-added spurious features, in order to return
the site to how it may have appeared in prehistory ... The monument is now closer to its prehistoric appearance than at any other
time in historic times. This will hopefully negate future attempts at
ill-informed 'rebuilding' at the site.

(Barnatt 1997: 81–84)

The Doll Tor incident is not isolated or exceptional: when I visited the
Twelve Apostles stone circle on Ilkley Moor in July 1998 these stones also

had been disturbed. Neo-Shamans frequent sites on the moor for rituals (discussed further below), although it is unknown who attempted to 'restore' the stones to their original locations. Doll Tor and the Twelve Apostles are only the tip of the iceberg, however: archaeological sites, particularly prehistoric monuments, and interpretations of them, are increasingly the focus of neo-Shamanic interests. Until recently, such attentions have been written off as fringe by heritage managers, site custodians and archaeologists; the example of Druids – widely perceived as eccentric phoneys – campaigning for access to Stonehenge at the solstices is particularly well known. But despite its standing as a much publicised and enduring issue – at least in this Stonehenge example – only recently have such 'alternative' approaches to archaeological sites and the politics surrounding site management begun to be examined seriously (e.g. Chippindale *et al.* 1990; Bender 1998; Prendergast 2001).

In this chapter and that following it, I assess critically and contribute to this new discourse. Such commentary is timely since it is now incumbent on British archaeologists and their colleagues in heritage management to respond dialogically to these physical, intellectual and 'spiritual' interactions with the past. I begin by introducing the diversity of 'alternative' interests in archaeological sites and unpack a new term by which these places are increasingly becoming known, 'sacred sites'. I then examine why it is that certain people wish to engage with the sites, the complexities of engagement between themselves and heritage management, and the contentious debates within which these interest groups are implicated. The situations, past and present, at three major (at least in terms of public awareness) archaeological sites are explored as case examples: the well-documented politics of site access, use and re/presentation at Stonehenge in this chapter, and the less represented but now more heavily impacted Avebury, as well as the politics surrounding the excavations of 'Seahenge' in that following. Apart from the perhaps obvious fact that archaeologists and site managers cannot afford to ignore these contests over sites, I demonstrate how the situation is not polarised (i.e. heritage managers *vis-à-vis* neo-Shamans); rather the interest groups and their interactions with one another are diverse and there is a plurality of views; efforts towards resolving tensions are therefore challenging indeed.

Problematising the 'sacred'

It would be misleading to suggest all individuals and groups with alternative interests in archaeological sites are 'neo-Shamans' since there is great variety, from Goddess worshippers, Druids, Heathens, Wiccans and other Pagans, to New Agers, Dowsers, Earth Mysteries enthusiasts, modern antiquarians, free-festivalers and so-called 'New Age' travellers. But the sometimes close interactions and often clear connections between these interest groups mean it would also be misleading to examine them only in separation, divorced from the wider context of alternative site use. The thread I use to connect them – for there are many others, such as counter-cultural tendencies and ecological activism – is neo-Shamanisms. Greywolf, for instance, is a Druid whose practices are neo-Shamanic and who regularly makes pilgrimages to ancient sites. There has also been an upsurge of shamanic themes in Earth Mysteries and modern antiquarianism, including the work of Devereux (e.g. Devereux 1992b) and Cope (1998). Nonetheless, there is very little published material on neo-Shamanic interactions with so-called 'sacred sites' worldwide (e.g. Bensinger 1988; Finn 1997; Bender 1998).

The term 'sacred site' needs unpacking. Archaeologists and heritage managers typically apply such labels as 'archaeological', 'heritage', or 'ancient' to these 'prehistoric' sites. These terms are not fixed or non-negotiable, however; they are value laden and constructed. 'Prehistoric' and 'archaeological' suggest such places are in some sense dead, of the past, no longer in use, separate from the present, though perhaps useful in the present as a time window on the past. The term 'monument' on the other hand denotes something erected in memory or celebration of a person or event in the past. Pagans in particular might contest such terms because of these connotations that we are somehow separated from these material remains because meaningful use of the sites expired long ago. Barnatt comments on how the Doll Tor restoration event, mentioned at the outset of this chapter, allowed 'the circle to again act as a communal focus' (1997: 81), as if the archaeologists were the first to feel this since the 'original' builders left; the implication is that appropriate and authentic social and/or ritual use of the site ended in prehistory. Barnatt's perspective on the neo-Shamans and what they did is markedly relenting,[1] but the practitioners would no doubt feel belittled or at least sidelined by his comments. In response and in some ways to contest the archaeological terminology, the term 'sacred site' is increasingly popular among Pagans, particularly Druids, and other neo-Shamans, who may speak of 'coming home' or at least of returning to a well-known much-loved place, rather than 'visiting' it as a tourist; they wish to engage directly with these places – at Stonehenge, perhaps to touch the stones, to gather with other people, to party, to scatter ashes of loved ones, to dance around the circle, and so on. Since I am exploring practitioner meanings as well as archaeological interpretations here, I interchange use of 'sacred site' with that of 'archaeological monument' etc., in full knowledge that 'sacred site' requires problematising and theorising (see Wallis and Blain 2002), and that all these terms are constructed, not given.

Pagans, neo-Shamans, Druids and others approach these 'sacred sites' as places which are 'alive' today, perhaps where ancestors, goddesses and gods, nature spirits, and persons other than humans can be felt, engaged with or contacted, and where the 'spirit' or 'energy' of the land can be felt most strongly. I asked Greywolf why sites such as Avebury and Stonehenge are 'sacred' to him. He responded:

> Many Druids like to make ritual at ancient stone circles since there is a strong feeling that they are places where communion with our ancestors may be made more readily than elsewhere. There is also a sense that making ritual at such places energises and benefits both the sites themselves and the land around ... I am drawn to Avebury ... because it is my heartland, i.e. the place where I feel most spiritually 'at home'. The first time I visited, more than twenty years ago, I felt I belonged there. That feeling has never left me. I work with spirits of place. This is a strong part of Druid tradition. I feel the spirit of place most strongly most often in Avebury. Six years ago, I was asked to make a Druid rite for an eclectic gathering at Avebury. I composed a rite that left space for people of all traditions to experience their own faith together in one circle with those of other faiths. It worked so well that similar open, multi-faith ceremonies are still being held there and elsewhere, both in Britain and overseas. Avebury is a very welcoming place in which to make ritual. I am not the only person who has experienced the spirit of the place as a great mother with open arms, welcoming all who come.
>
> (Greywolf, pers. com.)

Greywolf's remarks give a personal but not atypical neo-Shamanic perspective on sacred sites. More and more people make pilgrimages to these places throughout the year, with a surge in numbers around the eight most common Pagan festivals[2] which celebrate the turning of the seasons. As well as having 'spiritual' significance for individuals, archaeological monuments often also provide a focus for community; indeed, ancient sites have perhaps been the focus of community interactions for millennia. The primary aim of Tim Sebastion's Secular Order of Druids (SOD), for instance, was to re-establish access to Stonehenge for solstice and other celebrations after the 'battle of the beanfield' in 1985 and subsequent demise of the Stonehenge festival. When approximately 14,500 people were at Stonehenge for the Summer Solstice in 2001 (after which all interest groups agreed the event had been a success), Sebastion suggested (pers. com.) that now SOD's aim had been achieved it was perhaps time for the order to disband. That a Druid order was formed around political action for community rights illustrates how there are not simply individual neo-Shamanic claims to archaeological sites. Taking this example and those discussed thus far into account, it is clear that just as there is not one sort of 'neo-Shaman', so there is not just one sort of neo-Shamanic engagement with 'sacred sites'; there is great diversity. Indeed, there is also diversity of use of the term 'sacred site'.

An interesting recent turn of events is the way in which the term 'sacred sites' – perhaps first used by indigenous peoples campaigning for repatriation, after which it may have filtered into use by neo-Shamans via their contact with indigenous literature and communities – has now entered heritage discourse in Britain. Note the words used by an English Heritage staff member during Summer Solstice access to Stonehenge in 1998 (cited in the journal *Pagan Dawn*):

> [He] spoke to one group of TV and newspaper men who had put their equipment on the altar stone. He said sternly 'Have some respect, these stones are sacred. This is an altar.' We were impressed, especially when he said 'This *is* an altar', and not '*That was*'.
>
> (Wise 1999: 12)

Perhaps more surprising is that when involved with Pagans during the excavation of Seahenge, David Miles, English Heritage Chief Archaeologist, said that he accepted Seahenge was a 'sacred site'. This is fascinating: not only is this an example of a leading professional archaeologist using the term (almost an anachronism), but this is also the same term used by Pagans, with no doubt different understandings of how this sacredness is constituted. This apparent acceptance of the term as appropriate by the archaeological mainstream should not detract from its contentiousness. Without doubt, a neo-Shaman, Christian and heritage manager will perceive a 'sacred' site in very different ways. A Pagan, for example, may argue that other than human persons reside at these places and that such 'spirits' demand the site be used in a sacred way, a way which might even contradict conservation protocols (sites fenced off, buried, etc.). This implication of the 'sacred' in political contests of site marginalisation (not too remote from the situation in the USA – see Chapter 7) behoves site managers in particular to be explicit about what they mean by 'sacred site', lest they appear to be supporting ideas which, quite obviously, they do not.

Neo-Shamanic engagements with 'sacred' sites

The bulk of literature describing alternative interactions with sacred sites consists of personal accounts. One of these is written by the Keltic (*sic*) neo-Shaman Kaledon Naddair, in which he discusses his personal perspective on Keltic and Pictish 'shamanism' and rock art sites in Scotland (Naddair 1990). He suggests shamanic rituals at cup-and-ring mark sites – 'of major importance to my Ancestors' spirituality' – facilitated communication with 'Rock Spirits' which revealed the 'essential purpose' of the sites (we are not told what this purpose is, but can assume it is 'shamanic'). These other than human persons also improved Naddair's 'hand-dowsing' abilities, with an 'uncanny knack' of 'discovering new Cup and Ring mark sites long-buried'.

He also argues that 'much of the knowledge previously experienced at Cup and Ring mark sites was encoded upon the later Pictish symbol stones'. This was, apparently, enacted by the 'Pictish Druids' at the time of and after the 'Roman threat' and, 'I have also been given the "lost" meaning to certain Pictish symbols through my Wildman-Teacher' (all quotations Naddair 1990: 93–108). Archaeologists may have much to speculate and disagree with in Naddair's subjective experiences and interpretations, his uncritical use of the terms 'Pict' and 'druid' for instance, but his approach (and that of his Druidic group) to rock art is clearly neo-Shamanic and directly affects archaeological sites in Scotland. For example, are the buried rock art sites new discoveries, or are they recorded sites reburied by archaeologists for conservation purposes? In either case, such site use is of concern to archaeologists.

Shamanic experiences at Scottish rock art sites are also recounted in *Shamans' Drum* by MacEowen (1998), an American of 'Scots-Irish descent' who is reclaiming the ancient shamanic traditions of his 'ancestors' (a critical, self-reflective response to his paper is also provided by Blain 2001). MacEowen's use of Lakota-based Native American traditions ended during a sundance ceremony in which the vision he received was not of Native American teachers but the 'spirits' of his Scottish ancestors. This prompted him to re-explore Celtic 'shamanism', which he prefers (like Naddair) to call 'Pictish' and/or 'Gaelic': 'I believe it is possible to rekindle specific Gaelic shamanic methods and spiritual practices via a combination of deep remembrance and ancestral transmission' (MacEowen 1998: 36). Such comments might appear harmless enough to the editors of *Shamans' Drum*, but there are issues of uncompromising Eurocentrism and nationalism here. He argues that academics:

> [A]re able to accept the reality of ancestral transmission when it happens within indigenous tribes, yet they summarily discount this same possibility when it is within their own bloodlines – which were rooted in shamanic tribal cultures such as the Celts, Germans, and Norse ... My path has been to connect with those aspects of primal Celtic spiritual consciousness that best mirror my genetic propensities.
>
> (MacEowen 1998: 35–36)

Rationalist anthropologists do of course accept at least the *social* reality or effectiveness of religious traditions in indigenous contexts, but the ethnic categories he cites are contested rather than fixed in current academic thought, and the issue of 'bloodline' has troubling racist undertones even if MacEowen himself does not intend such. Biological determinism in 'spiritual' and religious ability is not something most neo-Shamans I have met entertain – though it is not uncommon and requires further study (e.g.

Gallagher 1997, 1999) – although his vague understanding of 'Pict' is more prevalent, covering a span of at least five thousand years of Scottish history and prehistory: according to MacEowen, all the Neolithic and Bronze Age monuments and medieval ruins in the Kilmartin Valley, Argyll, are 'Pictish'; he spent a night 'communicating' with 'Pictish ancestors' at one of these tombs.

Were it not for his obvious familiarity with the area (all the photographs are his) one could easily be mistaken for thinking he had never been to Kilmartin before. I was disappointed in not seeing the northern lights in Arctic Norway, let alone in southwest Scotland, yet MacEowen informs us: 'As I began inching my way into the grave, I noticed the aurora borealis, or northern lights, shimmering across the sky' (MacEowen 1998: 38). In all fairness, if MacEowen practises ancestral communication, then as all ethnographers should, I respect his beliefs. However, when he states 'to be sure, I am aware that poor scholarship and wishful thinking continue to plague many neo-pagan efforts to reclaim the past' (MacEowen 1998: 33), only to reify outmoded cultural migration models – 'it was not until I visited Spain (Celtiberia), the previous homeland of my ancestors of Milesian origin, that I realised my emotional experiences in Scotland had been a breakthrough' (MacEowen 1998: 39) – I have difficulty accepting that he is at all familiar with Iron Age prehistory or medieval Scottish history. In his idiosyncratic approach to the evidence MacEowen unfortunately associates the Picts with anything he likes, and romantically relegates the Celts to 'primal' times. Despite his capable qualifications in certain areas (he has an MA in counselling psychology), I think both the Celts and ancestral communication are approached more carefully by other neo-Shamans (see previous chapters).

Neo-Shamanic engagements with rock art sites also take place in England. My conversations with 'Gyrus' from Leeds revealed numerous instances of visionary experiences induced at the rock art sites of Ilkley Moor (Rombalds Moor) in West Yorkshire (see also Gyrus Orbitalis 1998, 2000; also Oakley 1998). Apparently, many Chaos Magickians (aka. technoshamans) in the area – Leeds was the birthplace of Chaos Magick in the works of Phil Hine (e.g. Hine 2001) and Peter Carroll (e.g. Carroll 1987), among others – use the monuments on the moor in their rituals (see also Dowson *et al.* in press). Gyrus classifies his approach to rock art and ancient sites as 'personal': 'I have to experience the place I'm involved in. I spend time there and immerse myself in it, meditate and do rituals, note dreams and synchronicities' (Gyrus 1998). He describes a first visit to the Badger Stone rock art site at which:

> I was too wet to care about the rain, a state which alters consciousness into a more receptive mode ... I did some spontaneous chanting and whirling ... My intuitive offerings to the Badger

Stone consisted of pouring some of my drink (water or whiskey) into the cups and watching it stream down the grooves.

(Gyrus Orbitalis 1998)

A torrent of hailstones at another time 'was blowing hard from behind me, hurting my head, and coming in at an almost horizontal angle, creating a tunnel-like effect before me – and an extremely conducive state of mind' (Gyrus Orbitalis 1998). Gyrus also mentioned an occasion where he experienced visions at the Badger Stone after ingesting an entheogen. While chanting into the rock he perceived that changes in tone affected the frequency of vision patterns, something he feels would be useful in determining how original creators of the engravings perceived them. He likened the experience to synaesthesia, a state often reported by shamans in which the senses blur into one another; the subject may see a taste, hear a smell or feel a sound. By interacting with the rock art and megalithic sites on Ilkley Moor, Gyrus – among others such as the Chaos Magickians – is engaging in neo-Shamanic activities which directly affect archaeology. Indeed, his experiences prompt and inspire him to write interpretative archaeological works (e.g. Gyrus Orbitalis 1998; Gyrus 1998) about the region. Furthermore, these modern practices re-establish folkloric rituals at rock art sites which appear to have been operating until very recently, certainly until the end of the nineteenth century (e.g. Crook 1998). This revival of tradition re-engages neo-Shamans with ancient sites in an active way, with experiences which challenge the passive and normative approaches to the sites encouraged by heritage management. To neo-Shamans, cup-and-ring marked rocks are not simply 'art-for-art's-sake' or ancient territorial markers, they are alive with 'spiritual' meanings today (Figure 5.1).

Neo-Shamanic interpretations of 'sacred' sites

Such engagements with and interpretations of ancient sites may be self-published by practitioners themselves or published by sympathetic publishers, and these neo-Shamanic interpretations of sites may draw on but also conflict with those of site curators and archaeology in general. The work of Paul Devereux is to the fore here, being read by many neo-Shamans but also notable for its filtering into academic archaeology (e.g. Devereux 1991). He is well known among enthusiasts of 'Earth Mysteries' as former editor of *The Ley Hunter* and for his research into ley-lines (coined by Watkins 1925), straight features in the landscape accentuated by human endeavours, such as the Nazca geoglyphs and cursus monuments (e.g. Devereux 2001), or invisible lines marked by features such as barrows, holy wells and churches. He is also published in academic journals, where he examines such ideas as the acoustic properties of rock art sites (Devereux and Jahn 1996). Twenty-five years of research have led him to reject the idea of dowsing the 'energy' of

Figure 5.1 Contemporary rock art on Ilkley Moor, Yorkshire. The large
image may portray a Gorgon's head. Enclosed in the
alchemical-like triangle is a pendant depicting a fish-tailed and
winged goat (the astrological/astronomical Capricorn image)
with the word 'Capricorn' underneath. The moor is used for
neo-Shamanic rituals, and there are numerous carvings of this
sort representing alternative 'spiritual' themes, although
responses to the appropriateness of this are mixed (e.g. Bowers
1999/2000)

ley-lines, suggesting instead they were used as 'spirit tracks' by trancing
shamans on out of body travel (pers. com.). This idea is gaining acceptance
among academics (e.g. Millson 1997), and I have applied a similar interpretation of spirit tracks in the shamanic landscape to the rock art of
Twyfelfontein, Namibia, based on ethnographic records and analogy, and a
shamanistic approach (Wallis 1996).

Devereux devotes an entire volume to interpreting Avebury in *Symbolic
Landscapes: The Dreamtime Earth and Avebury's Open Secrets* (1992b), pointing
out hitherto unnoticed and intriguing considerations of these monuments
by exploring leys as shamanistic. He argues it is only possible to 'see'
important aspects of Avebury's landscape when Western rational and linear

perspectives are replaced by a 'way of seeing' the landscape (referring possibly to Castaneda's description of learning to use altered consciousness in an alternate reality) – an attempt to experience the landscape as Neolithic 'shamans' may have done. In this way, Devereux first saw the 'double sunrise' and 'Silbury glory' of Silbury Hill, and learned to appreciate the 'dreamstones' of the henge megaliths. Due to their 'subjectivity', the usefulness of these ideas might be questioned by some mainstream archaeologists, but Devereux's idea of 'sightlines' between monuments visible only from specific points in the landscape may be considered valuable (as published in *Antiquity*, Devereux 1991, and employed by academics, e.g. Tilley 1994; Bradley 1997, 1998). Devereux has certainly broken new ground by severing the link between dowsing and ley-lines, and exploring the polemical (in today's 'drug war' society) uses of altered consciousness in prehistory (e.g. Devereux 1992a; 1997; also Rudgeley 1993). But while some of Devereux's research may be too 'alternative' for orthodox archaeology, the work of another independent researcher, Michael Dames, who makes links between Silbury Hill and a Neolithic Goddess religion, could be perceived as even more 'fringe'.

Dames is an art historian whose interpretations of the Avebury complex greatly appeal to many Goddess worshippers, Druids, neo-Shamans and other Pagans. In dialogue with Bender (1998: 184–185), Hutton describes how Dames's ideas, published in the 1970s, were actually influenced by traditional archaeology: academic research in the 1950s proposed the existence of Neolithic Mother Goddesses (e.g. Crawford 1957; Childe 1958; Daniel 1958; thereafter popularised by Gimbutas, e.g. 1974), a far more appealing and accessible suggestion than the scientised 'new' archaeology heralded by Binford (1962) and Clarke (1968). Dames tied these Goddess interpretations into findings from Atkinson's highly publicised Silbury Hill excavations of the late 1960s, which suggested construction of Silbury began around July, harvest time in the agricultural year. Since the Neolithic represented (to many old-school archaeologists and in popular imagination) an 'agricultural revolution', harvest must have been an auspicious time of the year. Dames then discovered people had celebrated the festival *Lammas* (Anglo-Saxon 'loaf-fest') or *Lughnasadh* until recent times, and in some places had built towers around which to celebrate the bounty of harvest. To this, adds Dames, Silbury looks from the air like a Goddess figure (see Dames 1976). Following the success of *The Silbury Treasure* (1976), which detailed these findings, Dames produced *The Avebury Cycle* (1977), bringing all the major elements of Avebury's prehistoric landscape together in a cycle of rituals which celebrated the Goddess and were enacted over one agricultural year. As Hutton states: 'they were ceremonies which people could perform, and so, within a year, people were there. That's why women dance on Silbury Hill at the August full moon' (in Bender 1998: 185). Dames's interpretations have had a major impact on many people who are inspired by this Goddess-oriented cosmology of the Avebury region: to cite Greywolf again, 'I am not the only person who has experienced the spirit of the place as a great mother with open arms, welcoming all who come.'

Dames's interpretations have been lauded since by Julian Cope, punk musician turned 'modern antiquarian', who wrote *The Modern Antiquarian: A Pre-Millennial Odyssey Through Megalithic Britain* (1998; see also Cope's web site http://www.headheritage.co.uk/). To archaeologists it might be more of a pre-millennial *oddity*, with statements like: 'Before the Romans foisted their straight lines upon us, these isles undulated with all that was the wonder of our Mother Earth' (Cope 1998: ix), and the notion that the Bronze Age apparently brought 'the clash' of Neolithic and Bronze working communities, 'the beginnings of patriarchal society', and,

> [M]ost importantly, the arrival of metals meant a severe shift in the possibilities of what violence could achieve. Whereas in the Neolithic period a successful stabbing would have been a considerable achievement, with the coming of bronze weapons bodies could be ripped asunder, limbs hacked off and enemies decapitated.
>
> (Cope 1998: 125)

Cope, alongside other popular writers such as Dames and Gimbutas, has been instrumental in promoting the idea among practitioners that the Neolithic was a period of matriarchal Goddess 'culture' followed and destroyed by the patriarchal warring 'culture' of the Bronze Age. And in Cope's eccentric, neo-Shamanic world-view there is room for almost anyone: 'Cliff Richard is a Pagan ... Cliff is a Pagan for Christ, but he's still a Pagan' (interviewed by Thompson 1998: 12). Alongside such odd remarks, sound advice is also given: 'megalithic adventurers should always leave with more rubbish than they came with', but more unusual a suggestion is that visitors should 'always hold shamanic experiments at non-gazetteer sites' (Thompson 1998: 12). Cope's idiosyncratic interpretations – such as the possibility that megaliths are juxtaposed with natural features in the landscape in the form of recumbent mother figures; e.g. Black Combe, Scotland (Cope 1998: 75–76) – may not sit well with archaeologists. But approaching Neolithic monuments and their locations in the landscape is also in vogue in archaeology, so Cope's linking of the Swallowhead Springs to the Avebury complex is pertinent (Cope 1998: 31). This blend of archaeological and neo-Shamanic approaches is on the one hand extremely refreshing, opening up British archaeology and alternative visions of sacred sites to a wider audience (beyond normative *Time Team*). On the other hand, the intellectual and physical implications of neo-Shamanic engagements with ancient sites are disquieting for archaeologists: Cope's and Dames's interpretations rely, in part, on outmoded interpretations, particularly singular notions of culture, material culture and goddesses in culture history; further, Naddair's finding of new rock art sites may precariously expose them to destructive elements. As a matter of course, then, archaeologists should be aware of and respond to these issues, yet they do not. An exceptional example is Darvill's (1999) favourable review of Cope's volume; Darvill's response to Cope is not to critique alternative interpretations but to criticise archaeologists for not being as successful in getting their approaches into the public domain: 'we need to realign our public outputs, to listen up and get real in what we present to the wider world' (Darvill 1999: 29). Widespread public belief is that megaliths are associated with the Earth Goddess(ess) and that such sites are in some way 'shamanic' and/or 'sacred'. Perhaps the most 'sacred' and famous of all, '*the* temple of the nation' (Sebastion 1990: 88) which has been at the centre of debates over alternative access to ancient monuments – spiritual, intellectual and physical – is Stonehenge.

'The temple of the nation' aka 'that site': Stonehenge

Stonehenge has, arguably, always been a site of political contest, but in a much-publicised recent incident (25 March 1997), the witch Kevin Carlyon 'illegally' entered the stones of Stonehenge to raise a Union Jack; he stated this was in reaction to the suggestion by archaeologists that Stonehenge was built by migrating people from what is now France 4,500 years ago. He stated 'it is my theory that those living in this country invaded Europe – and not vice versa' (cited in Gallagher 1997). Gallagher is one of very few researchers to address the nationalistic, sometimes racist, and often uncritical use of cultural boundedness by Paganisms (see also the nationalist comments by the Pagan group *Touta Dumnonioi* at http://www.homestead. com/dafydd/declaration2.html). But 'Every age has the Stonehenge it deserves – or desires' Jacquetta Hawkes famously told us (1967: 174), and in this age, the heritage industry's re/presentations of Stonehenge are no less political than those of Carlyon. The English Heritage leaflet to Stonehenge reliably informs us that the monument is the 'Greatest Mystery of the Prehistoric World'. Indeed, in the opening statement of this authoritative leaflet we learn 'Stonehenge is one of the wonders of the world, as old as many of the temples and pyramids of Egypt'. Ironically for the 'most important prehistoric site in the British Isles' (the text on an information panel at the entrance to Stonehenge) the standard of quality afforded its presentation today is, as noted by many, appalling. Comparisons with Dynastic Egypt are fatuous and misleading, recalling the culture-historic interpretation that megaliths are degenerate forms of pyramids. Indeed, the only possible meanings of Stonehenge described in the leaflet are that it may have been built by 'a sun-worshipping culture', or as 'a huge astronomical calendar', two explanations which are plausible but, arguably, functionalist and largely outdated. This simple leaflet provided for visitors is a first point of entry into meaning, so its informative potential is extremely high; therefore, its content should be very carefully constructed. It is somewhat embarrassing then, when visiting Stonehenge with family and friends as 'the archaeologist', to be confronted by 'sun-worshippers' and 'calendars' in a re/presentation without room for the possibility of polysemic meanings (in the past) and diversity of interpretation (in the present).

Among other interpretative devices, such as information panels, this leaflet does not and cannot be expected to tell us every possible interpretation, but, as stated, these are common first points of entry which visitors are likely to encounter, steering their earliest perceptions of the monument. The information panel at the entrance (specifically located by the car park toilets) states (with my interpretative parenthesis!):

> Stonehenge is over 5000 years old [what does this date actually mean and to which part of the landscape or many monuments dating from the Mesolithic to present day does it refer?] and is the most important prehistoric site in the British Isles [on what authority? Others might instead cite Les Fouillages in Guernsey, or Skara Brae, Orkney, or might avoid makings such sensationalist remarks altogether]. A World Heritage Site [this term is not explained; it is contested, but here reifies the global importance of the site], it is unique [as are all other sites: no single henge is the same as another] and there is nothing else like it in the world [that's a tautology, uniqueness twice!].

The result is that a very particular – if perceived as common-sense, well-known and enduring – even peculiar version of the past is presented. As Bender (1998: 180) suggests, it's the 'same old threnody: unique, incredibly old, British, world famous'. The much contested *Stonehenge Masterplan*[3] (e.g. Chippindale 1983, 1985; Golding 1989; Pryor 1998) 'focuses on conservation, presentation and packaging for tourists. But what of intellectual and spiritual access to Stonehenge? Alternative interest groups – Druids, travellers, free-festivalers – are again excluded' (Bender 1993: 269). Indeed, while physical access to Stonehenge is being negotiated (discussed in detail below) and may be accommodated by the management plan, the issue of diversity of interpretation on-site remains.

In contrast to the English Heritage re/presentation of Stonehenge (now and most probably in the future as well), the mobile *Stonehenge Belongs to You and Me* exhibition (Figure 5.2), produced by Barbara Bender at University College London (UCL) and members of the *Stonehenge Campaign*, is the only display of its kind: an academic has joined with travellers, Druids, and others to present an alternative re/presentation of Stonehenge which accommodates a diversity of non-English Heritage views (e.g. Bender 1998; *Stonehenge Campaign* 2000). Needless to say, we should not expect to see anything of its kind at Stonehenge itself. English Heritage's 'same old

Figure 5.2 The mobile *Stonehenge Belongs to You and Me* exhibition, produced by Barbara Bender (UCL) and the *Stonehenge Campaign*. This display accommodates a diversity of non-English Heritage views and appears here in the *Druid Space* dome at the 1998 Big Green Gathering in Wiltshire

threnody' will likely endure – it is simply too ingrained to remove. Despite its apparent harmlessness, and in comparison with other interpretations of world archaeology for political ends, it fits Ucko's (1990: xiv) discussion of nationalist uses of archaeology: 'an overt, political conjuring act [with] the complexities of the archaeological evidence being transformed into simple messages about national cultural identity'. As we all too often see in current affairs, this intellectually partisan view leads to opposition, and sometimes bloodshed. Even in modern Britain.

Since the 'Peoples Free Festival' (originally Windsor 1974) was disrupted by the authorities, and after the bloody 'battle of the beanfield' between travellers (and others) and police at the Summer Solstice of 1985, access to Stonehenge has been a hotly disputed subject (e.g. NCCL 1986; Hetherington 1992). I need not recount the events of 1985 as they have been well documented elsewhere (e.g. Chippindale 1986; Chippindale *et al.* 1990; Bender 1992, 1998; *Stonehenge Campaign* web site: http://www.geocities.com/SoHo/9000/stonecam.htm). C.J. Stone (1996) gives a very moving account of events at the 'beanfield' based on the TV documentary *Operation Solstice*: 'It is a film which should be seen by everyone ... so that they know that evil [in the form of the police under Thatcher's government] exists'

(1996: 153). Further violent confrontations happened the following year, and in 1995, when protestors commemorated the tenth anniversary of 'the beanfield' by attempting to gain access to Stonehenge at the Summer Solstice. The public face of English Heritage's reasoning for the restriction of access is a perceived physical threat to the monuments from the free festival. Some archaeologists, in contrast, argue 'there was very little vandalism' (Bender 1993: 275). Neo-Shamans, some Druids in particular, think that if the monument belongs to 'the nation', to everyone, then this should mean access is free and open, especially at such important spiritual/social events as the solstices. The curators feel they cannot privilege one group (i.e. Druids) over another (i.e. festivalers), although I do not know of any Druids, Pagans or others who think they deserve access over others. Of course some people are privileged: it is my view that no single group has a more authentic or legitimate claim on the henge, including archaeologists (see also Bender and Edmonds 1992; Bender 1998), yet everyone has to pay (but not all can) and no one is allowed into the stones without special access concessions. In effect, a human rights issue emerges: the groups most 'spiritually' connected to Stonehenge are marginalised (e.g. Crowley 1997) and, until recently, not allowed any admittance during annually auspicious dates. This exclusion is not the same for the dominating (in this country) Christian religion; we do not tell worshippers they must pay to enter Winchester Cathedral, for instance, or exclude them at Easter or Christmas because of its status as an ancient building and potential threats to its preservation. Indeed, it is not hard to see where priorities lie: tourist visitors bring huge financial gain to the heritage industry, yet pose a far more threatening impact on monuments such as Stonehenge and Winchester Cathedral than their 'alternative' counterparts. The site curators do not exclude *them*.

Concessions are made at Stonehenge: the curators allow the aforementioned 'special access' to the stones for a price substantially higher (£12, £8 for National Trust and English Heritage members) than the ordinary entrance fee of just under £5 (Summerley 1998: 14, based on 1998 figures). Druids and their Pagan colleagues are divided in opinion over this matter: some do not pay on principle, hoping their defiance may promote future opening up of access (e.g. Secular Order of Druids); others pay (e.g. British Druid Order), perhaps understandably apathetic after decades of waiting, but while also on good terms with the site custodians. The polemics behind Stonehenge are obfuscated, hyped by the press and far too complex for simple narratives: my discussion of events over the last three years as tensions of the past have softened and wider access has been negotiated, is therefore not definitive but personal, subject to my own biases as an archaeologist and neo-Shaman.

During the years of the exclusion zone, barbed wire and a police presence were added to the permanent perimeter fence, electric fence and rope cordoning off 'the stones', which are themselves enclosed by roads, physically, indeed forcibly, to exclude competing forms of access and engagement at the Summer Solstice. Nonetheless, English Heritage have, at least on one occasion, allowed a small number of people into the stones at the Summer Solstice. In the meantime, any group may pay for special access at most other times of the year, and Druids have paid to use Stonehenge at other auspicious dates such as the equinoxes. Occasionally, people have also been allowed into the stones in an impromptu manner for a short period over the Winter Solstice. Access at Summer Solstice is most contested, but in 1998 an English Heritage press release promised that despite an enforced police exclusion zone in the Stonehenge environs, one hundred people would be allowed into the stones on a (free) ticket only basis, brought into the site in coach-loads from outside the exclusion zone. This group, the first permitted officially to enter in fourteen years, would consist of English Heritage and National Trust persons, local interested individuals, archaeologists, the press, Druids and others. The event went peacefully – without violence or police arrests – although the opinions of some Druids do not attest to a particularly 'spiritual' occasion; their reports suggest the presence of the press was so intrusive that it was impossible to feel at ease and enjoy the solstice:

> As I stepped off [the coach] there was a TV camera in my face. I walked around the front of the coach into three or four camera flashes, and crossed the road to pass through two banks of massed press ... As we arrived at the stones, there was more press there as well; this was to be a total invasion. An E.H. member of staff was getting angry with a photographer who wouldn't shift their gear off a stone. There were journalists everywhere.
>
> (McCabe 1998/9: 20)

Add to that the internal politics of the various Druid orders represented, and the situation seems as fraught as ever:

> When the whole of the centre circle was then monopolised by one small group of antagonistic Druids ... celebrating a ritual which was to many deeply embarrassing, and in the full gaze of the media, any last vestige that the event was a victory for Druidry was lost ... For a group who claimed to be demanding access to the monument 'for the people of England' to then noisily claim the centre circle, unaware that the only members of the general public (including many Druids) who were at all interested in their ritual were the cynical media seems profoundly ironic ... For many the ritual that was performed in the centre was a very long way from any spirituality they could relate to. I would only pray that next year it is made very clear that Stonehenge is a site that belongs to the people:

everyone should have access without the intrusion of either the
media OR another group's spiritual practice.

(Restall Orr 1998/9: 23)

My eye-witness version of events the following year (Summer Solstice 1999)
follows (for another view, see 'Twitter of Blisted' 1998). Wiltshire Council's
application for the exclusion zone was turned down by the House of Lords
earlier in the year, and the police stated (in a phone call to Wiltshire
Constabulary) that despite a high profile they would not, therefore, be stop-
ping people from getting to Stonehenge, or more specifically, from getting
to the fence separating the henge from the road; the exclusion zone was
down for the first time in fifteen years. English Heritage doubled the
number of tickets for entry to the stones to two hundred, and the press
profile was tempered. People began arriving during daylight the evening
before solstice morning and at about 2 a.m. a group of people pushed down
the perimeter fence, reached the stones, and some of them climbed on top of
the trilithons. Just before dawn, I saw many more people jumping over the
fence to reach the stones. Half a dozen people or so ended up on the
trilithons, with around four or five hundred people standing within the
stones, 'illegally'. Where the so-called high police profile was when the
stones were first accessed in this way is uncertain, but when they did arrive
they did little to stop people getting in. Intimidation on their part in the
form of horse-mounted officers, riot gear and dog-handlers worked best on
most people who remained outside the fence, celebrating the sunrise on the
road and in the field of the Stonehenge avenue. This included those Druids
and others with tickets who at this point were not allowed into the stones;
in view of the 'illegal' actions of those in the circle, English Heritage
cancelled the ticket-holder event. Some Druids, including SOD, proceeded
to conduct their own ceremonies where they could, but the tension all
around could not be ignored. A police or press helicopter circled around
above us most of the night and morning, but the voices, shouts and whoops
of people on the ground almost drowned it out now and then. People on the
stones shouted about their success in 'seizing the stones' as people outside
encouraged or heckled them. Others still arrived, including further BDO
Druids, and attempted to have a peaceful time while watching the sunrise.
The road was filled with a carnival atmosphere; people played drums, sang,
danced and chatted.

Television and newspaper reporters painted a gloomy picture of the scene,
claiming the solstice was more about 'anarchy' than spirituality, but the
shouts and screams of celebration welcoming the rising sun testified to the
celebratory focus of the event. The press called those who 'invaded' the
stones 'smellies' (*The Sun*), 'hippies' (*The Daily Mail*), 'ravers' (*3rd Stone*
magazine), and 'New Age travellers' (*The Times*: De Bruxelles 1999: 13; *The
Daily Telegraph*: Fleet 1999: 4; *The Independent*: Davison *et al.* 1999: 3; Orr

1999: 5), stereotyping all present and recalling the headlines of 1985 such as 'sponging scum', 'invasion of the giro gypsies' and 'Stonehenge scarred in raid by travellers' (cited in Bender 1998: 162). The negative views of the press were inevitably coloured by, respectively, close timing of the miner's strike in 1985, and the presence of so-called 'New Age' travellers at the anti-capitalist protest in London a few days before the 1999 solstice. Mostly, people of all interest groups were annoyed about the actions of those rushing into the site since it did nothing to promote good relations and the opening up of access. But perhaps what happened was inevitable given that English Heritage had invited certain people and not others to enter the stones – ticket-holders would have been in full view of a large number of disgruntled people left on the tarmac outside the fence.

Some archaeologists (and Pagans) might agree with Clews Everard (site manager for English Heritage, Stonehenge) that climbing the trilithons may damage them, destabilise them and could result in them falling on people and killing them (television news interview). Others (alternative interest groups and some archaeologists included) might respond by pointing out that the site is heavily excavated and therefore not in an 'original' condition to allow it to be damaged, including having concrete supports implanted around the trilithons. And more than this, a few people on the stones can hardly compare with the past impact of Ministry of Defence forces on other Salisbury Plain monuments.[4] The heritage perspective in this instance is certainly value-laden and contestable, sanctioning certain sorts of destruction, i.e. archaeological investigation, but not others, i.e. alternative engagements: it is deemed acceptable to damage various archaeological sites by planning a cut and cover tunnel to replace the A303 (though see various objections to this, e.g. Fielden 1999), but not for travellers, Druids and others to touch or climb the stones. One conclusion to be drawn here is that safe, entrance-fee-paying middle England is most welcome where alternative interest groups are not, to a site that is an archetype for, and is owned by, 'the nation'.

It must be stressed that the views are not polarised (i.e. heritage managers vis-à-vis neo-Shamans) and that the site custodians are aware of positive forms of site engagement; positive here meaning any engagement which does not harm the archaeology. In an ideal world of fewer visitors, English Heritage would, I think, allow everyone into the stones, but in current times with such a huge volume of visitors, they are under considerable pressure simultaneously to 'protect' and to allow people to touch, make offerings and ritual at, drum, dance and sing around the stones. It is therefore a little surprising that proposals from Druids which address similar concerns over conservation and engagement have not been considered by Stonehenge's custodians. Suggestions have long been made by the Solstice Trust to have a Stonehenge festival some distance from Stonehenge at a new 'sacred site'. As well as engaging with ancient/archaeological sites, many neo-Shamans,

Pagans and others construct their own sacred sites, particularly stone circles, in some instances based on astronomical/astrological events. Examples include the two 1995 'Big Green Gathering' festival circles in Wiltshire, and the more recent circle on a farm in Masham, North Yorkshire (see *Pagan Dawn* 130, Imbolc/Spring 1999). In a similar vein, the Solstice Trust initially planned to reconstruct Woodhenge (Sebastion 1990), and although no landowner was forthcoming then, with the revised aim of reconstructing the Sanctuary (Avebury), Tim Sebastion (SOD) suggests the organic farmer and host of the Big Green Gathering festival has agreed to the proposals. Sebastion's (2001) argument is that the Stonehenge stones are not the central focus for many people who primarily go to Stonehenge for the festival atmosphere. If a new sacred site could be built away from Stonehenge, those wishing to attend the stones for solstice sunrise in whatever capacity (as a celebratory and/or spiritual event) can still do so, while the party-goers would be content with the festival at the new sacred site. The project would employ local people (particularly the young unemployed) and would be built with the intention of detracting attentions and pressures away from Stonehenge. Plausible as it may be, the Solstice Trust's proposal has not been seriously considered by any legislative or funding body, including English Heritage and the National Trust, who could have the most to gain, as the new site could help to achieve their aim of minimising the destructive impact on Stonehenge caused by direct engagements.

This is not to say that English Heritage have ignored the Druids (and others including traveller representatives), as their relations with certain parties of Druids have grown in amicability over the years. At meetings negotiating Summer Solstice access in 1998,

> Various agreements were reached between the parties present, which included Mr. Maughfling, Arthur Pendragon, the Police, English Heritage, Kevin Carlyon, myself, Emma Restall Orr, local councillors, and representatives of the ADO, OBOD, the PF and the traveller community ... English Heritage continue to engage in dialogue with all interested parties in an attempt to resolve outstanding problems over access.[5]
>
> (Shallcrass 1998/9: 18)

And as a result of this, negotiations at access meetings have been productive, according to the BDO:

> English Heritage obviously didn't see [the British Druid Order] as a problem. On the contrary, we began to develop a very good working relationship. We realised that we were in a position to move access discussions forward. We suggested to English Heritage that there were other groups in the Druid community who might bring some

rationality to the access meetings, notably the Order of Bards Ovates and Druids ... Having discovered that there were many more reasonable people in the Druid community than they had previously imagined ... English Heritage have made it clear that they are more than happy for Druids and others to celebrate peacefully at the stones, provided that the groups concerned conduct themselves in a way that does not represent a threat to public order, safety, or the stones.

(Shallcrass 1998/9: 18)

Druids instrumental in the opening up of access state categorically 'we would like to see access improved for all responsible groups, not just Druids, not just ourselves' (Shallcrass 1998/9: 17). Yet others do not see it quite like this. Many travellers have strong links with Stonehenge (e.g. Craig 1986; Bender 1998); the free festival marked a time when this nomadic group was able to gather together and celebrate their lifeway at a meeting place which is thousands of years old, a monument which may have been used for similar seasonal rituals in prehistory (Figure 5.3). Yet travellers are marginalised more than any other interest group, since they either will not (refuse) or cannot (financially) pay for entrance. Some travellers are at odds not only with English Heritage, but also the Druids. In the *Big Issue* article on Stonehenge released just before the 1999 solstice, one traveller argues:

Tourists are still allowed in all year round, but if you look funny and you haven't got money to spend they are not interested. They are turning an important historic and spiritual site into a theme park for tourists, a playground for the rich.

(Cited in Davies 1998: 24)

Another says,

I object to the druids monopolising the circle. English Heritage has cherry-picked a few pagan groups and witches who have no link with the place and a bunch of loonies in white cloaks. Why should the druids get access over everyone else?

(Cited in Davies 1998: 24)

But the situation is not as simple as defining insiders (those allowed in, including – but not exclusively – Druids) versus outsiders (those who refuse to pay, cannot pay or just could not get in due to the restricted number of tickets allowed at the 1998 and 1999 solstices), and traveller representatives have been involved in Stonehenge access meetings. Fortunately for all concerned, the events in 1999 were only a slight setback and English Heritage surpassed itself in 2000 when free and open access to the stones

Figure 5.3 Flyer advertising a Summer Solstice 'party' at Stonehenge for
the year 2000

was granted to all (described by Blain 2000; see also BBC news reports, e.g.
http://news.bbc.co.uk/hi/english/uk/newsid_797000/797689.stm, and the
divided opinions of archaeologists http://www.britarch.ac.uk/ba/ba54/
ba54news.html). With this success, the 2001 Summer Solstice attracted
approximately 14,500 people (Figure 5.4) from diverse backgrounds, and
the event passed peacefully (Blain and Wallis 2001; see also press coverage,
e.g. De Bruxelles 2001; http://www.thisiswiltshire.co.uk). A flyer from that
event, 'Stonehenge 2001: The Odyssey Continues', reflects the cautious
feeling of reconciliation and optimism radiated at the time (see also press
statement by The Truth and Reconciliation Commission for Stonehenge and
related issues, TRC, available online http://www.gaialive.co.uk, and
comments by Stonehenge Peace Process, available online http://www.green-
leaf.demon.co.uk):

> The Solstice Experiment ... A unique collaboration between
> English Heritage (our government) and the community at large. A

Figure 5.4 An estimated 14,500 people from all walks of life gathered at the Stonehenge for the Summer Solstice in 2001, an event which passed peacefully

Source: Courtesy of Jenny Blain.

brave experiment in healing the past, and embracing our future ...
The 'Summer Solstice Experiment' is a metaphor for our aspiration,
and an exercise in bringing that possibility into three-dimensional
reality ... This open access has been gained through years of
painstaking negotiations between English Heritage and interested
parties in the community, we believe that there is a sincere desire
for this 'free and open access to all' to continue and grow, but it is
dependent on us to keep to the agreements that have been made ...
and to leave promptly without fuss at 9am.

Both these events demonstrate that very large numbers of people can be
accommodated at Stonehenge without major damage caused to the archaeology. At first glance, this certainly looks towards good relations between
the interest groups in future; the situation is far from resolved, however.

The plurality of voices and history of events I have narrated thus far lead
me to suggest the central issue is not simply who owns Stonehenge (as raised
by Chippindale in the quotation opening this chapter), since travellers often
contest concepts of ownership and are more concerned with free access to
Stonehenge at the solstices than who its custodian is. It is also not contests
over access since, as we have seen, this appears to be opening up in recent
years. Rather, the central problem is *certain forms of access* to that place. And

events at the Winter Solstice in 2001 neatly encapsulate this core issue. As at the Summer Solstice, some Pagans and others wish to be at Stonehenge to watch and celebrate the Winter Solstice sunrise on the shortest day of the year. According to many Pagans, this was the morning of Friday 21 December, and a number of Druids (including Tim Sebastion of SOD), travellers and others planned to be at Stonehenge then. As stated earlier (note 2), Pagan festival dates are not hard and fast, and people may simply celebrate on the closest and/or most convenient day. Thus, while Sebastion *et al.* would celebrate on the 21st, 'as we always have done' (Sebastion, pers. com.), various Druids and others had already negotiated access with English Heritage for the following morning, Saturday 22nd. Indeed, Clews Everard stated, based on Druids she had spoken with, and according to the data obtained from astrology web sites, that Stonehenge would only be open on the Saturday morning (pers. com.). Sebastion and friends made it plain that a number of people, apart from themselves would be at Stonehenge on the morning of the 21st, but English Heritage categorically stated entrance would not be possible because they had preparations in place to facilitate access on the 22nd (specifically, regarding health and safety protocols, but also provision of hot food retailers).

This situation is particularly interesting: English Heritage are not only controlling the terms on which Stonehenge is accessed, but also stipulating which is the correct day of the festival – in effect telling Pagans and other celebrants when their festival days should be. Harvey (2001), writing soon after the event, stated: 'Without permission from Clews Everard ... [English Heritage] were doing nothing, insisting we were there on "the wrong day". So much for freedom of religion!'. So, people did turn out at Stonehenge on the 21st, myself included, and English Heritage, as they had stipulated, denied access. I watched a number of travellers wanting to scatter the ashes of a child on this occasion get very heated with the security guards who said English Heritage would not be allowing people into the stones. No one had expected such a large turnout and the security guards, along with the small police presence, were clearly perplexed at what to do. At one point, a security guard made it plain that he would not stop anyone if they tried to get in by climbing over the fence: needless to say, people began climbing over the fence. At this point, the police, who were obviously concerned about accidents on the A344 (juxtaposed with the fence to the northeast of Stonehenge), where some hundreds of people were gathered, prompted the security guards to open the gate. Those of us wanting to avoid trespass, a civil offence, now deemed we had been invited into the stones; the proceedings thereafter were, in my opinion, peaceful.

Feedback after the event – on various email lists, in person to various people involved, and gained from a conference[6] at which I delivered a paper addressing these issues – raises further points pertinent to my discussion over forms of access and engagement with Stonehenge. Clearly, English

Heritage were concerned that events had not proceeded as they, as site managers, would have liked. In a telephone interview, Clews Everard suggested: 'criminal damage' was caused to gain entry, with the electric fence and a padlock broken; further, glass bottles were left behind and people climbed on the stones 'with no regard for the sanctity of the place' (pers. com.). She added that the years of work negotiating access were compromised by these latest events, leaving English Heritage in the position of having to review how this would affect the future.

Press reports the following week were revealing, the description of the 'unofficial' Friday event – 'Revellers break into Stonehenge ... THREE hundred revellers broke a padlock in order to greet the dawning of the shortest day of the year ... in defiance of an order from English Heritage to stay away until the following day' (http://www.thisiswiltshire.co.uk, 27 December 2001) – contrasting with the description of the 'official' event which was so 'peaceful' the headline could say no more than 'Winter solstice is an all-weather event ... Druids ... were treated to snowflakes, a rainbow and a clear sunrise' (http://www.thisiswiltshire.co.uk, 28 December 2001).

There are clearly differences of opinion over appropriate behaviour at Stonehenge. Quoting Harvey (2001) again:

> Apparently, some people left bottles and cigarette butts in the circle, and some will interpret this as a desecration. Others will think it's stupid, unnecessary, very human and as easily tidied up as the nearby car-park that buries the earliest sacred site in this land-scape. Go and look at the three white blobs!

Everard suggested to me, on the other hand, that the site is not an appropriate place for 'a party' and 'drunken behaviour', and that this is an area they will be considering in depth regarding the organisation of access at future solstice events. But she also thought the notion of Stonehenge as a 'sacred site' could provide a suitable focus point around which the interest groups could negotiate (pers. com.). English Heritage evidently feel 'partying' and associated raucous behaviour compromise the preservation ethic: sacredness at Stonehenge, for them, is on a par with the sacredness conventionally associated with the passive, humble and serene Protestant sobriety many observe (congregation and tourists) at nearby Salisbury Cathedral, for instance. Sacredness, to others, means something else, as one Druid at the Summer Solstice 2001 event explains:

> [T]his is a holiday, it's a Holy Day, it's special, and people I think feel it's special. And I think the site likes us to be here, as well. Stonehenge wasn't built as a museum. It was built as a place for people to come, for worship, to use it ... I always think *this* is like New Year's Eve or Christmas or your birthday, all rolled into one.

And it is about – a lot of people partying. There's nothing wrong with that, that's a spiritual thing too, or can be.

(Interviewed by J. Blain for *Sacred Sites* Project, http://www.sacredsites.org.uk)

If 'partying' at Stonehenge is 'spiritual', if what is deemed as secular and non-spiritual by the authorities (English Heritage, who have facilitated the recent solstice 'events' nonetheless) can constitute 'sacred' practice by others (see especially comments by Pendragon 2000/2001b), then an analogy with nearby Salisbury Cathedral is again worthy of mention, but this time historically, in the pre-Reformation medieval period. In contrast to current, passive engagements with that 'sacred site', not only was this cathedral a regular location for the hustle and bustle of the marketplace in the Middle Ages – 'a horse-fair was held not only in the precincts but also in the cathedral itself' (Davies 1968: 56) – and the raucous 'feast of fools' (Davies 1968: 82, see also Billington 1984), but church buildings were also appropriate places for the drinking of 'church ales', for dancing, games and other, 'secular' events (Davies 1968). Camille suggests:

Clerics not only allowed folk festivities to happen, they condoned them ... This occurred not only on the feast of fools and in the boy bishop festivities, which were the clergy's own liminal escape into carnivalesque inversion ... [T]he case in the Lanercost Chronicle [describes how] villagers were compelled to dance around a statue of Priapus during Easter Week by their parish priest.

(Camille 1998: 263)

It would be misleading to suggest all the clergy condoned such wanton ribaldry: the chapter of Wells Cathedral, for instance, berated the damage caused to the cloisters during May games in 1338 (e.g. Camille 1998: 263), but nonetheless, as Pounds has recently argued:

[The] view of the church as a place far removed from the coarseness, the obscenities and the commercialism of daily life was a post-Reformation – specifically a Victorian – innovation. The villager drew no clear distinction, whatever the learned might think, between the spiritual and the otherworldly on the one hand, and the material life of the present on the other.

(Pounds 2000: 340)

After the Winter Solstice event(s) at Stonehenge in 2001 one Stonehenge Campaign activist commented '[W]hat they [English Heritage] want is tame druids' (communication to stonehengepeace email discussion list), meaning those Druids who are prepared to accept English Heritage's agenda

166

for the Winter Solstice and their concept of sacredness/heritage-cum-preservation ethic. The approaches of 'partying' Druids and others align more closely with the 'folk carnival' (e.g. Bakhtin 1968) in pre-Reformation churches, permeating the boundaries between Durkheimian definitions of 'sacred' and 'profane'. It is essential, I think, that round-table and other meetings at which these interest groups participate in the future not only discuss the enduring issue of access, but also how sacredness is constituted, on whose terms, and how differences of opinion over 'sacred' behaviour at Stonehenge and other sacred sites may be reconciled. Compromises will have to be made by all concerned.

The future of Stonehenge is, it seems, uncertain. Though things are changing rapidly at the site, particularly since its designation as a World Heritage Site, the management strategies aimed at revising the appalling visitor's centre, the location of the A33 road, etc. (e.g. English Heritage 2000; Wainwright 1996, 2000; and for views contesting Wainwright, including his response to them, see http://www.savestonehenge.org.uk/ deserve.html) are still far from being agreed, completed and implemented (e.g. Goodwin 1997a, 1997b; Clover 1997, 1998). While negotiations over the opening up of access are certainly improving, including at Pagan festival times, a recent document (Baxter and Chippindale 2002) suggests the Stonehenge Management Plan's 'promise' that people 'would ... be able to walk freely amongst the stones' has been 'cancelled'. And while both heritage managers and neo-Shamans appear to agree that this site and others are 'sacred', incidents at the 2001 Winter Solstice demonstrate that there are still clear differences of opinion over how this sacredness is constituted, how 'sacred sites' should be engaged with and how they should be managed. Indeed, the related issue of 'intellectual' access (which may not be distin-guishable from spiritual and physical access for Pagans) needs also to be scrutinised: that Bournemouth University Archaeology Group's 2001 Stonehenge Research Framework Project,[7] despite its aims for inclusivity and plurality – and despite discussing both 'physical access' and 'human experience' of the landscape – does not mention Pagan interests; and that there is only cursory mention of such interests in the Open Meeting convened by RESCUE to debate the Stonehenge Issue[8] speaks volumes, I think, about what is deemed to be the appropriate breadth of that inclu-sivity and plurality. In the next chapter I use the case examples of Avebury and 'Seahenge', and the growing issue of 'reburial', to explore these issues in wider contexts; specifically to further illustrate the diversity of alternative engagements with 'sacred sites', and the plurality of voices within heritage and Pagan communities.

6

WAKING NEOLITHIC ANCESTORS

Further controversies and 'reburial'

'Desecration' at Avebury

I opened this book with descriptions of destructive impact on the Avebury monuments, including graffiti on the stones, the lighting of fires and candle damage in West Kennet long barrow. The situation is perhaps reaching crisis point in a landscape which, with free and open access to a wide variety of monuments, is unlike 'the stones' of Stonehenge.[1] These examples of damage inevitably point towards future incidents of vandalism, and such direct and destructive engagements with 'sacred sites' are of concern to the alternative interest groups themselves, site curators and archaeologists. *Antiquity* suggests 'New age crazies' may be responsible (*Antiquity* 1996: 501) for the graffiti on the avenue stones in 1996, and that the enigmatic imagery used suggests the symbols have a 'magical' meaning rather than being associated with the 'tagging' of graffiti artists. According to *3rd Stone: The Magazine of the New Antiquarian*, the Pagan community may be aware of the individual who defaced the stones and 'it is hoped that those in the know will not remain silent in this latest desecration' (edition 35: 3). The proprietors of the *Henge Shop* told me a 'black witch' called Kevin claims to have made the markings, believing that by painting the avenue stones he tapped into the universal 'evil' energy in the earth at Avebury and chan-nelled it into the world to do its work. The shop owners were not convinced by this hearsay, but it seems no coincidence that the *Antiquity* article posits a link between the graffiti and similar defacement stating 'LIVE (= EVIL backwards)[2] at other mystic monuments' (*Antiquity* 1996: 501). At around the same time the ruin on Glastonbury Tor was adorned with a large anarchy 'A' in white paint in 1999, an incident linked by *The Ley Hunter* (no. 126 Spring 1997: 2) to Avebury's graffiti.

The National Trust and English Heritage, custodians of Avebury, have certainly not had their heads in the sand with regard to these issues and increasing Pagan, Druid and other alternative engagements with the monu-ments. Addressing the issues comprises a part of the National Trust Avebury Management Plan (1997)[3] and English Heritage Avebury World Heritage Site Management Plan (Pomeroy 1998),[4] and Bournemouth

University's Avebury Visitor Research (Calver 1998)[5] conducted for the National Trust reports on the significant numbers of 'spiritually motivated' visitors and their impact on the sites.[6] Outspoken archaeologists express concerns about the level of impact on Avebury during Pagan festivals and *Antiquity* has devoted considerable space to this topic (e.g. Pitts 1990; Fielden 1996; Gingell 1996; see also comments outside *Antiquity* by Pitts 1996). A string of events – including the graffiti – contributing to damage of the archaeology, prompted this discussion. Archaeologists cite incidents of damage to West Kennet long barrow during 'sleep-overs' when people celebrate the Pagan festivals, including concerns over the amount of litter (beer cans, cigarette butts, even – according to some reports, e.g. Prout 1998 – condoms and tampons) left after a night's celebration; this is offensive to the site managers who must clear up the mess, and to the public who visit the site the next day and who may feel intimidated by those still celebrating. There is the risk that parties in the barrow threaten its conservation since it is a small space for a lot of people; often it is impossible to get deeper than the first chambers at festival dates because so many people fill the tomb. A common example of damage is chalk markings, such as the tracings of a hand, pentagrams (sacred symbol to Wiccans in particular), runes and other graffiti. And it is graffiti: perhaps unbeknown to the 'artists', chalk can endure for many years. There is also the problem of fire damage in West Kennet, caused by mainly the lighting and thoughtless positioning of candles. Fires have also been lit in the entrance causing damage to the sarsens, as well as elsewhere in the Avebury region, including on top of Silbury Hill and on the henge banks; one forecourt stone of West Kennet was so badly damaged that a fractured piece of it had to be repaired with a gluing agent. Candles comprise an important part of some Pagan ceremonies so people will continue to use them, especially when it is dark, but as Christopher Gingell, until recently National Trust site manager for Avebury, states:

> There are large scars on the blocking stones, spalled by the heat of camp fires, and a great cavity in the oolitic walling of the main chamber burned by incessant placing of candles. We have carried out resin repairs to the blocking stones, but burned sarsen turns to the texture of lump sugar and will not last.
>
> (Gingell, http://www.rollrights.org.uk/chris.html)

Visitor impact extends to all Avebury's monuments. Since the mid-1970s, Silbury Hill has been closed officially by the National Trust. The sign explaining this situation, positioned on the fence erected at the bottom of the hill to stop access, has not stopped people climbing Silbury, however. On my visits to the area there has often been a handful or so of people – Pagan or otherwise – on the top, and during festivals dozens of people gather there to watch the sunset and sunrise, many of them resting in sleeping bags (I have yet to see a tent). Of the thousands of visitors who walk the paths around the banks of Avebury henge, Pagans must only contribute to foot weathering in a minor way (e.g. K. Jones 1998), but there are certainly examples of practice, as described, which implicate these practitioners in debates over conservation. Discussing the problems at Avebury, Clare Prout (now Clare Slaney), co-ordinator of Save Our Sacred Sites (SOSS) describes how:

> Back in October 1995 a Wiltshire local paper printed a story about the National Trust employing security guards to ensure that visitors to West Kennet long barrow behaved 'properly'. This was necessary, we were told, because of increasing damage to the barrow ... so I took a trip to the barrow to see the damage for myself ... The interior of the barrow ... was scorched and flaking. Greasy black grime from candle flame ran the height of the stones which were also covered in chalk symbols, and decomposed fruit, noisy with flies, at the back of the central chamber. The exterior bore witness to several fires, while beer cans and smokers' detritus littered the site.
>
> (Prout, http://www.rollrights.org.uk/cp.html)

This 'ritual litter' is in part a result of the votive offerings Pagans make at sacred sites. Though a simple song, poem, prayer or chant may suffice for some and leave no physical trace, offerings of material value are commonplace, from flowers, tobacco, food and drink to more permanent objects such as crystals, coins, feathers, unusual stones and other personal ritual objects. I have seen these in the tomb, piled against the back-stones of the main chamber and placed in every available crack and hollow elsewhere (Figure 6.1). They are also commonplace in the environs of Silbury Hill, at the foot of stones in the henge, and interlaced with the concrete markers of the Sanctuary. Those making the offerings have honourable intentions;[7] what they feel about the site managers and other volunteers clearing them away varies: some want their offerings to be left so that as they degrade the 'spirits' may benefit. Others hope individuals in need will use a crystal they have finished with, or hope their offering will encourage other people to do the same. For the most part it seems they would not wish their gifts to be collected and discarded as 'rubbish' (but contrast with Sam Fleming, a Pagan, discussed further below – 'I am one of those who remove your rubbish', http://www.ravenfamily.org/sam/pag/rrtart1/htm). Consequently, those people who consider the monument's 'spirituality' important are marginalised – their votive offerings to the place are not left alone and their opinions are not considered. While these considerations may appear minor, even amusing, to some readers, things are not so simple for practitioners themselves, whose rituals are sincere, or for site managers who keep the

Figure 6.1 Votive offerings at West Kennet long barrow, Avebury. An effigy of some kind rests on a bed of wild flowers

monuments 'clean', or tourists who may be offended at the sight of Pagan offerings.

A similar situation to this in the USA is at Chaco Canyon in New Mexico, where neo-Shamanic votive offerings are seen as significant archaeo-logically to the extent that they are collected and catalogued by site officials (detailed in Chapter 7). In a similar vein, neo-Shamanic 'offerings' at Avebury may not be a world apart from those made by Neolithic peoples studied by archaeologists today. Are the more permanent crystal, bone, coin and stone offerings aspects of modern material culture worthy of archaeolog-ical study in terms of contemporary ritual deposition and its relation to the past? A group of neo-Shamans enacted a ritual which disturbed the site when they ritually buried smashed flint fragments in the region of Neolithic pits in the henge. This act clearly meant more to the practitioners than simple interference with an archaeological site, than simple 'ritual litter' or offerings of degradable material: they knew of the pits' locations and were likely drawing on actions expressed during the Neolithic. Reasons for this may have been to connect themselves and their ceremony with Neolithic 'ancestors' who performed similar ritualised stone tool destruction, and for this connection to add power to their contemporary act. In these terms, then, perhaps this was not thoughtless 'vandalism', but more a legitimate continuation of tradition informed by on-site presentation boards.

171

Without doubt, open access and the considerable numbers of 'alternative' visitors are causing problems at Avebury. Prerequisites to the access deal are not succeeding: the curators state there should be no camping, lighting of fires or damage to the monuments, and the Criminal Justice Act and Public Disorder Bill deny 'raves', large gatherings and processions of certain people. These guidelines might seem reasonable because few people wish to deface the monuments or have the intention of creating unrest where locals are concerned. But where they are supposed to limit what people wish to do (or should not do) at the sites, the reality of the situation is altogether different. The best course of action the custodians ought to take is unchartered territory and there have been suggestions which worryingly mirror the Stonehenge situation, such as a National Trust ban on Druid ceremonies, an exclusion zone, filling the barrow with sand at the festivals, and hiring security guards to watch over the sites. Fortunately for all concerned (including the taxpayer), certain unofficial policies have been implemented instead.

Hands-on resolutions

The basic stance taken by the National Trust is that cordoning off Avebury during Pagan festivals would be impractical and expensive. The last thing anyone needs is another Stonehenge 'situation', so people may come and go as they please, at any time of day or night. To cater for those needing to sleep, the policy of 'no camping' is lifted in two areas: the henge and Silbury car parks. Dozens of tents are erected there at the festivals, and at the Summer Solstice of 1998 a sound system was set up in the henge car park – all this basically contravening the Criminal Justice Act (which, despite being rushed quickly through Parliament, has rarely been enforced by the police). Interestingly, the police presence at Avebury at these times is virtually nil. The National Trust is certainly making considerable concessions to keep clear air between themselves and alternative visitors, including free-festivalers. Allowing camping near Silbury seems to sanction the fact that people are going to climb the mound despite its closure, although Gingell informs me[8] that this policy aims to keep at least camping controlled.

The National Trust's strategy is well thought out: the spontaneity of Pagan festival events (which may begin and end at a variety of times in the run-up to and after the eight festival dates) means that strategies outlined in the management plan are not easily implemented. Instead, Gingell says, the National Trust is taking a 're-active' rather than 'pro-active' strategy. With this and the unpredictability of events in mind, precautions are taken as far as is possible and situations then responded to as they arise; in addition, Gingell comments that the events are effectively 'self-policed'. The National Trust's aim is not to exclude anyone from the region, but also not to give precedent to anyone else. This informal approach is certainly more pragmatic than the official strategies in English Heritage's management plan which are rather more conservative (perhaps reflecting their more distant role at Avebury): 'a minority of visitors believe that no owner or statutory body has any right whatsoever to regulate, manage, prevent access or use of the monuments' – this minority is not defined or sourced. English Heritage stress the importance of 'free access', but stress the need to 'respond' to 'inappropriate use ... through a variety of practices and measures'. In their favour, English Heritage argue for a balance between a 'non-confrontational management approach', and the 'risk of unrestricted growth in the use of the site', although there is still the perceived threat of this growth 'potentially leading to the development of free festivals' (all quotes Pomeroy 1998). These statements contrast with the unofficial and low-key re-active strategy of the National Trust, which is, currently, dealing with so-called 'free festivals' quite effectively:

[L]ocal groups wishing to use the [West Kennet long] barrow at night at certain hours for meditation and other spiritual uses have cooperated, seeking and willingly granted permission to remain in the barrow at night. We know they care for the place as we do, and we welcome the spirit in which they have worked with us.

(National Trust, http://www.rollrights.org.uk/chris.html)

Specific individuals stand out as those who have co-operated with the National Trust. The comments of Clare Prout (now Clare Slaney), founder of SOSS, are particularly noteworthy:

I'm a Pagan. That is, I try to honour the Land, perceiving it as a sacred and sentient creature, and I, along with an estimated 100,000 others, will make a pilgrimage to a sacred site, places like West Kennet, during one of Paganism's eight major festivals ... [W]e, along with many other visitors, need to learn new and less damaging ways of living with these delicate and vulnerable sites. At the same time, the managers of sites, often English Heritage or the National Trust, have got to come to terms with the fact that a large and growing percentage of the population view ancient monuments as places of worship, with good archaeological evidence to back us up ... [H]aving spoken with Chris Gingell ... it seemed that the time was right to begin an organisation that could be a forum for tourist organisations, land managers, Pagans and other spiritually-motivated visitors, Parish and local councils and so on, to discuss the future.

(Prout, http://www.rollrights.org.uk/cp.html)

Emerging from the success of SOSS has been the National Trust Guardianship Scheme at Avebury, as reported by 'Lorna':

Since the issue of damage to West Kennet Long Barrow first arose, I'm glad to say that things seem to have completely turned around. From mistrust, fears of more damage and possible closure, a positive situation has grown where negotiation and communication have led to a better understanding and cooperation ... Working on the fact that rubbish, graffiti and soot are likely to attract more of the same, we have tried to keep the site clean. Now and again we take cloths and buckets to give the stones a good scrub to remove soot.

('Lorna', http://www.rollrights.org.uk/cp.work.html)

According to Gingell, reports on the effectiveness of the scheme in the Pagan magazine *Pagan Dawn* (no. 124, Lammas 1997) resulted in many Pagans 'from all over Britain' offering their services, so many in fact that Gingell had to write a letter in a subsequent issue (no. 126, Imbolc 1998) pointing out that the National Trust was too 'decentralised' to deal with all the inquiries. In addition to individual Pagans and specific organisations such as SOSS, Druids have been at the front of negotiations with the National Trust, as Greywolf told me:

At Avebury, I was making ritual for a couple of years with increasingly large groups. It was when one of our rites attracted well over three hundred people that I thought I should get in touch with the National Trust there and see if they were OK about what we were doing. Fortunately, they are. We've never had a problem from them. My own interest in the archaeology of the site and its preservation as an open, welcoming place made it easy to build a rapport with the National Trust folks there. I've also maintained good relations with the local people.

(Greywolf, pers. com.)

Such evidence of co-operation and camaraderie encourage an optimistic assessment of the situation at Avebury, with positive implications for the management of other 'sacred sites'; but there is a significant issue underlying these constructive negotiations. All these people – Pagans, Druids and site custodians – agree the archaeology should be protected: they are united by the preservation ethic. The preservation ethic should not be viewed as common sense or non-negotiable, however. Central to the ethos of the heritage industry, it is promoted primarily by the National Trust and English Heritage, and marketed to, as well as aimed at, a middle-class audience; while suggesting these two organisations are somewhat elitist is not new, it is important to locate whose re/presentations of the past dominate in England, who their ideas are aimed at, and the dogmatic manner in which such ideas are privileged over others (e.g. Lowenthal 1996; Spencer 1997).

Unpacking the preservation ethic

The heritage industry, and archaeology more widely, like any other perspectives, are politically motivated and rooted in contemporary social circumstances (e.g. Lowenthal 1985; papers in Gathercole and Lowenthal 1990, Skeates 2000). Their theories on and approaches to the management and presentation of the past are an immediate reflection of prevailing sociopolitical ideas (e.g. papers in Cleere 1989; Moser 1996). The ideal view that archaeological monuments and remains are curated by the two heritage bodies but owned by 'the nation' is simplistic and a matter of increasing debate (e.g. Bender 1998; Skeates 2000). Pagans, neo-Shamans, Druids, travellers and others are approaching the past intellectually, experientially, spiritually and physically, in ways different from academic archaeologists and groups representing 'the nation'. Boniface and Fowler (1993) seek out such examples of 'culture clash' in terms of *Heritage and Tourism in 'the Global Village'*, but while other marginalised groups such as indigenous communities are represented in their discussion, neo-Shamans are not. In recent years this plurality of approaches to the past has, as I have discussed in relation to the example of Stonehenge, resulted in contest and even open conflict: everyone *should* have 'rights' to the past, but not everyone *does* or *can*.

The National Trust and English Heritage are the dominant groups 'caring' for British archaeological sites, and it is their versions of the past, and what about the past is important, which are available for consumption at these sites. While their views are, arguably, educated and informed, responding reflectively to the 'new', there are problematic issues with regard to their 'stories' of the past. In particular, these bodies model themselves as 'managers' and 'conservators'; themes which are themselves not longstanding but politically embedded in the present and which convey a fixed view of what the past is (e.g. Stanley Price 1989). English Heritage and the National Trust suggest archaeological remains should be preserved, or at least protected, with minimal disturbance for future generations of (Western) people to enjoy and learn from. Acceptable as this sounds, it assumes the archaeology is ours (occupiers of this country), that it belongs to us, a concept rooted in capitalist notions of property ownership: such views are not held, for example, by some indigenous communities and travellers (though I am not directly comparing the two). Preservation itself promotes misleading notions of archaeology as pristine and of an unchanging past, with archaeological sites in the role of the photograph; snap-shots of one moment in time which can be separated (framed) from the immediate environment and frozen in time.

For some Pagans, particularly those on good terms with the heritage bodies, the preservation ethic of the heritage industry is easily accommodated by their understanding of the term 'sacred sites'; the sacredness of these places means they should be preserved. Clare Prout argues:

We want to continue a heritage of ceremony, returning and receiving some spiritual nature through ritual. And that's really all right. Sacred places should be used for sacred purposes. It's just that archaeology doesn't often find evidence of prehistoric fires being lit against sacred stones. They don't find beer cans and condoms and tampons in long barrows ... I started *Save Our Sacred Sites* 3 years ago after a visit to West Kennet long barrow. Avebury National Trust (NT) were warning that security guards and closing times may have to be imposed on the site to preserve it from the ravages of visitors and I didn't believe them. After visiting the barrow I did. Chalk graffiti is one thing but piles of putrid fruit was quite another.

(Prout 1998: 6–7)

The perspective that sites should not be harmed is as much imposing a context as leaving 'putrid fruit' behind; the preservation ethic just seems so common sense that it is promoted as the natural order of things. Latham and Norfolk go further, specifically to address the deluge of visitors to ancient sites in Cornwall at the time of the 1999 solar eclipse:

[W]e are informed that the world and his wife will be visiting our land [in August 1999] to experience the total eclipse of the sun ... Local Pagans, who care lovingly for the sites all year round, have decided that the best way to minimise the possibility of any damage to the sites is to hold celebrations in order to focus the energy appropriately. For this reason we are working to co-ordinate eclipse celebrations at the major sacred sites in West Penwith. These open rituals will also be a way of protecting these special places from the over-enthusiastic, under-educated and ignorant visitor who may be thinking of altering them. This decision has the full support of local landowners, Penwith District Council, Cornwall Archaeology Unit and English Heritage ... We realise the land belongs to no-one and that no-one can claim rights over it, however, we do appeal to people's sense of courtesy and respect for the sacredness of the land and for the genius loci at these places.

(Latham and Norfolk 1998/9: 27)

Their strategy is a clever alliance of 'please do not' and Terry Pratchett-like tongue-in-cheek humour which resonates well with Pagan sensibilities:

We can't be held responsible for the consequences to anyone who crassly blunders into sacred places with the intent of taking over to become part of a media circus. Which brings us neatly to the subject of Spriggans ... from the Cornish 'sperysyan' meaning spirits ... They can be particularly vicious and live only in Penwith in West Cornwall, for which the rest of Britain should be very relieved. Spriggans haunt all the ancient places ... and what they hate more than anything, and will attack without quarter, are those who are miserly, mean-spirited and who threaten their homes ... [W]e will be working rituals to wake up – slowly, gently and very carefully all the wild elemental spirits in which Cornwall abounds ... We intend Britain to have a magically throbbing big toe by August ... If the European Community was up for it we'd also be applying for Magical Objective One Status to get our fair share of European Magical subsidy ... WARNING. Be afraid – be very afraid – if you have any ideas of being disrespectful to any of our sacred sites ... You are advised to add nothing nor take anything away. Spriggans like their homes just the way they are.

(Latham and Norfolk 1998/9: 27)

SOSS, ASLaN and their ilk are more and more prominent in their aim to steer alternative engagements towards greater respect and care for archaeological sites, but the dogmatic tone of their argument is clear. As well as concerns over the archaeology, such organisations wish to limit most forms of direct engagement, even touching the megalithic stones in case 'rare lichens' are damaged; this same 'lichen damage' argument is used by English Heritage's Clews Everard regarding access to the Stonehenge stones, and the Pagan Sam Fleming (founder of Cruithni, 'an organisation providing contacts and resources for concerned people and groups to help protect our heritage ... [with] the aim of preservation and protection of sacred sites and their setting, and maintenance of access to them', http://www.cruithni.org) regarding all megaliths. The nature of the 'sacred site' is clearly defined in these instances: sacredness=preservation ethic. There are a variety of views on what constitutes appropriate behaviour, 'spiritual' and physical, at sacred sites, from the preservationist extreme of waking Spriggans to deter destructive practices, to the opposite end of the spectrum with damaging instances of graffiti on Avebury's sarsen stones or napalm on the stones of Men-an-Tol. With regard to 'harnessing' the energy of an ancient site, some suggest 'a sacred site's energy should be harnessed to "clear away energy blocks that may be holding you back"' (cited in Finn 1997: 175). Gordon 'the toad' MacLellan thinks ancient sites 'offer places of stillness, connection with ancestors' (pers. com.), while Barry, also a neo-Shamanic environmental educator, suggests there are dangers: 'too much activity of the wrong kind can cause harm to the natural energies of a famous or popular place ... I've found a lot of sites that were closed down or seriously abused because they were well known' (pers. com.). This abuse may, according to some, also take place on a 'spiritual' level. Fleming suggests meddling with a site's energies is 'psychic vandalism' (Fleming 1999) and argues – in a markedly fundamentalist tone – that most forms of Pagan ritual constitute site damage:

> I find it unnecessary to perform any ritual at a prehistoric site unless the site is actively involved in the ritual ... [I]f the ritual could be performed in exactly the same way in any other location then the site is providing no more than an atmospheric backdrop and that is insufficient reason to expose a delicate and unique monument to the risk of damage.
>
> (Fleming n.d.a; see also n.d.b)

Not only are the terms 'delicate' and 'unique' here reminiscent of those used by the heritage bodies, but also the primary concern is that ritual at a site 'will ... change its character' (Fleming n.d.a); so both heritage managers and some Pagans agree sacred sites exist in some sort of common-sense preservationist vacuum, *ex nihilo*, and must be 'protected' and 'preserved', while not accounting for the fact that sites have doubtless had many meanings and contexts since erection – the fear is of 'imposing a context' on the sites, yet such an attitude of course also imposes a context of a different sort. Organisations such as SOSS and Cruithni can only be good news for the heritage bodies. A kindred organisation is Hallowed Ground 2000, not so much providing site visitor guidelines but being representative of the sensitive respect these preservation-ethic-supporting Pagans have for what they perceive to be sacred places:

> As we approach the millennium, places that were marked as special by our Ancestors – neolithic long barrows, Bronze Age stone circles and standing stones, Iron Age fogous, holy wells and sacred groves – are being visited by increasing numbers of people for whom these places have a spiritual significance. Hallowed Ground 2000 has been set up to record this spiritual and cultural relationship between people and the Sacred Landscape of Britain. Hallowed Ground 2000 will be a definitive contemporary record of British ancient Sacred Sites still in use today, an atlas of living folklore and spiritual belief, and a Domesday record of places which are still hallowed at the millennium.
>
> (Hallowed Ground 2000,
> http://www.rollrights.org.uk/hallow.html)

Andy Norfolk, who has pioneered Hallowed Ground 2000 with Clare Prout, comments on how the scheme works and its potential benefits for archaeologists and Pagans:

> We have a basic record sheet for volunteers to fill out about their local sacred site or sites. This will give us a snap-shot of the condition of these places with information on any threats to them. We can use this to alert those with responsibilities for the care of the

site to any problems. We also ask about the spiritual significance of the site(s). This should help make the 'authorities' and owners aware of the great significance these places have to all kinds of people, but especially Pagans. This will fit in well with the NT's new policy of preparing 'Statement of Significance' for all their properties. We also hope that the project will have value as a record of beliefs relating to ancient sacred sites.

(Andy Norfolk, pers. com.)

Clearly, many Pagans, Druids and others are aware of the issues facing their engagements with ancient sites. And, reflecting on the problems, some of them have chosen to take an active step towards raising awareness and changing attitudes in their communities. The Sacred Sites Charter produced by ASLaN (available online: http://www.symbolstone.org/archaeology/aslan/docs/charter_en.html), however, is not freely available at the sites themselves, appearing mainly in popular Pagan journals such as *Pagan Dawn* and *The Druid's Voice* (but see Scott 1999: 70–74), or small-scale publications (e.g. Burl 2000). It clearly should be on site – if this 'don't change the site, let the site change you' agenda (perhaps inspired by, the US 'take only photographs, leave only footprints', see Chapter 7) is to be promoted – to target those people who are less supportive of the preservation ethic and whose site etiquette (or lack of it) may require refinement. On the other hand, such guidelines align Pagan viewpoints with those of the site managers, to the extent that some Pagans, such as Sam Fleming (Fleming n.d.a), even suggest certain rituals should not be conducted at sacred sites because of their 'spiritual'/psychical effects.

Contests to the preservation ethic

While some Druids and other Pagans are on good terms with heritage managers, there are certainly those who contest the preservation ethic. Contrary to the preservationist ethos, archaeological remains do not stand still and are understood in very different ways over time. Heritage managers and archaeologists understand this too, of course: a wide range of factors, including current socio-politics, informs which story of the past is supported and how it is portrayed. At different times in their histories, remains were defined and redefined, located and relocated, a process which continues today (e.g. approaches to and the removal of Seahenge, discussed below). Nonetheless, the overriding impression most people have – and this includes archaeologists, heritage managers and popular culture – is that archaeological remains are a time-window on the past, a past which must be protected and preserved for posterity. Alternative writer and neo-Shamanic practitioner, Gyrus (introduced in the previous chapter), raises concerns – in 'The Last Museum' – over this 'museumification' of the landscape:

Will our culture's 'museum-consciousness' never stop? Are we so
pissed off at managing to alienate ourselves from our environment,
our art and our sense of the sacred that we're going to make damn
sure that no evidence of less cut-off and boxed-in cultures escapes
becoming an 'exhibit'? Is the whole landscape of this country and
this planet to be infected by our self-divided civilisation, turning it
into an all-embracing, terminal museum? Turning us all into
'observers' and 'visitors' whether we like it or not?

(Gyrus 1998b: 79)

Here we have 'sacredness' presented in a different way to that of the preservation
-ethos-supporting heritage managers and Pagans, advocating direct, hands-on
engagement. In a similar vein, *Festival Eye* magazine (1997, vol. 11 (Summer):
46) takes issue with the way in which issues of conversation compromise engagement, coining the satirical 'English Heriticage'.

Fencing off monuments, as at Stonehenge currently, is of course no less
legitimate a presentation than is open access (Ucko in Bender 1998: 140) –
both impose a context on the site. But the separation between monument
and experient imposed by a fence makes the way that monument is 'lived-
in', or not, very Western. With distance, the past can only be viewed, a
mode of interaction which exemplifies our 'specular' (Thomas 1993) civilisation: the past is framed and frozen to give plenty of time for gazing (e.g.
Urry 1990). Consequently, the onus is on a need to protect the past at the
expense of four other senses. A further reason for framing monuments must
be for financial gain. Payment for access to Stonehenge was perhaps first
demanded in 1901 (Sebastion 1990: 103), and since there is an emphasis on
tourism in English Heritage's aims and objectives, Stonehenge is essential to
the heritage and tourist industries: 'Stonehenge has to make money' (Bender
1993: 268). In terms of physical access, Stonehenge is atypical: many of the
sites neo-Shamans wish to frequent have free and open access, and most
people involved promote this situation (but see Fowler 1990a, 1990b,
1997). But while we see both heritage managers and Pagans using the term
sacred site, there remain disagreements – within both heritage management
and Paganisms – as to how these sacred sites should be engaged with and
managed. I have drawn attention to this in the previous chapter with the
example of Stonehenge, but perhaps the best example with which to illustrate the plurality of voices is that of 'Seahenge'.

Buster and bulldozers: 'Seahenge'

Contests over a small timber circle (or more correctly ellipse) surrounding an
upturned tree stump, dubbed 'Seahenge' (on construction 4,000 years ago it
was not so close to the sea, and since it is not enclosed by a bank and ditch,
it is not a henge), were documented in a special edition of *Time Team* (see

also various press reports, e.g. *British Archaeology* December 1998, February 2001, http://www.northcoastal.freeserve.co.uk/whatnextforseahenge.htm, report 20 February 2000; http://www.24hourmuseum.org.uk/nwh/ART 10705.htm, report 9 January 2002). It was interesting to watch how the views of archaeologists, particularly those with the preservation ethic in mind, were regarded as matter of fact and 'normal', whereas the Druids and other protesters were presented as fringe and, as the grins on many an archaeologist's face testify, laughable. As Moser comments, 'Archaeology is a political and social enterprise. This is always avoided in the [*Time Team*] programme ...' (in an interview with Mower 2000: 3), and local people felt the programme avoided their views in 'an advert for English Heritage' (cited in Champion 2000: 74). My narrative and critical discussion of the Seahenge fiasco are, as ever, not definitive, but personal (a well-balanced and detailed examination is provided by Matthew Champion, 2000, while Pryor's 2001 approach to Druids and other protestors attempts to be understanding, but is confused and stereotypical).

Some local people in the village of Holme-next-the-Sea say they had long known about this site as well as other timber structures on the beach of Holme Dunes Nature Reserve, but Seahenge came to the attention of archaeologists in summer 1998 following the nearby discovery of a Bronze Age axe head earlier in the year. Hopeful that the axe head and timbers were linked chronologically, Norfolk Archaeological Unit applied for funding from English Heritage, and in November 1998 a small investigative excavation began. Seahenge was certainly a remarkable find, a rare Bronze Age timber construction, but the expense of excavation, and other factors such as fragile environs, meant a full, follow-up excavation was deemed impractical; English Heritage decided to monitor the timbers closely but, having carefully recorded them *in situ*, left them to the damaging effects of the sea.

Various people were critical of this decision and this came to the attention of the national press who described it as the Stonehenge of the sea. Such comparisons could not go unverified and from the spring of 1999 increasing numbers of people turned up to see Seahenge for themselves. Perplexed by the 'meaning' of this idiosyncratic monument, a neo-Shaman says she 'didn't feel any particular energy coming from it', and wonders, 'maybe it'll come to me in a dream?' (Michelle Brown 1998: 15). Concerns were raised that visitor impact threatened the timbers and disrupted wildlife on the quiet nature reserve, and the public pressure, particularly due to the huge and perhaps disproportional press coverage, was on for the timbers to be excavated, conserved and exhibited. Pagans, such as Clare Prout of SOSS, were prominent in this regard, as were archaeologists including Francis Pryor (Director of Archaeology at Flag Fen Archaeological Centre, Cambridgeshire), and some local people who were concerned that visitors to the timbers *in situ* threatened the nature reserve and/or that any future exhibition would end up too far from Holme, with a subsequent loss of their heritage and tourism. Shortly after a correspondence (which may have been significant, though likely not the determining factor alone) between Philip Carr-Gomm (Chief of the Order of Bards, Ovates and Druids) and Jocelyn Stevens (Chairman of English Heritage), English Heritage made a u-turn on their decision to leave Seahenge, scheduling excavations for May 1999. It is pertinent to note that not only did English Heritage change their minds at this point, but that we also see here a number of people – some Pagans and English Heritage included – united by the preservation ethic.

Not everyone wanted Seahenge excavated and preserved, however. Some local people were greatly angered that English Heritage had not consulted them before announcing its turnaround decision. *The Times* reported how protesters (local and non-local) turned out to halt the proceedings; some Druids claimed the site's location on a ley-line meant that it should not be moved lest its spiritual essence be lost (Morrison 1999: 20). So we clearly have a diversity of views here, notably, for the purposes of my discussion, among Pagans, from those campaigning for excavation and preservation to those demanding the circle be left *in situ*. The excavation by Norfolk Archaeological Unit (funded by English Heritage) went ahead but was fraught with bitter wrangling both on- and off-site. Local youth worker, painter and spiritual healer Sam Jones was instrumental in the Friends of Seahenge anti-excavation campaign, feeling 'strongly that none of the academics involved with the decision making process had taken any account of the spiritual and religious aspects of the monument' (Champion 2000: 45). In her approach: 'Rather than seeing the site ... it was the feelings of a very calm feminine energy. It's a sign of natural harmony and thus only nature can decide its fate. I seek to honour nature and spirits above science' (cited by Champion 2000: 45–46). Jones's calls for action were answered by various people such as Hazel (a spiritualist and environmental campaigner from Cambridge) and Des Crow, as well as various Druids including Rollo Maughfling (GOD) and Buster Nolan, the latter being particularly prominent in press coverage. Furthermore, one local businessman, Mervyn Lambert, helped fund the protestors' legal action against the archaeologists – eventually unsuccessful but certainly disruptive to the excavations. Druids and other protestors made concerted efforts to halt or at least slow down excavations by peaceful protest, such as removing sand bags and sitting on the timbers (Figure 6.2).

In an attempt to avoid these setbacks, extraction of the central upturned stump with a bulldozer was planned for the early morning, before protestors arrived. This incident was called a 'Dawn Raid' (*Sacred Hoop News*, 1999, vol. 25 [Summer]: 8) by some neo-Shamans, and the archaeologists had to face protesting Druids nonetheless: this confrontation 'sent shock waves across the pagan and shamanic communities not only in Britain but also the US' (*Sacred Hoop News*, 1999, vol. 25 [Summer]: 8). As with the example of

Figure 6.2 Druids and other protestors at Seahenge slowed down and
attempted to halt the excavation of the timbers by means of
peaceful protest

Source: Courtesy of Eastern Counties Newspapers Ltd.

Stonehenge, archaeologists are viewed very negatively at such times, 'as
manifestations of imperialism' and 'an uncaring discipline, typical of a
dominant elitist society' (Ucko 1990: xv). Attempts to resolve the power
struggle at Seahenge were made by Clare Prout (now Slaney) who,

> [A]sked if I could arrange a meeting with all of them, in a sacred
> manner. They all agreed so last Tuesday [22 June 1999] we had
> eleven people from wildly different backgrounds holding hands,
> invoking our Ancestors and Great Spirit (which saves a lot of expla-
> nation and debate) and Awen'ing.[9] And within five hours we had a
> remarkable agreement. The timbers would be removed and
> preserved but returned to the village, possibly within a new Bronze
> Age village that would be built to house them. In the meantime,
> the site would be recreated with new timbers, with the proviso that
> if it caused tourism that impacted the birds it would be removed.
> And any ceremony for the removal of the timbers would be

welcome ... [A]ll those who were in the meeting were gracious and giving and we got a fabulous result.

(Prout in submission to Nature Religions
email discussion list, 7 July 1999)

Seven points of agreement were drawn up as a result of this meeting; two of them are noteworthy – (1) the site should be treated with respect, and (2) the site was sacred to the people who created it (cited in Champion 2000: 54) – for their unproblematised use of the term 'sacred'. Needless to say, the preservation ethic aligning view expressed by Prout was not acceptable to everyone (see especially comments by protestors Des Crow and Sam Jones in Champion 2000: 54) and in the final stages of the excavation Rollo Maughfling made what he claimed was 'an official druid proclamation' with eight articles outlining why the circle should remain *in situ*: 'Seahenge is a national monument ... not a museum piece', arguing that the excavation of the timbers is 'the greatest act of controlled vandalism', and 'Trying to remove Sea Henge, is like trying to move Stonehenge or Canterbury Cathedral' (Maughfling 2000/2001b: 11).

It is worth examining how archaeologists on site responded to such opposition to their objectives (Figure 6.3) – indeed these perspectives on alternative interests are only evidenced thanks to *Time Team*; reports in the archaeological literature skirt the issue, with Brennand and Taylor's (2000) report in *Current Archaeology* focusing on the archaeological 'facts', stating only that the excavations 'were enlivened, and sometimes delayed, by the activities of a number of "Druids"' – photographs of Druids are deployed to add colour to the article, nevertheless (see also revealing comments by Plouviez 2000). Note one particular comment by Maisie Taylor during the *Time Team* coverage: 'What's interesting is the people who are objecting to us digging the circle don't actually seem to want to know any more about it.' But of course it is not that Druids, Pagans and other neo-Shamans do not want to know about the past, it is that they want to know about the past and engage with it in ways which contrast markedly with those of archaeologists (see also Dowson 2001b). The very significant issue raised here concerns forms of knowledge and power: power over which approach to the past determines how sites are managed and presented. Rollo Maughfling recalls Buster's conversations with him:

[H]e (Buster) rightly foresaw that the authorities were going to intervene in the fate of Seahenge, and not in any manner that either local people or religious interests were going to find acceptable ... [he said] 'they don't seem interested in what its for or why it's where it is, they just want to rip it up and pack it off to some museum where no one can use it and all that will ever happen is that it gathers dust.'

(Cited in Champion 2000: 46)

Figure 6.3 Contests over Seahenge were heated: here, Buster Nolan, a
Druid, and Bill Boismeyer, project manager of the Seahenge
excavations, meet in a clash of world-views

Source: Courtesy of Eastern Counties Newspapers Ltd.

Indeed, there was considerable dissent amongst archaeologists. An article
in the widely read journal *British Archaeology*, by its editor, Simon Denison,
expresses disgust with the way Seahenge was 'yanked out of the sands': 'The
excavation ... was destruction, nothing short of vandalism' (Denison 2000:
28). Controversially perhaps, for an archaeologist versed in the preservation
– or at least conservation – ethic, Denison argues:

> [T]he only way to truly cherish an ancient monument or other
> historic feature is to leave it alone, avoid it, plan round it. And if it
> is necessary, *absolutely necessary*, to plough a road through it, or
> abandon it to the waves, then my judgement is we should photo-
> graph it, film it, write about it – and let it go.
>
> (Denison 2000: 28, original emphasis)

This view aligns with that of one Druid interviewed on the *Time Team*
programme, who argued we would learn more from Seahenge by leaving it

where it is in the landscape – however long it lasts – rather than disarticu-lating it and then absconding it to some alien location. Similarly, at a recent conference at which we discussed these issues, Professor Richard Bradley suggested, referring to Stonehenge, that we must:

[G]et used to monuments, spend time with them, be patient with them, and contemplate them before insights arise. There is an analogy between our instant consumption of monuments like Stonehenge, and the deficiencies of traditional archaeology; we have no patience. We have no patience as tourists, and we have no patience as academics. Its no good having forty-five minutes access to Stonehenge whether you pay or not. What you need is the possi-bility for spending a long time at it, of being able to look at it in different lighting conditions, for instance. And that goes for all monuments, not just Stonehenge. The health of the discipline as a whole depends on a change in mindset and the way we expect people to experience these sites.[10]

Bradley is saying that we need to have patience: the implication is that we need to have patience with ancient sites, *and* patience and tolerance with each other. High Court Judge Mrs Justice Arden, in addition to ruling in favour of English Heritage, had the following to say regarding lack of toler-ance and consultation at Seahenge:

'Their actions (English Heritage) have been perceived as provocative by a number of people ... [T]here has been ... no local meeting, and ... this is a religious place of worship for the druids' ... The judge then went on to rule that ... English Heritage ... should take into account such points as the need for public consultation at a local level and the wishes of genuine religious groups such as the Council for British Druid Orders.

(Champion 2000: 102)

So there are important lessons to be learned from Seahenge – 'perhaps to the extent that Seahenge will be the last disturbance of a sacred site without prior consultation and compromise' (Bannister 2000: 13) – but there still remains the issue of appropriate behaviour at sacred sites, since not everyone thinks preservation protocols necessarily compromise direct engagement.

In a similar vein to those demanding Seahenge be left *in situ*, to be destroyed, are those who suggest alternative forms of site management which are rather more conservationist (or at least reconstructionist) than preservationist. At the aforementioned conference in Southampton Tim Sebastion (SOD) argued that erosion of Avebury's banks (though not exclu-sively a result of Druid processions), a major problem for the site managers, need not be an issue for concern. If, unlike the sheep-grazed grass of the present, the banks did once consist of polished chalk, as archaeologists suggest, then, he commented, let the grass be worn down. When the banks begin to wear, working parties of Druids and other Pagans would then help restore the henge in a contemporary re-use of the site which, he argued, legitimately compares with Neolithic use. Unsurprisingly, this argument did not wash well with David Miles, the heritage spokesperson.

Since excavation, the timbers of Seahenge have been curated by Flag Fen. Unfortunately, there is much indecision over what should be done with them, particularly regarding the cost of conservation. In further twists and turns of decision-making on the part of English Heritage, plans were made towards the end of 2001 to re-bury the timbers, much to the approval of many Pagans and local people of Holme, but this has since been retracted. My own view is that the needs of each site must be judged on its own merits; we require a 'situational pragmatism' (Strathern 1998: 217) in our management of sacred sites, as is already in effect and successful at Avebury. The words of the neo-Shaman Gyrus also resonate with me, despite the tensions created for me by being both an archaeologist and a neo-Shaman:

> How important is conservation? I want to conserve these sites, but how far should we go? Even if going to sites is respectful, some 'damage' is done by human presence, as in the erosion of Silbury Hill in Avebury, caused by people going up it. Here I think we need to ask ourselves a big question: do we want to preserve these sites *absolutely as long as possible*, but experience them from a distance (unless you're a scientist); or do we want to accept a slightly increased rate of erosion and decay – and *actually* experience them? How does conservation and the acquirement of increasingly accurate scientific information weight up against the right to experience ancient sites as they were actually intended – i.e., without a bloody great fence between you and them? ... Do we value *data* over *experience*?
>
> (Gyrus 1998b: 80)

Furthermore, on the need for tolerance between archaeologists and Pagans, and the need for some pragmatic guidelines for reciprocal action, we might reflect on the 'stepping stones to common ground' agreed on by some archaeologists and Native Americans (following Swidler *et al.* 1997):

1 We must take each other seriously, and make constructive attempts to challenge negative stereotypes, by:
2 embarking on productive, collaborative dialogues, establishing:
3 research ethics
4 joint stewardship programmes, and
5 informed consent protocols.

Such suggestions are already in effect in some instances: Bender, Dowson, myself and other archaeologists I have cited do take neo-Shamans seriously; collaborative and reciprocal dialogues are happening at Stonehenge and the Rollright Stones; and the National Trust's guardianship scheme is a form of joint-stewardship. But in terms of research ethics and informed consent protocols, the example of Seahenge indicates that there is some way to go before archaeologists are prepared to give up or at least negotiate some of their power. And, while on paper these guidelines are attractive and optimistic, the reality of implementing them in practice in the US situation is rather different, subject to personal interpretations by those with power (e.g. archaeologists), personality clashes, etc. A highly controversial issue at the interface between Native American 'spirituality' and custodian interests, where stepping stones to common ground may meet resistance, is reburial. This highly disputed subject strikes a blow at the very heart of conventional archaeological practice, and, as the debates over reburial of the Seahenge timbers indicate, the reburial of human and other archaeological remains is now – perhaps surprisingly – coming to Britain.

A British reburial issue?

'Reburial' has been a central issue for archaeologists and anthropologists in the USA, Australia and elsewhere where the lobbying of indigenous communities for the repatriation and/or reburial of human remains and artefacts held by museums (and other institutions) has met increasing successes (e.g. Biolsi and Zimmerman 1997; Dongoske and Anyon 1997). In the USA, NAGPRA (Native American Graves Protection and Repatriation Act 1990) and in Australia the 1988 South Australian Aboriginal Heritage Act mark examples of policy which have enabled some indigenous communities to make legal claims on 'their' pasts. For archaeologists and anthropologists the implications have been immense, with opinion varying from those who largely support the indigenous claims (e.g. Dongoske and Anyon 1997) to those, particularly osteoarchaeologists and physical anthropologists who argue vital scientific data are being lost irretrievably (e.g. Chatters in Radford 1998). But such issues are not only controversial in indigenous contexts: the reburial issue is now on the agenda in Britain.

Increasing numbers of contemporary Pagans, neo-Shamans, Druids and others 'feel' they are native to the British Isles. They may claim to be 'Celtic' even if they have no immediate Scots, Irish, Cornish or Manx parentage (e.g. MacEowen 1998, discussed in the previous chapter). Just as there are 'wannabe' Indians (e.g. Green 1988), these are wannabe Celts, or 'cardiac celts' as Bowman (1995b) terms them, who 'know in their hearts' they are Celtic (e.g. Bowman 2000). There are also Pagans, contemporary Heathens in particular, who make ceremonies to honour Anglo-Saxon and other northern 'ancestors' (e.g. Blain 2002). Others still feel that through ritual, particularly at sacred sites, they are identifying themselves as 'spiritually' allied with the prehistoric peoples who built 'sacred sites' such as Stonehenge, Avebury and Seahenge. Closeness to the sites (frequent engagement is conducive to a feeling of closeness to the builders) denotes, for them, an affiliation with the prehistoric communities which constructed the monuments. Thus, issues of 'ancestor' welfare – i.e. concerns over the archaeological excavation and storage of human remains and artefacts – are now gaining in popularity (e.g. Wallis 2000).[11]

Such claims to indegineity are complex, but concerns over what archaeologists do with human remains is not just an issue for 'alternative' Pagans, however: a *British Archaeology* news article (November 1997: 5) discusses the 'Public Disquiet Over Digging of Graves', referring specifically to an excavation at an Anglo-Saxon cemetery in Suffolk. One remark is rather striking:

> How short a time do we have to be buried before it is permissible, even acceptable, for grinning archaeologists to dig out our bones, prod among our teeth, disperse our possessions, take the head off our horse and lay us, not to rest, in boxes in museums?
>
> (*British Archaeology*, November 1997: 5)

Indeed, 'When does sanctity, afforded to graves, cease to be an issue?'. In the article this criticism is levied at 'Britain's planning culture which appears to treat cemeteries, especially out-of-use non-Christian cemeteries, with little respect'. It seems people other than Pagans also express a sense of responsibility to these 'ancestors'.

Even so, it is neo-Shamans and their Druid and Pagan associates who are most vocal on the issue of reburial – increasingly so – and who are taking active roles in effecting change. Such interests seem to have been directly influenced by claims to the past by indigenous communities, particularly the high public profile of Native American repatriation and reburial of human remains and artefacts – in 2000 Glasgow's Kelvingrove Museum returned a Wounded Knee massacre Ghost Dance shirt to the Lakota. With their own interests in indigenous peoples and drawing on such a precedent, Pagans have framed their approaches to British reburial in language similar to that of Native Americans. The words of British Druid Order member Davies are particularly striking:

> Every day in Britain, sacred Druid sites are surveyed and excavated, with associated finds being catalogued and stored for the archaeological record. Many of these sites include the sacred burials of our ancestors. Their places of rest are opened during the excavation, their bones removed and placed in museums for the

voyeur to gaze upon, or stored in cardboard boxes in archaeological archives ... As far as archaeologists are concerned, there are no cultural implications to stop them from their work. As far as Druids are concerned, guardians and ancestors still reside at cere-monial sites such as Avebury and the West Kennet Long Barrow ... I believe we, as Druids, should be saying 'Stop this now. These actions are disrespectful to our ancestors. These excavations are digging the heart out of Druidic culture and belief.' When archae-ologists desecrate a site through excavation and steal our ancestors and their guardians, they are killing me as well as our heritage. It is a theft. I am left wounded. My identity as a Druid is stolen and damaged beyond repair. My heart cries. We should assert our authority as the physical guardians of esoteric lore. We should reclaim our past.

(Davies 1997: 12–13)

Davies's view clearly has an indigenous-inspired tone to it. Given that many Pagans, neo-Shamans in particular, engage actively with indigenous reli-gious practices – however contentious this may be – such rhetoric is not surprising. His view also compares with the so-called 'New Age traveller' opinion that archaeologists are contemporary society's 'looters of graves' (Bender 1993: 271), just as contemporary archaeologists perceive many of the early antiquarians. Whatever the influences, such Druidic claims to the past may be written off as 'fringe' by most people. This reaction, while understandable, is, however, short-sighted and in no small way arrogant: the example of Kennewick Man in the USA illustrates how the claims of contemporary Pagans – however controversial – have been included along-side those of archaeologists and indigenous groups (e.g. Radford 1998; Thorpe 2000/2001). In this famous case, not only were claims made on prehistoric 'ancestral' remains by both local Native American communities and a local right-wing Asatru organisation, the Asatru Folk Assembly, but also both groups were granted access to the remains to perform ceremonies which honoured the 'ancestral' remains, while the archaeologists had their scientific analyses halted by law (strangely, barely referred to in Chatters's 2000 discussion; Chatters being the physical anthropologist who first exam-ined the remains and thereafter campaigned for continued scientific analysis). Clearly, British archaeologists must be mindful of such (albeit exceptional) cases: simply put, the heightened interest in reburial in the neo-Shamanic community at present indicates the British reburial issue will not go away, cannot be ignored; Druids especially are prepared to act on their intentions. To Davies, reburial of these looted bones 'makes perfect sense; bones are living people and should therefore be respected and ceremo-nially reburied' (Davies 1998/9: 11), and he outlines how neo-Shamans can get directly involved in this issue:

I speak for the ancestors and guardians of the land, those spirits not currently represented in the archaeological record ... The Druid or Pagan shaman can use their gifts as 'harmonic bridges' to communicate between the realities of archaeology, land developers and Pagan Druids ... Druids should join together and encourage debate between archaeologists and museums in the reburial issue.

(Davies 1998/9: 10–12)

At first glance, individual neo-Shamans and Pagan groups do not have agreed core beliefs or practices, let alone centralised 'spiritual' beliefs concerning disposal of the dead. Nonetheless, in the 'time of tribes' (Maffesoli 1996), the reburial issue is gathering momentum and coherency, as indicated by Greywolf:

The question of respect for our ancestors has been very much to the fore with me lately ... My interest is personal, in that I've worked with the spirits in and around Stonehenge. I also find the display or shoddy storage of human remains a source of pain and sorrow. Given that obviously Christian remains are almost always given a Christian reburial when disturbed, it seemed reasonable that the same courtesy should be accorded our pagan ancestors. I'm aware of the increasing notice museums and others are taking of the reburial issue where it concerns native people in America and Australia. There's a small but growing voice within the pagan community calling for similar respect for our own ancestors.

(Greywolf, pers. com.)

The 'Stonehenge Masterplan' that has been under discussion at the Stonehenge solstice access meetings, particularly proposed changes to the landscape which will inevitably affect the archaeology detrimentally.[12] Initial field surveys indicate the cut and cover tunnelling work will damage or destroy sixteen archaeological sites, of which eleven would be ploughed out (virtually nothing remains). Only two of the remaining five sites would have any visible trace above ground, but, of these, approximately four burials would be disturbed. Concerned about this disturbance, Greywolf asked a National Trust representative:

if there was any possibility that priests used to working with the spirits of our ancestors could get access when such burials were uncovered and could make ritual for the spirits of the dead. He said that he knew re-burial was an issue in Australia and the US, but didn't know it was over here. I told him that it is a 'live' issue amongst the pagan community and was likely to become increasingly so. He expressed his personal sympathy to the idea. Inspired

191

by this initial contact, I wrote a letter to some appropriate folk in English Heritage and the National Trust. In it, I expressed my concern that any burials found might simply end up in boxes in a museum basement. I asked for access to burials on site when they were uncovered, for permission to make ritual before burials were removed, and also whether it would be possible to re-bury the ancestral remains after a suitable period of study, preferably within the Stonehenge area. The latter seems important since our ancestors clearly didn't select their burial places at random and I felt they should be returned to the earth as close to the original grave sites as possible. Both English Heritage and the National Trust replied very promptly and favourably. The National Trust are putting my letter forward to the next meeting of the Stonehenge Archaeology Group and I'm awaiting developments.

(Greywolf, pers. com)

More recently, negotiations have moved forward. A liaison group which includes representatives from the Highways Agency, the National Trust, English Heritage, Friends of the Earth, the Pagan Federation, the Ramblers Association, CPRE, local government, farmers, etc. has been established to discuss the future of Stonehenge, specifically at present the proposed road closures and development. After attending an initial meeting of this group in March 2000, and a second in September 2001, Greywolf had this to say:

I'm hoping to see sympathetic noises translating into action and will keep plugging away until it happens. From being involved in discussions about the road plans for Stonehenge and from making ritual and spirit journeys in and around the site, I've come to focus on respect and reburial as my primary reasons for being involved in the talks. I don't like the idea of any remains that may be uncovered during the work ending up either in a museum display or filed away in a cardboard box in a storeroom. I have been, and will continue asking for any remains that are found to be treated with respect and then returned to the earth as near as possible to their original burial sites, preferably with any accompanying grave goods and with suitable ritual.

(Greywolf, pers. com.)

Pagan calls for the 'reburial' of human remains and artefacts are as much politically motivated as they are spiritually so, particularly when concepts of 'ancestors' – who are unlikely to be directly related to us and who are separated from us by thousands of years – are deployed. Note the tone in the following quotation, again from Greywolf: following discussion of economic arguments for supporting the cut and cover tunnel over the long-bore option to reduce traffic on the A303 near Stonehenge, he outlines the BDO's 'spiritual' reasoning:

> [W]e support the cut and cover tunnel ... because the spirits of the land seem to be at worst indifferent to it ... I've connected with the spirits of the land and of our ancestors partly to assess how they feel about the proposals for the roads ... [T]he spirits are in no way opposed to the Stonehenge Master Plan as it stands. There are spirit pathways that are presently disrupted by the existing roads that will flow freely again should the tunnel be built, whether it is cut and cover or long bore. In either case, there will be damage. In either case, the spirits of the land are strong enough, tolerant enough, resilient and flexible enough to deal with it.
> (Greywolf, http://www.druidry.co.uk)

Here, a spiritual authority founded on ancestral communication is used to promote a political agenda (though the two are clearly entwined). On the face of it, this is little different from the use of the same sort of spiritual authority by various religions worldwide, when mobilised to further political, national or other aims. There are serious implications in the use of such terminology, and archaeologists cannot avoid addressing the issues – writing them off as fringe – by claiming scientific immunity or citing science over politics or 'spirituality', since their interpretations of the past are also constructions. Ucko, with indigenous claims on the past in mind, suggests that a challenge for archaeologists today is to avoid being seen as the enemy by insisting 'they have the right to disturb and desecrate burial sites and to make decisions about the disposal of other people's dead' (Ucko 1990: xvi). Indeed, while indigenous communities can demonstrate genetic or cultural links to satisfy the law, addressing the extent to which Pagans can claim British prehistoric remains are 'theirs' is to miss the point, for two reasons. First, it is interesting that the issue here is one of respect and reburial rather than repatriation. Most Pagans, whatever their claims on the past, generally do not claim to be exclusively related to the 'ancestors'. And, second, as pointed out in my Introduction, the issue here – rather than being one solely of academic discourse versus public understanding, of authenticity versus inauthenticity (following papers in Bromley and Carter 1996), or validity/invalidity (e.g. De Mille 1976) – is of multi-vocality and forms of knowledge and power. More conservative archaeologists may assume they have the power to make such charges because 'scientific' archaeological claims are perceived to be more objectively substantive. But the positivist dichotomies (of authenticity/authenticity, validity/invalidity, etc.) constructed, and the staunchly empiricist approaches taken by some academic critics of neo-Shamans (e.g. Kehoe 2000) are incompatible with contemporary reflexive archaeologies and with current social research methods generally. In the current 'post-processual' climate of archaeology, at least, there is need for archaeologists, heritage managers and others to be reflexive and transparent, and for them to open up their research/data to external scrutiny. So the issue is really whether archaeologists are prepared to address such pluralities and engage with them dialogically, rather than dismiss them as 'fringe' and 'eccentric'.

This protracted discussion of the situation regarding neo-Shamans and 'sacred' sites in Britain, developed in the previous chapter and continued here, demonstrates that further problematising and theorising of these issues are required, particularly with regard to influencing policy and praxis. Having recently drawn attention to the USA with regard to reburial, the final chapter explores the situation across the Atlantic where neo-Shamanic engagements with prehistoric sites (and with shamanisms) compete not only with the heritage industry, but also with another interest group: Native Americans.

7

INVADING ANTHROS, THIEVING ARCHOS, WANNABE INDIANS

Academics, neo-Shamans and indigenous communities

Today, as we approach the millennium a new ethnological term has been coined: *neoshamanism* ... However, neoshamanism has nothing to do with the shamanism that was born in traditional societies.

(Taksami 1998: 26)

And now, after all that, they've come for the very last of our possessions; now they want our pride, our history, our spiritual traditions. They want to rewrite and remake these things, to claim them for themselves. The lies and theft just never end.

(Margo Thunderbird 1988; cited by Kehoe 1990)

[T]he Zuni people have said that Estevan came into their Pueblo impersonating a medicine man. He demanded women as well as riches. Since the things Estevan requested were immoral and improper for medicine men to request, the Zunis killed him. Since that time our people have been in constant contact with non-Indian cultures.

(Zuni Pueblo[1] display, Our Land Our Culture Our Story exhibition, Indian Pueblo Cultural Center, Albuquerque, New Mexico)

Many (though not all) Native Americans argue that neo-Shamans 'impersonating' medicine people today are following in Estevan's imperialist footsteps. A study of neo-Shamanisms would therefore be incomplete if: first, it neglected to discuss these Native American claims that neo-Shamans are committing 'spiritual genocide' when engaging with their 'religions' (e.g. Smith 1994); second, without locating these issues in the wider global context of neo-Shamanisms and inidigineity; and third, if as a neo-Shamanic practitioner and archaeologist producing this study I failed to examine issues in which I am implicated. For such analysis is politically sensitive, neo-Shamanic and archaeologist practitioner or not, negotiating complex

195

relationships between indigenous peoples and 'Westerners'; indeed, it is hard to avoid comparisons between neo-Shamanic neo-colonialism and the colonialist approaches of archaeologists and anthropologists, who have, similarly, been accused of appropriating – even stealing from – indigenous cultures (e.g. Deloria 1988 [1970]). To compare and contrast with my examinations of neo-Shamanisms and archaeology in Britain, this chapter explores relationships between archaeologists, anthropologists, neo-Shamans and indigenous peoples, particularly within the context of 'sacred' sites, with the case study of Ancient Pueblo[2] 'ruins' in the American Southwest (Figures 7.1–7.3). Fieldwork (primarily participant-observation, interviewing, archive research and rock art recording) was conducted over six weeks in April 1998 at Chaco Culture National Historic Park (CCNHP), New Mexico, which is one of the most popular sites in the region for neo-Shamans and other tourists.

Chaco's monuments, dated principally via dendrochronology, were constructed around 900–1130 CE and it seems likely that a building boom was followed by abandonment, possibly related to environmental factors, and/or trade, ritual or other social changes (e.g. Lister and Lister 1981; Crown and Judge 1991; Sebastian 1996). Research has tended to focus, in the vein of processual/new archaeology, on economic and environmental

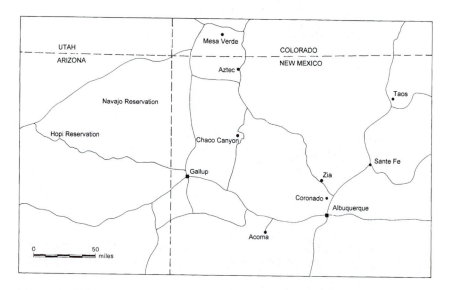

Figure 7.1 The Four Corners region of Southwest USA, where the states of New Mexico, Colorado, Utah and Arizona meet. Fieldwork was conducted in this region in April 1998. Places mentioned specifically in the text include: Ancient Pueblo remains in Chaco Canyon National Historic Park in New Mexico, Mesa Verde and Aztec National Monuments in Colorado, and the Native American reservations of Acoma, Hopi, Navajo and Zia

Source: Line drawing by Sophia Jundi.

Figure 7.2 Chetro Ketl, a complex 'Great House' in Chaco Canyon National Historic Park. The circular structures are 'kivas', probably used by Ancient Pueblo for ceremony and therefore favourite places for neo-Shamanic rituals and votive offerings today

Figure 7.3 Ancient Pueblo peoples of the Southwest also built cliff dwellings. The 'Cliff Palace' at Mesa Verde, Colorado, is one of the most famous and most visited, and is sacred to contemporary Native Americans

explanations for the region's success and subsequent decline (e.g. Earle 2001; Mathien 2001). There was certainly also a strong 'religious', or at least socio-religious involvement: the monumental architecture is thought to have been a focus for ritual, astronomical and/or calendrical observations (e.g Noble 1984; Frazier 1986; Pepper 1996), and/or pilgrimage (e.g. Renfrew 2001). But the Chacoans themselves, their day-to-day social relations, and the ways in which 'religious' practices were actively constituted are often lost sight of in such discussions. And while the precise purpose of 'kivas', pit-like structures common to Ancient Pueblo sites where intimate ritual occasions were likely orchestrated (as they are in contemporary Pueblos), is elusive (Figure 7.2), numerous enigmatic rock engravings[3] (e.g. Schaafsma 1980; Young 1988; Patterson-Rudolph 1997) add greater 'mystery' to the region's archaeology. As a consequence of this ambience, neo-Shamans are drawn to Chaco to conduct rituals and engage with the *genius loci*.

Further participant-observation and interviewing fieldwork was undertaken around Chaco, in the 'Four Corners region', the area at which the four states of New Mexico, Colorado, Utah and Arizona meet. Interviews were conducted with National Parks Service (NPA) officials at Chaco and elsewhere, and with various Native American tribal council spokespersons, principally from the Pueblos of Acoma, Zia and Hopi: Clay Hamilton, Hopi Cultural Preservation Office; Petuuche Gilbert and Daniel Sanchez, Tribal Councilman Reality Officer and Tribal Secretary, respectively, Acoma Pueblo; and Celestino Gachupin, Natural Resources Manager, Zia Pueblo.

I have sought to emphasise diversity thus far in this book; this concern is especially pressing in this chapter: contests over ancient sites and artefacts, meanings and practices, and complexities of relations between archaeologists, anthropologists, indigenous communities and neo-Shamans are particularly marked in Native America. There is no single Native American, neo-Shaman or archaeologist viewpoint; instead there is, by all accounts, a plurality of views, heated argument and controversy. As a result, the text is multi-vocal, and many sensitive and difficult issues are addressed. Issues dealt with in this chapter, perhaps more so than the others, might easily comprise a single volume in their own right. But exploring one issue without comparison can result in a myopic vision of neo-Shamanisms writ large; sweeping examinations without case examples, on the other hand, tend to universalise the situation – it is vital to avoid homogenising the issues. Building on and complementing previous chapters, this chapter constitutes a locative and multi-sited analysis in an effort to represent idiosyncrasies and diversity.

An 'Anthros' dilemma

Neo-Shamanic interests in indigineity worldwide are diverse indeed. Dance of the Deer Foundation, Center for Shamanic Studies in California organises

'Experience Huichol Shamanism' programmes (advertised in *Shaman's Drum*), while other organisations co-ordinate 'spiritual excursions' with shamans in Peru, Mexico and Hawaii. There are also reports of Westerners learning from San (Bushman) shamans and Bantu *Sangomas* in South Africa (Donna Voss, 1997 President of South Africa's Pagan Federation, pers. com.; see also Hall 1994), the Andean *paqo* (e.g. Wilcox 1999), Australian Aborigines (e.g. Mulcock 1997, 1998), and Siberian shamans (e.g. Kharitidi 1996; Beaumont and Kharitidi 1997; Kelly 1997). Of these, perhaps Native American 'religion' has been most affected by neo-Shamans: North America is where neo-Shamanisms have boomed, perhaps partly due to the close proximity of indigenous people.

Neo-Shamanic engagements with indigenous shamans are especially challenging for anthropologists, as Joralemon's experiences illustrate (1990; see also Villoldo and Jendresen 1990). Joralemon comments on the controversy surrounding Peruvian shaman Eduardo Calderon, informant to anthropologist Douglas Sharon (Sharon 1978). Following Sharon's anthropological studies which brought Calderon to public attention, Calderon was 'commercialised' by neo-Shaman and psychologist Alberto Villoldo, who now conducts 'spiritual tours' for neo-Shamans to meet and practise with the shaman (see also Dummigan 1997). For conventional (pre-experiential and pre-insider) anthropology, Calderon's involvement with neo-Shamans brings his reliability as an 'authentic' ethnographic informant into question, perhaps even jeopardising the credibility of Sharon's research. Equally alarming for Joralemon is how Calderon responds to the neo-Shamans' requirements by altering his 'traditional' practice substantially for them. Calderon thus becomes both a shaman, practising local, 'traditional' Peruvian healing, and a neo-Shaman, blending New Age terminology with local beliefs.

Joralemon's initial reaction to the situation is fourfold: First, embarrassment, for the neo-Shamans who believe Calderon's eclectic performance is 'real' shamanism, and for Calderon 'adopting the role of a shamanic clown in a New Age circus' (Joralemon 1990: 109). Second, anger, at Calderon for allowing the exploitation of himself and his tradition, and at Villoldo's motives, 'this travel agent to the spirit world'. Third, empathy for his fellow anthropologist (Sharon) who has been betrayed by this sell-out informant – an informant whose authenticity is now in question. And finally, anthropological superiority over Villoldo because, 'I am a serious student of culture, not a two week tourist pilgrim. I know TRADITION when I see it … My shaman informant never led any tour groups!' (all quotations Joralemon 1990: 109–110). After some reflection Joralemon reconsiders his motives for discontent and sees things anew: he is impressed with the way Calderon shifts between local Peruvian and neo-Shamanic modes of understanding sickness and the supernatural. Issues over 'tradition' are also negotiable: Calderon is dealing with local Peruvians in one context and neo-Shamans who have no knowledge of traditional Peruvian healing in the other, so he presents his obscure tradition in a way that neo-Shamans will understand, blending local knowledge with what they might perceive – *à la* Harner – as 'universal' shamanistic concepts. Of course, adapting to new social and cultural circumstances is what Calderon and countless other shamans have been doing with their 'traditions' for generations.

In the next instance, Joralemon considers the ethnographic value of the neo-Shamanistic rituals: 'Why weren't these also ethnographic facts?' (Joralemon 1990: 112), and his self-reflective discussion illustrates how the legitimacy of the shaman is not corrupted by neo-Shamanisms, but actually brings a new dimension to the relationship between shaman and anthropologist:

> [Neo-Shamans] have the spiritual 'fashions' from virtually every nation on which to model their own cosmic conceptions. Rather than pretending superiority, anthropologists might well study the choices of these culture consumers and the way the resulting mosaics reformulate local traditions to express the shopper's implicit premises.
>
> (Joralemon 1990: 112)

Joralemon's choice of terminology betrays his unfamiliarity with neo-Shamanisms: as I have demonstrated, not all neo-Shamans can be simply written off as culture-hungry consumers with superficial cosmologies. But his statement is not way off the mark and agrees with Atkinson's more sensitive suggestion: 'The reworking of shamanic traditions from around the world in terms of American and European cultural idioms and concerns is a significant development that anthropologists would do well to study' (Atkinson 1992: 322). It remains for me to examine these idioms, of the so-called 'wannabes'.

The 'Wannabes'

Hobson, a Cherokee critic, coined the term 'whiteshaman movement' to describe 'white' poets who assume the persona of Native American shamans in their writings (Hobson 1978; but see Hamayon 1994; for discussion of the White-Red 'fiction', see Simard 1990). Many Native Americans, alongside Hobson, critique strongly these 'wannabe Indians' (Green 1988) for marketing their work as if it were actually by a native author (see comments by Hogan and Rose in Coltelli 1990; Rose 1978, 1992, 1994); 'simulations of tribal identities in the literature of dominance' (Vizenor 1994: 59). Andy Smith (Cherokee member of Women of all Red Nations) suggests, furthermore: 'the New Age movement is part of a very old story of white racism and genocide against the Indian people' (Smith 1994: 168; see also Jacobs 1994). According to this view, cultural imperialism continues, with the 'spirituality' of indigenous peoples now up for grabs by 'plastic medicine-men' (Churchill 1992). Castile (1996) considers this a 'commodification of Indian identity' by neo-Shamans, and suggests it creates a commercial market for Indian teachers: 'The audience of these teachers is not the Indian communities they claim to represent, but the book-, lecture-, and even ordeal-buying public' (Castile 1996: 745). In response, 'real' Indians endeavour to expose 'the falsity of the unreal' (Castile 1996: 745), the 'Great Pretenders' (Rose 1992). Russell Means, American Indian Movement activist, states:

> Our religions are ours. Period. We have very strong reasons for keeping certain things private, whether you understand them or not. And we have every human right to deny them to you ... If you do not [respect our requests], then you are at best a thief ... And believe me when I say we're prepared to deal with you as such.
>
> (cited by Churchill 1992: 221)

Churchill joins the chant: 'shut down the [neo-Shamanism] movement's meetings, burn its sweat lodges, impound and return the sacred objects it desecrates' (cited in Buhner 1999).

In 'borrowing' indigenous traditions and marketing them in workshops, some neo-Shamans (though they may not realise it) reify imperialist approaches, 'defining for themselves the mission of bringing their "know-ledge" of American Indian spirituality to the peoples of modern Europe and America' (Kehoe 1990: 195). Others, such as Hungry Wolf (actually a German), go a step further to assume 'Indian' identities which reinforce racist stereotypes of Native Americans. Taking a similar figure to account, Root (1996) and a BBC documentary (*Grey Owl: The Great White Hoax* 1998; see also G.H. Davies 1999) assess 'Honky shaman' Grey Owl, aka Englishman Archie Belaney. A majority of neo-Shamans 'playing Indian' (P.J. Deloria 1998) are certainly ignorant of the implications of their actions and claims. The 'channels' Brown (1997) interviewed, for instance, all agreed that it would be wrong to become rich by using Native American religions and that benefits should be returned to indigenous communities. Despite Native American calls for them to stop appropriating their trad-itions, however, the channels steadfastly stated they would continue their practice because of its 'planetary significance' regarding environmental destruction (Brown 1997: 163–164). There are more disturbing claims, though, for a 'birthright' to Native American spirituality, with the impera-tive that 'this information is so important that it can no longer be kept a secret' (Brown 1997: 163–164). Worse still,

> Ken Carey, the white author of the New Age best-seller *The Return of the Bird Tribes*, suggests in an interview that computer-literate

white people are the most appropriate heirs to Native spiritual
traditions because the poverty of the reservations has 'debased' the
culture and made it unworthy of the spiritual traditions that have
always been part of Native community life ... [This represents a]
new version of Manifest Destiny, with the belief that white people
are entitled to possess ... any spiritual practice that happens to
catch their fancy.

(Root 1996: 93–94)

When foreigners such as Belaney and non-Native Americans such as Ken
Carey, Castaneda and Lynn Andrews impersonate Native Americans or
appropriate their traditions, the situation is clearly a neo-colonial one; all
the more so for being insidious. It deeply offends many Native Americans,
who, at one time, according to the Zuni quotation opening this chapter,
would have killed such impostors. The scenario is also neo-imperialist since
there is no agreed method of exchange – some neo-Shamans simply 'take'
what they want. As Graham Harvey points out, 'some Pagans appropriate
shamanic techniques without returning any benefit to the "donors" ... and
some even insult the "Indians" by continuing to use the derogatory term
"Red Man"' (Harvey 1997b: 120). Since they rarely engage directly with
Native Americans, most of the information neo-Shamans obtain about
'shamanism', particularly those in Britain and Europe, is gleaned from
ethnographic and neo-Shamanic texts, so that misunderstandings and negative stereotypes are perpetuated. This is not to say neo-Shamans do not
respect Native Americans; the difficulty is with the form this respect takes
in some instances, frequently drawing on romantic stereotypes, and the fact
that the respect is from a distance with demonstrable benefits rarely
returned to the tribes.

The authenticity of some teachers is questionable, as are their teachings:
'women's mysteries' for instance, are in vogue in neo-Shamanisms at present
and a concomitant surge of female neo-Shamans has emerged, Andrews
among them (e.g. Andrews 1982; and criticisms by Orenstein 1994; Morris
1995). Native American women were not afforded the same attentions
Western women are now afforded, however, so that 'women's mysteries' neo-
Shamanisms are obviously a recent invention. Separating the 'fakes' from
'genuine' shamans – obvious examples being Andrews and Castaneda – is
only simple in some instances, however, and the situation is complicated
when certain teachings are understood by some (including Native
Americans) to accommodate non-natives. A prime example is Lakota (Oglala
Sioux) elder Black Elk's sacred vision of Buffalo Calf Woman who brought
the sacred pipe to the tribes, which was popularised by Christian ethnographer John Neihardt. *Black Elk Speaks* (1993 [1932]) has had considerable
influence on natives and non-natives (e.g. papers in Deloria 1984). There is,
however, conflict over the interpretation of Buffalo Calf Woman's words: 'I

bring this pipe for all the common people'; do they mean the pipe is for Lakota people only, as native critics of neo-Shamanisms argue, or might they refer to all people, as native teachers of non-natives suggest? Lakota opinion is divided: Frank Fool's Crow, late ceremonial chief of the Teton Sioux said the sacred pipe is 'the key to the world's survival today' (Buhner 1999), words echoed by Joseph Chasing Horse and other Lakota elders who are friendly to neo-Shamanisms. But recently Lakota tribal statute stated that no aspects of Teton Sioux religion be used by or taught to non-natives, including sweat lodges, sundances, vision quests, sage, tobacco and animal parts (*Sacred Hoop* 23, Winter 1998/9: 8). The statute also vilifies those Lakota tribal members who teach neo-Shamans: 'Any White person or tribal member who knowingly encourages or have [*sic*] non-Indians in any ceremony, Sundance, or Vision Quest as participants will be liable and will be prosecuted in tribal or Federal Court for Fraud' (*Sacred Hoop* 23, Winter 1998/9: 8).

The use of the term 'fraud' in the Lakota statute raises issues of cultural copyright, implying there is an 'authentic' native tradition which has been 'copied' without authority by non-natives. The problem here rests with where 'tradition' begins and ends, and I think use of 'fraud' raises more questions than solutions. Is the movement towards a Pan-Indian religion including use of the sweat lodge in many parts of Native America 'traditional' or a fraudulent reworking of localised practices? The logical implication of terminology in the statute is that culture, particularly indigenous religions and other aspects of non-material culture, can somehow be copyrighted. Zuni Pueblo has used intellectual property rights to stop appropriations of Zuni culture (Brown 1997: 166–167), and Zia Pueblo recently demanded compensation for the appropriation of a tribal symbol in New Mexico's flag. This commodification of spirituality is rather troubling, appearing to fix 'tradition' so that any change to it (indigenous or neo-Shamanic) denotes inauthenticity or fraud. The paradox is that despite the inappropriateness of Western legal terminology, it is only within this framework that the Lakota, Zuni, Zia and other tribes can assert their rights.

Similar to the Lakota example, the Hopi (Arizona) lifeways are well documented by anthropologists and are popular consequently with neo-Shamans. Some Hopi 'traditionalists' have been teaching non-natives their 'religious' teachings, a situation which greatly angered many 'progressives' who demanded the teachings be kept secret. Since the official tribal council has opposed the teachings of non-natives, tribal consensus overrides the aims of the so-called traditionalists. No doubt the situation is far more complex than I can do it justice here, and it may seem cut and dry to side with those Native Americans shutting out the neo-Shamans who use their traditions and those Indians who side with them or 'misrepresent' these teachings; but it is important to be aware of the political nature of these 'spiritual' concerns. The case of Hopi traditionalists versus progressives, for instance, is a divide over many issues including land rights and mineral prospecting, not just neo-Shamanic appropriation (Geertz 1994).[4]

In an attempt to ensure authenticity of tribal membership, some Native American rituals now require 'roll cards' (stipulating Native American descent) and sufficient blood purity; one-quarter blood denotes a 'genuine' Native American in some tribes, but agreed quantities vary from tribe to tribe. Such a mandate is certainly unsettling for Europeans, for whom 'race', and by extension, ethnic cleansing, have been a recurring theme, even within the last decade. But it also seems bizarre to discriminate on 'racial purity' alone, since a multi-cultural, multi-racial America now has many 'mixed bloods', or metis, those with part Native American blood. The metis issue is a difficult one to tackle, since the concept of Indian racial purity is a Federal invention (Castile 1996: 744) rather than a classification Native Americans might choose to employ. Genuineness denoted by blood purity alone marks a significant barrier for those 'mixed bloods' with too little 'Indianness' to be involved in tribal life and its rituals. Consequently, in some instances where indigenous teachers encourage neo-Shamans, the teachers are metis. Listing some famous names, such as Jamie Sams (author of the 'Medicine Cards'), Ed 'Eagle Man' McGraw, Rolling Thunder, Freesoul, Brooke Medicine Eagle (e.g. 1988) – also known to the American Indian Movement as Brooke Medicine Ego – and Swiftdeer (e.g. Halifax 1979; Heinze 1991; Cruden 1995), demonstrates the extent of 'mixed blood' involvement in the teaching of neo-Shamans. Harley Swiftdeer-Reagan is particularly notable for having founded the Deer Tribe Metis Medicine Society Shamanic Lodge of Ceremonial Medicine, a 'mixed blood, mixed tradition shamanic path' (Wood and Wood 1993: 10). Apparently, Swiftdeer 'became the first non-full-blood Native American to join the Twisted Hairs Council of Elders, and was given permission to make their knowledge available to anyone who wanted it' (Wood and Wood 1993: 10). No doubt not all Native Americans would support such an edict of 'sharing wisdom: to all races and colours' (Rutherford 1993: 8–9).

Adopting a similar freedom of information policy is the Bear Tribe Medicine Society, founded by Sun Bear, who had visions directing him to 'share the knowledge of his people with contemporary men and women of all races. He felt the long neglected wisdom of indigenous peoples has much to teach the technologically orientated civilisations' (Wood and Wood 1993: 10). Sun Bear is of both Chippewa (Ojibwa) and Euro-American descent, and spent his early life on the White Earth Indian Reservation in northern Minnesota. In the late 1970s Sun Bear established the Bear Tribe, a 'group of native and non-native people sharing the same vision, philosophy, and direction toward the Earth and the Creation around us' (cited by Albanese 1990: 155). In his vision, Sun Bear saw the 'medicine wheel', perceived as a symbol of nature: a circle with four quarters representing creation and people's (human or otherwise) relation to it. In a second vision Sun Bear saw different coloured lights representing the diverse peoples who would learn from the medicine wheel teachings: 'it confirmed my belief that those who would come to me to learn would be of all colours, of all races, and of many nationalities' (cited by Albanese 1990: 233). There is growing attendance at medicine wheel gatherings, where participants can undertake sweat lodges, pipe rituals and crystal healing ceremonies, all themes from Plains Indian and Ojibwa traditions adapted by Sun Bear and fused with environmentalism and neo-Shamanic self-help themes to form the 'medicine wheel teachings'. Without doubt, Sun Bear's teachings have inspired countless people and provided them with empowering methods for living their lives in a 'sacred manner'.

Nonetheless, metis teachers like Sun Bear have been ostracised and criticised by Native American activists, who question his ancestry, the authenticity of his teachings, and have even disrupted his workshops with violence. Sun Bear has certainly introduced new, non-indigenous elements into his teachings, as well as redefined old ones. Perceiving nature as a powerful focus for religious and political activism, for example, may be quite a recent addition since the culture–nature distinction may not have been so pronounced before European engagement with Native America. Furthermore, Kehoe traces the idea of the 'medicine wheel' to what was originally 'a minor item in Cheyenne life, little wooden hoops used primarily in a game of skill ... [T]his practice of spiritual license continues' (Kehoe 1990: 200; see also Moore 1973; Rose 1992). But whatever the origins of Sun Bear's 'tradition', both Native Americans and neo-Shamans adhere to it; thus Kehoe (see also Townsend 1998, 1999) ends up in a neo-colonialist position herself,[5] informing Native Americans that their medicine wheels are a recent invention and, by implication, inauthentic and invalid. This presents a dangerous concept of what is 'tradition': the naïve and outmoded 'old is real, new is not' understanding here misunderstands the way in which traditions are actively constituted. Such an approach identifies Kehoe not as a champion of Native American rights, but as a neo-colonial arbiter over what is and what is not 'tradition'. Rather more interesting in the medicine wheel teachings is, as Albanese states:

> Amerindian immersion in nature lives on in a traditionalist version as well as in a New Age incarnation that is decidedly eclectic ... What unites traditionalists (who politicize the past) and New Agers (who transcendentalize it) is an abiding conviction of the centrality of nature and a continuing enactment of their concern.
>
> (Albanese 1990: 154–155)

Nature has become the prime focus for many Native Americans and neo-Shamans over the last century, and rather than deriding it as Kehoe does, I think it a development worthy of further study. The pertinent issue Kehoe does raise for my discussion of neo-Shamanisms and Native Americans is that teachings are being released by the Bear Tribe and other organisations which, some would argue, should not be taught to non-indigenes.

The perspective of those practising 'indigenous British shamanisms' is interesting at this juncture. During a visit to the States, two British Druids (Greywolf and Bobcat of the British Druid Order) were introduced to a Native American woman by a third party in terms of their teaching Native American spirituality (Restall-Orr 1997). The response was angry to say the least, but there was a misunderstanding: the Druids were bringing their 'native' Druid tradition from the UK to those non-natives in America wishing to learn it, primarily those of 'Celtic' ancestry (as I have discussed, in Britain especially emphasis is on reviving shamanisms indigenous to this country – though with other complications). For Native American critics this steering of 'whiteshamans' away from their religions might be refreshing. Indeed, many neo-Shamans I have met (such as Greywolf and Paxson) suggest popular authors with spurious credentials and who claim authority on teaching native ways are a minority; most practitioners are well aware of the sensitivities surrounding the non-native use of indigenous religions, and would not claim to use or teach them. The meeting of Druids and Native Americans cited above illustrates the – ofttimes justified – hostility of Native Americans to those presumed to be practising *their* traditions. But as the examples of Sun Bear, Black Elk and others make plain, matters of 'genuine' shamans and the 'authenticity' and 'validity' of shamanistic teachings are very grey areas indeed. Contemporary debates in anthropology over such terminology notwithstanding, one very real consequence of the enthusiastic consumption of popular literature and workshops on 'Native American spirituality' is that the often harsh social realities facing many contemporary Native Americans are obscured by stereotypical images of wise and 'noble savages' of a bygone age, and/or by genuinely fake neo-Shamans such as Castaneda and Andrews.

Neo-Shamans and the capitalist ethic

Besides attempts to expose 'inauthentic' traditions and 'fake' teachers, the issue of payment for teaching is a common reason for critiquing neo-Shamanisms. Kehoe is damning of the Bear Tribe, perceiving an easy to consume spirituality purely for profit making, an 'enterprise ... for the sale of packaged Indian rituals and easy-to-read books on Indian spirituality' (Kehoe 1990: 200). She similarly denounces Wallace Black Elk, who is 'genuine' Lakota but charges for sweat lodges, healing pipe-ceremonies, seminars and workshops. Similarly, Smith states:

> True spiritual leaders do not make a profit from their teachings, whether it's through selling books, workshops, sweat lodges, or

otherwise. Spiritual leaders teach the people because it is their responsibility to pass what they have learned from their elders to the younger generations. They do not charge for their services.

(Smith 1994: 168)

And, Deloria motions: 'Real and imagined "medicine men" have become hawkers of spirituality, breaking the old circle of the people and introducing anyone who can pay the entrance fee' (Deloria 1997: 212–213). Native Americans angry with those charging for teachings may be correct in identifying a break in traditional modes of dissemination. For shamans in other parts of the world, though, a 'payment in kind' is commonplace. As Joralemon states,

I suspect one would be hard-pressed to find a modern shaman for whom earning a livelihood from his/her occupation is not a central concern. All of the seven curanderos with whom I have worked in Peru ... are quite pragmatic about the business side of their practices ... they all expect to be rewarded for their expertise.

(Joralemon 1990: 110–111)

This may well be symptomatic of the arrival of capitalism in such circumstances (e.g. Allen-Mills 1997): the growth of democracy, capitalism and Western values in many parts of the world has an inevitable effect on shamanisms, but it would be naïve to contrast traditional- and neo-Shamanisms in terms of the West doing all the transformation. There are, for instance, super-star shamans in Korea whose proficiency is matched in terms of capital gains (Kendall 1996), and to whom clients pay huge sums of money (as well as to the shrines of ancestral spirits). To Drury and other neo-Shamans this may be deemed 'fake shamanism' (Drury 1982): I think it a transformation of indigenous practices in response to challenging social circumstances. Elsewhere, San/Bushman shamans of southern Africa began to assume elite status and charged for healings with the arrival of European settlers (Dowson 1994a, 1994b). Traditional modes of existence are always in flux and adapt to new circumstances. For many shamans, operating within increasing pressures of a rapidly spreading capitalist milieu, this means charging money for their services. Neo-Shamans charging for workshops are clearly not so different from their 'traditional' contemporaries where *both* are inevitably affected by the capitalist ethic. Indeed, at the root of the issue over payment might be the substance of the exchange – money – rather than exchange *per se*. As Brown suggests, it is difficult for Native Americans to hold neo-Shamans accountable on the subject of payment when the forces of capitalism in the modern world compel some of them to run casinos, deal in so-called 'art' (ritual) objects, and so on (see Brown 1997: 176). This is not to let neo-Shamans off the hook, of course: Johnson's judgement of Harner's Foundation for Shamanic Studies (FSS) is particularly astute, when it:

> awards monetary contributions to those they designate 'Living Treasures of Shamanism', such as Wangchuk, a 68-year-old Tibetan shaman living in exile in Nepal. While the award serves the admirable goals of enabling the shaman to continue to practise his 'traditional' form and preserving the rituals on tape for archives both in Tibet and at the Foundation, it also, in an ironic twist, promotes itself to arbiter and authority over who is and who is not a 'true shaman'.
>
> (Johnson 1995: 172)

With the 'Living Treasures' award, the Foundation decides who receives the title and stipend. The shaman's community may honour the shaman, but still, it is the FSS's criteria which hold influence. Of course, this award offers huge benefits for some shamans, but what of the shamans whom the FSS perceive to be not quite up to the mark?

As my discussion of the so-called 'wannabes' has illustrated, there are, without doubt, neo-Shamans whose engagements with indigenous shamans are blatantly neo-colonialist. There is a danger of over-simplifying a very complex situation, however; to explore these nuances further, I next examine neo-Shamanic engagements with Chaco Canyon in New Mexico; I first set the scene with some necessary discussion of historical context, and ways in which Native Americans in the region might also charge archaeologists and anthropologists with neo-colonialism.

Native Americans, 'Anthros' and 'Archos'

Historically volatile relationships between indigenous communities and anthropologists and archaeologists are well documented worldwide (e.g. Lurie 1988; Layton 1989a, 1989b; Nichols *et al.* 1989; Carmichael *et al.* 1994; Biolsi and Zimmerman 1997; Swidler *et al.* 1997). During the colonial era native communities were subject to genocide, cultural assimilation and religious suppression (e.g. Simard 1990); acts partly legitimated by anthropological notions of cultural evolution which classified indigenous peoples 'below' Westerners of 'higher civilisation' and barely above 'animals'. The American Southwest was a favourite location for the 'insidious salvage paradigm' (Root 1996: 74): early ethnographers, recognising a demise in tribal cultures such as the Pueblo and Navajo, determined to 'record' these practices for 'posterity' (and individual prestige) before they were lost 'forever'. For early archaeologists, on the other hand, monumental 'ruins' built by ancestors of the contemporary Pueblo were thought to have been constructed by prehistoric Mexican 'civilisations'; that 'primitive' Pueblo Indians were the architects was unthinkable.[6]

The situation is, mercifully, very different today, with increasing dialogic and collaborative relationships between anthropologists and archaeologists, and Native Americans (e.g. Ferguson *et al.* 1993; Herle 1993; Glass-Coffin 1994; McManamon 1994; Biolsi and Zimmerman 1997; Jameson 1997; Swidler *et al.* 1997; Fixico 1998; Smith 1999; Watkins 2000; http://www.canadianarchaeology.com/ahc/eprinciples.html). On the ground in the Southwest where archaeological remains outside reservations are 'managed' by the NPS (National Parks Service), for instance, there are, alongside or in place of their non-indigenous colleagues, Pueblo and Navajo rangers, and in some instances, archaeologists. And on a larger scale, NAGPRA (Native American Graves Protection and Repatriation Act, 1990), following its predecessor, the National Museum of the American Indian Act (1989), has enabled Native Americans to make claims for the repatriation of material culture, including human remains (e.g. Merrill *et al.* 1993), despite the protests of physical anthropologists, who largely depend on skeletal remains for their research (e.g. Meighan 1986; American Committee for Preservation of Archaeological Collections, ACPAC, http://www.adlestrop.com/acpac). At Aztec National Monument Museum, two signs read:

> [T]he artefact once displayed here came from a burial. Although in the past we commonly displayed burial items, we have since learnt from American Indians that this is not appropriate. Now more sensitive to their concerns, Aztec Ruins has removed all burial signs from display.

Gene Adams, a ranger at Aztec, told me these displays were adjusted in 1997 and seven tribes local to Aztec meet with the NPS once a month to discuss issues of repatriation and to develop strategies for negotiation (pers. com.). This is clear proof that sensitive dialogue is opening up in some instances between archaeologists and Native Americans (see also Roberts 1997).

Despite such encouraging advances, both interest groups express dissatisfaction with NAGPRA's terminology. The advent of NAGPRA, for instance, brought claims of 'cultural affiliation' on Ancient Pueblo material culture from the Navajo (Diné) peoples who may have had contact with Ancient Pueblo (e.g. McPherson 1992: 96) but arrived in the four corners region two to three hundred years after the monuments became 'ruins'. Appealing to the strength of oral history as a legitimate basis for repatriation, the Diné now comprise another interest group with claims on Ancient Pueblo archaeology including Chaco Canyon (for competing arguments for and against the use of oral histories as valid information for archaeologists, see, for example, Echo-Hawk 2000 and Mason 2000, respectively). Meanwhile, pressure from scientific archaeologists to alter NAGPRA in their favour is extremely worrying for those Native

Americans and archaeologists developing constructive relationships (Dongoske 1998, see also Stone *et al.* 1998); NAGPRA's terminology complicates advances in dialogue and policy making is greatly challenged by the diversity of Native American voices.

NAGPRA and the repatriation of human remains and artefacts mark one difficult issue, but ancient monuments chart different terrain altogether. The Executive Order Indian Sacred Sites (1996) (available online, http://www.cr.nps.gov/local-law/eo13007.htm) and 36 CFR Part 800 Protection of Historic Properties (available online, http://www.achp.gov/regs.html) address Native American concerns over access to and the management of their 'sacred sites' (especially those off reservation), while section 106 of the NHPA (National Historic Resources Act, amended 30 October 1992) requires consultation with Native Americans when such remains are affected (e.g. Ferguson *et al.* 1993). In the case of Fajada Butte, for example, a major astronomical Ancient Pueblo site in Chaco Canyon, there has been major damage as a result of tourist pressures so that:

> [I]n 1982 access to Fajada Butte was limited to research, monitoring and traditional American Indian Use ... NPS preservation efforts were limited because this is a sacred site. After scientific study and consultation with American Indian groups [certain repairs were made].
>
> ('The Sun Dagger display, CCNHP)

While this may appear sensitive to the Native American viewpoint, it is important to note how their interests are listed below the objectives of science. Indeed, archaeologists and Native Americans consistently take very different approaches to 'archaeological' remains. NPS management plans, for example, are at odds with some 'traditional' views. Summarised by the Organic Act of 1916 the NPS aim is:

> to conserve the scenery of the natural and historic objects and the wildlife therein and to provide for the enjoyment of the same in such manner and such means as will leave them unimpaired for the enjoyment of future generations.
>
> (Organic Act 1916)

But ideas of 'ownership', 'conservation', and 'preservation for posterity' are peculiarly Western (e.g. Murray 1996), and despite the good intentions behind the statutes cited above, Ancient Pueblo remains off reservation are often under the jurisdiction of the NPS, whose aim, like that of its British counterparts English Heritage and the National Trust, is 'protection' and 'preservation'. Hence, the valley was designated a 'National Monument' in 1907, its boundaries were expanded in 1980, and it was then heralded as a

'World Heritage Site' in 1987; such labels are meaningful principally to Westerners educated in the preservation ethic. For them,

> [T]he legislated purpose of Chaco ... is the preservation, protection and interpretation of the prehistoric cultural resources that it contains. In addition the park is committed to providing opportunities for visitors from all over the world to enjoy the remoteness, quiet, clear air and natural resources.
>
> (NPS 1996a)

Certainly some Native Americans (e.g. Pueblo and Navajo rangers) share this view, but other perspectives, particularly those which are more 'traditional' and expressed by elders, are ignored: for some Diné, for example, the sites have been appropriated by archaeologists:

> As the ruins are mapped, excavated, and turned over to the public in the name of preservation, a destructive act occurs by unintentionally denying the medicine man religious access to sites and objects that had previously been available ... [pointing out] the irony of preserving a 'dead' culture while on the other hand inadvertently helping to deny a 'living' one.
>
> (McPherson 1992: 126)

Some Diné ritualise at Ancient Pueblo and use artefacts in their 'medicine' (e.g. McPherson 1992: 103–111). Significantly, though, these people are mostly medicine men, ritually prepared and purified before and after engagement with the remains. And for the Pueblo and Navajo people I met, Chaco is a living place rather than an outdoor museum of 'preserved' (read dead) artefacts for tourist consumption. Chaco figures prominently in Navajo oral recollections (see, for example, Locke 1976: 81–83) and it is central to Pueblo cosmologies, for the Hopi in particular:

> The Hopis call Pueblo Bonito [in Chaco Canyon] 'The place beyond the horizon'. In our Hopi migration stories, Pueblo Bonito and other villages in the valley were resting places for many clans prior to their final journey to the Mesas. Clans that have ancestral ties to the area include the Parrot, Katsina, Sparrow-Hawk, Squash, Crane, Bow, Sand, Lizard and Eagle. When I visit the area, I feel the mystery and the significance. Pueblo people still pay spiritual homage to this 'footprint' for no spiritual/archaeological site is ever considered 'abandoned'. Pueblo Bonito is still a living legacy to us and other Pueblo.
>
> (Leigh J [Jenkins] Kuwanwisiwma, Hopi; quoted in an Indian
> Art and Culture Museum display, Santa Fe, New Mexico)

211

In one of the museum displays in the Chaco visitor centre we are told:

> [Ancient Pueblo] beliefs and practices may have been similar to those of modern Pueblo people … [but they] may never be shared with outsiders. If they were, would we understand the relationship to the whole? … Chaco Canyon, the ruins and the artefacts left behind deserve our respect. They were sacred to the people who once lived here – and they still are to Pueblo descendants today.
>
> ('Ceremony: Chaco as a Center' display, CCNHP)

This is a sensitive representation of Chaco in the past and its connections with the modern Pueblo people, who might agree with Ed Natay, Chief Regulations Officer of American Indian Programmes: 'Ancestors are still there. Spirits are still there. The Pueblo people still visit, still consider it the same as going to a lived-in place. And there is respect for all these sites among the Indian people' (NPS 1992). The Hopi Cultural Preservation Office, among other Pueblo tribal organisations, is at the centre of discussions over the significance of archaeological remains (as well as ethnographic and ethno-historical records) to archaeologists and anthropologists, on the one hand, and Hopi cultural preservation, on the other, and is involved in negotiations towards developing strategies for mutual reciprocation, particularly when sacred sites are impacted by development (e.g. Ferguson *et al.* 1993). Indeed, Ferguson *et al.* (1993: 32) state, 'Nondestructive osteological analyses and studies of artefacts are seen as appropriate means to collect the data of interest to the Hopi Tribe.'

But the Pueblo do not speak with a single voice: for some, at least the tribal council members I met, the handling of human remains is potentially dangerous, and visiting sacred sites at all is deeply problematic. In contrast to the archaeological view that sites were 'abandoned', traditions teach that 'spirits' reside at these places and that disturbance – from non-natives and most natives – is a violation. Both Pueblo and Navajo traditions teach that Ancient Pueblo remains should be avoided by all but the suitably prepared – usually medicine men or their equivalents – but in the current climate where such views are challenged by heritage management, the ambivalent view of one Pueblo woman is fitting: some mornings she wakes up thinking the NPS are correct in preserving the ruins, other mornings she agrees with her grandparents who told her the place was meant to be left alone to decay and that preservation actually harms the 'spirits' residing there (related to me by the Chaco ranger G.B.).

I discussed these issues in detail with Pueblo spokespersons at the centre of the debate and they expressed deep concern over archaeological custodianship of the monuments. Petuuche Gilbert (Acoma) said of Chaco: 'people died there, people's remains are there, the spirits' power is still there'. Celestino Gachupin (Zia) suggested archaeological measures to stabilise ruin walls have malevolent effects on the site's spirits, and reinforced this by adding: 'we say everything has life. Some longer, some short … if a building is meant to last five hundred or a thousand years then collapse, it is meant to'. In addition to conflicts over site use, what archaeologists classify as 'utilitarian tools' are to some Pueblo sacred, only to be handled by specific ritual specialists:

> The handling of these objects by others ... can have negative physical and spiritual consequences for those individuals ... [sacred artefacts are ritually retired, so their excavation] violates that ceremonial retirement [and] could result in the release of the negative spiritual force contained [within them].
>
> (Dongoske and Anyon 1997: 190)

Clay Hamilton (Hopi) stated that women archaeologists dealing with human remains are particularly at risk and even touching pottery sherds is potentially damaging.

These comments challenge significantly conventional archaeological practice and rhetoric: Ancient Pueblo structures are meant to decay, a view anathema to the preservation ethic. These Pueblo spokespersons also argue that archaeologists and tourists are in danger when near to or in direct contact with the remains. To most archaeologists these views need not be taken seriously, and perhaps in light of this they are not represented in site presentations. At Chaco's museum, specialist archaeologists provide the interpretation, mediated by the NPS, sanitising the polemics over access to provide neatly packaged 'education' for tourist consumption. Educational benefits aside, the interpretative displays in a National Park such as Chaco are constructed, defined and presented by the dominant custodians. The sites are presented as 'sacred' to the Pueblo with the implication that 'respect' is due, but how this sacredness and respect are constituted is not specified: to non-indigenes, on the one hand, this may stipulate preservation in the form of a 'take only photographs, leave only footprints' site etiquette; for Native Americans not espousing the preservation ethic, on the other, the same terms stipulate avoidance of remains so they may deteriorate.

By virtue of their managerial powers, archaeologists are – to Celestino – a 'necessary evil': their interests and practices conflict with traditional views, but their 'authority' enables the closure of sites and the repatriation of archaic remains. The change in Native American perception of archaeologists from 'grave-robber' to 'necessary evil' suggests collaborative dialogue is still begging. In some instances the hegemony is quite explicit, as policy at Chaco stipulates: 'concerning the "American Indian Religious Freedom Act" ... American Indian ceremonies or religious use *will be regulated* through the Superintendent with the issue of special use permits' (Belli 1993: 9, Superintendent CCNHP, emphasis mine). So although the NPS is making indigenous concerns part of its management strategy, further negotiation is necessary; but if the situation were not already complicated and fraught enough, negotiations are also required with a third interest group: it is now time to introduce the neo-Shamans who – controversially – conduct rituals at Ancient Pueblo sites, leave votive offerings, and remove artefacts.

Ancient Pueblos and neo-Shamans

Many of the thousands of visitors drawn to Chaco each year have 'alternative' interests. In 1987 huge numbers of people visited the park to celebrate a major astronomical/astrological event known as the 'Harmonic Convergence'. Neo-Shamans still go there, albeit to a lesser degree in recent times, but while tourists break a Pueblo site visitation taboo (to use an anthropological construct), neo-Shamans go one step further, to perform rituals and leave votive offerings at the sites. Brown also reports on the damage to sacred sites in Sedona, Arizona – reputedly a focus for 'energy vortexes' – caused by non-natives having 'virtually taken over' while 'imitating Native American vision quests' (Brown 1997: 161–162, 211–212). While there are various popular books chronicling the Harmonic Convergence at Chaco (e.g. Bensinger 1988) and neo-Shamanic activity at other sites (e.g. Grant 1997), only Christine Finn has provided documentation and discussion in the academic domain (Finn 1997). Finn describes the opinions of site managers, New Age visitors and Native American groups with connections to Chaco, and examines modern votive offerings left at the site in particular. Testimonies of the tribal spokespersons I met agreed with her descriptions.

The perspective held by some Native Americans that it is dangerous to be in close proximity to ancestral material culture implicates archaeologists, tourists, and neo-Shamans (see also Whiteley 1997). The American Indian Movement (AIM) suggests mimicking Native American rituals exposes 'ignorant non-Indians to potential harm and even death' (AIM Leadership Conference 1984, cited in M.F. Brown 1998: 201). Since earliest contact, however, Native American 'religions', Pueblo religion – especially Hopi – in particular, has fascinated Westerners for its exoticism, complexity and obscurity. There are numerous ethnographic records of Pueblo life and religion (e.g. Tyler 1964), but when Frenchman Robert Boissiere (1986) claimed he was adopted by a Hopi Kiva Clan in the 1970s, the *practice* of the religion was now promoted. Boissiere claimed he had a vision instructing him to found a kiva clan in Santa Fe composed entirely of non-Indian people. The Hopi response was mixed, particularly oppositions between the 'traditionalists' and 'progressives', as discussed by A.W. Geertz (1983): two 'traditionalist' elders endorsed Boissiere's publication and practice of previously secret religious knowledge. According to Clay Hamilton, though, a majority of Hopi people compare 'white' kiva clans with early anthropological intrusions in terms of 'theft'. Geertz (1987: 44) damns them as 'self-righteous spiritual imperialists who embody the "Pahana Syndrome"'

(Geertz 1994); that is, wanting to be the returned benevolent 'white brother' spoken of in Hopi oral tradition. Following centuries of intrusions, accelerated during the 'Hippie invasion' (Geertz 1994), Hopi villages are now reticent to discuss issues with outsiders: photography is banned, tourists are no longer allowed to watch some ceremonial dances – it is even an offence to take notes in their museum. Indeed, as stated in my Introduction, until I made my (autoarchaeological) purposes very clear – in that I was neither a Pahana Syndrome-suffering neo-Shaman, nor a culture-thieving 'anthro' – Clay Hamilton was extremely reluctant to meet and talk with me.

All the tribal council members I spoke with expressed concerns with outsiders being exposed to aspects of the Pueblo lifeway, be it rituals or material culture. Among the Pueblo there is no religious hierarchy: everyone has a precise place in 'religion' so that one individual cannot possess complete knowledge; through this socio-religious set-up, community is reciprocated and reproduced, each person's office sanctioned, and individual participation contributes towards the complete ritual. Essentially, 'everyone in turn is responsible for the total tribal life' (entrance sign, Acoma Museum). Clay Hamilton suggested that those neo-Shamans in Sedona practising what they believe is an authentic Hopi snake dance could therefore be at risk: the workshop teacher cannot know everything about, or be an 'authority' on, Hopi religion, so elements missing could leave the practitioners in danger; a matter of spiritual responsibility and consequence. Petuuche Gilbert and Daniel Sanchez agreed:

> Do respect our religion, don't use it ... you cannot use our religion because you are not Acoma and to be Acoma you have to be born here. From day one you become Acoma and the teaching must begin at birth.
>
> (Gilbert and Sanchez, pers. com.)

Suggesting anthropological texts on Pueblo religion – specifically Waters (1963) – are 'fake', these Pueblos stated that neo-Shamanic practices drawing on these records are also false, an insensitive mockery of Pueblo religion; the intent a naïve travesty.[7] As archaeological practices are perceived by them as sacrilegious, then, so for these Pueblos neo-Shamanic interactions are viewed as an intrusion, profane and hazardous – imitations by 'Wannabe Pueblos' is disrespectful, and Celestino Gachupin anticipates that the situation with neo-Shamans visiting Zia Pueblo in search of elders and wisdom '*will* worsen'.

To these Pueblos, then, neo-Shamans, archaeologists and anthropologists are comparable: in terms of their neo-colonial actions and because they are at risk when engaging with Pueblo culture. No doubt, archaeologists would see themselves differently, and at Chaco, though not explaining that many

Pueblo and Diné would rather the sites were not visited at all by non-natives, signs erected by the NPS reflect explicitly Pueblo concerns regarding neo-Shamans when stating 'kivas are sacred places, leave nothing behind'. The Pueblo tribal council members I met stated the removal of artefacts or leaving behind of votive offerings is comparable with all other non-indigenous interactions with the sites: it is offensive. Celestino Gachupin stated that the leaving behind of artefacts by neo-Shamans is actually 'destructive to the spiritual fabric of the place'; not only are votive acts offensive and disrespectful, they also detrimentally impact the site's spirits who in turn may pose a threat to the visitors. The Pueblo view is not singular, however, and on site at Chaco, some of the Pueblo visitors I met thought anyone who was respectful to the site should be allowed to visit, so long as they don't take anything or leave anything behind. Nonetheless, since the Harmonic Convergence, the NPS have collected, curated and catalogued large numbers of neo-Shamanic offerings, many imitative of Native American ritual objects; Pueblo prayer sticks, for instance. Unlike the votive offerings discarded as 'ritual litter' in Britain, these items – from crystals and shells, to burnt sage and feathers – are perceived to represent a continuity of site use and are therefore worthy of archaeological curation (Finn 1997: 176). Finn questions: 'Are they "junk" or archaeological objects of meaning and value? ... [W]hile extrapolation from 20th-century to prehistoric behaviour is problematic, there is resemblance between the "modern" and the artefacts gathered from traditional archaeological excavation' (Finn 1997: 169).

Having commented that many British Pagans would most likely rather their votive offerings were not cleared up as 'litter', while others condemn most forms of offering, it is worth considering how US neo-Shamans visiting Chaco feel about the 'appropriation' of their material culture by the NPS. G.B. Cornucopia, a ranger at Chaco for many years, told me that people who leave votive offerings are unaware of the NPS policy to curate them. One individual who did hear about the NPS 'tidying up' returned to Chaco's visitor centre demanding the return of his crystal offerings; to the amusement of the Navajo rangers, he claimed to be 'Native American'. The New Agers at Chaco – claiming to be 'Indian' or not – may have good intentions when leaving their offerings and otherwise engaging with the sites, but their practices are deeply offensive for some Pueblo and Navajo: while G.B. was monitoring a neo-Shamanic ritual in Casa Rinconada, a Navajo guide passing by wryly commented 'any Indians down there?'.

The situation at Casa Rinconada, where most neo-Shamanic activities were focused, escalated when a trend for depositing cremated human remains in the kiva emerged. In response, the NPS decided to deny access to the interior: George Esber, the region's ethnographer stated 'kivas are places for the living, not the dead' (NPS 1992), and contact with human remains is particularly offensive to the Diné[8] (see also Gabriel 1992; Martin 1997). Chaco borders the Navajo reservation and consultation programmes (Swidler

and Cohen 1997) – in part, apparently, a result of neo-Shamanic activities –
allow the collection of religious and medicinal herbs in the region:

> In 1988 the Resource Management Plan for Chaco Culture National
> Historic Park addressed the issue of Native American use of park
> resources, and proposed a special regulation concerning the
> continued medico-religious practices by Navajo and Pueblo Indians
> ... Contemporary native American practice, rock art and finds of
> prehistoric and historic prayer sticks attest to the importance of the
> site for healing ceremonies ... the NPS insists it is actively seeking a
> harmonious relationship with the traditional – the native American
> Indian users – in the light of an increase in New Age activity.
>
> (Finn 1997: 176)

In an NPS press release, it transpires that a Navajo Site Maintenance Crew
discovered the cremations at Casa Rinconada and consequently removed and
returned the ashes to the families who deposited them. Regional Director
John Cook stated:

> The problem is a serious one that can have an adverse affect on both
> the Navajo and Pueblo people, as well as other American Indians.
> Navajo belief dictates that the dead must be avoided and their
> burial places left undisturbed. To expose themselves to locations or
> things associated with the dead could adversely affect their personal
> health and well-being.
>
> (NPS 1992)

An example narrated by G.B. makes this perspective very plain: during one
neo-Shamanic ritual in Chaco, the leader of the ceremony died from an
aneurysm. The Diné reasoning was that the dead man had been thoughtless
to conduct such a ritual, had offended the 'spirits' of the place; essentially,
'that served him right'. As some Diné say: 'the dead must be treated with
the same respect as the living and ... failure to do so will lead to heart
attacks or nightmares brought by the wind ... To antagonise the spirits of
the deceased is to tamper with one's health' (McPherson 1992: 102–103).

The NPS response to neo-Shamanic engagement with Ancient Pueblo
remains has involved difficult decisions. In addressing the problem at Casa
Rinconada, for instance, the NPS established a 'policy on the spreading of
cremated remains'. However, 'even as the policy was being formalised,
cremated remains again were spread on the Great Kiva' (NPS 1992). To the
NPS, the implementation of 'special use permits' to enable natives only to
visit and conduct rituals at Casa Rinconada might be a suitable way of
addressing the situation. But, they cannot partition parts of the canyon for
the exclusive use of a few, nor can they privilege one religion over another.

And the protocol seems decidedly patronising, if not neo-colonialist, the NPS allowing certain concessions where *they* see fit. Following consideration of how best to resolve the problems (NPS 1996a), Casa Rinconada was eventually closed to the public in July 1996 (NPS 1996b; Finn 1997: 177). 'Visitor impact' was cited as the reason for this action, but neo-Shamanic impact was clearly the specific reason. We should also not be surprised to learn, 'Some Indians have objected to the public being allowed into the kiva, although McLean [CCNHP Chief of Interpretation] said *that was not a factor in the decision to close it'* (*The Albuquerque Tribune*, 11 December 1996, my emphasis). In the same vein as Fajada Butte, then, closure of Casa Rinconada was for the purpose of preservation rather than in view of Native American wishes. On my visit I observed people crossing over the barriers to enter the kiva, and site rangers reported that offerings are still found there (and elsewhere); in one instance a neo-Shamanic 'shrine' was discovered at Penasco Blanco (G.B. Cornucopia, pers. com.).

This continued disregard for Native American wishes not to leave offerings behind is deeply concerning. For their part, NPS closing of sites to all users might be read as a way of avoiding the need to address differences among the interest groups over issues of site management. And simply cataloguing neo-Shamanic offerings as artefacts and storing them in cardboard boxes does not respond effectively to issues presented by neo-Shamans. In this the NPS are not required to acquiesce to one interest group or another – the reality is far too complex for such simple decisions (though of course archaeologists and tourists are privileged nonetheless). But just as is in effect at Stonehenge and other sites managed by English Heritage and the National Trust, the NPS do have a mandatory role, as custodians, to *negotiate* with the interest groups and perhaps facilitate round table dialogue. Perhaps more challenging is their obligation (which also holds for English Heritage and the National Trust) to represent the plurality of interests – including Native Americans, tourists, neo-Shamans and archaeologists – in site presentation. The curated neo-Shamanic offerings, for instance, might provide a suitable, if contentious, focus point for a carefully constructed exhibition which not only narrates the diversity of perceptions of Chaco, but also delivers guidelines for reciprocal action. Pueblo demands that the monuments be avoided could be set beside those of Pueblo rangers and others adhering to the preservation ethic, or at least ambivalent to it; and these alongside those of neo-Shamans who leave the offerings despite requests by Native Americans and the NPS not to. In this way, informed individuals can make up their own minds about how they will or will not approach Chaco.

Neo-Shamanic neo-colonialism?

Many neo-Shamans 'borrowing' elements of Pueblo religion – and charged by them with neo-colonialism – cause offence without intent and are shocked to realise they have; others respond less favourably: Celestino mimicked a neo-Shaman he had met, 'I'm an American, I'm in America, why can't I?'. Pueblo people I have met express an understanding of the neo-Shamanic spiritual quest, but think the 'stealing' of their rituals and direct engagement with sacred sites unacceptable. Outside Native America, in countries where Western colonial influence had a different impact, shamans have responded to neo-Shamans in other ways. South African sangomas may have been marginalised in a similar way to Native Americans, but as mentioned earlier, some of them have been open to neo-Shamanic interests (e.g. Hall 1994): perhaps the breakdown of apartheid and a gradual, if politically sensitive process of 'reconciliation' has facilitated this. The main difference between the Pueblo and sangoma examples concerns the internal systems of copyright and privacy operating in Pueblo communities. All my informants said they had the simple right to say 'no' to people seeking spiritual teaching from their elders. Petuuche and Daniel thought the attitudes and approaches of non-natives, particularly concepts of religious freedom and the right to knowledge – both of which seem to legitimate appropriation and commodification – problematic. The right to privacy is a central issue for them:

[W]e must maintain the privacy of elements of our beliefs and customs in order to preserve the strength and substance of our culture. There are things about Pueblo life which can only be discussed within our community for this reason. We ask that you respect this privacy ... There are still many more aspects of our lives which we are pleased to share.
(Introductory panel 'Our Land Our Culture Our Story', Indian Pueblo Cultural Center, Albuquerque; see also HCPO 1998)

A strong element of privacy in Pueblo lifeways maintains 'spiritual' community and continuity, and negotiates social cohesion; thus, Pueblo requests for privacy – based on tribal consensus – must be respected. In contrast, these systems do not operate among Hall's sangoma teachers, where openness to outsiders is acceptable. It would be simplistic to suggest all Native American traditions operate in a similar way to the Pueblo – as noted, opinion is divided within and between communities – but being aware of these socio-political arenas, their complexities and nuances, better enables analysis of the situation, and better places archaeologists and anthropologists as negotiators in the process of dialogue.

Tribal councils who must deal with issues of land rights, NAGPRA and neo-Shamans on a daily basis acknowledge that such processes of negotiation are inherently political (see Appendix). The intrinsic relationship between politics and spirituality is, problematically, denied by many neo-Shamans, on the other hand; they often appeal to a perceived universal 'spiritual truth', and the right to know, in their claims on indigenous religions, thereby imposing (perhaps in some cases unwittingly) their own peculiarly Western concepts of universality. Such neo-colonialist and universalist comments are voiced by a neo-Shaman in *Shaman's Drum*, who argues that excluding non-natives from Native American religion would be the same as Christians saying blacks cannot become Christian (Buhner 1999). Buhner's argument is flawed by the fact that Christianity is an evangelical religion where Native Americans traditions are not. He suggests sweat lodges and sage like those in Native America are used worldwide, so that his use of them cannot be 'theft'. He might also claim his position is a spiritual rather than a political one, thereby authenticating his argument on 'higher' grounds. But as Brown argues, neo-Shamanic appropriation of Native American religions has a detrimental and undermining effect on other claims such as land rights (Brown 1997: 166). Neo-Shamans therefore cannot have their cake and eat it too. Buhner's simplistic methodology is easily deconstructed. There may be these 'universal' trappings of 'shamanism' worldwide, to him at least, but if neo-Shamans also mimic a Native American format, as many do, then the sweat and the sage *are* 'borrowings' from Native America. Buhner's perspective is naïvely neo-imperialist since it appeals to the peculiarly Western (though increasingly acceptable) notion of a global village, when we are actually dealing with the diversity of Native American 'religions', among distinct tribes, in specific areas. The richness of tradition is lost in his monolithic and neo-colonialist narrative of his right to know and what constitutes 'real' 'shamanism'.

Nonetheless, foregrounding diversity and nuance over metanarrative inevitably challenges universal application of 'neo-colonialism'; in some instances, neo-Shamanic engagements with shamans can be seen as a positive force for indigenous peoples, agreeing with Harvey's (1997b) notion of 'extra pay' (utilised in Chapter 2). Some neo-Shamans ideologically and financially support, publicise and draw considerable attention to, the rights and acts of cultures formerly and currently suppressed. The FSS's 'Living Treasures' award and teaching of core-shamanism at the request of indigenous groups mark examples where neo-Shamanisms are giving back to the cultures 'borrowed' from, albeit controversial ones. Also, Harner *does* emphasise the complexity of shamanic cultures (they are not evolutionarily simple) and the value of their modes of awareness (altered states are not just for 'hippies' and the 'insane'). On a smaller though not insignificant scale, Leo Rutherford of Eagle's Wing for Contemporary Shamanism in London reports:

> I am delighted to tell you that our tape and booklet 'FORTY-FOUR CHANTS, WORDS AND MUSIC' has sold nearly seven hundred copies and raised over £3,000 for Native American charities. Most of this has gone ... to Native American peoples, and

£1,000 went to the Tairona Heritage Trust to help the Kogi of Columbia to buy land.

(*Sacred Hoop* 1, 1993: 9)

Furthermore, widespread consensus among neo-Shamans I have met is that the term 'shaman' is honorific; to call *oneself* a shaman in the West is egotistical – the term is used sensitively and neo-Shamans thereby endeavour to respect traditional shamans. Also, according to Harvey, where neo-Shamanic Pagans are active in environmental education (MacLellan 1995) they move 'towards being properly shamanic ... the word is paid extra: it is honoured as a force for change, an imperative in the growth and evolution of Paganism[s]' (Harvey 1997b: 117). The socio-political context for neo-Shamanisms and its benefits are recognised here, engendering 'an important part of the postmodern critique of society' (Harvey 1997b: 122). In this respect, neo-Shamanisms are far more intelligent and socially aware than many critics give credit, and they move beyond the 'hermeneutic failures' Jocks (1996) and others perceive in them.

The issue of neo-colonialism is, in all regards, complex, as Merete Demant Jakobsen points out:

> [o]n one of the courses [on which] I did my research, there was a young [indigenous] Greenlandic woman. When I interviewed her she told me that she did not draw on her tradition in her own journeys but that of Native Americans – is she committing cultural imperialism?
>
> (Jakobsen, pers. com.)

In such instances, the monolithic charge of neo-colonialism is disrupted and issues of cultural 'borrowing' or 'stealing' complicated. Elsewhere, Serge Kahili King's handbook of the Hawaiian way of the adventurer describes contemporary Hawaiian 'shamanism' as follows:

> [T]he great healing, metaphysical, and shamanic traditions of Hawaii are being kept alive primarily by the same race that almost destroyed them completely. Without the audiences of white mainlanders, even the few Hawaiian teaching *kahunas* would have virtually no one to teach.
>
> (King 1990: 33–34)

In a bizarre twist, it is the neo-colonial actions of neo-Shamans which have facilitated the survival of Hawaiian 'shamanism' in modern form. In another instance, Michael Harner told me that representatives from Native American, Sami and Inuit groups have approached his Foundation, requesting that he teach core-shamanism to restore their sacred knowledge formerly disrupted due to conquest and missionisation (Harner, pers. com.; see also FSS newsletters 1988–1997):

> Prompted by pressure for such a service, Harner will demonstrate the shamanic practice he has developed for peoples or communities where earlier – perhaps even as late as the beginning of the century – shamanism was still alive, but where it has been forgotten since then (thus, for instance, among certain North American Indian tribes, the Eskimos of Alaska, and the Lapps of Sweden and Norway). The White Shaman reintroduces the healing ritual, teaching it to the youth of the formerly shamanic peoples. In this work, Michael teaches only 'core-shamanism', the minimal general methods consistent with those once used by their ancestors, so that members of these tribal societies can elaborate and integrate the practices on their own terms in the context of their traditional cultures.
>
> (Hoppál 1992b: 201; see also, Drury 1989: 99)

Taking these examples into account, distinctions between 'shamanisms' and 'neo-Shamanism' begin to blur. The FSS is not entirely off the neo-colonial hook, however.

The FSS has, most recently, been involved in the revival of shamanisms in post-Soviet Siberia. Kenin-Lopsan, president of the Society of Tuvan Shamans, for instance, recently received a 'Living Treasures' grant, and the FSS have other contacts in Tuva, Buryatia, Khakassia and China (e.g. Uccusic 1996; Grimaldi 1996; Brunton 1997; Van Deusen 1997a, 1997b). The FSS say:

> A distinct feature of the Urgent Tribal Assistance Project is that it responds to requests for help rather than initiating assistance, because the Foundation does not want to be in a position of being yet another outsider imposing something on a tribal culture.
>
> (Shamanism 7(1): 22)

Behind the benevolent façade, though, the UTA project and FSS's approach more generally do just that. First, the FSS portrays its core-shamanism as 'shamanism' to indigenous people, when it is, I have argued, a Western construction – indeed its appeal to 'core' features is reminiscent of Buhner's universalist approach. The shamanisms revival in Siberia should involve traditions idiosyncratic to Buryatia, Tuva, Khakassia and so on, not a universal American or Western neo-Shamanism. The FSS is, by good intent, encouraging the 'traditional' shamans to teach the younger generation and suggests they can put cultural meat onto the bare core-shamanism bones, but assuming these bare bones are a given in the first place is deeply problematic; the risk is of imposing Western views of what 'shamanism' should be onto these communities. On seeing core-shamanism at work, for instance, and comparing it with their own methods, the Buryat shamans suggest 'the Foundation's methods were immensely faster, our students learning in two days what had taken them years to learn' (Poncelet and Poncelet 1994: 21). It seems no coincidence that Harner's manual states: 'what a shaman [he means, I argue, a core-shaman] can do in a few minutes takes a yogi many years' (Harner 1990 [1980]: xiii). In contrast to Townsend's positive reading of FSS involvement in Siberia (1999), the organisation is at risk of promoting Western quick-fix shamanism where a 'traditional'[9] form already exists; core-shamanism weekend workshops then replace traditional shamanic inheritance and arduous training over many years. Two core-shamans state: 'we met several individuals introduced to us as "shamans", who attended the workshop. While some of them were clearly good healers, none journeyed or communicated directly with spirits' (Poncelet and Poncelet 1994: 21). The implicit assumption made here is that indigenous criteria for being a 'shaman' do not fit FSS criteria of the core-shaman. The notion of core-shamanism does not sit happily with my argument for a diversity of culturally nuanced 'shamanisms' – those shamans not 'journeying' are in fact just as much shamans as those who do – and the FSS publication *Shamanism* makes little reference to diversity of practice; indeed, it appears mostly concerned with furthering the Foundation's aims and core-shamanism in particular. In 1993, the FSS held a joint conference with the Republic of Tuva 'for the rehabilitation of shamanism' (Harner 1994: 1), and the FSS journal portrays its role as instrumental in the president of Tuva's public declaration following the conference 'that both [Shamanism and Buddhism] would be equally respected in the modern Tuvan Republic' (Harner 1994: 2).

On the one hand, it seems the FSS's actions illustrate how neo-colonialism is more insidious and difficult to detect than colonialism; on the other, it is difficult to ignore benefits the FSS brings to shamanisms. Leslie Conton, a Foundation member involved with presentation of Wangchuk's 'Living Treasures' award, told me the stipend enables shamans to continue in their profession full-time without other employment, so stalling the disintegration of shamanic traditions. She argues the award makes a powerful statement: the West, who formerly discredited shamans as superstitious, now values the profession; and rather than getting a patronising pat on the back from 'the West', it is Wangchuk's community which values him as a proficient shaman, not just the Foundation. The award appears well meant, if a little naïve; a financial stipend alone does not solve the long-term social injustices which many indigenous shamans and their communities face, and the implicit assumption is still made that the West knows what real 'shamanism' is like – would the Buryat shamans who do not 'journey' qualify for an award as well as Wangchuk? Some shamans undoubtedly benefit from the FSS, and, whether we like it or not, the approval of the West is welcomed by the indigenous shamans. Since the request for teaching comes from the indigenous groups rather than the other way round, neo-colonialism is perhaps too harsh or at least too simplistic a term in this instance.

Western influences on indigenous shamanisms are occurring in other parts of the world without Harner's influence, from the syncretism of Roman Catholicism and shamanisms in Peru to the case of the Sakha (Yakut) of Siberia. The Sakha have been reviving 'shamanism' as part of a nationalist revivalist statement in the post-Soviet era (e.g. Balzer 1993) in notable contrast to the 'traditional' practices subjugated by communist Russia. 'Shamanism' of the Sakha revival is comparable with Western neo-Shamanisms in, as Vitebsky puts it, a shared 'crisis of literal belief. They know their knowledge about shamanic ideas, not as *habitus* but as facts' (Vitebsky 1995b: 190–191). Vitebsky argues a radical environmentalism influences their perception of the Siberian landscape, and that as well as shifting their locative indigenous ideology to a more global level, the Sakha are psychologising and de-religionising their shamanism (Vitebsky 1995b: 195); all concepts markedly 'Western' in origin and equally influential on neo-Shamans. For the Sakha, 'shamanism' – and in this case the boundaries between shamanisms and neo-Shamanisms are clearly more permeable – is now providing an empowering socio-religious link to a past formerly inter-rupted by communism.

Elsewhere in Siberia/Central Asia, Brown reports on the revitalisation of shamanisms in post-Soviet Tuva (though no mention is made of Harner's involvement): 'In the shamans' clinic at 41 Lenin Street, fees start at 5,000 rubles, or about a dollar, and go up' (Brown n.d.). He describes how the clinic resembles a GP's practice, with treatment rooms and signs on each door, one of which reads 'Sarayglar Borbakhol, 7th generation shaman'. But while the treatment begins with the shaman taking the pulse of each patient and lasts around fifteen minutes, the shaman's instruments of healing consist of 'a shiny brass disk he uses as a mirror, the clawed feet of animals, seeds, feathers, rattles and what appears to be the shoulder blade of a deer. A shaman's drum leans up against the wall' (Brown n.d.). Another shaman 'diagnoses illness by studying skin colour and pulse, and by detecting "bioenergy" ... .In the rebirth of old traditions in Tuva, this is a new synthesis ... He combines shamanism, lamaism and modern medicine' (Brown n.d.). Brown quotes Kenin-Lopsan (mentioned above) who tells him

there are 34 registered shamans, and more than a hundred studying. He holds up the card all board-certified shamans get once they are approved. It's in a folding red leatherette case just like the ones that used to hold Communist Party membership cards.

(Brown n.d.)

In situations like these in Siberia (see also Humphrey's 1999 discussion of Buryat shamans) it is no longer possible to make rigid distinctions between 'shamanisms' and 'neo-Shamanisms' (see also Vitebsky 1995b: 184): the boundaries between 'shamans' and 'neo-Shamans', 'local' and 'global' (see papers in Fardon 1995), 'authentic' and 'inauthentic' are permeated. Vitebsky is correct to argue against 'any smooth model of "globalisation" as a one-way current, an acculturation leading implicitly to a cultural homogenisation. Rather, it compels us to regard the global process as a 'continual realignment of a system of epistemological and political relationships' (Vitebsky 1995b: 183). As indigenous shamans revitalise their own traditions with 'borrowed' Western (core-shamanic) elements, as they enter the 'global village', the neo-colonialism charge levelled at neo-Shamans becomes too simplistic; mechanisms of colonialism have never been purely one-sided and these shamans in Siberia, like those in Taussig's (1987) study of colonial and contemporary era shamans in Colombia, illustrate how 'the oppressed' negotiate colonial relations and indeed have power over 'the oppressors'. Johnson (1995: 165) regards the actions of some neo-Shamans (particularly Harnerism) as a 'unilineal appropriation, from them to us'. Such transferral of knowledge from local contexts to global ones certainly effects changes of meaning, but the examples I have cited indicate such a comment is monolithic, indeed representative of the myopic critique of neo-Shamanisms.

In this light, I have argued it is essentialist, simplistic and naïve to deconstruct neo-Shamanisms out of hand: monolithic criticisms of neo-Shamanic engagements with indigeneity, and vice versa, fail to take account of diversity. The more nuanced approach I have advocated, and examples I have cited, challenge and disrupt restrictive terminology, from 'classic' or 'authentic' 'shamanism' and 'the shaman' vs 'the neo-Shaman' to what constitutes 'the West' and 'indigeneity', and 'colonialism' and 'neo-colonialism'. Amongst the competing indigenous voices, many shamans – metis or otherwise – *are* willing to teach neo-Shamans. And without doubt, neo-Shamans gain 'spiritual' and other benefits from a variety of indigenous teaching, and in some instances return benefits to the tribes. But following the argument I have made, as both neo-Shaman and archaeologist, I think it imperative that we – all the interest groups – are acutely aware of the polemics of such relationships. To many tribal members, these benefits are outweighed by the threats neo-Shamans pose to the integrity of their teachings and to their right to say 'no'. There are demonstrable instances where neo-Shamans, unwittingly or otherwise, are involved in neo-colonial practices. Yet it is clear, as M.F. Brown argues (1998: 195), that the situation is by no means as simple as saying 'Give the natives their culture back' – not all neo-Shamans can be called, fairly, 'culture stealers', and, as Welch (2002: 35) states: '[I]ndigenous peoples are not unambiguously victims. The colonialist presentation is refuted by indigenous agency.' Approaching these issues in a binary 'us vs them' way is to miss the point: we need a common-sense approach rather than extremes, a careful balancing act between the West's freedom of information and indigenous people's cultural privacy. A much needed first step in the process of education, understanding and recon-ciliation is to recognise that the situation is far more complex than misleading stereotypes allow, and to encourage 'round table' programmes of communication and negotiation.

8

CONCLUSION
Neo-Shamanisms in post-modernity

Pray now for how long
we're falling from ecstasy
Like changelings
Freedom returned for new souls
here or after
well enrapture me and I'll change ...
(From the song 'Psychonaut' written by Carl McCoy,
performed by *Fields of the Nephilim* and *The Nefilim*)

After the initial and perhaps somewhat quizzical reaction 'What have neo-Shamanisms got to do with me?' readers will by now, I expect, have formulated some of their own answers. A great many people from all walks of life are implicated in the issues neo-Shamanisms raise, many even unaware of the fact. This research area, my approach to it and assessment of it, are new, challenging and in no small part controversial. Each of the chapters is a discrete case study of neo-Shamanic practices, but also a 'blurred genre' (C. Geertz 1983) or 'pastiche' (Strathern 1987a) of neo-Shamanisms in its own right, with its own specific conclusions. From these conclusions, it might be overstretching the point to suggest, as I have done in the past (Wallis 2001), that an 'archaeology of shamanisms' must begin not with shamanisms in the past but with neo-Shamanisms in the present. But the point is not invalid: if, as Rainbird and Hamilakis (2001: 91) suggest, archaeologists 'should interrogate (the archaeological and broader) "regimes of truth", and the links of knowledges with power, and intervene critically in the modern battle-fields of cultural production and consumption', then the sense of urgency in my comment at least does not seem misplaced. Academics and other professionals cannot remove themselves from the social contexts in which they live, in which they are embedded; neo-Shamanisms, therefore, cannot be neglected or written off by them as 'fringe' and 'harmless'.

Neo-Shamanisms, like shamanisms, have a socio-political imperative. The claims by some practitioners that particular neo-Shamanic paths are unbiased, non-cultural or apolitical are erroneous and facilitate elitist avoidance of the polemics. Frequently, neo-Shamans attempt to disengage themselves from the problematic aspects of their practices by claiming universal spiritual truth (e.g. Grimaldi 1997, critiqued by Noel 1998). In other cases, neo-Shamans are evidently market-orientated and/or disconnected from day-to-day social relations – the 'New Age' stereotype – having little in common with indigenous shamanisms, indeed often completely misrepresenting these. 'Wannabe Indians' perpetuate notions of the 'Indian' as Other, and romanticise Native Americans of the present into an idyllic mould. In so doing, real living Indians are ignored, distanced further from the present into a 'dead' and 'primitive' past. Other neo-Shamans, in contrast, directly engage with native communities in beneficial ways. I argue, therefore, that a fuller understanding of shamanisms is only achieved when neo-Shamanisms are also explored.

When 'shaman-*ism*' is deconstructed as an untheorised Western term with, all too often, a nebulous meaning (or range of meanings), and when the nuances of indigenous–neo-Shamanic interaction in a global setting are taken into account, some differences between shamanisms and neo-Shamanisms start to fade. The diversity of shamanic and neo-Shamanic practices and their meeting might best be explored without the prejudicial assumptions of 'real' versus 'new' shamanisms; in this way specific instances of appropriation/neo-colonialism or 'extra pay' can be appraised. In place of a judgmental relativist stance in which everyone calling themselves 'shamans' are shamans, I think a 'situational pragmatism' (Strathern 1998: 217) is more appropriate: in some instances there are demonstrable differences (e.g. core-shamans *vis-à-vis* community-specific indigenous shamans), while in others neo-Shamans are more like indigenous shamans, principally when the positive transformations their practices bring about in themselves have an agentic effect in their day-to-day social relations, and particularly when there are reciprocal community benefits (for other than human and human communities, and indigenous communities in particular). Neo-Shamans are, in some instances, powerful forces for social and political critique, not simply consumers promoting individualistic psychological and/or 'spiritual' betterment; they thereby give 'extra pay' to shamanisms and empower neo-Shamanisms in new ways.

Assuming all neo-Shamans are the same is not only a dangerous misrepresentation but also extremely naïve. I have therefore promoted a nuanced assessment of neo-Shamanisms, bringing previously marginalised voices into an arena which has ignored them or treated them insensitively. This work appraises and builds on previous approaches to neo-Shamans; but where previous researchers have made only brief and often monolithic remarks, I have undertaken a 'multiple positioning' (see papers in Fardon 1995) and represented the diversity of practitioners both in overview and with detailed case examples. In all their diversity, neo-Shamans reject any of the attempts at generalisation which derisive critics impose. Jakobsen's impression of 'neo-Shamanism' is not 'that it is a confused disillusioned group with a sense of impotence. Several of the people I have encountered in courses are highly articulate and very well informed' (Jakobsen 1999: 150). My experiences agree: the well-grounded and educated perceptions and ideas of some neo-Shamans may be atypical, but they certainly challenge popular, negative stereotypes and generalisations.

Anthropologists, archaeologists and others are inextricably embedded in these issues and must reassess critically their own position *vis-à-vis* neo-Shamans. Indeed, I have demonstrated how neo-Shamanisms have heavily influenced anthropological and archaeological perceptions of shamanism: the historical and socio-political locations of 'shamanism studies' and neo-Shamanisms are linked. By virtue of having intertwined histories, some neo-Shamans share their romantic yearnings and primitivist tendencies with academics, albeit those of earlier generations. Where academics can revise the work of their forebears, however, it is vital to express current ideas in the popular realm so that stereotypes embedded in public imagination can be addressed, be they misinformed neo-Shamanic concepts of the 'red man', or, on the other hand, monolithic concepts of 'New Age' shamanism. My publishing efforts in this area in both academic (e.g. Wallis 1999, 2000, 2001) and popular (e.g. Wallis 1998, 2002a; Blain and Wallis 1999) texts, participation in negotiations over access to Stonehenge, co-organisation of the 'Permeability' conference bringing key representatives of the interest groups as well as independent researchers/persons together for debate, as well as attendance at Pagan, Druid and other neo-Shamanic events to present my findings (e.g. BroomCon, Pagan Federation South, Strange Attractor), mark first steps, as 'culture broker' (Blain 1997), in this direction; localised attempts to address real issues and forge paths towards reciprocal, if compromised, change.

Neo-shamanic variability, active participation in indigenous shamanisms, and engagements with shamanisms past behove implicated academics (including those in archaeology, anthropology, religious studies and history), field workers (such as archaeologists, anthropologists and heritage managers), indigenous communities and other interest groups to engage with neo-Shamans, and I intend here to have contributed to this dialogue between the interest groups. In an era of transparency in which academic authority is no longer absolute, in which the ivory tower must increasingly 'open up' to external scrutiny, in an era of globalisation, pluralisation and multivocality in which academics are forced to negotiate, broker and indeed give up some of their hold over knowledge – if they are to transform populist stereotypes (of both shamans and neo-Shamans) – archaeologists and implicated scholars must not only be aware of these neo-Shamanic approaches but also engage with such 'alternative' histories and respond to them dialogically, a matter of social inclusivity and permeating the boundaries between academia and popular culture.

I could not have reached these conclusions were it not for a multi-sited method, with comparison of a variety of neo-Shamanisms in the two geographically and socially separated case studies of North America and the UK. Since the UK and USA are not the whole story, I do not suggest this research is exhaustive. In the interests of avoiding metanarrative, future research might approach the neo-Shamanisms I have discussed from another standpoint which is other than archaeologist and practitioner. And moving beyond my examples, neo-Shamanisms in Australia, central Europe and other Western countries, as well as the revival of shamanisms in indigenous cultures and the neo-Shamanic involvement in these, require much closer analysis. The rapidly transforming political climate in South Africa, for instance, is clearly having a dramatic impact on relations between neo-Shamans and black sangomas (e.g. Hall 1994). Exploring this situation may shed new light on the diverse socio-political engagements between neo-Shamans and indigenous shamans. Perhaps most pressing of all, the process of globalisation and associated dissolutions of some cultural divides but reification of others challenges us to address the relevance of neo-Shamanisms to current debates on community identity, constructions of personhood, and power discourse.

I close my discussion in this specific context by addressing an issue I have only touched upon briefly and which demands further analysis: ancient *seiðr*, contemporary seidr, and the issue of gender in both. This ties together various strands running through this book, from post-colonial discourse, alternative archaeologies and queer theory to multi-sited ethnography and the contrasting examples of Britain and North America. Many Heathen neo-Shamanic practices in Britain and North America, in contrast to being 'safe' and 'Westernised', confront and challenge conservatism both in Heathenry and wider society. Heathenry writ large is a conservative Paganism with moral, ethical and 'spiritual' values adhering to 'middle' England and America. 'Traditional' family values are sacred and the issue of same-sex relations remains controversial. Associations with nationalism, racism and homophobia do not typify Heathenry,[1] but the unfortunate history of associations between Northern religions and Nazism last century is seized upon by groups motivated by politics of the far right. They, in turn, are picked out by the tabloid press so that the liberal attitudes of others are eclipsed.

The seidr practices of largely liberal-minded Heathens are not always regarded favourably because many in the Heathen community find notions of 'spirits' and practices involving direct communications with deities and ancestors to be dubious, verging on the blasphemous (Blain, pers. com.). Similarly, at the time of the Icelandic Sagas a millennium ago, *seiðr* was a disreputable practice, especially in the later texts written down by Christians (the majority of all the literature) in which magical workings are generally associated with antisocial behaviour. The insult *ergi* (also *argi* or *ragr*) is used in the myths and sagas to describe a male *seiðr*-worker or *seiðr-maðr* (*seiðr*-man) of human or divine status. Loki the trickster deity, for instance, calls Odin (in some respects a warrior god) *ergi* when he practises the *seiðr* techniques taught by the goddess Freyja (*Locasenna* 24; Larrington 1996: 89). *Ergi* may refer to an 'effeminate man' or to being 'unmanly', and possibly also to passive male homosexuality, reflecting the pejorative sentiments surrounding a man or god taught 'women's magic' (for detailed discussion, see Sørensen 1983).

Seiðr and *ergi* contrast significantly with the sort of 'strong warrior' male role model deemed conventional and desirable during the unpredictable and uncertain times of Viking migration and conflict, and among some contemporary Heathens. Their own experiences have led Paxson, Blain and other seidr-workers, however, to re-appraise the negative associations of *seiðr*/seidr and *ergi*. They suggest that perhaps in earlier times, certainly before Christian prejudice, *seiðr* may have been a more acceptable practice. Northern society may have contained a more 'shamanistic' element, particularly at the local level of small isolated communities, and the status of a *seiðrmaðr* and his *ergi* might even compare with the shaman *berdache* in some Native Americans societies (for discussion of the *berdache*, see for example, Roscoe 1991, 1996, 1998; Whitehead 1993). In similarity to *seiðr* and *ergi*, *berdache* is a loaded term, a colonial construction which imposed Eurocentric understandings of gender and sexual relations onto indigenous cultures (e.g. papers in Jacobs *et al.* 1997) – Europeans judged the *berdache* in simplistic terms and assumed 'men' dressed in women's clothes were simply despicable transvestites. In contrast to Western values, *berdache*-type shamans (e.g. Czaplicka 1914; Taylor 1989; D'Anglure 1992), gender-crossing priests such as the Hindu hijras (e.g. Nanda 1993a, 1993b), multiple-gender conceptions (e.g. Herdt 1996) and same-sex relations (e.g. Sparkes 1998) are cross-culturally consistent. Such consistency deconstructs the simplistic Western conflation of gender and sex and construction of gender based on binary oppositions. So rather than use the binary 'two-spirited people' (Kehoe 1998), or the binary and androcentric 'men-women' (Knüsel and Ripley 2000), 'changing ones' (Roscoe 1998) may be the most applicable replacement for *berdache*.

As evidence for changing ones in ancient northern Europe, archaeologists have recently noted significant anomalies in grave goods associated with Anglo-Saxons, particularly pagans (e.g. Wilson 1992), such as 'male' skeletons buried with 'female' objects (especially those identified as amuletic in function, including crystal balls: e.g. 10 per cent of adult 'males' had 'female' grave goods at Norton, Cleveland, Knüsel and Ripley 2000: 170). This not only challenges conventional methods of determining sex from grave goods (challenged, for example, by Härke 1990), an issue much discussed in the archaeology of sex and gender (e.g. Lucy 1997), and gender from sex, but also the imposition of Western binary sex-gender classifications onto past peoples. Heathens, in turn, may cite Tacitus, who describes (*Germania* 43) how: '[i]n the territory of the Naharvali one is shown a grove, hallowed from ancient times. The presiding priest dresses like a woman'

231

(Mattingly 1948: 136). Similarly, Saxo Grammaticus remarks on the 'changing ones' type priests or 'wives' of Freyr (a male 'fertility' god) at Uppsala in Sweden. They are said to have worn dresses fringed with little bells, and Saxo was 'disgusted by the effeminate gestures ... and by the unmanly clatter of bells' (*Gesta Danorum*, book 6, translated by Elton 1999 [1905]). Finally, some scholars and practitioners (e.g. Blain 2002) locate Odin, as warrior and/or death god as well as seidr-practitioner *par excellence*, as a deity with enigmatic, queer gender (unlike Blain's discussion, rather more simplistic and binary readings are given by Grambo 1989, and more recently Solli 1999). Challenges to normativity are also presented to us, according to Coles (e.g. 1998), in the form of prehistoric wooden figurines which may exhibit ambiguous genitalia, three of which Coles tentatively links to Odin due to the lack or distortion of one eye. It does not seem unreasonable to conclude from this rather limited number of examples that third and/or multiple conceptions of gender may have existed in some Northern communities, although these sources – both archaeological and historic/literary – must be approached with caution, and certainly deserve closer scrutiny (e.g. following in the vein of Stoodley 1999).

In full knowledge that there are negative associations associated with *seiðr* (e.g. the insult *ergi*), this evidence from the past is used by contemporary seidr-workers, who, simply by practising seidr today, engage in a dissonant act which receives prejudice from within their own communities and from wider culture. Paxson suggested to me that the 'opening up' of oneself psychically to be successful in seidr might be regarded as rather more a female ability than a male one. Binaries aside, in the community this means only certain men generally want to be involved with seidr, particularly gay men. The high proportion of gay men in the Hrafnar community is quite unrepresentative of Heathenry in general, so the combination of gay men and seidr places Hrafnar further into a marginal category in Heathenry, perhaps reflective of its geographical location in liberal San Francisco. Being gay and practising seidr present a significant challenge to conventional Heathenry and the normative West nonetheless. Not all men practising seidr are gay, however. Over time, Paxson says more 'straights' have begun to practise seidr. For heterosexual male seidr-workers, experiences with seidr challenge conventional classifications of gender with a domino effect for other masculist Western attitudes. Bil is a seidr-worker in New Mexico who works with the dying to ease their spiritual transition and has various 'ghosts' as spirit-helpers. He points out that:

My sexuality is heterosexual. I was never approached by the ghosts who follow me to change that in any way. I was, however, severely 'lambasted' for carrying too much of a 'macho attitude' and was forced to make changes in that area – so much so, that folks often wonder, now, if I am homosexual or not. They usually figure it out soon enough when they meet my family and friends. My eccentricity doesn't stem from sexuality or sexual preference but mainly from the fact that I have no emotional reactions any longer (I have emotions; I just don't demonstrate reaction with them, that's all).

(Blain and Wallis 2000: 404)

In a similar vein, 'James', a newcomer to seidr practice in Britain, says:

In my own practices, seiðr focuses on both 'male' and 'female' deities, Woden and Freyja, in rituals of possession ... I think many people (especially men) would find seiðr disturbing because of how it makes them feel (apart from the radical change into shamanic consciousness), going beyond stereotypes of male, female, gay, etc. For me, seiðr with Freyja allows an integrating understanding of what it is to be male, female and other, multiple possibilities. That is empowering and affects how I live with my reality, world, local and spiritual communities. It changes who I am.

(Blain and Wallis 2000: 405)

Agreeing with Harvey's assertion that neo-Shamans in environmental education are agents in the post-modern critique of society, I argue that these seidr-workers and their subsequent disputing and altering of normative Western stereotypes present a significant disruption of and protest against modernity. Dowson argues 'the very practice of archaeology provides the foundations of social and epistemological privilege by authorizing a heterosexual history of humanity' (1999b: 4). Conservative Heathens follow this line and cultivate their perceived closeness to 'ancestors' by assuming ancient Heathen communities consisted of heterosexual family units as we – it is widely perceived – have them today. In direct contrast, these seidr-workers are mobilising their own experiences in an alternative history of seidr and Heathenry which challenges conventional understandings of the past, and normativity in the present. Where archaeologists underwrite homophobia in their reification of familial units and heterosexual relations, gay and straight seidr-workers disrupt these biases; they indirectly but 'actively challenge the manner in which epistemological privilege is negotiated in archaeology' (Dowson 1999b: 4). In their engagements with neo-Shamanic practices, they also challenge both the atheistic and often homophobic stance of contemporary Western society and the aversion to interactions with spirits or other than human beings in their Heathen communities.

These seidr-workers are not simply going on shamanic trips for fun or profit, as critics of neo-Shamans largely suggest, but are radically reorienting their world-views. In terms of consciousness alterations, gender conceptions, sexual orientation and community interactions, these neo-Shamans are more

like some indigenous shamans. Rather than appropriating aspects of indigenous shamanisms, or romanticising shamanisms past, these neo-Shamans
give significant 'extra pay' to shamanisms in the past and the present. I
argue they accord with Taussig's understanding of shamanisms (first
discussed in Chapter 2) in which there is always tension and dissonance, and
the potential for 'dismantling all fixed notions of identity' (Taussig 1989:
57). As changing ones, seidr-workers give extra pay to neo-Shamanisms as
well, empowering this term and practices associated with it in ways beyond
the negative stereotypes critics impose on them. My discussion of contemporary seidr and gender exemplifies the complex ways with which
neo-Shamans are negotiating their worlds. Clearly, despite my appraisal of a
wide variety of neo-Shamanisms and their implications for a multitude of
interest groups, this book is by no means comprehensive; there is still great
scope for further academic investigation and discussion.

APPENDIX

Resolution of the 5th Annual Meeting of the Tradition Elders Circle and AIM resolution[1]

Resolution of the 5th Annual Meeting of the Tradition Elders Circle

Northern Cheyenne Nation, Two Moons' Camp
Rosebud Creek, Montana
October 5, 1980.

It has been brought to the attention of the Elders and their representatives in Council that various individuals are moving about this Great Turtle Island and across the great waters to foreign soil, purporting to be spiritual leaders. They carry pipes and other objects sacred to the Red Nations, the indigenous people of the western hemisphere.

These individuals are gathering non-Indian people as followers who believe they are receiving instructions of the original people. We, the Elders and our representatives sitting in Council, give warning to these non-Indian followers that it is our understanding this is not a proper process, that the authority to carry these sacred objects is given by the people, and the purpose and procedures are specific to time and the needs of the people.

The medicine people are chosen by the medicine and long instruction and discipline are necessary before ceremonies and healing can be done. These procedures are always in the Native tongue; there are no exceptions and profit is not the motivation.

There are many Nations with many and varied procedures specifically for the welfare of their people. These processes and ceremonies are of the most Sacred Nature. The Council finds the open display of these ceremonies contrary to these Sacred instructions.

Therefore, be warned that these individuals are moving about playing upon the spiritual needs and ignorance of our non-Indian brothers and sisters. The value of these instructions and ceremonies is questionable, may be meaningless, and hurtful to the individual carrying false messages. There are questions that should be asked of these individuals:

1. What nation does the person represent?
2. What is their Clan and Society?
3. Who instructed them and where did they learn?
4. What is their home address?

If no information is forthcoming, you may inquire at the address listed below, and we will try to find out about them for you. We concern ourselves only with those people who use spiritual ceremonies with non-Indian people for profit. There are many other things to be shared with the four colors of humanity in our common destiny as one with our Mother the Earth. It is this sharing that must be considered with great care by the Elders and the medicine people who carry the Sacred Trusts, so that no harm may come to people through ignorance and misuse of these powerful forces.

Signed,

Tom Yellowtail
Wyoloa, MY 59089.

Larry Anderson
Navajo Nation
PO Box 342
Fort Defiance
AZ 86504.

Izadore Thom
Beech Star Route
Bellingham
WA 98225.

Thomas Banyacya
Hopi Independent Nation
Shungopavy Pueblo
Second Mesa
via AZ 86403.

Philip Deere (deceased)
Muskogee (Creek) Nation (in tribute).

Walter Denny
Chippewa-Cree Nation
Rocky Boy Route
Box Elder
MT 59521.

Austin Two Moons
Northern Cheyenne Nation
Rosebud Creek
MT.

Tadadaho
Haudenasaunee
Onondaga Nation
via Nedrow, NY 13120.

Chief Fools Crow (deceased)
Lakota Nation (in tribute).

Frank Cadinal, Sr.
Chateh, PO Box 120
Assumption, Alberta
Canada TOM OSO.

Peter O'Chiese
Entrance Terry Ranch
Entrance, Alberta
Canada.

AIM (American Indian Movement) resolution

Sovereign Diné Nation
Window Rock, AZ
May 11, 1984.

Whereas the Spiritual wisdom which is shared by the Elders with the people has been passed on to us through the creation from time immemorial; and

Whereas the spirituality of Indian Nations is inseparable from the people themselves; and

Whereas the attempted theft of Indian ceremonies is a direct attack and theft from Indian people themselves; and

Whereas there has been a dramatic increase in the incidence of selling Sacred ceremonies, such as the sweat lodge and the vision quest, and of Sacred articles, such as religious pipes, feathers and stone; and

Whereas these practices have been and continue to be conducted by Indians and non-Indians alike, constituting not only insult and disrespect for the wisdom of the ancients, but also exposing ignorant non-Indians to potential harm and even death through the misuse of these ceremonies; and

Whereas the traditional Elders and Spiritual leaders have repeatedly warned against and condemned the commercialisation of our ceremonies; and

Whereas such commercialisation has increased dramatically in recent years, to wit:

- the representations of Cyfus McDonald, Osheana Fast Wolf, and Brooke Medicine Ego, all non-Indian women representing themselves as "Sacred Women," and who, in the case of Cyfus McDonald, have defrauded Indian people of Sacred articles;
- A non-Indian women going by the name of "Quanda" representing herself as a "Healing Women" and charging $20 for sweat lodges;
- Sun Bear and the so-called "Bear Tribe Medicine Society," who engage in the sale of Indian ceremonies and Sacred objects, operating out of the state of Washington, but traveling and speaking throughout the United States;
- Wallace Black Elk and Grace Spotted Eagle, Indian people operating in Denver, Colorado, charging up to $50 for so-called "Sweat Lodge Workshops;"
- A group of non-Indians working out of Boulder, Colorado, and throughout the Southwest, and audaciously calling itself "Vision Quest, Inc.," thereby stealing the name and attempting to steal the concept of one of our most spiritual ceremonies;

Therefore, let it be resolved that the Southwest AIM Leadership Conference reiterates the position articulated by our Elders at the First American Indian Tribunal held at D.Q. University, September 1982, as follows:

Now, to those who are doing these things, we send our third warning. Our Elders ask, "Are you prepared to take the consequences of your actions? You will be outcasts from your people if you continue these practices" ... Now, this is another one. Our young people are getting restless. They are the ones who sought their Elders in the first place to teach them the Sacred ways. They have said that they will take care of those who are abusing our Sacred ceremonies and Sacred objects in their own way. In this way they will take care of their Elders.

We Resolve to protect our Elders and our traditions, and we condemn those who seek to profit from Indian Spirituality. We put them on notice that our patience grows thin with them and they continue their disrespect at their own risk.

NOTES

INTRODUCTION: A NATIVE AT HOME – PRODUCING
ETHNOGRAPHIC FRAGMENTS OF NEO-SHAMANISMS

1 In producing an ethnographic analysis of neo-Shamanisms it is unnecessary to
reproduce the exhaustive argument over defining 'shamanism' (e.g.
Bourguignon 1967, 1974, 1976; Dowson 1999a, in press; Eliade 1989 [1964];
Gilberg 1984; Hamayon 1993; Holmberg 1989; Hultkrantz 1973, 1978; Lewis
1984, 1989, 1993; Porterfield 1987; Shirokogoroff 1935; Voigt 1984; Walsh
1989, 1990; Winkelman 1989; Wright 1989; Hoppál 1992a; Hoppál and
Howard 1993; Bowie 2000; Price 2001a). Suffice to say, for the moment,
'shamanism' is an anthropologically constructed concept (e.g. Taussig 1987,
1989: 57; Noel 1997: 37; Harvey 1998: 23) used to approach and interpret
certain practices in 'indigenous' societies which negotiate community
healing/sickness and other day-to-day social relations via engagements with
'spirits' or 'other than human persons'. For the specific approach taken to
shamanisms in this book, see discussion of 'elements of shamanisms', below.
And on the orthography and reasoning behind my use of the term 'neo-
Shamanisms', in comparison and contrast with 'shamanisms', see Chapter 1.
2 In contrast to Sherratt, who argues the term 'psychoactive' is 'neutral' (Sherratt
1995a: 9), I suggest that the term along with 'hallucinogen' and 'psychedelic' is
value-laden. They denote or have connotations of mental aberration (illness) in
the prefix 'psycho', and/or a perceived hedonistic 'drug' use among a disaffected
Western youth. This not only marginalises the indigenous religious use of
consciousness-altering plants, fungi and animals but also negatively stereotypes
Westerners who use such substances (from alcohol and tobacco to ayahuasca) in
rituals. 'Entheogens' (e.g. Forte 1997. See also the *Council on Spiritual Practices*,
online document: http://www.csp.or) less pejoratively describes substances with
consciousness-altering properties. Etymologically, entheogen derives from Greek
entheos, 'possessed by a god' (and is related to the modern English 'giddy', Old
English *gidig*, 'possessed by a god/spirit'), and *genous*, 'produced'. Hence
'entheogen' is literally 'generate god or spirit within'. While this may be unacceptable to some, I think it more sensitive and accurate, particularly in
indigenous contexts. Entheogens such as the *Ayahuasca* vine and *Peyote* cactus are
utilised by shamans and other specialists as sacraments. Many neo-Shamans may
also use entheogens, or entheogenic substances, in rituals for spiritual empowerment, that is in a sacramental rather than recreational arena.
3 Orthography aside, it is worth stating that pronunciation of the term 'shaman'
is variant as both anthropological construct and indigenous Siberian reality,
despite wide neo-Shamanic claims – disseminated most visibly via Harner (e.g.

Harner 1990 [1980]: 20) and his workshops – for emphasis on the first syllable, thus 'shar-man'. The Evenki emphasised the second syllable, 'sha-márn', while both 'sháy-man' and 'shár-man' are common today (Price 2001b: 4), with the anglicised 'shay-man' most prominent in British academia.

4 Such terms as 'Western', 'indigenous', etc. are value-laden, contentious and may suggest homogeneity and clear-cut divisions when in reality none exist (see Harvey 2000a and 2003 for deconstruction of these and related terms).

5 This neglect is related to what might be called 'neo-Shamanophobia', the sardonic reaction from opponents to neo-Shamanisms which negatively stereotypes them as either harmless or dangerous crackpots. Hunt's sensationalised sentiments are typical:

> [T]he ancient shamanic techniques for contacting spirit guides have been introduced to the masses ... [S]eemingly unaware of the grave danger, America, once the world's leader in finance, business, science and technology, is reasserting its leadership position, but now in a new enterprise – the rise of New Age shamanism ... the implications are staggering.
>
> (Hunt 1988: 294)

and reproduced in slightly more critical form by Kehoe (2000). A more nuanced assessment is long overdue.

6 I use inverted commas around 'spiritual' and 'spirit' since these are extremely vague terms with a variety of meanings; a Catholic priest and Heathen neo-Shaman will no doubt conceive of a 'spirit' differently. This unhelpful and mystifying metanarrative – spirit – locates such transcendent beings outside day-to-day social relations. In place of it, Harvey (2003) following Hallowell (2002 [1960]) uses the phrase 'other than human persons' which, despite being cumbersome, more sensitively reflects the complex relationships humans (including shamans and neo-Shamans) have with other beings (e.g. tree people, rock people), and the way in which such beings are perceived to be active social agents. I adhere to their view but retain use of 'spirit' alongside 'other than human persons' since the former endures as the term neo-Shamans use themselves.

7 I do, however, take issue with Young and Goulet's avowed search for a 'metamodel' of reality (Young and Goulet 1994b: 12; Goulet and Young 1994: 329–330), which betrays a positivist stance that scientifically devalues their emphasis on the multiplicity of shamanic experience.

8 Challenging monolithic and dichotomous views of science vs non- or pseudoscience, Wylie (2000) proposes a far more nuanced understanding of these areas, which is of methodological value to archaeology and other social sciences.

9 Díaz-Andreu (2002: 162, 171) notes that all too often such terms as 'shaman', 'sorcerer' and 'medicine men' are left 'untheorised' in the literature, and that 'shaman' is especially 'charged' and therefore 'unacceptable in my opinion', only to suggest, in my opinion, the apparently 'neutral', but more vague and indeed desperately untheorised, 'ritual specialist'.

10 Use of the terms 'trance', 'altered states' or 'ecstasy' as the major defining characteristic of shamanisms, as Eliade (1989 [1964]) and Lewis (1989 [1971]) have done, is contested by Humphrey (1996: 30–31). As well as the presence of altered consciousness (arguably a more nuanced term than 'altered state' or 'altered state of consciousness'), the approach advocated here requires two other 'elements of shamanisms' to infer shamanisms. Of course not all of a shaman's practices require altered consciousness; this approach accommodates such diversity but stresses that altered consciousness is present consistently in the shaman's vocation.

11 I differ from Young and Goulet (1994a) in henceforth avoiding use of 'extraordinary' experience. 'Extraordinary' is a value-laden judgement that inappropriately measures shamanic experiences in relation to a perceived 'normal' Western reality.

12 For example 'Discussion: Relativism, Objectivity and the Politics of the Past', *Archaeological Dialogues* 1998, 1: 30–53.

13 Of course all language is composed of metaphors, and the usefulness of 'metaphor' for exploring material culture has been aptly demonstrated by Tilley (e.g. Tilley 1999). Still, I argue that approaching shamanisms and neo-Shamanisms in terms of metaphors and textual readings is inappropriate and misleading, failing to take shamanic experiences *seriously*.

14 A representative, but not exhaustive list of workshops attended include a Michael Harner *The Way of the Shaman: The Shamanic Journey, Power and Healing; The Basic Workshop* (for literature, see, Harner 1990 [1980]; Johnson 1995; Jakobsen 1999) co-ordinated by his Foundation for Shamanic Studies (FSS); a *Shamanic Trance Postures* workshop based on the work of anthropologist Felicitas Goodman (1986, 1990) conducted by Howard Charing of Eagle's Wing for Contemporary Shamanism, London; a *Shamanic Trance Dance* workshop held by the Kokopelli Company; a workshop based on the Five Rhythms shamanic trance dances pioneered by Gabrielle Roth (1990, 1997), led by a shamanic business consultant; a Faerie workshop held by neo-Shaman Gordon 'the toad' MacLellan; and a medicine wheel ceremonial conducted by 'Native American' Willy Lone Bear. Rituals attended include a shamanic healing conducted by Jonathan Horwitz of the Scandinavian Center for Shamanic Studies; a *Bear Tribe* drumming ritual based on the controversial work of Sun Bear (see Chapter 7); sweat lodge ceremonies orchestrated by Shivam O'Brien of Spirit Horse Nomadic Circle in the UK, and a Native American elder of the 'River People' in Oregon, USA; a *Hrafnar* god possession ritual in San Francisco, reconstructed Seidr séances in Southampton (Chapter 3); a Native American-based pipe ceremony orchestrated by British neo-Shamans Nick and Jan Wood (editors of *Sacred Hoop* magazine, the most widely disseminated neo-Shamanic journal in Britain); and a 'Heathen' neo-Shamanic trance dance held by 'Runic John' and associates (Chapter 3). I have also attended numerous Pagan, Druid, Wiccan and Heathen ceremonies which have associations with shamanisms and neo-Shamanisms (Chapter 3).

15 A select list of interviewees includes the neo-Shamans Michael Harner (FSS); Leo Rutherford and Howard Charing (Eagle's Wing); Shivam O'Brien (Spirit Horse); Diana Paxson and Rauðhildr (Heathen *Hrafnar* community, San Francisco); Malcolm, 'Runic John' and 'James' (Heathen neo-Shamans in Britain); and Greywolf (a.k.a. Philip Shallcrass, joint-chief of the *British Druid Order*). Christopher Gingell (National Trust site manager, Avebury), and G.B. Cornucopia (ranger at Chaco Canyon) among others were interviewed on the subject of neo-Shamanisms and archaeological sites. Interviews were conducted on Native American reservations with Clay Hamilton (Hopi Cultural Preservation Office), Petuuche Gilbert and Daniel Sanchez (Tribal Councilman Reality Officer and Tribal Secretary, respectively, Acoma Pueblo), and Celestino Gachupin (Natural Resources Manager, Zia Pueblo).

1 'WHITE SHAMANS': SOURCES FOR NEO-SHAMANISMS

1 Hereafter, then, my preference is to use plural forms consistently. When using 'shamanism' or 'neo-shamanism' in the singular I refer only to specific instances

in which, either I am critiquing the use of singular terms, or these terms are used by other researchers, hence the inverted commas.

2   In contrast, I consider this singling out of 'soul flight' or 'shamanic journey' as the exemplary feature of shamanism to misleadingly reify metanarrative, and think it foregrounds similarity at the expense of specific social contexts and conflicts, conceptually, with the emphasis on diversity I have hitherto promoted.

2 PLASTIC MEDICINE MEN? APPRAISING THE 'GREAT PRETENDERS'

1   The 'wounded man' scene is a favourite source for neo-Shamanic interpretations, such as Moore and Gillette's (1993: 9–11) gross romantic speculation presented as fact that the scene is a narrative of a 'magician' transforming into a bird, 'a soaring being of pure spirit'. This is largely because the imagery, like much enigmatic archaeological 'art', lends itself to the whims of 'the Western' observer.

2   The Foundation for Shamanic Studies (FSS) nominates 'Living Treasures' of Shamanism, awards that include recognition of certain 'outstanding' shamans, and provide a financial stipend. The neo-colonial implications of this and other activities of the FSS are discussed towards the end of this chapter and in Chapter 7.

3   Many core-shamanists I have met suggest that beyond attendance at more work-shops, the FSS provides no follow-up support or community activity following the basic workshop. 'Drumming circles' have emerged, but while the FSS may advertise them, they are not an integral part of the Foundation's structure or course prospectus, being run by enthusiastic practitioners rather than faculty members.

4   'Berdache' is a pejorative term that emerged in the colonial era and reifies Eurocentric concepts of sex and gender, but alternatives are also problematic (for further discussion, see Conclusion).

3 TALIESIN'S TRIP, WYRD WODEN: DRUID AND HEATHEN NEO-SHAMANS

1   Dividing up aspects of 'social' life as if they were discrete entities is heavily influenced by, if not directly derived from, the Enlightenment and its distinctions between science, magic and religion (Tambiah 1990). In many non-Western cultures what we call 'religion' is an integral part of the everyday actions of 'economics', 'politics', and so on. In this I follow in the vein of Stuart Piggott, who, some forty years before me, mentions a 'Wessex Culture battle-axe': 'we can be sure that the authority it denoted was as much spiritual as temporal, for priests and kings, magicians and princes, were not in the ancient world so sharply separated as they are in our latter-day scientific minds' (Piggott 1962: 96).

2   In their use of the term 'Heathen', practitioners are arguably reclaiming a pejorative term, in similarity to the use of 'Indian' by Native Americans and 'Nigger' by Black and Asian Europeans and Americans.

3   As stated in the introductory chapter, it would be misleading to suggest my discussions comprise a comprehensive ethnography of neo-Shamanisms or to suggest that such an ethnography is possible; neo-Shamanisms are simply too disparate and diverse. It seems more correct to speak of 'partial' ethnographies or 'ethnographic fragments', which is in keeping with the post-modern nature

of most neo-Shamanisms and current reflexive endeavours in anthropology and archaeology – in short, it is essential to this autoarchaeology.

4 Given widespread public perceptions of contemporary Paganism which are often confused, derogatory and blatantly incorrect, such as those by Logan (1988) and McLaughlin (2000), it seems necessary to make clear that Pagans are not Satanists, and that Paganism is largely a liberal, tolerant and ethically conscious 'new religion'.

5 As an aside, Hutton mentions a nineteenth-century Welsh 'cunning man' who may have got the idea for his costume from accounts from 'Siberian tribal shamans' (Hutton 1999: 90) – an early neo-Shaman? The same may also be true for the 'modern Druid' Dr William Price,

> a natural shaman and a dedicated revolutionary against every political, religious and moral institution. Free love and the worship of nature were his main doctrines. In wizard's robes topped by a fox-skin head-dress he performed the seasonal Druid rites at his altar on the Pontypridd rocking stone.
>
> (Michell 1997: 6; see also Green 1997: 152)

6 As mentioned in my introductory chapter, acknowledging the influence of academia on Paganism and vice versa is an important component of my auto-archaeology and other reflexive approaches. It is interesting to note therefore that where Pagans have suffered job loss and child custody legalities due to erroneous accusations of satanic child abuse (see the Home Office report on religious discrimination by Weller *et al.* 2001), Hutton has made statements in court demonstrating, historically and ethnographically, that Paganism has no links to Satanism (pers. com.).

7 See Shallcrass (1997a: 18–19).

8 I use the terms 'Heathen', 'Heathenry' and 'Heathenism' here to refer only to contemporary practitioners. No Heathens I have met claim their religion is part of an unbroken tradition, and I think it appropriate to clearly differentiate between modern and ancient forms.

9 These terms are covered by the conventional umbrella term 'Northern', hence my use of 'Northern shamanisms' (still emphasising plurality) as a general term rather than 'Viking shamanism', 'Nordic shamanism', 'Anglo-Saxon' shamanism, etc., since in correct use these are culture- and region-specific.

10 I use the Old Norse *seiðr* to refer to the ancient practice and the anglicised seidr for the modern. While practitioners today may not make such a strong distinction I think it appropriate to differentiate ancient from modern as I have done with ancient/indigenous and (post-)modern in terms of shamanisms and neo-Shamanisms. The classic work on *seiðr* is by Strömbäck (1935), but there is unfortunately no English translation – see instead Morris (1991); Näsström (1995); Dubois (1999).

11 Odin has linguistic variations including: ON Oðinn, OE Woden, OF Wodan, OHG Wutan, Wuotan.

12 Many Heathens believe the Christian 'hell' was corrupted from the ancient Norse realm of the dead and the Goddess Hel associated with that realm. In Norse mythology, Hel is not purgatory but simply a home for the dead. Contemporary Heathen convention is to use the term Helheim (Hel home or world) to avoid associations with the Christian Hell. The world Nifelhel also appears in the mythology, a darker and deeper world than Helheim where the souls from Helheim die. This concept is also thought to be Christian-influenced, combining elements of the distinct worlds of Helheim, home of the dead,

and Nifelheim, the world of primal cosmic Ice that, in opposition to Muspelheim, the world of primal cosmic fire, produces a fog that gives rise to life (and seven other worlds).

13 On the other hand, or in addition – for each interpretation is not mutually exclusive – Blain (pers. com.) suggests the possibility that a 'spirit-marriage' is described, similar to the Siberian shamanic examples (e.g. Czaplicka 1914), with the wife as the 'shaman': she has a spirit-spouse, Freyr, and a human-spouse, Gunnar, which is customary for the Swedes but is incomprehensible to the Norwegians, who assume Gunnar must be impersonating Freyr. And if Freyr is said to speak, this must 'really' be Gunnar speaking, rather than the gyðja relaying Frey's messages.

14 In Norse mythology, *Sleipnir* is associated with the world-tree *Yggdrasil* meaning 'terrible steed'. As related in the Eddic poem *Havamal*, Odin hangs himself on the tree in an ordeal that culminates in his receiving the wisdom of the runes and other esoteric knowledge. These instances mark the evidence *par excellence* for Odin being a shamanistic god, though of course such an interpretation is not accepted universally.

15 In Heathen possession rituals other than Hrafnar's, the deity does not want to 'party' and may instead 'deliver stiff reprimands' (Blain, pers. com.).

16 This idiosyncratic way of presencing 'ancestors' directly (which readers will have noted is also prevalent in Greywolf's comments), who are most likely not kin relations and who hail from millennia ago, is not exclusive to Druids; the implications of such a concept are addressed in Chapter 6.

17 P. Jones (1998) makes the pertinent point that in Western Europe contemporary Pagans have a long, documented history of nature religions to draw on which can be considered 'their' history in the sense of a shared 'European Heritage' (as the heritage industry promotes it). This is in contrast to Albanese's discussion of persistent primitivism and cultural appropriation by the New Age and others in the USA, and while there are Pagans in Western Europe who can be neo-colonialist, most obviously those practising in a Native American style, for the most part the issue of appropriation surrounds use of the European past, which is itself contested, as explored later in this chapter.

18 The issue of 'purity' of tradition is important to some Heathens in that Hrafnar's borrowings are not seen as 'pure'. Apart from reflecting the conservatism in Heathenism generally and a lament for an idyllic and unchanging past, this also reflects widespread disquiet in the community about the practice of shamanistic rituals such as deity possession and *seiðr*.

4 'CELTIC' AND 'NORTHERN' SHAMANISMS? CONTESTING THE PAST

1 Classical authors were referring to diverse localised communities, rather than a homogeneous entity, that came to be called 'Keltoi'.

2 Of course, the 'conventional' understanding of shamanisms is inadequate since it is all too often based on Eliade's noble savage mythos. The way to elucidate whether the 'Celts' or any other society utilised shamanisms is, I argue, according to the elements of shamanisms.

3 Shapiro (1998) discusses the problems of using the term hunter-gatherer in the history of religions. So-called hunter-gatherers are by no means the only communities to utilise shamanistic practices.

4 Ross may, on the other hand, be presenting her own colourful perception of Druidry as shamanistic.

5 Graves's chapters on 'The Tree-Alphabet' (Graves 1961 [1948]: 165–204) discuss the *Ogham* system of writing. His mythological interpretations, not attested to academically, have been elaborated upon by neo-Shamans to produce divination devices, such as Pennick and Jackson's (1992) *Celtic Oracle*.

6 Sexually ambiguous imagery is not uncommon in Iron Age and Romano-British 'art' and has recently been interpreted by Aldhouse Green (2001) in terms of multiple genders and shamanisms.

7 Links between metal-workers and shamans have been made in other areas of archaeology, particularly for the Bronze Age (e.g. Shell 2000, following analysis by Piggott 1962, and Budd and Taylor 1995).

8 J.D. Hill was Lecturer in Archaeology, University of Southampton, at the time of this communication and is now Keeper of Prehistoric and Romano-British Antiquities, The British Museum.

9 On the yew theme, MacKillop also notes that Corc mac Luigthig, ancestor of many kings of Munster, had a vision of a burning yew bush with angels dancing over it – a further vestige of shamanistic practice cloaked in Christian mythology?

10 A list of translations used in this section appears in the references.

11 The Old Norse *fylgja* and *hamingja* (plausibly translated as 'fetch' and 'protective-spirit', respectively) may, in some circumstances, be associated with shamanic spirit-helpers. Such a slight suggestion requires further, detailed analysis. There is much evidence of these entities in Northern literature (e.g. Kelchner 1935).

12 It is interesting to note that the mead of poetry, or the vessel that contains it, from which Odin gains 'shamanic' wisdom is called *Óðrœrir*, 'the one that stimulates to ecstasy'. The mead therefore relates, by its properties and etymology, to the 'shamanic' derivation of Odin's name, as mentioned in the previous paragraph.

13 Høst (1999) remarks that Strömbäck (1935: 137) links accounts of *noaide* (sami) shamans being called back from trance by 'a song apparently of tempting or erotic character delivered by a young girl' to the *varðlokkur* ('tempter of the soul', Simek 1993: 353 – a 'magic song' aka. *galdr* and *seiðælti* in other sagas) sung for the seeress in *Eiríks Saga rauða*.

14 It is unsurprising that Nässtrom (1996b) describes Freyja as a 'goddess of many names', although the situation is by no means a simple one. As Grundy (1996) points out, the plausible identification of Gullveig and Heidr with Freyja – as suggested by such authorities as Turville-Petre 1964: 159) – has not been contested, nor for that matter Freyja's possible manifestations as Hildr and Gifjon, although other scholars (e.g. Simek 1993) may afford separate status for them. The mixed bag of dates for various manuscripts hinders any certainty, but there are certainly strong conjectural similarities between these figures and the persona of Freyja.

15 Pollington (2000: 49) cites Meaney's (1989) interpretation of the pouches as 'elf bags', used in the cure of 'elf-shot', a phenomenon mentioned below in the context of Bates's research into Anglo-Saxon shamanism. The Fyrkat find is reminiscent of Gregory of Tours's description of a bag belonging to an 'impostor': 'filled with the roots of various plants … mole's teeth, the bones of mice, bear's claws and bear's feet … recognised … as witchcraft' (trans. Thorpe 1974: section IX.6, 485).

16 Pollington comments further on these henbane seeds:

> They may have been intended for use in brewing – the word *pilsener* used in relation to beer derives from the city of Pilsen, itself named from the

cultivation of Henbane, German *Bilse*. The effects of Henbane as a flavouring for beer are said to be that ... in high doses it causes severe mental disturbance, dementia, delirium and confusion.

(Pollington 2000: 130)

17 That Celtic neo-Shamans use the same Tacitus quotation as evidence for Ogham rather than runic 'signs', demonstrates the problematic nature of this source.
18 The term 'Dark Ages' and its connotations are more a modern fabrication based on how researchers have perceived this period rather than on the evidence itself. Indeed numerous recent works make clear that the evidence is by no means lacking (or 'dark') and that the Romans by no means left a land empty of 'civilisation' (e.g. Hinton 1993; Arnold 1997).
19 Hutton (1991, 1993) and L. Jones (1994, 1998) are refreshingly atypical in addressing neo-Shamanisms as well as ancient shamanisms in their research.

5 'SACRED' SITES? NEO-SHAMANS AND PREHISTORIC HERITAGE

1 It does not seem coincidental that Barnatt was a contributor to *The Ley Hunter* journal in the 1970s and 1980s. Other archaeologists, such as Barbara Bender, Thomas Dowson and Julian Thomas, are also prepared to engage with alternative interest groups, with the former involved with Druids, travellers and festivalers at Stonehenge (e.g. Bender 1998), and the latter two having articles published in *The Ley Hunter* (e.g. Dowson 1999c; Thomas 1996).
2 Eight specific Pagan festivals mark and celebrate the seasonal changes seen in nature during the ever-turning 'wheel of the year'. There is an emphasis on the agricultural cycle, and adherents use these times to connect with the land, reflect on how the changes in nature reflect changes in self and community, observe long-term patterns of stability and change, and to make ritual and celebration. The following dates are somewhat arbitrary since they may depend on other factors such as planetary alignments (at the equinoxes and solstices), the proximity of sunrise and sunset, since the festivals tend to last for some days (particularly when happening at a weekend) and since not all of the eight festivals are celebrated or accepted by all Pagans. In order, these festivals are: Samhain (Halloween), 31 October; Yule (Winter Solstice), 21 December; Imbolc, 2 February; Spring Equinox, 21 March; Beltane (May Day), 1 May; Summer Solstice, 21 June; Lammas, 31 July; Autumnal Equinox, 21 September. For full discussion of their meanings, see Harvey (1997b).
3 The Stonehenge Masterplan can be viewed on the English Heritage web site: http://www.stonehengemasterplan.org/.
4 At the same time, it might also be argued that the military have, more recently, safeguarded many monuments under their jurisdiction.
5 For clarification, 'Mr. Maughfling' is Rollo Maughfling, Arch-Druid of Glastonbury and self-styled Arch-Druid of Britain, a title recognised by some Druids, but not all of them. The BDO in particular believe his tactics have alienated the druid community from English Heritage and the authorities, rather than promoted developments, and accuse him of 'monopolising' the stones at the 1998 solstice. Nonetheless, Maughfling has been deeply involved in Stonehenge access negotiations (e.g. Maughfling 1997, 2000/2001a). 'Arthur Pendragon' is widely recognised by alternative groups as the returned/reincarnated King Arthur of medieval legend; he professes the Druid faith and has made repeated demonstrations for free access at Stonehenge by crossing the exclusion zone each year (e.g. Pendragon 2000/01a), resulting in his immediate

arrest (for further discussion, also relating to the trial of Arthur at Southwark Crown Court, November 1997 regarding his right to carry the sword Excalibur, see Hutton 1998b). 'Kevin Carlyon' is self-proclaimed High Priest of British White Witches and founder member of the Covenant of Earth Magic. The ADO is the Ancient Druid Order, the original group to hold Druid ceremonies during the free festival, OBOD is the Order of Bards Ovates and Druids, and the PF is the Pagan Federation.

6 The Development of Paganism: Histories, Influences and Contexts c.1880–2002; 'Belief Beyond Boundaries', The Open University Religious Studies Research Group, Milton Keynes, 12 January 2001. The paper was entitled 'Sacred Sites / Archaeological Sites: Contestations and Contexts of Ancient Places in Developments of Contemporary Paganisms'.

7 Available online: http://apollo5.bournemouth.ac.uk/consci/stonehenge/intro. htm. Note that the *Archaeological Research Agenda for the Avebury World Heritage Site* (Chadburn and Pomeroy-Kilinger 2001) also neglects to address Pagan interests. This apparently overlooks Bournemouth University's *Avebury Visitor Research* (Calver 1998) which suggests 'some groups expressed disappointment that there was not more information about ley lines and other astrological features that is felt by some to be the original purpose of the site' (ibid.: 21). Such an oversight is frustrating, given that Pagans comprise one of the most prominent interest groups at the site, as Calver's report concludes:

> Avebury ... is still an important centre of pantheist worship ... These groups use the monuments extensively and return on many occasions for the various celebrations that have significance to them ... [Indeed] at certain times of the year/day this group can be in the majority within the WHS.
>
> (Calver 1998: 22–32)

8 Avaliable online: http://www.rescue-archaeology.freeserve.co.uk/rescuenews. rn79/shengmtg.htm.

6 WAKING NEOLITHIC ANCESTORS: FURTHER CONTROVERSIES AND 'REBURIAL'

1 It is interesting to note that the Coach House pub near Avebury has recently been granted a licence for conducting civil weddings (*Pagan Dawn* 1999: 8); this reflects and perhaps anticipates the number of people who would like to marry lawfully, having conducted their Pagan hand-fasting in the locale.

2 Bender suggests the LIVE graffiti at Stonehenge in 1989 might also be 'a proclamation about the life-force, or a political credo, or – as rumoured – the unfinished logo of a certain football team' (1998: 128). The 1999 graffiti at Avebury, on the other hand, may be related to protests surrounding genetically modified (GM) foods (Gingell, pers. com.; see also news reports, e.g. http://news.bbc.co.uk/hi/english/uk/newsid_372000/372326.stm).

3 The National Trust plan states their strategy is to:

> Continue to attempt to accommodate 'new religious' and other visitors drawn to Avebury at Solstice and other calendar events, on the understanding that the National Trust does not discriminate on the basis of why people come but is concerned with how they respect the sites and other users.
>
> (Objective H, section H.10: 29–30)

247

Also: to '[e]ncourage pagan, druid and other new religious groups to avoid concentrating their ceremonies at vulnerable "honeypot" sites like Avebury' (Objective L, section L.6, p. 42).
4 The English Heritage plan reports that

> Spiritually, Avebury is still a 'temple' for many people who visit … Paganism may well be the fastest growing religion in Britain, and this is linked with the increasing interest mystical [sic] significance of Avebury as a 'sacred' place … [A] growing proportion of visitors do visit Avebury for spiritual reasons.
>
> (Section 3.5.2: 27)

Also, Issue 41 states 'At certain times of the year when large numbers of people gather at Avebury … the conservation of the monuments and the freedom of all visitors to enjoy them, as well as safety and security issues, are of paramount importance.' Furthermore:

> [m]any people stay at the monuments for several hours, or for one or several nights. At the same time, unauthorised parking and camping overnight or over several days can potentially cause damage to the monument (especially through the lighting of fires and visitor erosion), disruption to the local community, and detract from the enjoyment of other visitors. In addition, a wide range of safety and security issues, such as large numbers of people gathering on Silbury Hill or in West Kennet Long Barrow, are of paramount importance.
>
> (Section 8.1.7: 64–65)

5 Bournemouth's research suggests 16 per cent of their sample of user groups expressed 'spiritual motivation' as their reason for visiting Avebury and 11 per cent said 'personal meditation' was the purpose of their visit. Also, 'some groups expressed disappointment that there was not more information about ley lines and other astrological features that is felt by some to be the original purpose of the site' (Calver 1998: 21). The report concludes: 'Avebury … is still an important centre of pantheist worship … These groups use the monuments extensively and return on many occasions for the various celebrations that have significance to them' (ibid.: 22). Indeed, 'At certain times of the year/day this group can be in the majority within the WHS' (ibid.: 32).
6 In addition, 193 people responded to a questionnaire supplied in the spring of 1995 by Stones Restaurant in Avebury (Pitts 1996), of which 63 per cent agreed 'the stones still have some mysterious power' (ibid.: 130). Alongside the management plan for the Rollright Stones in Oxfordshire (Lambrick 2001), which addresses similar issues, these surveys and reports illustrate the way in which neo-Shamanisms are influencing site management protocols.
7 Other offerings might be left for rather more perplexing reasons, such as the plastic Christmas tree with baubles and tinsel I found in West Kennet Long Barrow at Yule in 2000!
8 Unless otherwise indicated, I gained the opinions of Chris Gingell when interviewed at Avebury on 8 September 1999. The situation at Silbury escalated when cereologists (crop circle enthusiasts) cum UFOlogists abseiled down the shaft (a result of antiquarian excavations of the eighteenth century) which had collapsed in the spring of 2001 due, apparently, to the unusually wet weather (see press reports, e.g. http://news.bbc.co.uk/hi/english/uk/newsid_1511000/

1511488.stm), an event they videoed and enthusiastically reported on the Internet (e.g. http://www.cropcircleconnector.com/Bert/bert2001a.html; with comments on Britarch email list). The abseilers promoted heated controversy in heritage and alternative communities but English Heritage were unable to prosecute due to insufficient evidence. Over the 2001 Summer Solstice, Pagans joined heritage managers to dissuade pilgrims from climbing the hill for their own safety and for the preservation of the hill, and various people (Pagans included) co-ordinated a march scheduled for 8 September 2001 to campaign for a more immediate response from heritage management towards repairing the collapsed shaft (advertised on ukheathenry email list 1 August 2001; see also http://www.cruithni.org/issues/silbury/). This event was cancelled (as stated on ukpagans email list 4 September 2001) because English Heritage stepped up their plans for investigations just as the march was advertised. Silbury is undergoing seismic and other investigations to determine appropriate conservation measures (e.g. *White Dragon* 30, 2001: 30; http://news.bbc.co.uk/hi/english/uk/newsid_1493000/1493535.stm).

9 Many Druids chant the 'Awen' during their ceremonies. One description of its meaning, though not necessarily definitive, is by Shallcrass (2000: 48): 'a feminine noun variously translated as "muse", "genius", "inspiration", "poetic furore", and "poetic frenzy". It is made up of two words: "aw" meaning "flowing", and "en" meaning "spirit". So, literally, Awen is the "flowing spirit".'

10 Speaking in the Alternative Archaeology, has it Happened Yet? Debate at the New Approaches to the Archaeology of Art, Religion and Folklore: A Permeability of Boundaries? conference, Department of Archaeology, University of Southampton, 11–12 December 1999 (Wallis and Lymer 2001).

11 A session at the European Association of Archaeologists (EAA) meeting 1999 (Ethics and the Excavation and Treatment of Human Remains: A European Perspective) discussed the European reburial issue. Unsurprisingly, the 'alternative' voices of Pagans and others with spiritual concerns over the past were not discussed because the session organisers either hadn't heard of such concerns, or, if they had, they were not seen as a serious threat to archaeology. My paper did raise this issue, but in a different session, 'The Archaeology of Shamanism' (Wallis 2001).

12 A web site opposing the Stonehenge Masterplan but offering views from both sides of the argument, *Stonehenge Under Threat! World Heritage Site Threatened by Road Building Scheme*, can be found at http://www.savestonehenge.org.uk.

7 INVADING ANTHROS, THIEVING ARCHOS, WANNABE INDIANS: ACADEMICS, NEO-SHAMANS AND INDIGENOUS COMMUNITIES

1 The Spanish term Pueblo, meaning 'town', has become the generic term for the contemporary Pueblo 'Indian' people, the villages in which they live, as well as the remains of their 'Ancient Pueblo' ancestors such as Pueblo Bonito ('beautiful village') in Chaco Canyon, New Mexico.

2 The Navajo term 'Anasazi' is a more familiar and commonly used term. Its meaning is contested, however, and may be translated as 'ancient enemy' or 'ancient ones'. This political ambiguity leads modern Pueblo 'Indians' considered to be descendants of these communities, and archaeologists sensitive to their concerns (e.g. Dongoske *et al.* 2000), to prefer 'Ancient', 'Ancestral' or 'prehistoric' Pueblo, over 'Anasazi', so I use the former here. On a similar note, while Diné may be preferable, Navajo is the accepted popular term; I use them interchangeably. 'Native American' describes the indigenous population of USA,

as most indigenous people of the USA prefer, instead of 'Indian' or 'American Indian', colonial residues which are essentially pejorative. It is interesting to note, however, that not all Native Americans approve of this politically correct terminology, and that 'Indian' is being used by Native American indigenism theorists 'fully aware of its colonial origins' in a reclaiming of terminology 'to draw upon the past to create a new future' (Dirlek 1996: 19–20). 'Indigenous people' is also a politically correct term, although Béteille (1998: 190–191) suggests it is a moral signification reversal of the colonial 'native'. He is right to guard against 'moral excitation', as exemplified by Root's (1996: 96) sweeping generalisation 'the greatest threat facing Native survival today is the spiritual appropriation of the New Age movement', which is naïvely judgmental and potentially damaging to both interest groups. I hope my discussion provides a more nuanced appraisal.

3   Many contemporary Navajo avoid such rock art sites because of their links with the dead. Handprints represent lost, wandering and potentially malevolent 'spirits': if someone dies and is not buried properly, their 'spirit' will look for a different body to inhabit.

4   The traditionalist vs progressive issue is deeply convoluted. The scope of the work by A.W. Geertz (1983, 1987, 1994) attests to its magnitude, so to attempt a synopsis in a single paragraph or so would not do justice to the complexity of Hopi perspectives, nor to Geertz's accounts. Readers are instead referred to Geertz's exhaustive and absorbing research.

5   Kehoe's and other papers in Clifton's controversial *Invented Indian* (1990) are roundly critiqued by Vine Deloria Jr (1998) since their consensus that current perceptions of Indianness are invented can be perceived as neo-colonialist – Churchill (1992) might label it a 'new racism'.

6   My focus is on perspectives on Ancient Pueblo remains, but many Native Americans, the Pueblo in particular, consider all *Hisatsinom* (Anasazi/Ancient Pueblo, Hohokam, Mogollon, and Fremont) remains 'sacred'.

7   It is worth noting the irony that Waters's book was on sale in the museum shop on some reservations; this exemplifies the complexity of these issues.

8   My Diné guide in Monument Valley who is training to be a Peyote 'medicine man' in the Native American Church kept a 'respectful distance' from the Ancient Pueblo remains because getting too close 'brings bad luck'. Fences had been erected around the ruins, he said, to keep out younger Navajo who broke this taboo. This use of fencing to keep people out and to allow the sites to decay, for *spiritual* reasons, contrasts markedly with the NPS (and in England, English Heritage) fencing to restrict visitor impact in the interests of *conservation*. The Navajo archaeology unit, on the other hand, would perhaps also argue the fences are erected in the interests of protection and preservation.

9   I must point out again here that by 'tradition' I do not mean 'static' and 'unchanging' or 'more authentic', but rather a tradition continually changing and adapting to new circumstances. The melding of Siberian shamanisms with core-shamanism is another example of the process of transculturation when two cultures meet, resulting in hybridity, or more properly synergy or syncretism (e.g. Ashcroft *et al.* 1998): the Siberian shamanisms emerging now cannot be judged as any better or worse than those that came before; they simply exist now, and work for the present.

8 CONCLUSION: NEO-SHAMANISMS IN POST-MODERNITY

1   Certain groups, however, such as the Odinic Rite and Hammarens Ordens Sällskap in Britain, and the Asatru Folk Assembly in the USA, are more explic-

itly caught up in issues of racism, nationalism (British and/or European) and homophobia.

APPENDIX

1   Cited by Churchill (1992: 223–228).

BIBLIOGRAPHY

A note on translations

A number of translations from Old Norse are cited in Chapters 2, 3 and 4. The list below indicates the reference for each translation. In addition, many of the Norse Myths are made very accessible in Crossley-Holland (1980).

Egils saga see Scudder (2001).
Flateyjarbók see Guðbrandur Vigfússon and Unger (1860–1868)
Gísla saga see Johnston and Foote (1963)
Grímnismál see Dronke (1998) and Larrington (1996)
Gylfaginning see Faulkes (1998)
Hávamál see Dronke (1998) and Larrington (1996)
Laxdœla saga see Kunz (2001)
Saga of Eiríkr the Red see Magnusson and Pálsson (1965)
Skáldskaparmál see Faulkes (1998)
Þrymskviða see Dronke (1998) and Larrington (1996)
Vafþrúðnismál see Dronke (1998) and Larrington (1996)
Vatnsdœla saga see Wawn (2001)
Voluspá see Dronke (1998) and Larrington (1996)
Ynglinga saga see Hollander (1999)

Adler, M. 1986. *Drawing Down the Moon: Witches, Druids, Goddess-Worshippers and Other Pagans in America Today*. Boston: Beacon Press.

Ahmed, A.S. and C.N. Shore 1995. Introduction: Is Anthropology Relevant to the Contemporary World? In: A.S. Ahmed and C.N. Shore (eds) *The Future of Anthropology: Its Relevance to the Contemporary World*: 12–45. London: Athlone.

Albanese, C.L. 1990. *Nature Religion in America: From the Algonkian Indians to the New Age*. Chicago: University of Chicago Press.

Aldhouse Green, M. 2001a. Gender Bending Images: Permeating Boundaries in Ancient European Iconography. In: R.J. Wallis and K.J. Lymer (eds) *A Permeability of Boundaries: New Approaches to the Archaeology of Art, Religion and Folklore*: 19–29. BAR International Series 936. Oxford: British Archaeological Reports.

—— 2001b. Cosmovision and Metaphor: Monsters and Shamans in Gallo-British Cult-expression. *European Journal of Archaeology* 4(2): 203–232.

Allen, B. 2000. *Last of the Medicine Men*. London: BBC Worldwide Limited.

Allen-Mills, T. 1997. Tribe Torn as Tradition Fights Greed. *The Sunday Times*, 12 October: 19.

Andrews, L. 1982. *Medicine Woman*. San Francisco: Harper and Row.

Antiquity. 1996. Reports: The Future of Avebury, Again. *Antiquity* 70: 501–502.

Arent, A.M. 1969. The Heroic Pattern: Old Germanic Helmets, *Beowulf*, and *Grettis saga*. In: E.C. Polome (ed.) *Old Norse Literature and Mythology*: 130–199. Austin: University of Texas Press.

Armstrong, E.A. 1944. Mugwort Lore. *Folk-Lore* 55(1): 22–27.

Arnold, A. 1990. The Past as Propaganda: Totalitarian Archaeology in Nazi Germany. *Antiquity* 64: 464–478.

Arnold, C.J. 1997. *An Archaeology of the Anglo-Saxon Kingdoms*. London: Routledge.

Ashcroft, B., G. Griffiths and H. Tiffin 1998. *Key Concepts in Post-Colonial Studies*. London: Routledge.

Aswynn, F. 1994. *Leaves of Yggdrasil*. St Paul, Minnesota: Llewellyn.

Atkinson, J.M. 1989. *The Art and Politics of Wana Shamanship*. Berkeley and Los Angeles: University of California Press.

—— 1992. Shamanisms Today. *Annual Review of Anthropology* 21: 307–330.

Ausenda, G. 1995. *After Empire: Towards An Ethnology of Europe's Barbarians*. Woodbridge, Suffolk: The Boydell Press.

Bahn, P.G. 1993. The Archaeology of the Monolithic Sculptures of Rapanui: A General View. In: S.R. Fischer (ed.) *Easter Island Studies: Contributions to the History of Rapanui in the Memory of William T. Mulloy*: 82–85. Oxford: Oxbow Books.

—— 1996. Comment on: Dronfield, J. Entering Alternative Realities: Cognition, Art and Architecture in Irish Passage-Tombs. *Cambridge Archaeological Journal* 6(1): 55–57.

Bakhtin, M.M. 1968. *Rabelais and his World*. Cambridge, Massachusetts: Massachusetts Institute of Technology Press.

—— 1993. *Towards a Philosophy of the Act*. Austin, Texas: University of Texas Press.

Balzer, M. 1993. Two Urban Shamans: Unmasking Leadership in Fin-de-Soviet Siberia. In: G.E. Marcus (ed.) *Perilous States: Conversations on Culture, Politics, and Nation*: 131–164. Chicago: University of Chicago Press.

—— 1997. Introduction. In: M. Balzer (ed.) *Shamanic Worlds: Rituals and Lore of Siberia and Central Asia*: xiii–xxxii. New York: North Castle Books.

Bannister, V. 2000. A Load of Old Rubbish. *Pagan Dawn: The Journal of the Pagan Federation* 135(Beltane): 12–13.

Barfield, L. and M. Hodder 1987. Burnt Mounds as Saunas, and the Prehistory of Bathing. *Antiquity* 61: 370–379.

Barley, N. 1972. Anglo-Saxon Magico-Medicine. *Journal of the Royal Anthropological Society of Oxford* 3: 67–76.

Barnatt, J. 1997. Excavation and Restoration of the Doll Tor Stone Circle, Stanton, Derbyshire, 1994. *Derbyshire Archaeological Journal* 117: 81–85.

Basilov, V. 1992. *Shamanism of the Peoples of Central Asia and Kazakhstan*. Moscow: Nauka (in Russian).

Bates, B. 1983. *The Way of Wyrd: Tales of an Anglo-Saxon Sorceror*. London: Arrow.

—— 1996. *The Wisdom of the Wyrd: Teachings for Today from Our Ancient Past*. London: Rider.

—— 1996/7. Wyrd: Life Force of the Cosmos. *Sacred Hoop* 15(Winter): 8–13.

Baxter, I. and C. Chippindale 2002. *A Sustainable and Green Approach to Stonehenge Visitation: The 'Brownfield' Option*. Pdf file available on request: contact info@moffatcentre.com.

Beals, R.L. 1978. Sonoran Fantasy or Coming of Age? *American Anthropologist* 80: 355–362.

Beaumont, R. and O. Kharitidi 1997. The Secrets of Siberian Shamanism. *Kindred Spirit Quarterly* 38: 47–50.

Bell, C. 1998. Performance. In: M.C. Taylor (ed.) *Critical Terms for Religious Studies*: 205–224. Chicago: Chicago University Press.

Belli, L.A. 1993. Concerning 'American Indian Religious Freedom Act'. In: *Public Notice: Closures and Public Use Limits, Chaco CNHP Authority*. 36 CFR – Points 1, 2, 3, 4. 1 April: 9.

Bend, C. and T. Wiger 1987. *Birth of a Modern Shaman*. St Paul, Minnesota: Llewellyn.

Bender, B. 1992. Theorising Landscapes, and the Prehistoric Landscapes of Stonehenge. *Man* 27: 735–755.

—— 1993. Stonehenge – Contested Landscapes (Medieval to Present Day). In: B. Bender (ed.) *Landscape: Politics and Perspectives*: 245–280. Oxford: Berg.

—— 1998. *Stonehenge: Making Space*. Oxford: Berg.

Bender, B. and M. Edmonds 1992. De-romancing the Stones. *The Guardian* 15 June.

Bensinger, C. 1988. *Chaco Journey: Remembrance and Awakening*. Santa Fe, New Mexico: Timewindow.

Berg, D. 2001. Modern Pagans (interview with Jörmundur Ingi, head of Ásatrú in Iceland). *Iceland Review* 39(2): 42–46.

Berger, P. 1980. *The Heretical Imperative*. New York: Anchor Books.

Bernard, H.R. 1988. *Research Methods in Cultural Anthropology*. London: Sage.

Biehl, J. 2000. *Ecology and the Modernization of Fascism in the German Ultra-right*. Available online: http://www.spunk.org/library/places/germany/sp001630/janet.html.

Billington, S. 1984. *A Social History of the Fool*. Brighton: The Harvester Press.

Binford, L.R. 1962. Archaeology as Anthropology. *American Antiquity* 28: 217–225.

Biolsi, T. and L.J. Zimmerman (eds) 1997. *Indians and Anthropologists: Vine Deloria Jr. and the Critique of Anthropology*. Tucson: University of Arizona Press.

Blacker, C. 1975. *The Catalpa Bow: A Study of Shamanistic Practices in Japan*. London: George Allen and Unwin.

Blain, J. 1997. On the Knife-edge: Seidr-working and the Anthropologist. Unpublished paper presented at 'Re-Enchantment: An International Conference on Contemporary Paganism and the Interface Between Nature and Religion(s)', King Alfred's College, Winchester.

—— 1998a. Seidr as Women's Magic: Shamanism, Journeying and Healing in Norse Heathenism. Unpublished paper presented at CASCA (Canadian Anthropology Society) annual conference, May 1998, University of Toronto.

—— 1998b. Presenting Constructions of Identity and Divinity: Ásatrú and Oracular Seidhr. In: S. Grills (ed.) *Fieldwork Methods: Accomplishing Ethnographic Research*: 203–227. Thousand Oaks, California: Sage.

—— 1999a. The Nine Worlds and the Tree: Seiðr as Shamanistic Practice in Heathen Spirituality. *Spirit Talk: A Core Shamanic Newsletter* 9 (Early Summer): 14–19.

—— 1999b. Seidr as Shamanistic Practice: Reconstituting a Tradition of Ambiguity. *Shaman* 7(2): 99–121.

—— 2000. *Stonehenge Solstice 2000: Audio Diary*. Available online on the *Megalithic Mysteries* pages edited by Andy Burnham: http://easyweb.easynet.co.uk/~aburnham/pers/sounds.htm.

—— 2001. Shamans, Stones, Authenticity and Appropriation: Contestations of Invention and Meaning. In: R.J. Wallis and K. J. Lymer (eds) *A Permeability of Boundaries: New Approaches to the Archaeology of Art, Religion and Folklore*: 47–55. BAR International Series 936. Oxford: British Archaeological Reports.

—— 2002. *Nine Worlds of Seidr-Magic: Ecstasy and Neo-shamanism in North European Paganism*. London: Routledge.

Blain, J. and R.J. Wallis. 1999. Men and 'Women's Magic': Gender, Seidr, and 'Ergi'. *The Pomegranate: A New Journal of Neopagan Thought* 9: 4–16.

—— 2000. The 'Ergi' Seidman: Contestations of Gender, Shamanism and Sexuality in Northern Religion Past and Present. *Journal of Contemporary Religion* 15(3): 395–411.

—— 2001. Stonehenge Solstice Access, 20–21 June 2001. Report submitted to English Heritage by the Sacred Sites, Contested Rights/Rites Project, 5 July 2001. Available online: http://www.sacredsites.org.uk.

—— In preparation. Ritual Reflections, Practitioner Meanings: 'Performance' Disputed. Manuscript submitted to *Cultural Anthropology*.

Boddy, J. 1994. Spirit Possession Revisited: Beyond Instrumentality. *Annual Review of Anthropology* 23: 407–434.

Boissiere, R. 1986. *Meditations with the Hopi*. Santa Fe, New Mexico: Bear and Company.

Boniface, P. and P. Fowler 1993. *Heritage and Tourism in the 'Global Village'*. London: Routledge.

Bonser, W. 1925. The Significance of Colour in Ancient and Mediaeval Magic. *Man* 25: 194–198.

—— 1926. Magical Practices Against Elves. *Folk-Lore* 37: 350–363.

—— 1962. Animal Skins in Magic and Medicine. *Folk-Lore* 73: 128–129.

Bourguignon, E. 1967. World Distribution and Pattern of Possession States. In: R. Prince (ed.) *Trance and Possession States*. Montreal: R.M. Bucke Memorial Society.

——1974. Cross-cultural Perspectives on the Religious use of Altered States of Consciousness. In: I.I. Zaretsky and M.P. Leone (eds) *Religious Movements in Contemporary America*: 228–243. New Jersey: Princeton University Press.

—— 1976. *Possession*. San Francisco: Chandler and Sharp.

Bowers, P. 1999/2000. On Ilkley Moor: Letter from Paul Bowers, September 1999. *Northern Earth* 80: 30.

Bowie, F. 2000. *The Anthropology of Religion*. Oxford: Blackwell.

Bowman, M. 1993. Reinventing the Celts. *Religion* 23: 147–156.

—— 1994. The Commodification of the Celt: New Age/Neo-Pagan Consumerism. *Folklore in Use* 2: 143–152.

—— 1995a. The Noble Savage and the Global Village: Cultural Evolution in New Age and Neo-Pagan Thought. *Journal of Contemporary Religion* 10(2): 139–149.

—— 1995b. Cardiac Celts: Images of the Celts in Paganism. In: G. Harvey and C. Hardman (eds) *Paganism Today: Wiccans, Druids, the Goddess and Ancient Earth Traditions for the Twenty-first Century*: 242–251. London: Thorsons.

—— 2000. Contemporary Celtic Spirituality. In: A. Hale and P. Payton (eds) *New Directions in Celtic Studies*: 69–91. Exeter: University of Exeter Press.

Boyer, L.B. 1969. Shamans: To Set the Record Straight. *American Anthropologist* 71: 307–309.

Boyle, M. 1990. *Schizophrenia: A Scientific Delusion?* London: Routledge.

Bradley, R.J. 1989. Deaths and Entrances: A Contextual Analysis of Megalithic Art. *Current Anthropology* 30: 68–75.

—— 1997. *Signing the Land: Rock Art and the Prehistory of Atlantic Europe*. London: Routledge.

—— 1998. *The Significance of Monuments: On the Shaping of Human Experience in Neolithic and Bronze Age Europe*. London: Routledge.

Branston, B. 1957. *The Lost Gods of England*. London: Thames and Hudson.

Brennand, M. and M. Taylor 2000. Seahenge. *Current Archaeology* 167: 417–424.

Bromley, D.G. and L.F. Carter (eds) 1996. *Religion and the Social Order: The Issue of Authenticity in the Study of Religions*. Official Publication of the Association for the Sociology of Religion, vol. 6. Greenwich, Connecticut: JAI Press.

Brown, D. n.d. *Traditional Healing Returns to Tuva*. Available online: http://www.fotuva.org/misc/shamanism/clinic.html.

Brown, M. 1998. In February of this Year I Received a Curious and Completely Unexpected Invitation ... Would I Like to Interview Carlos Castaneda? *Daily Telegraph Saturday Magazine* (1 August): 38–42.

Brown, Michelle. 1998. Henge of the Sea. *Sacred Hoop* 24(Spring): 15.

Brown, M.F. 1988. Shamanism and Its Discontents. *Medical Anthropology Quarterly* 2(2): 102–120.

—— 1989. Dark Side of the Shaman. *Natural History* November: 8–10.

—— 1997. *The Channeling Zone: American Spirituality in an Anxious Age*. Cambridge, Massachusetts: Harvard University Press.

—— 1998. Can Culture Be Copyrighted? *Current Anthropology* 39(2): 193–222.

Brück, J. 1999. Ritual and Rationality: Some Problems of Interpretation in European Archaeology. *European Journal of Archaeology* 2(3): 313–344.

Brunton, B. 1997. Shamans and Shamanism by the Lake: Reawakened Traditions in Buryatia. *Shamanism* 10(1): 3–7.

Buchholz, P. 1971. Shamanism – The Testimony of Old Icelandic Literary Tradition. *Mediaeval Scandinavia* 4: 7–20.

Budd, P. and T. Taylor 1995. The Faerie Smith Meets the Bronze Industry: Magic Versus Science in the Interpretation of Prehistoric Metal-making. *World Archaeology* 27(1): 133–143.

Buhner, S. 1999. Open Dialogue: Do-Earth Based Ceremonies Belong to Natives Only? *Shaman's Drum* 51(Spring): 4–12.

Burl, A. 2000. *The Rollright Stones*. Banbury, Oxfordshire: Tattooed Kitten Publications.

Butler, B. 1996. The Tree, the Tower and the Shaman: The Material Culture of Resistance of the No M11 Link Roads Protest of Wanstead and Leytonstone, London. *Journal of Material Culture* 1(3): 337–363.

Butler, J. 1993. *Bodies That Matter: On the Discursive Limits of 'Sex'*. London: Routledge.

—— 1994. Against Proper Objects. *Differences: A Journal of Feminist Cultural Studies – 'More Gender Trouble: Feminism Meets Queer Theory'* 6: 1–26.

Calver, S. 1998. *Avebury Visitor Research 1996–1998*. Bournemouth: Bournemouth University Report on Behalf of the National Trust.

Camille, M. 1998. *Mirror in Parchment: The Luttrell Psalter and the Making of Medieval England*. London: Reaktion Books.

Campbell, M. 1999. Ergi: A Personal Perspective on Men and Seiðr. *Spirit Talk: A Core Shamanic Newsletter* 9(Early Summer): 22–24.

Carmichael, D.L., J. Hubert, R. Reeves and A. Schanche (eds) 1994. *Sacred Sites, Sacred Places*. London: Routledge.

Carpenter, D. 1998. Symbolic Stupidity. *The Right Times* 2(Summer Solstice): 24.

Carrasco, D. and J.M. Swanberg (eds) 1985a. *Waiting for the Dawn: Mircea Eliade in Perspective*. Boulder, Colorado: Westview Press.

—— 1985b. Introduction: Other Eliades. In: D. Carrasco and J.M. Swanberg (eds) *Waiting for the Dawn: Mircea Eliade in Perspective*: 1–7. Boulder, Colorado: Westview Press.

—— 1985c. Comment on: M. Eliade 1985a. Waiting for the Dawn. In: D. Carrasco and J.M. Swanberg. (eds) *Waiting for the Dawn: Mircea Eliade in Perspective*: 17. Boulder, Colorado: Westview Press.

—— 1985d. Comment on: M. Eliade 1985b. A New Humanism. In: D. Carrasco and J.M. Swanberg (eds) *Waiting for the Dawn: Mircea Eliade in Perspective*: 35. Boulder, Colorado: Westview Press.

Carr-Gomm, P. (ed.) 1996. *The Druid Renaissance*. London: Thorsons.

Carroll, P. 1987. *Liber Null and Psychonaut: An Introduction to Chaos Magic (Two Complete Volumes)*. York Beach, Maine: Samuel Weiser, Inc.

Castaneda, C. 1968. *The Teachings of Don Juan: A Yaqui Way of Knowledge*. Berkeley: University of California Press.

—— 1971. *A Separate Reality: Further Conversations with Don Juan*. London: The Bodley Head.

—— 1972. *Journey to Ixtlan: The Lessons of Don Juan*. New York: Simon and Schuster.

—— 1974. *Tales of Power*. New York: Penguin Books.

Castaneda, M.R. 1997. *A Magical Journey with Carlos Castaneda*. Victoria, British Columbia: Millennia Press.

Castile, G.P. 1996. The Commodification of Indian Identity. *American Anthropologist* 98(4): 743–749.

Chadburn, A. and M. Pomeroy-Kilinger 2001. *Archaeological Research Agenda for the Avebury World Heritage Site*. Avebury/London: Avebury Archaeological and Historic Research Group, Trust for Wessex Archaeology/English Heritage.

Chadwick, N.K. 1934. 'Imbas Forosnai'. *Scottish Gaelic Studies* 4: 98–135.

—— 1936a. Shamanism among the Tatars of Central Asia. *Journal of the Royal Anthropological Institute of Great Britain and Ireland* 66: 75–112.

—— 1936b. The Spiritual Ideas and Experiences of the Tatars of Central Asia. *Journal of the Royal Anthropological Institute of Great Britain and Ireland* 66: 291–329.

—— 1942. *Poetry and Prophecy*. Cambridge: Cambridge University Press.

—— 1966. *The Druids*. Wales: University of Wales Press.

Champion, M. 2000. *Seahenge: A Contemporary Chronicle*. Aylsham, Norfolk: Barnwell's Timescape.

Chapman, M. 1992. *The Celts: The Construction of a Myth*. New York: St Martin's Press.

Chatters, J.C. 2000. The Recovery and First Analysis of an Early Holocene Human Skeleton from Kennewick, Washington. *American Antiquity* 65(2): 291–316.

Childe, V.G. 1958. *The Prehistory of European Society*. Harmondsworth: Penguin.

Chippindale, C. 1983. What Future for Stonehenge? *Antiquity* 57: 172–180.

—— 1985. English Heritage and the Future of Stonehenge. *Antiquity* 59: 132–137.

—— 1986. Stoned Henge: Events and Issues at the Summer Solstice, 1985. *World Archaeology* 18(1): 38–58.

Chippindale, C., P. Devereux, P. Fowler, R. Jones and T. Sebastion 1990. *Who Owns Stonehenge?* Manchester: Batsford.

Churchill, W. 1992. *Fantasies of the Master Race: Literature, Cinema and the Colonization of American Indians*. Monroe, Maine: Common Courage Press.

Clarke, D.L. 1968. *Analytical Archaeology*. London: Methuen.

Cleere, H.F. (ed.) 1989. *Archaeological Heritage Management in the Modern World*. London: Routledge.

Clifford, J. and G. Marcus (eds) 1986. *Writing Culture: The Poetics and Politics of Ethnography*. Cambridge, Massachusetts: Harvard University Press.

Clifton, C.S. 1989. Armchair Shamanism: A Yankee Way of Knowledge. In: T. Schultz (ed.) *The Fringes of Reason, A Whole Earth Catalogue*: 43–49. New York: Harmony Books.

—— 1994. Shamanism and Neoshamanism. In: C. Clifton (ed.) *Witchcraft and Shamanism: Witchcraft Today, Book Three*: 1–13. St Paul, Minnesota: Llewellyn.

Clifton, G. (ed.) 1990. *The Invented Indian: Cultural Fictions and Government Policies*. New Brunswick: Transaction.

Clottes, J. and J.D. Lewis-Williams 1998. *The Shamans of Prehistory: Trance and Magic in the Painted Caves*. New York: Harry N. Abrams, Inc.

Clover, C. 1997. Stonehenge Fails to get £22m Grant from Lottery. *The Daily Telegraph*, 14 June: 7.

—— 1998. Traffic will be hidden by £125m Stonehenge Tunnel. *The Daily Telegraph*, 1 August: 4.

Cohen, A.P. 1994. *Self Consciousness: An Alternative Anthropology of Identity*. London: Routledge.

Coles, B. 1998. Wooden Species for Wooden Figures: A Glimpse of a Pattern. In: A. Gibson and D. Simpson (eds) *Prehistoric Ritual and Religion*: 163–173. Stroud, Gloucestershire: Sutton.

Collis, J. 1997 [1984]. *The European Iron Age*. London: Routledge.

Coltelli, L. 1990. *Winged Words: American Indian Writers Speak*. Nebraska: University of Nebraska Press.

Conrad, J. 1989 [1902]. *Heart of Darkness*. London: Penguin.

Conway, D.J. 1995. *By Oak, Ash, and Thorn: Modern Celtic Shamanism*. St Paul, Minnesota: Llewellyn.

Cope, J. 1998. *The Modern Antiquarian: A Pre-millennial Odyssey Through Megalithic Britain*. London: Thorsons.

Cowan, T. 1993. *Fire in the Head: Shamanism and the Celtic Spirit*. San Francisco: HarperCollins.

Craig, S. (ed.) 1986. *Stonehenge '85: Souvenir Issue – A Collection of Material to Commemorate 'The Battle of the Beanfield' June 1st 1985*. Glastonbury: Unique Publications.

Crapanzano, V. 1980. *Tuhami: Portrait of a Moroccan*. Chicago: University of Chicago Press.

Crawford, J. 1963. Evidences for Witchcraft in Anglo-Saxon England. *Medium Aevum* 32(2): 99–116.

Crawford, O.G.S. 1957. *The Eye Goddess*. London: Phoenix House.

Creighton, J. 1995. Visions of Power: Imagery and Symbols in Late Iron Age Britain. *Britannia* 26: 285–301.

—— 2000. *Coins and Power in Late Iron Age Britain*. Cambridge: Cambridge University Press.

Crook, S. 1998. Away with the Fairies: Rock Art and Psychic Geography in West Yorkshire. Unpublished MA Thesis, Department of Archaeology, University of Southampton.

Crossley-Holland, K. 1980. *The Penguin Book of Norse Myths: Gods of the Vikings*. London: Penguin.

Crowley, V. 1994. *Phoenix from the Flame: Pagan Spirituality in the Western World*. London: Aquarian.

Crowley, V. 1997. Pagan Faiths Excluded from the Sacred Land Project. *The Independent*, 26 April.

—— 1998. Wicca as Nature Religion. In: J. Pearson, R.H. Roberts and G. Samuel (eds) *Nature Religion Today: Paganism in the Modern World*: 170–179. Edinburgh: Edinburgh University Press.

Crown, P.L. and W.J. Judge (eds). 1991. *Chaco and Hohokam: Prehistoric Regional Systems in the American Southwest*. Santa Fe, New Mexico: School of American Research Press.

Cruden, L. 1995. *Coyote's Council Fire: Contemporary Shamans on Race, Gender, and Community*. Rochester, Vermont: Destiny Books.

Cunningham, S. 2001 [1988]. *Wicca: A Guide for the Solitary Practitioner*. St Paul, Minnesota: Llewellyn.

Cushing, F.H. 1897. Remarks on Shamanism. *American Philosophical Society Proceedings* 36: 183–192.

Czaplicka, M.A. 1914. *Aboriginal Siberia: A Study in Social Anthropology*. Oxford: The Clarendon Press.

Dames, M. 1976. *The Silbury Treasure*. London: Thames and Hudson.

—— 1977. *The Avebury Cycle*. London: Thames and Hudson.

D'Anglure, S. 1992. Rethinking Inuit Shamanism Through the Concept of 'Third Gender'. In: M. Hoppál and J. Pentikäinen (eds) *Northern Religions and Shamanism*: 146–150. Budapest: Akadémiai Kiadó.

Daniel, G. 1958. *The Megalith Builders of Western Europe*. London: Hutchinson.

Darvill, T. 1999. Music, Muses, and the Modern Antiquarian: A Review Article. *The Archaeologist* 34: 28–29.

Davidson, H.E. 1950. The Hill of the Dragon: Anglo-Saxon Burial Mounds in Literature and Archaeology. *Folk-Lore* 61(4): 169–184.

—— 1964. *Gods and Myths of Northern Europe*. London: Pelican.

——. 1980. The Germanic God of the Dead. In: M. Pye and P. McKenzie (eds) *Proceedings of the Thirteenth Congress for the History of Religions, Lancaster 1975*: 96–97. Leicester Studies in Religion II. Leicester: Department of Religion, University of Leicester.

—— 1993. *The Lost Beliefs of Northern Europe*. London: Routledge.

Davies, A. 1998. Return of the Men in White. *The Big Issue* 288(15–21 June): 22–26.

Davies, C.A. 1999. *Reflexive Ethnography: A Guide to Researching Selves and Others*. London: Routledge.

Davies, G.H. 1999. 'Brave Heart, Forked Tongue': Timewatch – Grey Owl, the Great White Hoax. *Radio Times* 17–23 April: 30–32.

Davies, J.G. 1968. *The Secular Use of Church Buildings*. London: SCM Press.

Davies, P. 1997. Respect and Reburial. *The Druid's Voice: The Magazine of Contemporary Druidry* 8(Summer): 12–13.

—— 1998/9. Speaking for the Ancestors: The Reburial Issue in Britain and Ireland. *The Druid's Voice: The Magazine of Contemporary Druidry* 9(Winter): 10–12.

Davison, J., M. Brace and A. Mullins 1999. Mayhem at Midsummer's Dawn as Travellers Storm Stonehenge Fence. *The Independent* 22 June: 3.

De Bruxelles, S. 1999. Violence Wrecks the Solstice Celebration. *The Times* 22 June: 13.

—— 2001. Magic of Stonehenge Summons up the Sun. *The Times* 22 June: 9.

De Heusch, L. 1982. Possession and Shamanism. In: L. de Heusch *Why Marry Her? Society and Symbolic Structures*: 151–164. Cambridge: Cambridge University Press.

De Lauretis, T. 1991. Queer Theory: Lesbian and Gay Sexualities – An Introduction. *Differences* 3 (2): iii–xviii.

Deloria, P.J. 1998. *Playing Indian*. New Haven, Connecticut: Yale University Press.

Deloria, V., Jr. (ed.). 1984. *A Sender of Words: Essays in Memory of John G. Neihardt*. Salt Lake City, Utah: Howe Brothers.

—— 1988 [1970]. *Custer Died for Your Sins: An Indian Manifesto*. New York: Macmillan.

—— 1997. Anthros, Indians and Planetary Reality. In: T. Biolsi and L.J. Zimmerman (eds) *Indians and Anthropologists: Vine Deloria Jr. and the Critique of Anthropology*: 209–221. Arizona: The University of Arizona Press.

—— 1998. Comfortable Fictions and the Struggle for Turf: An Essay Review of *The Invented Indian: Cultural Fictions and Government Policies*. In: D.A. Mihesuah (ed.) *Natives and Academics: Researching and Writing about American Indians*: 65–83. Lincoln: University of Nebraska Press.

De Mille, R. 1976. *Castenada's Journey: The Power and the Allegory*. Santa Barbara, California: Capra Press.

—— (ed.) 1980. *The Don Juan Papers: Further Castaneda Controversies*. Santa Barbara, California: Ross-Erikson.

Denning, K. 1999a. Archaeology and Alterity. Unpublished paper presented in the 'Method and Theory 2000' session at the Society for American Archaeology Annual Meeting, Chicago.

—— 1999b. Apocalypse Past/Future: Archaeology and Folklore, Writ Large. In: C. Holtorf and A. Gazin-Schwartz (eds) *Archaeology and Folklore*: 90–105. London: Routledge.

Denison, S. 2000. Issues: One Step to the Left, Two Steps Back. *British Archaeology* 52(April): 28.

Denzin, N.K. 1997. *Interpretive Ethnography: Ethnographic Practices for the 21st Century*. Thousand Oaks, California: Sage.

Deren, M. 1975. *The Voodoo Gods*. St Albans, Hertfordshire: Paladin.

De Rios, M.D. 1974. The Influence of Psychotropic Flora and Fauna on Mayan Religion. *Current Anthropology* 15: 147–164.

—— 1984. *Hallucinogens: Cross-cultural Perspectives*. Shaftesbury, Dorset: Prism Press.

Devereux, G. 1956. Normal and Abnormal: The Key Problem of Psychiatric Anthropology. In: J.B. Casagrande and T. Gladwin (eds) *Some Uses of Anthropology: Theoretical and Applied*: 22–48. Washington: Anthropological Society of Washington.

—— 1961. Shamans as Neurotics. *American Anthropologist* 63: 1088–1090.

Devereux, P. 1991. Three-dimensional Aspects of Apparent Relationships Between Selected Natural and Artificial Features within the Topography of the Avebury Complex. *Antiquity* 65: 249.

—— 1992a. *Shamanism and the Mystery Lines: Ley Lines, Spirit Paths, Shape-shifting and Out-of-body-travel*. London: Quantum.

—— 1992b. *Symbolic Landscapes: The Dreamtime Earth and Avebury's Open Secrets*. Glastonbury: Gothic Image.

—— 1997. *The Long Trip: A Prehistory of Psychedelia*. New York: Arkana.

—— 2001. Did Ancient Shamanism Leave a Monumental Record on the Land as well as in Rock Art? In: R.J. Wallis and K. J. Lymer (eds) *A Permeability of Boundaries? New Approaches to the Archaeology of Art, Religion and Folklore*: 1–7. BAR International Series 936. Oxford: British Archaeological Reports.

Devereux, P. and R.G. Jahn 1996. Preliminary Investigations and Cognitive Considerations of the Acoustic Resonances of Selected Archaeological Sites. *Antiquity* 70: 665–666.

Díaz-Andreu, M. 2002. Making the Landscape: Iberian Post-Palaeolithic Art, Identities and the Sacred. In: G G. Nash and C. Chippindale (eds) *European Landscapes of Rock-art*: 158–175. London: Routledge.

Dickinson, T.M. 1993a. Early Saxon Saucer Brooches: A Preliminary Overview. *Anglo- Saxon Studies in Archaeology and History* 6: 11–44. Oxford: Oxford University Committee for Archaeology.

—— 1993b. An Anglo-Saxon 'Cunning Woman' from Bidford-on-Avon. In: M. Carver (ed.) *In Search of Cult: Archaeological Investigations in Honour of Philip Ratz*: 45–54. Woodbridge, Suffolk: The Boydell Press.

Diderot, D. *et al.* 2001 [1765]. 'Shamans Are Imposters Who Claim They Consult the Devil – And Who Are Sometimes Close to the Mark'. In: J. Narby and F. Huxley (eds) *Shamans Through Time: 500 Years on the Path to Knowledge*: 32–35. London: Thames and Hudson.

Dietler, M. 1994. Our Ancestors the Gauls: Archaeology, Ethnic Nationalism, and the Manipulation of Celtic Identity in Modern Europe. *American Anthropologist* 96 (3): 584–605.

Dirlek, A. 1996. The Past as Legacy and Project: Postcolonial Criticism and the Perspective of Indigenous Historicism. *American Indian Culture and Research Journal* 20(2): 1–31.

Dongoske, K.E. 1998. Annual Report of the Committee on Native American Relations. *Society for American Archaeology Bulletin* March: 2, 33.

Dongoske, K.E. and R. Anyon 1997. Federal Archaeology: Tribes, Diatribes and Tribulations. In: N. Swidler, K.E. Dongoske, R. Anyon and A.S. Downer (eds) *Native Americans and Archaeologists: Stepping Stones to Common Ground*: 197–206. Walnut Creek, California: AltaMira Press.

Dongoske, K.E., D.L. Martin and T.J. Ferguson 2000. Critique of the Claim of Cannibalism at Cowboy Wash. *American Antiquity* 65(1): 179–190.

Doty, W. 1990. Writing the Blurred Genres of Postmodern Ethnography. *Annals of Scholarship: Studies of the Humanities and Social Sciences* 6(3–4): 267–287.

Douglas, M. 1980. The Authenticity of Castaneda. In: R. De Mille (ed.) *The Don Juan Papers: Further Castaneda Controversies*: 25–32. Santa Barbara, California: Ross-Erikson.

Downton, J. 1989. Individuation and Shamanism. *Journal of Analytic Psychology* 34: 73–88.

Dowson, T.A. 1994a. Reading Art, Writing History: Rock Art and Social Change in Southern Africa. *World Archaeology* 25(3): 332–345.

—— 1994b. Hunter-gatherers, Traders, and Slaves: The 'Mfecane' Impact on Bushmen, their Ritual and Art. In: C. Hamilton (ed.) *The Mfecane Aftermath: Reconstructive Debates in South Africa's History*: 51–70. Johannesburg and Pieter-maritzberg: Witwatersrand University Press and Natal University Press.

—— 1996. Review of P. Garlake 1995. The Hunter's Vision: The Prehistoric Rock Art of Zimbabwe. *Antiquity* 70: 468–469.

—— 1998a. The Relationship of Theory and Sexual Politics in the Representation of Rock Art. Paper presented at the Alta Rock Art Conference, Norway.

—— 1998b. Homosexualitat, teortia queer i arqueologia [Homosexuality, Queer Theory and Archaeology]. *Cota Zero* 14: 81–87 (in Catalan with English transla-tion).

—— 1998c. Like People in Prehistory. *World Archaeology* 25(3): 332–345.

—— 1999a. Rock Art and Shamanism: A Methodological Impasse. In: A. Rozwad-owski, M.M. Kośko and T.A. Dowson (eds) *Rock Art, Shamanism and Central Asia: Discussions of Relations*: 39–56. Warsaw: Wydawnictwo Academickie (in Polish).

—— 1999b. An Archaeologist's Reflections on Homophobia. Unpublished manuscript.

—— 1999c. Interpretation in Rock Art Research: A Crisis in Confidence. *The Ley Hunter* 133: 21–23.

—— 2001a. Queer Theory and Feminist Theory: Towards a Sociology of Sexual Politics in Rock Art Research. In: K. Helskog (ed.) *Theoretical Perspectives in Rock Art Research*: 312–329. Oslo, Norway: Institutett for sammenlignende kultur-forskning.

—— 2001b. Afterword: Permeating Boundaries. In: R.J. Wallis and K.J. Lymer (eds) *A Permeability of Boundaries: New Approaches to the Archaeology of Art, Religion and Folklore*: 137–138. BAR International Series 936. Oxford: British Archaeo-logical Reports.

Dowson, T.A., E. Evans, S. Crook, D. Murphy, S. Elliot, P. Haupt, J. Kirby, L. McDermot and R.J. Wallis. In preparation. Spirits of the Moor: Neo-Shamanism at Rock Art Sites in Britain. In: Dowson *et al. Ever Increasing Circles: Re-considering Problems and Perspectives for the Rock Art of the Irish and British Isles*. International Rock Art Monographs 1. Series Editor: T.A. Dowson. Cambridge: Cambridge University Press.

Dronke, U. (ed. and trans.). 1998. *The Poetic Edda: Vol. II Mythological Poems*. Oxford: Oxford University Press.

Drury, N. 1982. *The Shaman and the Magician: Journeys Between the Worlds*. London: Routledge.

—— 1989. *The Elements of Shamanism*. Shaftesbury, Dorset: Element Books.

—— 1993. *Pan's Daughter: The Magical World of Rosaleen Norton*. Oxford: Mandrake of Oxford.

Dubois, T.A. 1999. *Nordic Religions in the Viking Age*. Philadelphia: University of Pennsylvania Press.

Dummigan, G. 1997. A Sniff of Magic in the Witching Hour. *Weekend Telegraph* 3 May: 31.

Earle, T. 2001. Economic Support of Chaco Canyon Society. *American Antiquity* 66(1): 26–35.

Echo-Hawk, R.C. 2000. Ancient History in the New World: Integrating Oral Traditions and the Archaeological Record in Deep Time. *American Antiquity* 65(2): 267–290.

Eilberg-Schwartz, H. 1989. Witches of the West: Neopaganism and Goddess Worship as Enlightenment Religions. *Journal of Feminist Studies in Religion* 5(1): 79–95.

Eliade, M. 1961. Recent Works on Shamanism. *History of Religions* 1(1): 152–186.

—— 1985a. *Waiting for the Dawn*. In: D. Carrasco and J.M. Swanberg (eds) *Waiting for the Dawn: Mircea Eliade in Perspective*: 11–16. Boulder, Colorado: Westview Press.

—— 1985b. Literary Imagination and Religious Structure. In: D. Carrasco and J.M. Swanberg (eds) *Waiting for the Dawn: Mircea Eliade in Perspective*: 17–24. Boulder, Colorado: Westview Press.

—— 1989 [1964]. *Shamanism: Archaic Techniques of Ecstasy*. London: Penguin Arkana.

Elliott, R.W.V. 1989 [1959]. *Runes: An Introduction*. Manchester: Manchester University Press.

Ellis, C. and A.P. Bochner (eds) 1996. *Composing Ethnography: Alternative Forms of Qualitative Writing*. Walnut Creek, California: AltaMira Press.

—— 2000. Autoethnography, Personal Narrative: Reflexivity Researcher as Subject. In N.K. Denzin and Y.S. Lincoln (eds) *Handbook of Qualitative Research*: 733–769. Thousand Oaks, California: Sage.

Ellis, H.R. 1943. *The Road to Hel: A Study of the Conception of the Dead in Old Norse Literature*. Cambridge: Cambridge University Press.

Elton, O. (trans.) 1999 [1905]. *Saxo Grammaticus' Gesta Danorum, Book 6*. Available online: http://www.inform.umd.edu:8080/EdRes/ReadingRoom/Nonfiction/Saxo/Danes/book06.

Emboden, W. 1978. The Sacred Narcotic Lily of the Nile: *Nymphaea caerulea*. *Economic Botany* 32: 395–407.

—— 1989. The Sacred Journey in Dynastic Egypt: Shamanistic Trance in the Context of the Narcotic Water Lily and the Mandrake. *Journal of Psychoactive Drugs* 21: 61–75.

English Heritage. 1995. *The Monuments at Risk Survey of England 1995 (MARS): Pathways to Protecting the Past – An English Heritage Strategy Document*. Available online: http://www.cruithni.org/resources/publications/eh/monuments_at_risk/index.html.

—— 2000. *Stonehenge World Heritage Site Management Plan*. Available online: http://www.english-heritage.org.uk/.

Ewing, K.P. 1994. Dreams from a Saint: Anthropological Atheism and the Temptation to Believe. *American Anthropologist* 96(3): 571–583.

Fabian, J. 1983. *Time and the Other: How Anthropology Makes its Object*. New York: Columbia University Press.

Fardon, R. (ed.) 1995. *Counterworks: Managing the Diversity of Knowledge*. London: Routledge.

Farrar, J. and S. Farrar 1984. *The Witches' Way: Principles, Rituals and Beliefs of Modern Witchcraft*. London: Robert Hale.

Fatunmbi, A.F. 1991. *Ìwa-pèlé: Ifá Quest; The Search for the Source of Santería and Lucumí*. Bronx, New York: Original Publications.

Faulkes, A. 1998. *Edda by Snorri Sturluson*. London: J.M. Dent.

Favret-Saada, J. 1980. *Deadly Words: Witchcraft in the Bocage*. Cambridge: Cambridge University Press.

Feder, K.L. 1996. *Frauds, Myths and Mysteries: Science and Pseudoscience in Archaeology*. Mountainview, California: Mayfield Publishing Company.

Ferguson, T.J., K. Dongoske, L. Jenkins, M. Yeatts and E. Polingyouma 1993. Working Together: The Roles of Archaeology and Ethnohistory in Hopi Cultural Preservation. *Cultural Resources Magazine* 16: 27–37.

Fielden, K. 1996. Avebury Saved? *Antiquity* 70: 503–507.

—— 1999. Stonehenge – The Masterplan. *Pagan Dawn: The Journal of the Pagan Federation* 131(Beltane): 23–24.

Fikes, J.C. 1993. *Carlos Castaneda, Academic Opportunism and the Psychedelic Sixties*. Victoria, British Columbia: Millennia Press.

Finn, C. 1997. Leaving More than Footprints: Modern Votive Offerings at Chaco Canyon Prehistoric Site. *Antiquity* 71: 169–178.

Firth, D. and H. Campbell 1997. *Sacred Business: Resurrecting the Spirit of Work*. Oxford: Odyssey.

Fischer, M.M.J. 1986. Ethnicity and the Post-modern Arts of Memory. In: J. Clifford and G. Marcus (eds) *Writing Culture: The Poetics and Politics of Ethnography*: 194–223. Cambridge, Massachusetts: Harvard University Press:

Fixico, D.L. 1998. Ethics and Responsibilities in Writing American Indian History. In: D.A. Mihesuah (ed.) *Natives and Academics: Researching and Writing about American Indians*: 84–99. Lincoln: University of Nebraska Press.

Flaherty G. 1988. The Performing Artist as the Shaman of Higher Civilisation. *Modern Language* 103(3): 519–539.

—— 1989. Goethe and Shamanism. *Modern Language* 104(3): 580–596.

—— 1992. *Shamanism and the Eighteenth Century*. New Jersey: Princeton University Press.

Flaherty, R.P. 1991. T.M. Luhrmann and the Anthropologist's Craft: Differential Identity and the Ethnography of Britain's Magical Subculture. *Anthropological Quarterly* 64: 152–155.

Fleet, M. 1999. A Midsummer Nightmare at Stonehenge. *The Daily Telegraph* 22 June: 4.

Fleming, S. 1999. Psychic Vandalism. *The Right Times* 5(Spring Equinox): 12–14.

Fleming, S. n.d.a. *Organising Ritual at Prehistoric Sites*. Available online: http://www.ravenfamily.org/sam/pag/ritualmeths.html.

—— n.d.b. The Effects of Physical Damage to Sites. Available online: http://www.ravenfamily.org/sam/pag/site_dam.html.

Forte, R. (ed.) 1997. *Entheogens and the Future of Religion*. San Francisco: Council on Spiritual Practices.

Fowler, P. 1990a. Stonehenge: Academic Claims and Responsibilities. In: C. Chippindale, P. Devereux, P. Fowler, R. Jones and T. Sebastion (eds) *Who Owns Stonehenge?*: 120–138. Manchester: Batsford.

—— 1990b. Stonehenge in a Democratic Society. In: C. Chippindale, P. Devereux, P. Fowler, R. Jones and T. Sebastion (eds) *Who Owns Stonehenge?*: 139–159. Manchester: Batsford.

—— 1997. Why Public Access Must Be Controlled. *British Archaeology* April: 11.

Frazer, W.O. and A. Tyrell (eds) 2000. *Social Identity in Early Medieval Britain*. London: Leicester University Press.

Frazier, K. 1986. *People of Chaco: A Canyon and Its Culture*. New York: W.W. Norton and Company.

French, P.J. 1972. *John Dee: The World of an Elizabethan Magus*. London: Routledge and Kegan Paul.

Fries, J. 1993. *Helrunar: A Manual of Rune Magic*. Oxford: Mandrake Press.

—— 1996. *Seidways: Shaking, Swaying and Serpent Mysteries*. Oxford: Mandrake Press.

Furst, P.T. (ed.) 1972. *Flesh of the Gods: The Ritual Use of Hallucinogens*. London: George Allen and Unwin.

Gabriel, K. 1992. *Marietta Wetherill: Life with the Navajos in Chaco Canyon*. Albuquerque, New Mexico: University of New Mexico Press.

Gallagher, A.-M. 1997. Weaving a Tangled Web? History, Nation, 'Race' and Other Issues in Pagan Ethnicity. Paper presented at 'Re-Enchantment: An International Conference on Contemporary Paganism and the Interface Between Nature and Religion(s)', King Alfred's College, Winchester.

—— 1999. Weaving a Tangled Web? Pagan Ethics and Issues of History, 'Race' and Ethnicity in Pagan Identity. *The Pomegranate: A New Journal of Neopagan Thought* 10(November): 19–29.

Gantz, J. 1981. *Early Irish Myths and Sagas*. London: Penguin.

Gatens, M. 1991. Power, Bodies and Difference. In: M. Barrett and A. Phillips (eds) *Destabilizing Theory: Contemporary Feminist Debates*: 120–137. Stanford, California: Standford University Press.

Gathercole, P. and D. Lowenthal (eds) 1990. *The Politics of the Past*. London: Unwin and Hyman.

Geertz, A.W. 1983. Book of the Hopi: The Hopi's Book? *Anthropos* 78: 547–556.

—— 1987. Prophets and Fools: The Rhetoric of Hopi Indian Eschatology. *Native American Studies* 1(1): 33–45.

—— 1993. Archaic Ontology and White Shamanism. *Religion* 23: 369–372.

—— 1994. *The Invention of Prophecy: Continuity and Meaning in Hopi Indian Religion*. Berkeley, California: University of California Press.

—— 1996. Contemporary Problems in the Study of Native North American Religions with Specific Reference to the Hopis. *The American Indian Quarterly* 20 (3 and 4): 393–414.

Geertz, C. 1983. Blurred Genres: The Refiguration of Social Thought. In: C. Geertz *Local Knowledge: Further Essays in Interpretive Anthropology*: 19–35. London: Collins.

—— 1988. *Works and Lives: The Anthropologist as Author*. Stanford, California: Stanford University Press.

Gell, A. 1998. *Art and Agency: An Anthropological Theory*. Oxford: Oxford University Press.

Gelling, M. 1962. Place-names and Anglo-Saxon Paganism. *University of Birmingham Historical Journal* 8: 7–25.

Giddens, A. 1991. *Modernity and Self-identity: Self and Society in the Late Modern Age.* Stanford, California: Stanford University Press.

—— 1995. Epilogue: Notes on the Future of Anthropology. In: A.S. Ahmed and C.N. Shore (eds) *The Future of Anthropology: Its Relevance to the Contemporary World*: 272–277. London: Athlone.

Gilberg, R. 1984. How to Recognise a Shaman among Other Ritual Specialists? In: M. Hoppál (ed.) *Shamanism in Eurasia*: 21–27. Göttingen: Edition Herodot.

Gimbutas, M. 1974. *The Goddesses and Gods of Old Europe: Myths and Cult Images.* London: Thames and Hudson.

Gingell, C. 1996. Avebury: Striking A Balance. *Antiquity* 70: 507–511.

Glass-Coffin, B. 1994. Viewpoint: Anthropology, Shamanism, and the 'New Age'. *The Chronicle of Higher Education*, 15 June: A48.

Glosecki, S.O. 1986. Wolf Dancers and Whispering Beasts: Shamanic Motifs from Sutton Hoo? *Mankind Quarterly* 26: 305–319.

—— 1988. Wolf of the Bees: Germanic Shamanism and the Bear Hero. *Journal of Ritual Studies* 2/1: 31–53.

—— 1989. *Shamanism and Old English Poetry.* New York: Garland Publishing.

Gmelin, J.G. 2001 [1751]. Shamans Deserve Perpetual Labor for Their Hocus-Pocus. In: J. Narby and F. Huxley (eds) *Shamans Through Time: 500 Years on the Path to Knowledge*: 27–28. London: Thames and Hudson.

Golding, F.N. 1989. Stonehenge – Past and Future. In: H.F. Cleere (ed.) *Archaeological Heritage Management in the Modern World*: 265–271. London: Routledge.

Goodman, F.D. 1986. Body Posture and the Religious Altered State of Consciousness: An Experimental Investigation. *Journal of Humanistic Psychology* 26(3): 81–118.

—— 1988. Shamanic Trance Postures. In: G. Doore (ed.) *Shaman's Path: Healing, Personal Growth, and Empowerment*: 53–61. Boston and London: Shambhala.

—— 1989. The Neurophysiology of Shamanic Ecstasy. In: M. Hoppál, and O. von Sadovsky (eds) *Shamanism Past and Present (Part 2)*: 377–379. Budapest: Ethnographic Institute, Hungarian Academy of Sciences and Fullerton, Los Angeles: International Society for Trans-Oceanic Research.

—— 1990. *Where the Spirits Ride the Wind: Trance Journeys and Other Ecstatic Experiences.* Bloomington: Indiana University Press.

Goodwin, S. 1997a. Druids to Go Free as Stonehenge Plans to Drop Entrance Charges. *The Independent* 6 June: 3.

—— 1997b. Stonehenge Restoration Plan Meets Brick Wall. *The Independent* 14 June.

Goulet, J.-G. and D. Young 1994. Theoretical and methodological issues. In: D.E. Young and J.-G. Goulet (eds) *Being Changed by Cross-cultural Encounters: The Anthropology of Extraordinary Experience*: 298–336. Peterborough, Ontario: Broadview.

Graham, M. 1998/9. Moseley Bog Sweat. *The Druid's Voice* 9(Winter): 24–25.

Grambo, R. 1989. Unmanliness and Seiðr: Problems Concerning the Change of Sex. In: M. Hoppál and O. von Sadovsky (eds) *Shamanism: Past and Present (Part 1)*: 103–113. Budapest: Ethnographic Institute, Hungarian Academy of Sciences and Fullerton, Los Angeles: International Society for Trans-Oceanic Research.

Grant, K. 1973. *Aleister Crowley and the Hidden God.* London: Frederick Muller Ltd.
—— 1975. *Cults of the Shadow.* London: Frederick Muller Ltd.
—— 1980. *Outside the Circles of Time.* London: Frederick Muller Ltd.
—— 1991 [1972]. *The Magical Revival.* London: Skoob Books.
Grant, K. and S. Grant 1998. *Zos Speaks: Encounters with Austin Osman Spare.* London: Fulgur Limited.
Grant, R. 1997. The New Age Goldrush. *Daily Telegraph Magazine* 22 November: 36–42.
Graves, R. 1961 [1948]. *The White Goddess.* London: Faber and Faber.
—— 1969. *The Crane Bag and Other Disputed Subjects.* London: Cassell.
Green, M. 1986. *The Gods of the Celts.* Dover: Alan Sutton.
—— 1997. *Exploring the World of the Druids.* London: Thames and Hudson.
Green, R. 1988. The Tribe Called Wannabee. *Folklore* 99(1): 30–55.
Greenwood, S. 2000. Gender and Power in Magical Practices. In: S. Sutcliffe and M. Bowman (eds) *Beyond New Age: Exploring Alternative Spirituality*: 137–154. Edinburgh: Edinburgh University Press.
Greywolf. n.d. *Awen: The Holy Spirit of Druidry.* Available online: www.druidorder.demon.co.uk/Awen.htm.
Griffiths, B. 1996. *Aspects of Anglo-Saxon Magic.* Frithgarth, Norfolk: Anglo-Saxon Books.
Grimaldi, S. 1996. Learning from a Master: An Ulchi Shaman Teaches in America. *Shamanism* 9(2): 7–11.
—— 1997. Open Dialogue: Observations on Daniel Noel's The Soul of Shamanism – A Defense of Contemporary Shamanism and Michael Harner. *Shaman's Drum* 46: 4–9.
Grimes, R.L. 2000. Ritual. In: W. Braun and R.T. McCutcheon (eds) *Guide to the Study of Religion*: 259–270. London: Cassell.
Grimshaw, A. and K. Hart 1995. The Rise and Fall of Scientific Ethnography. In: A.S. Ahmed and C.N. Shore (eds) *The Future of Anthropology: Its Relevance to the Contemporary World*: 46–64. London: Athlone.
Groesbeck, C.J. 1989. C.G. Jung and the Shaman's Vision. *Journal of Analytical Psychology* 34(3): 255–275.
Grof S. 1996 [1975]. *Realms of the Human Unconscious: Observations from LSD Research.* London: Souvenir Press.
Grundy, S. 1995. The Cult of Odhinn: God of Death. PhD Thesis, University of Cambridge.
—— 1996. Freyja and Frigg. In: S. Billington and M. Green (eds) *The Concept of the Goddess*: 56–67. London: Routledge.
Guðbrandur Vigfússon and Unger, C.R. (eds) 1860–68. *Flateyjarbok: en samling af norske konge-sagaer med indskudte mindre fortællinger om begivenheder i og udanfor Norge samt Annaler 1–3.* Kristiania: no publisher.
Guenther, M. 1999. From Totemism to Shamanism: Hunter-gatherer Contributions to World Mythology and Spirituality. In: R.B. Lee and R. Daly (eds) *The Cambridge Encyclopedia of Hunters and Gatherers*: 426–433. Cambridge: Cambridge University Press.
Gundarsson, K. 2001. *Spae-Craft, Seiðr, and Shamanism.* Available online: http://www.thetroth.org/resources/kveldulf/spaecraft.html.
Gyrus 1998. The Last Museum. *Towards 2012: Part IV 'Paganism'*: 77–80.

—— 2000. *On Prehistoric Rock Art and Psychedelic Experiences*. Available online: http://home.freeuk.net/rooted/2cb.html.

Gyrus Orbitalis 1998. *The Goddess in Wharfedale*. Available online: http://www.suresite.com/oh/v/verbeia/.

Halifax, J. 1979. *Shamanic Voices: A Survey of Visionary Narratives*. London: Arkana.

—— 1982. *Shaman: The Wounded Healer*. London: Thames and Hudson.

Hall, J. 1994. *Sangoma: My Odyssey into the Spirit World of Africa*. New York: Tarcher/Putnam.

Hallowell, A.I. 2002 [1960]. Ojibwa Ontology, Behaviour and World View. In: G. Harvey (ed.) *Readings in Indigenous Religions*, Chap. 1. London: Continuum.

Halperin, D.M. 1995. *Saint Foucault: Towards a Gay Hagiography*. Oxford: Oxford University Press.

Hamayon, R. 1993. Are 'Trance', 'Ecstasy' and Similar Concepts Appropriate in the Study of Shamanism? *Shaman* 1(2): 3–25.

—— 1994. The Eternal Return of the Everybody-for-himself Shaman: A Fable. *Diogenes* 166 (42/2): 99–109.

—— 1998. 'Ecstasy' or the West-dreamt Siberian Shaman. In: H. Wautischer (ed.) *Tribal Epistemologies: Essays in the Philosophy of Anthropology*: 175–187. Aldershot, Hampshire: Ashgate Publishing.

Hamilakis, Y. 2001. Afterword. In: M. Pluciennik (ed.) *The Responsibilities of Archaeologists*: 91–96. Lampeter Workshops in Archaeology 4. BAR International Series 981. Oxford: British Archaeological Reports.

Hammersley, M. 1992. *What's Wrong with Ethnography?: Methodological Explorations*. London: Routledge.

Handelman, D. 1967. The Development of a Washo Shaman. *Ethnology* 6: 444–464.

—— 1968. Shamanizing on an Empty Stomach. *American Anthropologist* 70: 353–356.

Haraway, D.J. 1991. *Simians, Cyborgs, and Women: The Reinvention of Nature*. London: Free Association Books.

Harding, S. 1991. *Whose Science? Whose Knowledge?: Thinking from Women's Lives*. Milton Keynes: Open University Press.

Härke, H. 1990. The Anglo-Saxon Weapon Burial Rite. *Past and Present* 126: 22–43.

Harner, M. 1972. *The Jivaro: People of the Sacred Waterfalls*. Berkeley: University of California Press.

—— (ed.) 1973a. *Hallucinogens and Shamanism*. Oxford: Oxford University Press.

—— 1973b. The Role of Hallucinogenic Plants in European Witchcraft. In: M. Harner (ed.) *Hallucinogens and Shamanism*: 125–150. New York: Oxford University Press.

—— 1988a. What is a Shaman? In: G. Doore (ed.) *Shaman's Path: Healing, Personal Growth, and Empowerment*: 7–15. Boston and London: Shambhala.

—— 1988b. Shamanic Counseling. In: G. Doore (ed.) *Shaman's Path: Healing, Personal Growth, and Empowerment*: 179–187. Boston and London: Shambhala.

—— 1990 [1980]. *The Way of the Shaman*. London: HarperCollins.

—— 1994. The Foundation's Expedition to Tuva. *Shamanism* 7(1): 1–2.

Harner, M. and G. Doore 1987. The Ancient Wisdom in Shamanic Cultures: An Interview with Michael Harner conducted by Gary Doore. In: S. Nicholson (ed.) *Shamanism: An Expanded View of Reality*: 3–16. Wheaton, Illinois: Quest Books.

Harrold, F.B. and R.A. Eve (eds) 1995. *Cult Archaeology and Creationism: Understanding Pseudoscientific Beliefs about the Past*. Iowa: University of Iowa Press.

Harvey, G. 1995. Heathenism: A North European Pagan Tradition. In: G. Harvey and C. Hardman (eds) *Paganism Today: Wiccans, Druids, the Goddess and Ancient Earth Traditions for the Twenty-first Century*: 49–64. London: Thorsons.

—— 1997a. The Authority of Intimacy in Paganism and Goddess Spirituality. *Diskus: Internet Journal of Religion* 4(1):1–7.

—— 1997b. *Listening People, Speaking Earth: Contemporary Paganism*. London: Hurst and Co.

—— 1998. Shamanism in Britain Today. *Performance Research 'On Ritual'* 3(3): 16–24.

—— 2000a. Introduction. In: G. Harvey (ed.) *Indigenous Religion: A Companion*: 1–19. London: Cassell.

—— 2000b. Boggarts and Books: Towards an Appreciation of Pagan Spirituality. In: S. Sutcliffe and M. Bowman (eds) *Beyond New Age: Exploring Alternative Spirituality*: 155–168. Edinburgh: Edinburgh University Press.

—— 2001. *News: Winter Solstice at Stonehenge*. Available online on the *Megalithic Portal* pages edited by Andy Burnham: http://www.megalithic.co.uk/article.php?sid=2146410508.

—— 2003. Introduction. In: *Shamanism: A Reader*: 1–23. London: Routledge.

Harvey, G. and C. Hardman (eds) 1995. *Paganism Today: Wiccans, Druids, the Goddess and Ancient Earth Traditions for the Twenty-first Century*. London: Thorsons.

Hassan, F.A. 1997. Beyond the Surface: Comments on Hodder's 'Reflexive Excavation Methodology'. *Antiquity* 71: 1020–1025.

Hawkes, J. 1967. God in the Machine. *Antiquity* 41: 174–180.

Hawkes, S.C., H.R.E. Davidson and C. Hawkes 1965. The Finglesham Man. *Antiquity* 39: 17–31.

HCPO (Hopi Cultural Preservation Office). 1998. *Respect for Hopi Knowledge, Intellectual Property Rights, Visitor Etiquette, HCPO Policy and Research*. Available online: http://www.nau.edu/~hcpo-p/current/hopi.

Heelas, P. 1992. The Sacralization of the Self and New Age Capitalism. In: N. Abercombie and A. Ward (eds) *Social Change in Contemporary Britain*: 139–166. Cambridge: Polity Press.

—— 1993. The New Age in Cultural Context: The Premodern, the Modern and the Postmodern. *Religion* 23: 103–116.

—— 1996. *The New Age Movement: The Celebration of the Self and the Sacralization of Modernity*. London: Blackwell.

Heinze, R.I. (ed.) 1991. *Shamans of the 20th Century*. New York: Irvington.

Heiser, B.H. 1987. *The Fascinating World of the Nightshades*. London: Dover Press.

Henry, H. 1999. Trends: Pagan Powers in Modern Europe. *Hinduism Today International* July: 1–3.

Herbert, K. 1994. *Looking for the Lost Gods of England*. Frithgarth, Norfolk: Anglo-Saxon Books.

Herdt, G. 1996. Mistaken Sex: Culture, Biology and Third Sex in New Guinea. In: G. Herdt (ed.) *Third Sex Third Gender: Beyond Sexual Dimorphism in Culture and History*: 419–445. New York: Zone Books.

Herle, A. 1993. Views: Shaman Insights. *Museums Journal* December: 24.

Herzfeld, M. 1991. *A Place in History: Social and Monumental Time in a Cretan Town*. Oxford: Princeton University Press.

Hess, D.J. 1993. *Science in the New Age: The Paranormal, Its Defenders and Debunkers, and American Culture*. Madison: University of Wisconsin Press.

Hetherington, K. 1992. Place, Space and Power: Stonehenge and the Travellers. *Here and Now* 12: 25–28.

Hill, J.D. 1995. *Ritual and Rubbish in the Iron Age of Wessex: A Study on the Formation of a Specific Archaeological Record*. BAR British Series 242. Oxford: British Archaeological Reports.

Hine, P. 2001. Perspectives on Mass Ritual. *Dragon Eco-Magic Journal* 1: 11–15.

Hinton, D. 1993. *Archaeology, Economy and Society: England from the Fifth to the Fifteenth Century*. London: Routledge.

Hiscock, P. 1996. The New Age of Alternative Archaeology in Australia. *Archaeology Oceania* 31: 152–164.

Hobson, G. 1978. The Rise of the White Shaman as a New Version of Cultural Imperialism. In: G. Hobson *The Remembered Earth*: 100–108. New Mexico, Albuquerque: Red Earth Press.

Hodder, I. 1992. *Theory and Practice in Archaeology*. London: Routledge.

—— 1997. 'Always Momentary, Fluid and Flexible': Towards a Reflexive Excavation Methodology. *Antiquity* 71: 691–700.

—— 2000. Developing a Reflexive Method in Archaeology. In: I. Hodder (ed.) *Towards Reflexive Method in Archaeology: The Example at Çatalhöyük*: 3–14. McDonald Institute Monographs: British Institute of Archaeology at Ankara Monograph 28. Cambridge: Cambridge University Press.

Hollander, L.M. (trans.). 1999. *Heimskringla: History of the Kings of Norway by Snorri Sturluson*. Austin, Texas: University of Texas Press.

Holm, N.G. 1980. Ecstasy Research in the Twentieth Century: An Introduction. In: N.G. Holm, *Religious Ecstasy*: 7–26. Stockholm: Almqvist and Wilksell.

Holmberg, D.H. 1989. *Order in Paradox: Myth, Ritual, and Exchange Among Nepal's Tamang*. Ithaca, New York: Cornell University Press.

Holtorf, C. 1998. The Life-histories of Megaliths in Mecklenburg-Vorpommern (Germany). *World Archaeology* 30(1): 23–28.

Holtorf, C. and H. Karlsson (eds) 2000. *Philosophy and Archaeological Practice: Perspectives for the 21st Century*. Lindome, Sweden: Bricoleur Press.

Holtorf, C. and T. Schadla-Hall 1999. Age as Artefact: On Archaeological Authenticity. *European Journal of Archaeology* 2(2): 229–247.

Hoppál, M. 1992a. Shamanism: An Archaic and/or Recent System of Beliefs. In: A. Siikala and M. Hoppál (eds) *Studies on Shamanism*: 117–131. Budapest: Akadémiai Kiadó and Finnish Anthropological Society, Helsinki.

—— 1992b. Urban Shamans: A Cultural Revival in the Postmodern World. In: A. Siikala and M. Hoppál (eds) *Studies on Shamanism*: 197–209. Budapest: Akadémiai Kiadó and Finnish Anthropological Society, Helsinki.

—— 1996. Shamanism in a Postmodern Age. *Folklore: An Electronic Journal of Folklore*. Avilable online: http://haldjas.folklore.ee/folklore/vol2/hoppla.htm.

Hoppál, M. and K. Howard (eds) 1993. *Shamans and Cultures*. Budapest: Akadémiai Kiadó.

Horwitz, J. 1989. On Experiential Shamanic Journeying. In: M. Hoppál, and O. von Sadovsky (eds) *Shamanism Past and Present (Part 2)*: 373–376. Budapest: Ethnographic Institute, Hungarian Academy of Sciences and Fullerton, Los Angeles: International Society for Trans-Oceanic Research.

—— 1998. *The Absence of 'Performance' in the Shamanic Rite: Shamanic Rites Seen from a Shamanic Perspective II*. Available online: http://www.users.dircon.co.uk/~snail/SCSS/Articles/Rites2.htm.

Høst, A. 1999. Exploring Seidhr: A Practical Study of the Seidhr Ritual. Paper presented at 'Religious Practices and Beliefs in the North Atlantic Area' seminar, Århus University.

—— 2001. What's in a Name? Neo Shamanism, Core Shamanism, Urban Shamanism, Modern Shamanism, or What? *Spirit Talk* 14: 1–4.

Houston, J. 1987. Foreword: The Mind and Soul of the Shaman. In: S. Nicholson (ed.) *Shamanism: An Expanded View of Reality*: vii–xiii. Wheaton, Illinois: Quest Books.

'How Green Is Our Magic?' Papers presented at the Dragon Eco-Magic Conference, special issue of the journal *Dragon Eco-Magic Journal* 2000.

Howard, M. 1985. *The Wisdom of the Runes*. London: Rider.

Hübener, G. 1935. Beowulf and Germanic Exorcism. *Review of English Studies* 11: 163–181.

Hultkrantz, Å. 1973. A Definition of Shamanism. *Temenos* 9: 25–37.

—— 1978. Ethnological and Phenomenological Aspects of Shamanism. In: V. Diószegi and M. Hoppál (eds) *Shamanism in Siberia*: 27–58. Budapest: Akadémiai Kiadó.

—— 1998a. On the History of Research in Shamanism. In: J. Pentikäinen, T. Jaatinen, I. Lehtinen and M.-R. Saloniemi (eds) *Shamans*: 51–70. Tampere Museums Publications 45. Tampere, Finland: Tampere Museums.

—— 1998b. The Meaning of Ecstasy in Shamanism. In: H. Wautischer (ed.) *Tribal Epistemologies: Essays in the Philosophy of Anthropology*: 163–173. Aldershot, Hampshire: Ashgate Publishing.

—— 1998c. Rejoinder. In: H. Wautischer (ed.) *Tribal Epistemologies: Essays in the Philosophy of Anthropology*: 188–190. Aldershot, Hampshire: Ashgate Publishing.

Humphrey, C. 1996. *Shamans and Elders: Experience, Knowledge, and Power among the Daur Mongols*. Oxford: Clarendon Press.

—— 1999. Shamans in the City. *Anthropology Today* 15 (3): 3–10.

Hungry Wolf, A. 1973. *The Good Medicine Book*. New York: Warner Paperback Library.

Hunt, D. 1988. *America the Sorcerer's New Apprentice: The Rise of New Age Shamanism*. Eugene, Oregon: Harvest House Publishers.

Hutton, R. 1991. *The Pagan Religions of the Ancient British Isles: Their Nature and Legacy*. Oxford: Blackwell.

—— 1993. *The Shamans of Siberia*. Glastonbury, Somerset: The Isle of Avalon Press.

—— 1996. Introduction: Who Possesses the Past? In: P. Carr-Gomm (ed.) *The Druid Renaissance*: 17–34. London: Thorsons.

—— 1997a. The Neolithic Great Goddess: A Study in Modern Tradition. *Antiquity* 71: 91–99.

—— 1997b. The New Druidry. *Druidlore* 1: 19–21.

—— 1998a. The Discovery of the Modern Goddess. In: J. Pearson, R.H. Roberts and G. Samuel (eds) *Nature Religion Today: Paganism in the Modern World*: 89–100. Edinburgh: Edinburgh University Press.

—— 1998b. Report upon Contemporary Druidry and the Role of Arthur Pendragon of the Loyal Arthurian Warband. *Druidlore* 2: 24–26.

—— 1999. *Triumph of the Moon: A History of Modern Pagan Witchcraft*. Oxford: Oxford University Press.

—— 2000. Paganism and Polemic: The Debate over the Origins of Modern Pagan Witchcraft. *Folklore* 111(1): 103–117.

Huxley, A. 1959. *The Doors of Perception, Heaven and Hell*. London: Penguin.

Ingerman, S. 1991. *Soul Retrieval: Mending the Fragmented Self*. San Francisco: HarperSanFrancisco.

Insoll, T. (ed.) 2001. *Archaeology and World Religion*. London: Routledge.

Jackson, A. (ed.) 1987. *Anthropology at Home*. London: Tavistock Publications.

Jackson, M. 1989. *Paths Toward a Clearing*. Bloomington, Indiana: Indiana University Press.

Jacobs, J. 1994. Earth Honouring: Western Desires and Indigenous Knowledges. *Meanjin* 53(2): 305–314.

Jacobs, S., W. Thomas and S. Lang (eds) 1997. *Two-spirit People: Native American Gender, Sexuality, and Spirituality*. Illinois: University of Illinois Press.

Jakobsen, M.D. 1998. Recognising Evil: Approaches to Spirits in Traditional and Contemporary Shamanism. Paper presented at Shamanism in Contemporary Society Conference, University of Newcastle.

—— 1999. *Shamanism: Traditional and Contemporary Approaches to the Mastery of Spirits and Healing*. Oxford: Berghahn Books.

James, S. 1999. *The Atlantic Celts: Ancient People or Modern Invention?* London: British Museum Press.

Jameson, F.H. (ed.) 1997. *Presenting Archaeology to the Public: Digging for Truths*. Walnut Creek, California: AltaMira Press.

Jencson, L. 1989. Neopaganism and the Great Mother Goddess. *Anthropology Today* 5(2): 2–4.

Jensen, A.F. 1996. Possible Criteriological Categories used in the Judgement of the Authenticity of Shamanism. In: D.G. Bromley and L.F. Carter (eds) *Religion and the Social Order: The Issue of Authenticity in the Study of Religions*: 191–206. Official Publication of the Association for the Sociology of Religion, vol. 6. Greenwich, Connecticut: JAI Press.

Jeter, K. 1990. The Shaman: The Gay and Lesbian Ancestor of Humankind. *Marriage and Family Review* 14(2–3): 317–334.

Jilek, W.G. 1971. From Crazy Witch Doctor to Auxiliary Psychotherapist: The Changing Image of the Medicine Man. *Psychiatric Clinician* 4: 200–220.

Jocks, C.R. 1996. Spirituality for Sale: Sacred Knowledge in the Consumer Age. *American Indian Quarterly* 20 (3): 415–431.

Johnson, P.C. 1995. Shamanism from Ecuador to Chicago: A Case Study in Ritual Appropriation. *Religion* 25: 163–178.

Johnston, G. (trans.) and P. Foote (notes and essay) 1963. *The Saga of Gisli*. London: Aldine Press/J.M. Dent and Sons Ltd.

Jolly, K.L. 1996. *Popular Religion in Late Saxon England: Elf Charms in Context*. Chapel Hill, North Carolina: The University of North Carolina Press.

Jones, K. 1998. The State of Large Earthwork Sites in the United Kingdom. *Antiquity* 72: 293–307.

Jones, L. 1994. The Emergence of the Druid as Celtic Shaman. *Folklore in Use* 2: 131–142.

—— 1998. *Druid, Shaman, Priest: Metaphors of Celtic Paganism.* Enfield Lock, Middlesex: Hisarlik Press.

Jones, P. 1998. The European Native Tradition. In: J. Pearson; R.H. Roberts and G. Samuel (eds) *Nature Religion Today: Paganism in the Modern World*: 77–88. Edinburgh: Edinburgh University Press.

Jones, P. and C. Matthews (eds) 1990. *Voices from the Circle: The Heritage of Western Paganism.* Wellingborough, Northamptonshire: The Aquarian Press.

Jones, P. and N. Pennick 1995. *A History of Pagan Europe.* London: Routledge.

Joralemon, D. 1990. The Selling of the Shaman and the Problem of Informant Legitimacy. *Journal of Anthropological Research* 46(2): 105–118.

Joralemon, D. and D. Sharon 1993. *Sorcery and Shamanism: Curanderos and Clients in Northern Peru.* Salt Lake City, Utah: University of Utah Press.

Karjala, M.Y. 1992. Aspects of the Other World in Irish Folk Tradition. In: M. Hoppál and J. Pentikäinen (eds) *Northern Religions and Shamanism*: 176–180. Budapest: Akadémiai Kiadó.

Karl, R. and A. Minard 2002. Eating Epona: Horses and Dogs as Food Animals in Celtic Culture. Paper presented at The Folklore Society Annual Conference 'Folklore and Archaeology', Departments of Welsh and Archaeology, University of Cardiff, 22–24 March 2002.

Katz, R. 1982. *Boiling Energy: Community Healing Among the Kalahari !Kung.* Cambridge, Massachusetts: Harvard University Press.

Katz, R., M. Biesele and V. St Denis 1997. *Healing Makes Our Hearts Happy: Spirituality and Cultural Transformation among the Kalahari Ju|'hoansi.* Rochester, Vermont: Inner Traditions International.

Kaye, Q. 2000. Conference Review: New Approaches to the Archaeology of Art, Religion and Folklore: 'A Permeability of Boundaries?', University of Southampton, 11–12 December 1999. *Papers from the Institute of Archaeology* 11: 95–97.

Kehoe, A.B. 1990. Primal Gaia: Primitivists and Plastic Medicine Men. In: J. Clifton (ed.) *The Invented Indian: Cultural Fictions and Government Policies*: 193–209. New Brunswick: Transaction.

—— 1998. Appropriate Terms. *Society for American Archaeology Bulletin* March: 23, 34.

—— 2000. *Shamans and Religion: An Anthropological Exploration in Critical Thinking.* Prospect Heights, Illinois: Waveland Press, Inc.

Kelchner, G.D. 1935. *Dreams in Old Norse Literature and their Affinities in Folklore.* London: Cambridge University Press.

Kelly, K. 1997. Blessing of the Reindeer Camps. *Sacred Hoop* 18: 24–25.

—— 1999. Close to Nature: An Interview with Annette Høst. *Spirit Talk: A Core Shamanic Newsletter* 9 (Early Summer): 5–9.

Kendall, L. 1996. Korean Shamanism and the Spirits of Capitalism. *American Anthropologist* 98(3): 512–527.

Kendrick, T.D. 1927. *The Druids.* London: Senate.

Kharitidi, O. 1997 [1996]. *Entering the Circle: Ancient Secrets of Siberian Shamanism Discovered by a Russian Psychiatrist.* London: Thorsons.

Khazanov, A.M. 1996. Nationalism and Neoshamanism in Yakutia. In: K. Lyon, L. Bilaniuk and B. Fitzhugh (eds) *Post-Soviet Eurasia: Anthropological Perspectives on a*

World in Transition: 77–86. Michigan Discussions in Anthropology, vol. 12. Ann Arbor, Michigan: Department of Anthropology, University of Michigan.

King, S.K. 1990. *Urban Shaman: A Handbook for Personal and Planetary Transformation Based on the Hawaiian Way of the Adventurer*. New York: Simon and Schuster.

Knüsel, C. and K. Ripley 2000. The *Berdache* or Man-woman in Anglo-Saxon England and Early Medieval Europe. In: W.O. Frazer and A. Tyrell (eds) *Social Identity in Early Medieval Britain*: 157–191. Leicester: Leicester University Press.

Krech, S. 1999. *The Ecological Indian: Myth and History*. New York: W.W. Norton and Company.

Kroeber, A.L. 1940. Psychotic Factors in Shamanism. *Character and Personality* 8: 204–215.

Kunz, K. (trans.) 2001. The Saga of the People of Laxardal. In: *The Sagas of Icelanders*: 270–421. London: Penguin.

La Fontaine, J. 1999. Heathenism/Odinism. In: W. De Blécort, R. Hutton and J. La Fontaine (eds) *Witchcraft and Magic in Europe, Volume 6: The Twentieth Century*: 110–114. London: The Athlone Press.

Lambrick, G. 2001. *Rollright Conservation and Management Plan*. Banbury, Oxfordshire: The Rollright Trust.

Larrington, C. (trans.) 1996. *The Poetic Edda*. Oxford: Oxford University Press.

Latham, C. and A. Norfolk 1998/9. A Press Release on Behalf of the Genius Loci of West Penwith. *The Druid's Voice: The Magazine of Contemporary Druidry* 9(Winter): 27.

Laufer, B. 1917. Origin of the Word Shaman. *American Anthropologist* 19: 361–371.

Laurie, E.R. and T. White 1997. Speckled Snake, Brother of Birch: Amanita Muscaria Motifs in Celtic Literature. *Shaman's Drum* 44: 52–65.

Layton, R. (ed.) 1989a. *Who Needs the Past?: Indigenous Values and Archaeology*. London: Routledge.

—— (ed.) 1989b. *Conflict in the Archaeology of Living Traditions*. London: Routledge.

—— 1997. *An Introduction to Theory in Anthropology*. Cambridge: Cambridge University Press.

Leach, E. 1969. High School. *New York Review of Books* 12(5 June): 12–13.

Leary, T. 1970. *The Politics of Ecstasy*. St Albans, Hertfordshire: Paladin.

Leigh, D. 1984. Ambiguity in Anglo-Saxon Style I Art. *The Antiquaries Journal* 64: 34–42.

Letcher, A. 2001. The Scouring of the Shire: Fairies, Trolls and Pixies in Eco-Protest Culture. *Folklore* 112: 147–161.

Leto, S. 2000. Magical Potions: Entheogenic Themes in Scandinavian Mythology. *Shaman's Drum* 54: 55–65.

Lévi-Strauss, C. 1963. The Effectiveness of Symbols. In: C. Lévi-Strauss (ed.) *Structural Anthropology*: 181–200. New York: Basic Books.

Lewis, I.M. 1984. What is a Shaman? In: M. Hoppál (ed.) *Shamanism in Eurasia*: 3–12. Göttingen: Edition Herodot.

—— 1986. *Religion in Context: Cults and Charisma*. Cambridge: Cambridge University Press.

—— 1989a [1971]. *Ecstatic Religion: A Study of Shamanism and Spirit Possession*. London: Routledge.

—— 1989b. South of North: Shamanism in Africa. *Paideuma* 35: 181–188.

—— 1991 [1988]. Shamanism. In: S. Sutherland and P. Clarke (eds) *The World's Religions: The Study of Religion, Traditional and New Religion*: 67–77. London: Routledge.

—— 1993. Malay Bomohs and Shamans. *Man* 28: 361.

Lewis, J.R. and J.G. Melton (eds) 1992. *Perspectives on the New Age*. Albany, New York: State University of New York Press.

Lewis-Williams, J.D. 1992. Ethnographic Evidence Relating to 'Trance' and 'Shamans' among Northern and Southern Bushmen. *South African Archaeological Bulletin* 47: 56–60.

Lewis-Williams, J.D. and T.A. Dowson 1988. The Signs of All Times: Entoptic Phenomena in Upper Paleolithic Art. *Current Anthropology* 29(2): 201–245.

—— 1999 [1989]. *Images of Power: Understanding Bushman Rock Art*. Johannesburg: Southern Book Publishers.

Lindholm, C. 1997. Logical and Moral Dilemmas of Postmodernism. *Journal of the Royal Anthropological Institute* 3: 747–760.

Lindquist, G. 1997. *Shamanic Performance on the Urban Scene: Neo-Shamanism in Contemporary Sweden*. Stockholm Studies in Social Anthropology 39. Stockholm: University of Stockholm.

Linsell, T. 1994. *Anglo-Saxon Mythology, Migration and Magic*. Pinner, Middlesex: Anglo-Saxon Books.

Linzie, B. 1999. Seething: Where Does a Seiðrman Go? *Spirit Talk: A Core Shamanic Newsletter* 9(Early Summer): 27–29.

Lister, R.H. and F.C. Lister 1981. *Chaco Canyon: Archaeology and Archaeologists*. Albuquerque, New Mexico: University of New Mexico Press.

Locke, R.F. 1976. *The Book of the Navajo*. California: Mankind Publishing.

Logan, K. 1998. *Paganism and the Occult: A Manifesto for Christian Action*. Eastbourne, East Sussex: Kingsway Publications.

Lommel, A. 1967. *Shamanism: The Beginnings of Art* (trans. M. Bulloch). New York: McGraw-Hill.

Lonigan, P. 1985. Shamanism in the Old Irish Tradition. *Eire-Ireland* 20(3): 109–129.

Lowenthal, D. 1985. *The Past is a Foreign Country*. Cambridge: Cambridge University Press.

—— 1996. *Possessed by the Past: The Heritage Crusade and the Spoils of History*. New York: The Free Press.

Lucas, G. 2001. *Critical Approaches to Fieldwork: Contemporary and Historical Archaeological Practice*. London: Routledge.

Lucy, S.J. 1997. Housewives, Warriors and Slaves? Sex and Gender in Anglo-Saxon Burials. In: J. Moore and E. Scott (eds) *Invisible People and Processes: Writing Gender and Childhood into European Archaeology*: 150–158. Leicester: Leicester University Press.

Luhrmann, T.M. 1989. *Persuasions of the Witch's Craft: Ritual Magic in Contemporary England*. Cambridge, Massachusetts: Harvard University Press.

Lurie, N.O. 1988. Relations Between Indians and Anthropologists. In: W.E. Washburn (ed.) *Handbook of American Indians, Volume 4*. Washington, DC: Smithsonian Institute.

Lyon, D. 1993. A Bit of a Circus: Notes on Postmodernity and New Age. *Religion* 23: 117–126.

Lyotard, J.-F. 1986. *The Postmodern Condition*. Manchester: Manchester University Press.

MacCulloch, J.A. 1911. *The Religion of the Ancient Celts*. London: Constable (reprint).

MacEowen, F.H. 1998. Rekindling the Gaelic Hearthways of Oran Mor. *Shaman's Drum* 49(Summer): 32–39.

MacKillop, J. 1998. *Dictionary of Celtic Mythology*. Oxford: Oxford University Press.

MacLellan, G. 1994. *Small Acts of Magic*. Manchester: Creeping Toad.

—— 1995. Dancing on the Edge: Shamanism in Modern Britain. In: G. Harvey and C. Hardman (eds) *Paganism Today: Wiccans, Druids, the Goddess and Ancient Earth Traditions for the Twenty-first Century*: 138–148. London: Thorsons.

—— 1997. *Sacred Animals*. Chieveley, Berkshire: Capall Bann.

—— 1998. A Sense of Wonder. *Performance Research 'On Ritual'* 3(3): 60–63.

—— 1999. *Shamanism*. London: Piatkus.

Maffesoli, M. 1996. *The Time of the Tribes: The Decline of Individualism in Mass Society*. London: Sage.

Magnusson, M. and H. Pálsson (trans.) 1965. *The Vinland Sagas: The Norse Discovery of America*. London: Penguin.

Marcus, G.E. 1995. Ethnography in/of the World System: The Emergence of a Multi-sited Ethnography. *Annual Review of Anthropology* 24: 95–117.

Marcus, G.E. and M.M.J. Fischer 1986. *Anthropology as Cultural Critique: An Experimental Moment in the Human Sciences*. Chicago: The University of Chicago Press.

Martin, R. 1997. How Traditional Navajos View Historic Preservation: A Question of Interpretation. In: N. Swidler, K.E. Dongoske, R. Anyon and A.S. Downer (eds) *Native Americans and Archaeologists: Stepping Stones to Common Ground*: 128–134. Walnut Creek, California: AltaMira Press.

Mason, R.J. 2000. Archaeology and Native North American Oral Traditions. *American Antiquity* 65(2): 239–266.

Mathien, F.J. 2001. The Organisation of Turquoise Production and Consumption by the Prehistoric Chacoans. *American Antiquity* 66(1): 103–118.

Matson, E.R. 1980. De Mille Does Not Exist. In: R. De Mille (ed.) *The Don Juan Papers: Further Castaneda Controversies*: 174–177. Santa Barbara, California: Ross-Erikson.

Matthews, C. 1995. *Singing the Soul Back Home: Shamanism in Daily Life*. Shaftesbury, Dorset: Element Books.

—— 1996 Following the Awen: Celtic Shamanism and the Druid Path in the Modern World. In: P. Carr-Gomm (ed.) *The Druid Renaissance*: 223–236. London: Thorsons.

—— 1997. Midwifing the Soul. *Sacred Hoop* 19: 14–17.

Matthews, J. 1991a. *Taliesin: Shamanism and the Bardic Mysteries in Britain and Ireland*. London: Aquarian.

—— 1991b. *The Celtic Shaman: A Handbook*. Shaftesbury, Dorset: Element Books.

—— 1991c. *The Song of Taliesin: Stories and Poems from the Books of Broceliande*. London: Aquarian.

—— 1999. *The Celtic Seer's Sourcebook: Vision and Magic in the Druid Tradition*. Blandford, Dorset: Brockhampton Press.

Mattingly, H. (trans.) 1948. *Tacitus on Britain and Germany*. London: Penguin.

Maughfling, R. 1997. Druids and Stonehenge. *Druidlore* 1: 8–10.

—— 2000/2001a. Stonehenge and Druidry in the Twenty-First Century. *Druidlore* 3: 4–6.

277

—— 2000/2001b. The Fight to Save Seahenge. *Druidlore* 3: 10–13.

Mauss, M. 1990 [1950]. *The Gift: The Form and Reason for Exchange in Archaic Societies*. London: Routledge.

McCabe, M. 1998/9. A Day at the Circus. *The Druid's Voice: The Magazine of Contemporary Druidry* 9(Winter): 20–21.

McLaughlin, B. 2000. *A Dangerous Spell of Toil and Trouble is Being Cast*. Available online: http://www.independent.ie/2000/113/e12c.shtml.

McManamon, F.P. 1994. Presenting Archaeology to the Public in the USA. In: P.G. Stone and B.L. Molyneaux (eds) *The Presented Past: Heritage, Museums and Education*: 61–81. London: Routledge.

McPherson, R.S. 1992. *Sacred Land, Sacred View: Navajo Perceptions of the Four Corners Region*. Charles Redd Monographs in Western History 19. Provo, Utah: Brigham Young University, Charles Redd Center for Western Studies.

Mead, S.M. 1997. *Landmarks, Bridges and Visions: Aspects of Maori Culture*. Victoria, Wellington: University of Wellington Press.

Meaney, A.L. 1981. *Anglo-Saxon Amulets and Curing Stones*. BAR British Series 96. Oxford: British Archaeological Reports.

—— 1989. Women, Witchcraft and Magic in Anglo-Saxon England. In: D.G. Scragg (ed.) *Superstition and Popular Medicine in Anglo-Saxon England*: 9–40. Manchester: Manchester Centre for Anglo-Saxon Studies.

Medicine Eagle, B. 1988. To Paint Ourselves Red. In: G. Doore (ed.) *Shaman's Path: Healing, Personal Growth, and Empowerment*: 209–216. Boston and London: Shambhala.

Megaw, R. and V. Megaw 1990. *Celtic Art: From its Beginnings to the Book of Kells*. London: Thames and Hudson.

Meighan, C. 1986. *Archaeology and Anthropological Ethics*. Calabasas, California: Wormwood Press.

Melia, D.F. 1983. The Irish Saint as Shaman. *Pacific Coast Theology* 18: 37–42.

Merrill, W.L., E.J. Ladd and T.J. Ferguson 1993. The Return of *Ahayu:da*: Lessons for Repatriation from Zuni Pueblo and the Smithsonian Institution. *Current Anthropology* 34(5): 523–567.

Meskell, L. 1995. Goddesses, Gimbutas and 'New Age' Archaeology. *Antiquity* 69: 74–86.

—— 1998a. Consuming Bodies: Cultural Fantasies in Ancient Egypt. *Body and Society* 4(1): 63–76.

—— 1998b. Oh My Goddess! Archaeology, Sexuality and Ecofeminism. *Archaeological Dialogues* 5(2): 126–143.

—— 1999. Feminism, Paganism, Pluralism. In: C. Holtorf and A. Gavin-Schwartz (eds) *Archaeology and Folklore*: 83–89. London: Routledge.

Metzner, R. 1994. *The Well of Remembrance: Rediscovering the Earth Wisdom Myths of Northern Europe*. Boston: Shambhala.

Michell, J. 1997. Stonehenge: Its Druids, Custodians, Festivals and Future. *Druidlore* 1: 4–6.

Millson, P. 1997. *Flightpaths to the Gods: An Investigation into the Mystery of the Nazca Lines*. Manchester: BBC/BSS.

Mitteilungen, K. 1935. Runic Rings and Old English Charms. *Archiv für das Studium der Neueren Sprachen* 67: 252–256.

Moore, J.H. 1973. Book Review: S. Hyemeyohsts 'Seven Arrows'. *American Anthropologist* 75: 1040–1042.

—— 1994. Putting Anthropology and Archaeology Back Together Again: The Ethnogenetic Critique of Cladistic Theory. *American Anthropologist* 96: 925–948.

Moore, R. and D. Gillette 1993. *The Magician Within: Accessing the Shaman in the Male Psyche*. New York: William Morrow and Cooper.

Moore, T.M. 1996. *The Re-Enchantment of Everyday Life*. London: Hodder and Stoughton.

Morris, K. 1991. *Sorceress or Witch? The Image of Gender in Medieval Iceland and Northern Europe*. New York: University of America Press.

Morris, R. 1998. Measuring the Destruction of Monuments. *British Archaeology* June: 15.

Morris, R.H. 1995. Woman as Shaman: Reclaiming the Power to Heal. *Women's Studies* 24: 573–584.

Morrison, R. 1999. Mad Dogs and Englishmen … . *The Times* 22 June: 20.

Moser, S. 1995. Archaeology and its Disciplinary Culture: The Professionalisation of Australian Prehistoric Archaeology. PhD Thesis, School of Archaeology, Classics and Ancient History, University of Sydney.

—— 1996. Science and Social Values: Presenting Archaeological Findings in Museum Displays. In: L. Smith and A. Clark (eds) *Issues in Management Archaeology*: 32–42. St Lucia, Queensland: Tempus Press.

Motzafi-Haller, P. 1997. Writing Birthright: On Native Anthropologists and the Politics of Representation. In: D.E. Reed-Danahay (ed.) *Auto/Ethnography: Rewriting the Self and the Social*: 195–222. Oxford: Berg.

Mower, J.P. 2000. Trench Warfare? Archaeologists Battle it Out. *Papers from the Institute of Archaeology* 11: 1–6.

Mulcock, J. 1997. Searching for Our Indigenous Selves: Creating New Meaning Out of 'Old Cultures'. Unpublished paper presented at Australian Anthropological Society Annual Conference 'Indigenous Societies and the Postcolonial State', Magnetic Island, Queensland.

—— 1998. Searching for Our Indigenous Selves: Following the Allegory of the Autocthonic Shaman (Fieldwork from Western Australia). Unpublished paper presented at Shamanism in Contemporary Society Conference, University of Newcastle.

Murphy, J.M. 1964. Psychotherapeutic Aspects of Shamanism on St. Lawrence Island, Alaska. In: A. Kiev (ed.) *Magic, Faith and Healing: Studies in Primitive Psychiatry Today*: 53–83. London: The Free Press.

Murphy, R. 1981. Book Review: M. Harner 'The Way of the Shaman'. *American Anthropologist* 83: 714–717.

Murray, T. 1996. Coming to Terms with the Living: Some Aspects of Repatriation for the Archaeologist. *Antiquity* 70: 217–220.

Myerhoff, B. 1974. *Peyote Hunt: The Sacred Journey of the Huichol Indians*. Ithaca, New York: Cornell University Press.

Naddair, K. 1990. Pictish and Keltic Shamanism. In: P. Jones and C. Matthews (eds) *Voices from the Circle: The Heritage of Western Paganism*: 93–108. Wellingborough, Northamptonshire: The Aquarian Press.

Nagy, J.F. 1981. Shamanic Aspects of the *Bruidhean* Tale. *History of Religions* 20: 302–322.

Nanda, S. 1993a. Hijras: An Alternative Sex and Gender Role in India. In: G. Herdt (ed.) *Third Sex Third Gender: Beyond Sexual Dimorphism in Culture and History*: 373–417. New York: Zone Books.

—— 1993b. Hijras as Neither Man Nor Woman. In: H. Abelove; M.A. Barde and D.M. Halperin (eds) *The Lesbian and Gay Studies Reader*: 498–527. London: Routledge.

Näsström, B.-M. 1995. *Freyja: The Great Goddess of the North*. Lund Studies in the History of Religions, vol. 5. Lund: Department of History of Religions, University of Lund.

—— 1996a. Freyja and Frigg: Two Aspects of the Great Goddess. In: J. Pentikäinen (ed.) *Shamanism and Northern Ecology*: 81–96. Berlin and New York: Mouton de Gruyter.

—— 1996b. Freyja: A Goddess with Many Names. In: S. Billington and M. Green (eds) *The Concept of the Goddess*: 69–75. London: Routledge.

National Trust 1997. *Avebury Management Plan, April 1997*. Avebury, Wiltshire: The National Trust.

NCCL (National Council for Civil Liberties). 1986. *Stonehenge: A Report into the Civil Liberties Implications of the Events Relating to the Convoys of Summer 1985 and 1986*. London: Yale University Press.

Neihardt, J.G. 1993 [1932]. *Black Elk Speaks: Being the Life Story of a Holy Man of the Oglala Sioux*. Lincoln: University of Nebraska Press.

Neu, J. 1975. Lévi-Strauss on Shamanism. *Man* 10(1): 285–292.

Nichols, D.L., A.L. Klesert and R. Anyon 1989. Ancestral Sites, Shrines and Graves: Native American Perspectives on the Ethics of Collecting Cultural Properties. In: P.M. Messenger (ed.) *The Ethics of Collecting Cultural Property: Whose Culture? Whose Property?*: 27–38. Albuquerque, New Mexico: University of New Mexico Press.

Nietzsche, F. 1983 [1893]. On the Uses and Disadvantages of History for Life. In: F. Nietzsche *Untimely Meditations* (ed. D. Breazeale, trans. R.J. Hollingdale): 57–123 Cambridge: Cambridge University Press.

Noble, D.G. (ed.) 1984. *New Light on Chaco Canyon*. Santa Fe, New Mexico: School of American Research Press.

Noel, D.C. 1997. *The Soul of Shamanism: Western Fantasies, Imaginal Realities*. New York: Continuum.

—— 1998. Open Dialogue: A Response to Susan Grimaldi's Critique of 'The Soul of Shamanism'. *Shaman's Drum* 48: 4–8.

Nolan, E.P. 1985. The Forbidden Forest: Eliade as Artist and Shaman. In: D. Carrasco and J.M. Swanberg (eds) *Waiting for the Dawn: Mircea Eliade in Perspective*: 108–122. Boulder, Colorado: Westview Press.

Noll, R. 1983. Shamanism and Schizophrenia: A State-specific Approach to the 'Schizophrenia Metaphor' of Shamanic States. *American Ethnologist* 10: 443–459.

—— 1989. What Has Really Been Learned about Shamanism? *Journal of Psychoactive Drugs* 21(1): 47–50.

Norfolk, A. 1998. Cornish Sacred Sites and Their Protection. *Pagan Dawn: The Journal of The Pagan Federation* 128(Lughnasadh): 15–18.

North, R. 1997. *Heathen Gods in Old English Literature*. Cambridge: Cambridge University Press.

NPS (National Park Service, United States Department of the Interior). 1992. *News Release: Southwest Region Establishes Policy on Spreading of Cremated Remains*. 25 August.

—— 1996a. *News Release: Chaco Culture National Historic Park Distributes Environmental Assessment on Closure of Casa Rinconada*. 5 December.

—— 1996b. *Protection of Casa Rinconada Interior Environmental Assessment, Chaco Culture National Historic Park, New Mexico*. December.

Oakley, G.T. 1988. *Verbeia: Goddess of Wharfedale*. Leeds: Rooted Media.

Odinic Rite. 1998. *The Way of the Rite: A Handbook for Members and Friends of the Odinic Rite*. London: Odinic Rite.

Ó'Drisceoil, D. 1988. Burnt Mounds: Cooking or Bathing? *Antiquity* 62: 671–680.

O'hOgain, D. 1988. *Fionn mac Cumhail: Images of the Gaelic Hero*. Dublin: Gill and Macmillan.

Olson, A.M. 1978. From Shaman to Mystic: An Interpretation of the Castaneda Quartet. *Soundings* 1: 47–66.

Oosten, J. 1989. Theoretical Problems in the Study of Inuit Shamanism. In: M. Hoppál, and O. von Sadovsky (eds) *Shamanism Past and Present (Part 2)*: 331–341. Budapest: Ethnographic Institute, Hungarian Academy of Sciences and Fullerton, Los Angeles: International Society for Trans-Oceanic Research.

Opler, M. 1936. Some Points of Comparison and Contrast Between the Treatment of Functional Disorders by Apache Shamans and Modern Psychiatric Practice. *American Journal of Psychiatry* 92: 1371–1387.

—— 1961. On Devereux's Discussion of Ute Shamanism. *American Anthropologist* 63: 1091–1093.

Orchard, A. 1997. *Cassell Dictionary of Norse Myth and Legend*. London: Cassell.

Orenstein, G.F. 1994. Toward an Ecofeminist Ethic of Shamanism and the Sacred. In: C. Adams (ed.) *Ecofeminism and the Sacred*: 172–190. New York: Continuum.

Orr, D. 1999. Do the Right Thing, Please. *The Independent* 22 June: 5.

Pagan Federation. 1996. *The Pagan Federation Information Pack*. London: Pagan Federation.

—— 1997a. *Update on Sacred Sites Around Britain*. Available online: http://www.pf_pd_sa.html.

—— 1997b. *Northern Tradition Information Pack*. London: Pagan Federation.

Page, R.I. 1964. Anglo-Saxon Runes and Magic. *Journal of the Archaeological Association* 27: 14–31.

—— 1970. *Life in Anglo-Saxon England*. London: B.T. Batsford.

—— 1995. *Runes and Runic Inscriptions: Collected Essays on Anglo-Saxon and Viking Runes*. Woodbridge, Suffolk: The Boydell Press.

Patterson-Rudolph, C. 1997. *On the Trail of Spider-Woman: Petroglyphs, Pictographs, and Myths of the Southwest*. Santa Fe, New Mexico: Ancient City Press.

Paxson, D.L. 1992. The Seid Project: A Report on Experiences and Findings. Unpublished manuscript: Hrafnar Monograph 1.

—— 1993. *Heide: Witch-Goddess of the North*. Available online: http://www. hrafnar.org/godesses/heide.html. Originally published in *Sagewoman*, Fall 1993.

—— 1997. *The Return of the Volva: Recovering the Practice of Seidh*. Available online: http://www.vinland.org/heathen/hrafnar.seidh.html.

—— 1998. 'This Thou Dost Know ...': Oracles in the Northern Tradition. *Idunna: A Journal of Northern Tradition*: no page numbers.

—— 1999. Seeing for the People: Working Oracular Seiðr in the Pagan Community. *Spirit Talk: A Core Shamanic Newsletter* 9(Early Summer): 10–13.

Pearce, J.C. 1976. Don Juan and Jesus. In: D.C. Noel (ed.) *Seeing Castaneda: Reactions to the 'Don Juan' Writings of Carlos Castaneda*: 191–219. New York: Capricorn Books.

Pearson, J. 1998. Assumed Affinities: Wicca and the New Age. In: J. Pearson, R.H. Roberts and G. Samuel (eds) *Nature Religion Today: Paganism in the Modern World*: 45–56. Edinburgh: Edinburgh University Press.

—— 2001. Going Native in Reverse: The Insider as Researcher in British Wicca. Paper presented at BASR (British Association for the Study of Religion) Annual Conference 'Religion and Community', Faculty of Divinity, University of Cambridge, September.

Pearson, M. and M. Shanks 2001. *Theatre/Archaeology*. London: Routledge.

Pedersen, M. 1999. The Return of the Seiðr: Experiences of Seiðr in Modern Denmark. *Spirit Talk: A Core Shamanic Newsletter* 9(Early Summer): 25–27.

Pendragon, A. 2000/2001a. Boys in Blue in the Bluestones. *Druidlore* 3: 7.

—— 2000/2001b. Sacred Sites. *Druidlore* 3: 20–21.

Pennick, N. 1989. *Practical Magic in the Northern Tradition*. Wellingborough, Northamptonshire: The Aquarian Press.

—— 1992. *Rune Magic: The History and Practice of Ancient Runic Traditions*. London: Thorsons.

—— 1999. *The Complete Illustrated Guide to Runes*. Shaftesbury, Dorset: Element Books.

Pennick, N. and N. Jackson 1992. *The Celtic Oracle: A Complete Guide to Using the Cards*. London: Aquarian.

Pepper, G.H. 1996. *Pueblo Bonito*. Albuquerque, New Mexico: University of New Mexico Press.

Peters, L.G. 1997. The Tibetan Healing Rituals of Dorje Yüdronma: Fierce Manifestation of Feminine Cosmic Force. *Shaman's Drum* 45: 36–47.

Peters, L.G. and D. Price-Williams 1980. Towards an Experiential Analysis of Shamanism. *American Anthropologist* 9: 21–46.

Petrovich, A. 2001 [1672]. The Shaman: 'A Villain of a Magician Who Calls Demons'. In: J. Narby and F. Huxley (eds) *Shamans Through Time: 500 Years on the Path to Knowledge*: 18–20. London: Thames and Hudson.

Piggott, S. 1962. From Salisbury Plain to South Siberia. *The Wiltshire Magazine* 58: 93–97.

—— 1968. *The Druids*. London: Pelican.

—— 1989. *Ancient Britons and the Antiquarian Imagination: Ideas from the Renaissance to the Regency*. London: Thames and Hudson.

Pitts. M. 1990. What Future for Aveburry? *Antiquity* 64: 259–274.

—— 1996. The Vicar's Dewpond, the National Trust and the Rise of Paganism. In: D. Morgan, P. Salway and D. Thackray (eds) *The Remains of Distant Times: Archaeology and the National Trust*: 116–131. Woodbridge, Suffolk: The Boydell Press for the Society of Antiquaries of London and the National Trust.

Plouviez, J. 2000. Debating Seahenge: Archaeology and Emotion. *Rescue News* 81: 3.

Pluciennik, M. (ed.) 2001. *The Responsibilities of Archaeologists: Archaeology and Ethics*. Lampeter Workshop in Archaeology 4. BAR International Series 981. Oxford: British Archaeological Reports.

Poewe, K. 1999. Scientific Neo-Paganism and the Extreme Right: From Ludendorff's *Götterkenntnis* to Sigrid Hunke's *Europas Eigene Religion*. *Journal of Contemporary Religion* 14(3): 387–400.

Pollington, S. 2000. *Leechcraft: Early English Charms, Plantlore and Healing*. Hockwold-cum-Wilton, Norfolk: Anglo-Saxon Books.

Pomeroy, M. 1998. *Avebury World Heritage Site Management Plan*. London: English Heritage.

Poncelet, C. and N. Poncelet 1994. Expedition to Buryatia. *Shamanism* 7(1): 21.

Porterfield, A. 1987. Shamanism: A Psychosocial Definition. *Journal of the American Academy of Religion* 55(4): 721–739.

Pounds, N.J.G. 2000. *A History of the English Parish: The Culture of Religion from Augustine to Victoria*. Cambridge: Cambridge University Press.

Powell, T.G.E. 1958. *The Celts*. London: Thames and Hudson.

Prendergast, K. 2001. The Great Circle: Stonehenge, the Sacred and the Problem of Authority. In: C. Finn and M. Henig (eds) *Outside Archaeology: Material Culture and Poetic Imagination*: 97–102. BAR International Series 999. Oxford: British Archaeological Reports.

Press, I. 1971. The Urban Curandero. *American Anthropologist* 73: 741–756.

Price, N. 2000. Shamanism and the Vikings? In: W.W. Fitzhugh and E.I Ward (eds) *Vikings: The North Atlantic Saga*: 70–71. Washington, DC: Smithsonian Institute.

—— (ed.) 2001a. *The Archaeology of Shamanism*. London: Routledge.

—— 2001b. An Archaeology of Altered States: Shamanism and Material Culture Studies. In: N. Price (ed.) *The Archaeology of Shamanism*: 3–16. London: Routledge.

Prout, C. 1998. Saving Sacred Sites. *The Right Times* 2(Summer Solstice): 6–7.

Pryor, F. 1998. The Great Prize of Starlit Stonehenge. *British Archaeology* December: 15.

—— 2001. *Seahenge: New Discoveries in Prehistoric Britain*. London: HarperCollins.

Puttick, E. 1998. Paganism and Shamanism: How Are they Related? Unpublished paper presented at Shamanism in Contemporary Society Conference, University of Newcastle.

Rabinow, P. 1988. Beyond Ethnography: Anthropology as Nominalism. *Cultural Anthropology* 3/4: 355–364.

Radford, T. 1998. *Equinox: Homicide in Kennewick*. London: Channel Four Television.

Rainbird, P. and Y. Hamilakis (eds) 2001. *Interrogating Pedagogies: Archaeology in Higher Education*. Oxford: Archaeopress.

Reed-Danahay, D.E. (ed.) 1997. *Auto/Ethnography: Rewriting the Self and the Social*. Oxford: Berg.

Rees, A. and B. Rees 1961. *Celtic Heritage: The Ancient Tradition in Ireland and Wales*. London: Thames and Hudson.

Reide-Wolfe, A. 1997. Teach An Alais. *Sacred Hoop* 18: 28–29.

Reinhard, J. 1976. Shamanism and Spirit Possession: The Definition Problem. In: J.T. Hitchcock and R.L. Jones (eds) *Spirit Possession in the Nepal Himalayas*: 12–20. Warminster, Wiltshire: Aris and Phillips, Ltd.

Reinharz, S. 1992. *Feminist Methods in Social Research*. Oxford: Oxford University Press.

Renfrew, C. 2001. Production and Consumption in a Sacred Economy: The Material Correlates of High Devotional Expression at Chaco Canyon. *American Antiquity* 66(1): 14–25.

Restall-Orr, E. 1997. Druidry Without Bounds. Unpublished paper presented at Re-Enchantment: An International Conference on Contemporary Paganism and the Interface Between Nature and Religion(s), King Alfred's College, Winchester.

—— 1998/9. Not My Faith. *The Druid's Voice: The Magazine of Contemporary Druidry* 9(Winter): 23.

—— 2000. *So What is the BDO?* Available online: http://www.druidorder.demon.co.uk/bdo_what.htm.

Richardson, A. 1998. Strong Medicine. *Pagan Dawn: The Journal of the Pagan Federation* 126(Imbolc): 23–25.

Riches, D. 1994. Shamanism: The Key to Religion. *Man* 29: 381–405.

Ring of Troth (Europe) 1997. *Elder Troth: An Introduction to the Northern Tradition.* London: Ring of Troth.

Roberts, A. 1997. Tribal Consultation in the National Park Service: A Personal Perspective. In: N. Swidler, K.E. Dongoske, R. Anyon and A.S. Downer (eds) *Native Americans and Archaeologists: Stepping Stones to Common Ground*: 227–234. Walnut Creek, California: AltaMira Press

Root, D. 1996. *Cannibal Culture: Art, Appropriation, and the Commodification of Difference.* Boulder, Colorado: Westview Press.

Roscoe, W. 1991. *The Zuni Man-Woman.* Albuquerque: University of New Mexico Press.

—— 1996. How to Become a Berdache: Toward a Unified Analysis of Gender Diversity. In: G. Herdt (ed.) *Third Sex Third Gender: Beyond Sexual Dimorphism in Culture and History*: 329–371. New York: Zone Books.

—— 1998. *Changing Ones: Third and Fourth Genders in North America.* London: Macmillan.

Rose, W. 1978. An Old-time Indian Attack Conducted in Two Parts: Part One: Imitation 'Indian' Poems, Part Two: Gary Snyder's Turtle Island. In: G. Hobson (ed.) *Remembered Earth: An Anthology of Contemporary Native American Literature*: 211–216. Albuquerque, New Mexico: Red Earth Press.

—— 1992. The Great Pretenders: Further Reflections on White Shamanism. In: M.A. Jaimes (ed.) *The State of Native America: Genocide, Colonisation and Resistance*: 403–421. Boston: South End.

—— 1994. Just What Is All This Fuss About Whiteshamanism Anyway? In: B. Schöler (ed.) *Coyote Was Here: Essays on Contemporary Native American Literary and Political Mobilization*: 13–24. The Dolphin 9. Århus, Sweden: Seklos.

Rosenthal, B.G. 1997. Introduction. In: B.G. Rosenthal (ed.) *The Occult in Russian and Soviet Culture*: 1–32. London: Cornell University Press.

Ross, A. 1967. *Pagan Celtic Britain.* London: Constable.

Roszack, T. 1970. *The Making of a Counter Culture: Reflections on the Technocratic Society and Its Youthful Opposition.* London: Faber and Faber.

Roth, G. 1990. *Maps to Ecstasy: Teachings of an Urban Shaman.* Wellingborough, Northamptonshire: Crucible.

—— 1997. *Sweat Your Prayers: Movement as a Spiritual Practice.* New York: Tarcher/Putnam.

Rothenberg, J. (ed.) 1985. *Technicians of the Sacred: A Range of Poetry from Africa, America, Asia, Europe, and Oceania* (2nd edn). Los Angeles and London, Berkeley, California: University of California Press.

Rouget, G. 1987. *Music and Trance.* Chicago: Chicago University Press.

Rudgeley, R. 1993. *The Alchemy of Culture: Intoxicants in Society.* London: British Museum Press.

Rutherford, L. 1993. To All Races and Colours: About the Release of the Ancient Teachings. *Sacred Hoop* 1: 8–9.

—— 1996. *Principles of Shamanism.* London: Thorsons.

Ryan, J.S. 1963. Othin in England: Evidence from the Poetry for a Cult of Woden in Anglo-Saxon England. *Folk-Lore* 74: 460–480.

Saler, B. 1979 [1967]. Nagual, Witch, and Sorcerer in a Qhiché Village. In: J. Middleton (ed.) *Magic, Witchcraft and Curing*: 69–100. Austin and London: University of Texas Press.

Sales, K. 1992. Ascent to the Sky: A Shamanic Initiatory Engraving from the Burrup Peninsula, Northwest Western Australia. *Archaeology Oceania* 27: 22–35.

Salomonsen, J. 1999. Methods of Compassion or Pretension? Anthropological Fieldwork in Modern Magical Communities. *The Pomegranate: A New Journal of Neopagan Thought* 8: 4–13.

—— 2002. *Enchanted Feminism: The Reclaiming Witches of San Francisco.* London: Routledge.

Samson, R. 1991. *Social Approaches to Viking Studies.* Glasgow: Cruithne Press.

Schaafsma, P. 1980. *Indian Rock Art of the Southwest.* Santa Fe, New Mexico: School of American Research Press.

Schmidt, P.R. and T.C. Patterson (eds) 1995. Introduction: From Constructing to Making Alternative Histories. In: P.R. Schmidt and T.C. Patterson (eds) *Making Alternative Histories: The Practice of Archaeology and History in Non-Western Settings*: 1–24. Santa Fe, New Mexico: School of America Research Press.

Scott, N. 1999. *Total Eclipse: Souvenir Guide to the Once in a Lifetime Event.* London: Highbury House Communications PLC.

Scudder, B. (trans.) 2001. Egil's Saga. In: *The Sagas of Icelanders*: 3–184. London: Penguin.

Sebastian, L. 1996. *The Chaco Anasazi: Sociopolitical Evolution in the Prehistoric Southwest.* Cambridge: Cambridge University Press.

Sebastion, T. 1990. Triad /|\: The Druid Knowledge of Stonehenge. In: C. Chippindale, P. Devereux, P. Fowler, R. Jones and T. Sebastion (eds) *Who Owns Stonehenge?*: 88–119. Manchester: Batsford.

—— 2001. Alternative Archaeology: Has it Happened? In R.J. Wallis and K.J. Lymer (eds) *A Permeability of Boundaries?: New Approaches to the Archaeology of Art, Religion and Folklore*: 125–135. BAR International Series 936. Oxford: British Archaeological Reports.

Semple, S. 1998. A Fear of the Past: The Place of the Prehistoric Burial Mound in the Ideology of Middle and Later Anglo-Saxon England. *World Archaeology* 30(1): 109–126.

Senn, H. 1989. Jungian Shamanism. *Journal of Psychoactive Drugs* 21(1): 113–121.

Shallcrass, P. 1995. Druidry Today. In: G. Harvey and C. Hardman (eds) *Paganism Today: Wiccans, Druids, the Goddess and Ancient Earth Traditions for the Twenty-first Century*: 65–80. London: Thorsons.

—— 1996. The Bardic Tradition and the Song of the Land. P. In Carr-Gomm (ed.) *The Druid Renaissance*: 52–67. London: Thorsons.

—— 1997a. *The Passing of the Year: A Collection of Songs and Poems, Spells and Invocations*. St Leonard's on Sea, Sussex: British Druid Order.

—— 1997b. *The Story of Taliesin*. St Leonard's on Sea, Sussex: British Druid Order.

—— 1997c. Insanity or Inspiration: A Pagan Perspective. Unpublished paper presented at Re-Enchantment: An International Conference on Contemporary Paganism and the Interface Between Nature and Religion(s), King Alfred's College, Winchester.

—— 1998. A Priest of the Goddess. In: J. Pearson, R.H. Roberts and G. Samuel (eds) *Nature Religion Today: Paganism in the Modern World*: 157–169. Edinburgh: Edinburgh University Press.

—— 1998/9. English Heritage, Stonehenge and Some Druids. *The Druid's Voice: The Magazine of Contemporary Druidry* 9: 16–20.

—— 2000. *Druidry*. London: Piaktis.

Shapiro, W. 1998. Ideology, 'History of Religions' and Hunter-gatherer Studies. *Journal of the Royal Anthropological Institute* 4(3): 489–510.

Sharon, D. 1978. *Wizard of the Four Winds: A Shaman's Story*. New York: The Free Press.

Shaw, S. In preparation a. *Deep in the Heart*.

—— In preparation b. *Lose Touch with the Earth, and You Lose Touch with Life*.

Shell, C.A. 2000. Metalworker or Shaman: Early Bronze Age Upton Lovell G2a Burial. *Antiquity* 74: 271–272.

Shepherd, C. 1998. *A Study of the Relationship Between Style I Art and Socio-Political Change in Early Medieval Europe*. BAR International Series 745. Oxford: British Archaeological Reports.

Sherratt, A. 1991. Sacred and Profane Substances: The Ritual Use of Narcotics in Later Neolithic Europe. In: P. Garwood, D. Jennings, R. Skeats and J. Toms (eds) *Sacred and Profane: Conference Proceedings*: 50–64. Oxford: Oxford Monograph 32.

—— 1995a. Introduction: Peculiar Substances. In: J. Goodman, P.E. Lovejoy and A. Sherratt (eds) *Consuming Habits: Drugs in History and Anthropology*: 1–10. London: Routledge.

—— 1995b. Alcohol and its Alternatives: Symbol and Substance in Pre-industrial Cultures. In: J. Goodman, P.E. Lovejoy and A. Sherratt (eds) *Consuming Habits: Drugs in History and Anthropology*: 11–46. London: Routledge.

Shetelig, H. and Hjalmur Falk 1937. *Scandinavian Archaeology* (trans. E.V. Gordon). Oxford: Clarendon Press.

Shirokogoroff, S. 1935. *Psychomental Complex of the Tungus*. London: Kegan and Paul.

Siikala, A.-L. 1978. *The Rite Technique of the Siberian Shaman*. Helsinki, Finland: FF Communications 220.

Silverman, J. 1967. Shamans and Acute Schizophrenia. *Americal Anthropologist* 69: 21–31.

Simard, J.-J. 1990. White Ghosts, Red Shadows: The Reduction of North American Natives. In: G. Clifton (ed.) *The Invented Indian: Cultural Fictions and Government Policies*: 333–370. New Brunswick: Transaction.

Simek, R. 1993 [1984]. *A Dictionary of Northern Mythology*. Bury St Edmunds, Suffolk: St Edmundsbury Press.

Skeates, R. 2000. *Debating the Archaeological Heritage*. London: Duckworth.

Smith, A. 1994. For All Those Who Were Indian in a Former life. In: C. Adams (ed.) *Ecofeminism and the Sacred*: 168–171. New York: Continuum.

Smith, J.Z. 1987. *To Take Place: Toward Theory in Ritual*. Chicago: University of Chicago Press.

Smith, L.T. 1999. *Decolonizing Methodologies: Research and Indigenous Peoples*. London, New York and Dunedin, New Zealand: Zed Books/University of Otago Press.

Solli, B. 1999. Odin the *Queer?* On *Ergi* and Shamanism in Norse Mythology. In: A. Gustafsson and H. Karlsson (eds) *Glyfer och arkeologiska rum – en vänbok till Jarl Nordbladh*: 341–349. Gotarc Series A, vol. 3. Göteborg, Sweden: University of Göteborg.

Sørensen, P.M. 1983. *The Unmanly Man: Concepts of Sexual Defamation in Early Northern Society*. Odense, Denmark: Odense University Press.

Spare, A.O. 1993. *From the Inferno to Zos: The Writings and Images of Austin Osman Spare (Volume 1)*. Seattle: First Impressions.

Sparkes, B.A. 1998. Sex in Classical Athens. In B.A. Sparkes (ed.) *Greek Civilisations: An Introduction*: 248–262. Oxford: Blackwell.

Speake, G. 1980. *Anglo-Saxon Animal Art and its Germanic Background*. Oxford: Clarendon Press.

Spence, L. 1995 [1945]. *The Magic Arts in Celtic Britain*. London: Constable (reprint).

Spencer, V. 1997. The New Style of Old Values: Enterprise Culture and the National Heritage. *Diatribe: A Postgraduate Journal from the Centre for Language and Cultural Theory* 7 ('Flashbacks'): 97–109.

Spicer, E. 1969. Review of C. Castaneda 1968. *The Teachings of Don Juan: A Yaqui Way of Knowledge*. *American Anthropologist* 71(2): 320–322.

Spilman, S. 1999. Lhamo Dolkar: A Tibetan Exorcist in Nepal. *Shaman's Drum* 51: 51–57.

Stafford, G. 1990. The Medicine Circle of Turtle Island. In: P. Jones and C. Matthews (eds) *Voices from the Circle: The Heritage of Western Paganism*: 83–92. Wellingborough, Northamptonshire: The Aquarian Press.

Stanley, E.G. 1964. *The Search for Anglo-Saxon Paganism*. Cambridge: Brewer.

Stanley Price, N.P. 1989. Conservation and Information in the Display of Prehistoric Sites. In: H.F. Cleere (ed.) *Archaeological Heritage Management in the Modern World*: 284–290. London: Routledge.

Starhawk 1989. *The Spiral Dance*. San Francisco: Harper and Row.

Steele, J. 1996. 'Eco-noble Savages' Who Never Were. *British Archaeology* March: 8–9.

Stoll, D. 1987. Smoky Trails: On Taussig's 'Shamanism, Colonialism and the Wild Man'. *Anthropology Today* 3(6): 9–10.

Stone, C.J. 1996. *Fierce Dancing: Adventures in the Underground*. London: Faber and Faber.

Stone, P.K., V.R. Perez and D. Martin 1998. Review of Video by N. Nicastro 1996. Science or Sacrilege: Native Americans, Archaeology and the Law. *American Anthropologist* 100(4): 1022–1024.

Stonehenge Campaign 2000. *'Stonehenge Belongs to You and Me': A Record of the Travelling Exhibition 1993–2000*. Stonehenge Campaign Publication.

—— News Website. Available online: http://www.geocities.com/SoHo/9000/stonecam.htm.

Stonehenge Under Threat! World Heritage Site Threatened by Road Building Scheme. Available online: http://www.stonehenge.care4free.net/.

Stoodley, N. 1999. *The Spindle and the Spear: A Critical Enquiry into the Construction and Meaning of Gender in the Early Anglo-Saxon Burial Rite.* BAR British Series 288. Oxford: British Archaeological Reports.

Storm, H. 1972. *Seven Arrows.* New York: Ballantine.

Storms, G. 1948. *Anglo-Saxon Magic.* The Hague: Martinus Nijhoff.

Stout, A. 2001. Making the Past: The Politics of Prehistory. *3rd Stone: Archaeology, Folklore and Myth – The Magazine of the New Antiquarian* 40(Summer/Autumn): 34–42.

Strathern, M. 1987a. Out of Context: The Persuasive Fictions of Anthropology. *Current Anthropology* 28(3): 251–281.

—— 1987b. The Limits of Auto-anthropology. In: A. Jackson (ed.) *Anthropology at Home*: 16–37. London: Tavistock Publications.

—— 1987c. An Awkward Relationship: The Case of Feminism and Anthropology. *Signs* 12(2): 276–292.

—— 1998. Comment on: M.F. Brown, Can Culture Be Copyrighted? *Current Anthropology* 39(2): 193–222.

Strömbäck, D. 1935. *Sejd: textstudier i nordisk religionshistoria.* Nordiska texter och undersökningar 5. Stockholm: Hugo Gebers Förlag.

Stuart, H. 1976. The Anglo-Saxon Elf. *Studia Neophilogica* 48: 313–320.

Stuart, J. 2000. The Home Counties Witch Project. *The Independent on Sunday/The Sunday Review* 7 May: 20–22.

Summerley, N. 1998. My Private Stonehenge. *The Telegraph* 20 June: 14.

Swidler, N. and J. Cohen 1997. Issues in Intertribal Consultation. In: N. Swidler N., K.E. Dongoske, R. Anyon and A.S. Downer (eds) *Native Americans and Archaeologists: Stepping Stones to Common Ground*: 197–206. Walnut Creek, California: AltaMira Press.

Swidler, N., K.E. Dongoske, R. Anyon and A.S. Downer (eds) 1997. *Native Americans and Archaeologists: Stepping Stones to Common Ground.* Walnut Creek, California: AltaMira Press.

Taksami, C. 1998. Siberian Shamans. In: J. Pentikäinen; T. Jaatinen, I. Lehtinen and M.-R. Saloniemi (eds) *Shamans*: 11–26. Tampere Museums Publications 45. Tampere, Finland: Tampere Museums.

Tambiah, S.J. 1990. *Magic, Science, Religion and the Scope of Rationality.* Cambridge: Cambridge University Press.

Taussig, M. 1987. *Shamanism, Colonialism and the Wild Man: A Study in Terror and Healing.* Chicago: The University of Chicago Press.

—— 1989. The Nervous System: Homesickness and Dada. *Stanford Humanities Review* 1(1): 44–81.

Taylor, J.G. 1989. Shamanic Sex Roles in Traditional Labrador Inuit Society. In: M. Hoppál and O. von Sadovsky (eds) *Shamanism Past and Present (Part 2)*: 297–306. Budapest: Ethnographic Institute, Hungarian Academy of Sciences and Fullerton, Los Angeles: International Society for Trans-Oceanic Research.

Taylor, P. 1992. The Message of the Runes: Divination in the Ancient Germanic World. In: J. Matthews (ed.) *The World Atlas of Divination*: 33–44. London: Tiger Books.

Taylor, T. 1994. Thracians, Scythians, and Dacians, 800 BC–AD 300. In B. Cunliffe (ed.) *The Oxford Illustrated Prehistory of Europe*: 373–410. Oxford: Oxford University Press.

—— 1996. Gundestrup Cauldron. In: B.M. Fagan (chief ed.) *The Oxford Companion to Archaeology*: 268–269. Oxford: Oxford University Press.

Tedlock, B. 1991. From Participant Observation to the Observation of Participation: The Emergence of Narrative Ethnography. *Journal of Anthropological Research* 47: 69–94.

Thomas, J. 1993. The Politics of Vision and the Archaeologies of Landscape. In: B. Bender (ed.) *Landscapes: Politics and Perspectives*: 19–48. Oxford: Berg.

—— 1996. Monuments Ancient and Modern. *The Ley Hunter* 125: 17–19.

Thomas, N. 1994. Marginal Powers: Shamanism and Hierarchy in Eastern Oceania. In: N. Thomas and C. Humphrey (eds) *Shamanism, History, and the State*: 15–31. Ann Arbor: University of Michigan Press.

Thompson, B. 1998. Cliff Richard is a Pagan. *The Independent Weekend Review*, 24 October: 12.

Thorpe, L. (trans.) 1974. *Gregory of Tours: The History of the Franks*. London: Penguin.

Thorpe, N. 2000/2001. Science vs. Culture: The Reburial Conflict in the USA. *3rd Stone: Archaeology, Folklore and Myth* 39: 43–51.

Thorsson, E. 1984. *Futhark: A Handbook of Rune Magic*. York Beach, Maine: Samuel Weiser.

—— 1987. *Runelore: A Handbook of Esoteric Runology*. York Beach, Maine: Samuel Weiser.

Thun, S. 1969. The Malignant Elves. *Studia Neophilologica* 41: 378–396.

Thurneysen, R. 1993 [1946]. *A Grammar of Old Irish*. Dublin: Dublin University Press.

Tilley, C. 1994. *A Phenomenology of Landscape: Places, Paths and Monuments*. Oxford: Berg.

—— 1999 *Metaphor and Material Culture*. Oxford: Blackwell Publishers.

Tingay, K. 2000. Madame Blavatsky's Children: Theosophy and its Heirs. In: S. Sutcliffe and M. Bowman (eds) *Beyond New Age: Exploring Alternative Spirituality*: 37–50. Edinburgh: Edinburgh University Press.

Tisdall, C. 1976. *Joseph Beuys – Coyote*. Munich: Schirmer Mosel.

—— 1979. *Joseph Beuys*. New York and London: Solomon R. Guggenheim Museum and Thames and Hudson.

—— 1998. *Joseph Beuys – We Go This Way*. London: Violette Editions.

Tomlinson, P. and A.R. Hall 1996. A Review of the Archaeological Evidence for Food Plants from the British Isles: An Example of the Use of the Archaeobotanical Computer Database (ABCD). *Internet Archaeology* 1. Available online: http://intarch.ac.uk/journal/issue1/tomlinson_toc.html.

Torgovnick, M. 1990. *Gone Primitive: Savage Intellects, Modern Lives*. Chicago: University of Chicago Press.

Torrey, E.F. 1974. Spiritualists and Shamans as Psychotherapists: An Account of Original Anthropological Sin. In: I.I. Zaretsky and M.P. Leone (eds) *Religious Movements in Contemporary America*: 330–337. Princeton, New Jersey: Princeton University Press.

Townsend, S. 1988. Neo-shamanism and the Modern Mystical Movement. In: G. Doore (ed.) *Shaman's Path: Healing, Personal Growth and Empowerment*: 73–83. Boston and London: Shambhala.

—— 1997. Core Shaman and Neopagan Leaders of the Mystical Movement in Contemporary Society. *Dialogue and Alliance: A Journal of the International Religious Foundation* 13(1): 100–122.

—— 1998. Shamanic Spirituality: Core Shamanism and Neo-shamanism in Contemporary Western Society. Unpublished manuscript.

—— 1999. Western Contemporary Core and Neo-shamanism and the Interpenetration with Indigenous Societies. *Proceedings of the International Congress: Shamanism and Other Indigenous Spiritual Beliefs and Practices* 5 (2): 223–231. Moscow: Institute of Ethnology and Anthropology of the Russian Academy of Sciences.

Trigger, B.G. 1989. *A History of Archaeological Thought*. Cambridge: Cambridge University Press.

Tucker, M. 1992. *Dreaming with Open Eyes: The Shamanic Spirit in Contemporary Art and Culture*. London: HarperCollins.

Turner, E. 1989. From Shamans to Healers: The Survival of an Inupiaq Eskimo Skill. *Anthropologica* 31: 3–24.

—— 1992. The Reality of Spirits. *Revision* 15(1): 28–32.

—— 1994. A Visible Spirit Form in Zambia. In: D.E. Young and J.-G. Goulet (eds) *Being Changed By Cross-cultural Encounters: The Anthropology of Extraordinary Experience*: 71–95. Peterborough, Ontario: Broadview Press.

Turville-Petre, E.O.G. 1964. *Myth and Religion of the North: The Religion of Ancient Scandinavia*. London: Weidenfeld and Nicolson.

'Twitter of Blisted'. 1998. Free Stonehenge. *The Right Times* 3(Autumn Equinox): 11–12.

Tyler, H.A. 1964. *Pueblo Gods and Myths*. Norman, Oklahoma: University of Oklahoma Press.

Uccusic, P. 1996. Second Foundation Expedition to Tuva: July 1994. *Shamanism* 8(1): 4–9.

Ucko, P.J. 1990. Foreword. In: P. Gathercole and D. Lowenthal (eds) *The Politics of the Past*: ix–xxi. London: Unwin Hyman.

Urry, J. 1990. *The Tourist Gaze: Leisure and Travel in Contemporary Societies*. London: Sage Publications.

Van Deusen, K. 1997a. Buryat Shamans and their Stories. *Shamanism* 10(1): 7–11.

—— 1997b. Shamanism in Khakassia Today. *Shamanism* 10(1): 11–16.

VanPool, C.S. and T.L. VanPool 1999. The Scientific Nature of Postprocessualism. *American Antiquity* 64(1): 33–53.

Villoldo, A. and E. Jendresen 1990. *The Four Winds: A Shaman's Journey into the Amazon*. New York: Harper and Row.

Villoldo, A. and S. Krippner 1986. *Healing States: A Journey into the World of Spiritual Healing and Shamanism*. New York: Simon and Schuster.

Vitebsky, P. 1995a. *The Shaman*. London: Macmillan.

—— 1995b. From Cosmology to Environmentalism: Shamanism as Local Knowledge in a Global Setting. In: R. Fardon (ed.) *Counterworks: Managing the Diversity of Knowledge*: 182–203. London: Routledge.

—— 1998. Shamanism Among the Sakha of Yakutia and Sora of India. Unpublished paper presented at Shamanism in Contemporary Society Conference, University of Newcastle.

—— 2000. Shamanism. In: G. Harvey (ed.) *Indigenous Religions: A Companion*: 55–67. London: Cassell.

Vizenor, G. 1994. *Manifest Manners: Post-Indian Warriors of Surveillance*. Hanover, New Hampshire: University Press of New England.

Voigt, V. 1984. Shaman – Person or Word? In: M. Hoppál (ed.) *Shamanism in Eurasia*: 13–20. Göttingen: Edition Herodot.

Wainwright, G.J. 1996. Stonehenge Saved? *Antiquity* 70: 9–12.

—— 2000. The Stonehenge We Deserve. *Antiquity* 74: 334–342.

Wallis, R.J. 1996. Footprints of the Rain: Rock Art and the Shamanic Landscape in the Twyfelfontein Valley, Namibia. MA thesis, Department of Archaeology, University of Southampton.

—— 1998. Journeying the Politics of Ecstasy: Anthropological Perspectives on Neo-shamanism. *The Pomegranate: A New Journal of Neopagan Thought* 6: 20–28.

—— 1999. Altered States, Conflicting Cultures: Shamans, Neo-shamans and Academics. *Anthropology of Consciousness* 10(2–3): 41–49.

—— 2000. Queer Shamans: Autoarchaeology and Neo-shamanism. *World Archaeology* 32(2): 252–262.

—— 2001. Waking the Ancestors: Neo-shamanism and Archaeology. In: N. Price (ed.) *The Archaeology of Shamanism*: 213–330. London: Routledge.

—— 2002a. Taliesin's Trip: Celtic Shamanisms? *The Druid's Voice*: in press.

—— 2002b. The 'Bwili' or 'Flying Tricksters' of Malakula: A Critical Discussion of Recent Debates on Rock Art, Ethnography and Shamanisms. *Journal of the Royal Anthropological Institute* 8: 753–778: in press.

—— In preparation. *Return to the Source: Neo-shamanism and Shamanism in Central Asia and Siberia*.

Wallis, R.J. and J. Blain 2002. *Sacred Sites, Contested Rights/Rites: Contemporary Pagan Engagements with the Past*. Available online: http://www.sacredsites.org.uk.

Wallis R.J. and K. J. Lymer (eds) 2001. *A Permeability of Boundaries: New Approaches to the Archaeology of Art, Religion and Folklore*. BAR International Series 936. Oxford: British Archaeological Reports.

Walsh, R. 1989. What is a Shaman?: Definition, Origin and Distribution. *Journal of Transpersonal Psychology* 21(1): 1–11.

—— 1990. *The Spirit of Shamanism*. New York: Tarcher and Putman.

Waters, F. 1963. *The Book of the Hopi*. New York: Viking Penguin.

Watkins, A. 1925. *The Old Straight Track*. London: Methuen and Company.

Watkins, J. 2000. *Indigenous Archaeology: American Indian Values and Scientific Practice*. Walnut Creek, California: AltaMira Press.

Wawn, A. (trans.). 2001. The Saga of the People of Vatnsdal. In: *The Sagas of Icelanders*: 185–269. London: Penguin.

Weir, A. 2000 *Irish Sweathouses and the Great Forgetting*. Available online: http://www.beyond-the-pale.co.uk/sweathouses.htm.

Welch, C. 2002. Appropriating the Didjeridu and the Sweat Lodge: New Age Baddies and Indigenous Victims? *Journal of Contemporary Religion* 17(1): 21–38.

Welch, M. 1992. *Anglo-Saxon England*. London: B.T. Batsford Ltd.

Weller, P. 1997. *Religions in the UK: Directory 1997–2000*. Mickleover, Derby: University of Derby.

Weller, P., A. Fieldman and K. Purdman 2001. *Religious Discrimination in England and Wales*. Home Office Research Study 220. Available online: www.homeoffice.gov.uk/rds/pdfs/hors220.pdf.

Werner, O. and G.M. Schoepfle 1987. *Systematic Fieldwork. Volume 1: Foundations of Ethnography and Interviewing*. Newbury Park, California: Sage Publications.

Whitehead, H. 1993. The Bow and the Burden Strap: A New Look at Institutionalized Homosexuality in Native North America. In: H. Abelove, M.A. Barde and D.M. Halperin (eds) *The Lesbian and Gay Studies Reader*: 498–527. London: Routledge.

Whitfield, N. 1999. Design and Units of Measure on the Hunterston Brooch. In: J. Hawkes and S. Mills (eds) *Northumbria's Golden Age*: 296–314. Stroud, Gloucestershire: Sutton Publishing.

Whiteley, P. 1997. The End of Anthropology (at Hopi)? In: T. Biolsi and J. Zimmerman (eds) *Indians and Anthropologists: Vine Deloria Jr. and the Critique of Anthropology*: 177–207. Tucson: University of Arizona Press.

Whitley, D.S. 1992. Shamanism and Rock Art in Far Western North America. *Cambridge Archaeological Journal* 2: 89–113.

Wilcox, J.P. 1999. *Keepers of the Ancient Knowledge: The Mystical World of the Q'ero Indians of Peru*. Shaftesbury, Dorset: Element Books.

Wilk, S. 1980. Don Juan On Balance. In: R. De Mille (ed.) *The Don Juan Papers: Further Castaneda Controversies*: 154–157. Santa Barbara, California: Ross-Erikson.

Williams, H. 1998. Monuments and the Past in Early Anglo-Saxon England. *World Archaeology* 30(1): 90–108.

—— 2001. An Ideology of Transformation: Cremation Rites and Animal Sacrifice in Early Anglo-Saxon England. In: N. Price (ed.) *The Archaeology of Shamanism*: 193–212. London: Routledge.

Williams, I. 1968. *The Poems of Taliesin*. Dublin: The Dublin Institute for Advanced Studies.

Williams, P. and L. Chrisman 1993. Colonial Discourse and Post-colonial Theory: An Introduction. In: P. Williams and L. Chrisman (eds) *Colonial Discourse and Post-colonial Theory: A Reader*: 1–20. London: Harvester Wheatsheaf.

Willis, R. 1994. Narrative: New Shamanism. *Anthropology Today* 10(6): 16–18.

Wilson, D. 1992. *Anglo-Saxon Paganism*. London: Routledge.

Wilson, D.M. 1959. A Group of Anglo-Saxon Amulet Rings. In: P. Clemoes (ed.) *The Anglo-Saxons: Studies in Some Aspects of their History and Culture Presented to Bruce Dickens*: 159–170. London: Bowes and Bowes.

Wilson, J.F. 1974. The Historical Study of Marginal American Religious Movements. In: I.I. Zaretsky and M.P. Leone (eds) *Religious Movements in Contemporary America*: 596–611. Princeton, New Jersey: Princeton University Press.

Winkelman, M. 1989. A Cross-cultural Study of Shamanistic Healers. *Journal of Psychoactive Drugs* 21(1): 17–24.

Wise, C. 1999. A Pagan Dawn: Summer Solstice Dawn at Stonehenge. *Pagan Dawn: The Journal of the Pagan Federation* 130(Imbolc/Spring): 12–14.

Wood, N. 1998. News From the Hoop: Carlos Castaneda – 19??–1998. *Sacred Hoop* 22: 8.

Wood, N. and J. Wood 1993. Who's Who? An Overview of U.K. Networks and Tribes. *Sacred Hoop* 1: 10–11.

Woodman, J. 1998. Conference Review of Shamanism in Contemporary Society, Department of Religious Studies, University of Newcastle upon Tyne, 23–26 June. *Anthropology Today* 14(6): 23–24.

Wright, P.A. 1989. The Nature of the Shamanic State of Consciousness: A Review. *Journal of Psychoactive Drugs* 21(1): 25–33.

Wylie, A. 1992. The Interplay of Evidential Constraints and Political Interests: Recent Archaeological Research on Gender. *American Antiquity* 57(1): 15–35.

—— 1995. Alternative Histories: Epistemic Disunity and Political Integrity. In: P.R. Schmidt and T.C. Patterson (eds) *Making Alternative Histories: The Practice of Archaeology and History in Non-Western Settings*: 255–272. Santa Fe, New Mexico: School of America Research Press.

—— 2000. Questions of Evidence, Legitimacy, and the (Dis)unity of Science. *American Antiquity* 65(2): 227–237.

Yates, T. 1993. Frameworks for an Archaeology of the Body. In: C. Tilley (ed.) *Interpretative Archaeology*: 31–72. Oxford, Berg.

Young, D.E. and J.-G. Goulet (eds) 1994a. *Being Changed by Cross-cultural Encounters: The Anthropology of Extraordinary Experience*. Peterborough, Ontario: Broadview Press.

—— 1994b. Introduction. In: D.E. Young and J.-G. Goulet (eds) *Being Changed by Cross-cultural Encounters: The Anthropology of Extraordinary Experience*: 7–13. Peterborough, Ontario: Broadview Press.

Young, M.J. 1988. *Signs from the Ancestors: Zuni Cultural Symbolism and Perceptions of Rock Art*. Albuquerque, New Mexico: University of New Mexico Press.

Zinser, H. 1987. Schamanismus im 'New Age': Zur Wiederkehr schamanistischer Praktiken und Seancen in Europa. *Zeitschrift für Religions und Geistes-Geschichte* 39(1): 319–327.

Zoëga, G.T. 1961 [1910]. *A Concise Dictionary of Icelandic*. Oxford: The Clarendon Press.

INDEX

INDEX